M & E HANDBOOKS

M & E Handbooks are recommended reading for examination syllabuses all over the world. Because each Handbook covers its subject clearly and concisely, books in the series form a vital part of many college, university, school and home study courses.

Handbooks contain detailed information stripped of unnecessary padding, making each title a comprehensive self-tuition course. They are amplified with numerous self-testing questions in the form of Progress Tests at the end of each chapter, each text-referenced for easy checking. Every Handbook closes with an appendix which advises on examination technique. For all these reasons, Handbooks are ideal for pre-examination revision.

The handy pocket-book size and competitive price make Handbooks the perfect choice for anyone who wants to grasp the essentials of a subject quickly and easily.

GW00750982

THE M & E HANDBOOK SERIES

Applied Economics

Edmund Seddon

MA

Senior Lecturer in Economics,
Faculty of Business and Management Studies,
Liverpool Polytechnic

J. D. S. Appleton

B.Sc(Econ), M.Sc,Dip.Ed

Principal Lecturer,
Faculty of Business and Management Studies,
Liverpool Polytechnic

THIRD EDITION

MACDONALD AND EVANS

Macdonald & Evans Ltd
Estover, Plymouth PL6 7PZ

First published 1972
Reprinted (with amendments) 1973
Reprinted 1975
Reprinted 1976
Second edition 1978
Third edition 1981

© Macdonald & Evans Ltd 1981

0 7121 01772

Filmset in Great Britain by Northumberland Press Ltd
Gateshead, Tyne and Wear
and printed by Richard Clay (The Chaucer Press) Ltd
Bungay, Suffolk

Preface to the First Edition

This Handbook sets out to analyse the main problems which confront the UK economy today and to test the validity of theoretical solutions to these problems against the results which have been achieved. It is intended for a very wide range of students, from those taking GCE "A" Level to those preparing for papers in Applied Economics in the examinations of both academic and professional bodies.

Part One establishes the theoretical framework of macro-economic analysis and appraises the techniques and effectiveness of fiscal policies designed to manage the level of demand.

Part Two continues this approach in the realm of monetary policy by way of examining the structure and operation of the whole monetary system.

Part Three considers the implications for domestic economic policy of external trade and payments transactions.

Part Four is concerned with *direct* government intervention in specific segments of the economy in an attempt to improve the efficiency of their operation.

The authors are conscious that this is a field of study in which there is continuous change. Old problems assume new forms and require fresh solutions. Moreover, the institutional apparatus of the economy is evolving at a rate which quickly dates written material. Nevertheless it is hoped that this book will provide the reader with a systematic and critical approach to the solutions put forward to current economic problems. Judicious reading of newspapers, periodicals, journals, and government and banking publications will enable the student to keep abreast of events.

Grateful acknowledgment is due to the following bodies for permission to reprint the examination questions which appear in Appendix III.

The Joint Matriculation Board of the Universities of Manchester, Liverpool, Leeds, Sheffield, and Birmingham (JMB). University of London.

Liverpool Polytechnic.

Institute of Bankers (IOB).

Savings Bank Institute (SBI).

Institute of Municipal Treasurers and Accountants (IMTA).

Institute of Cost and Management Accountants—formerly Institute of Cost and Works Accountants (ICWA).

Institute of Transport (IOT).

Chartered Institute of Secretaries (CIS).

January 1972

ES
JDSA

Preface to the Third Edition

The growing rejection of Keynesian orthodoxy has inevitably implied considerable shifts in the emphasis in textbooks upon different economic theories. This is reflected in the extension of Chapter I to include a detailed review of the thinking of the "Austrian" school of economists, Keynes's original critics. Their position is further elaborated in a new section in Chapter IV.

A new Chapter V critically examines the validity of the behavioural suppositions upon which Keynesian demand management was based and their implications for deficit public finance. The practical consequences are outlined in a substantial modification of the chapter on the National Debt.

The technical difficulties of implementing the new monetarism together with the major institutional developments which have occurred in banking and the financial markets have led to a major revision and extension of Part Two.

Amendments and modifications have again been made throughout the text to bring it into line with current theory, practice and institutional arrangements.

October 1981
ES
JDSA

Contents

payments disequilibrium in variable exchange rate
systems; International Monetary Fund (IMF); The
foreign exchange crisis of 1971; Managed floating;
Monetary union; The World Bank Group

PART FOUR: GOVERNMENT AND INDUSTRY

PART ONE
THE MACROECONOMIC APPROACH

CHAPTER I

An Outline of Developments in Economic Analysis

FROM COLLECTIVISM TO INDIVIDUALISM

1. Introduction. The objects of this introductory chapter are two-fold. Firstly it sets out to define the subject area by showing how it originated and developed in response to a changing economic environment. Secondly it seeks to demonstrate that unlike the physical sciences the subject does not comprise a body of theory universally agreed by all economists. There has always been dis-agreement both in terms of the methodology appropriate to the analysis of particular problems and in the interpretation of observed economic phenomena. Controversy continues at the present time on a number of issues, particularly with respect to the importance of money in the economy. (The neo-Keynesian/ monetarist controversy, *see* **37, 38.**)

2. Origins of economics as an independent area of study. As an independent discipline, economics emerged from the great political, social and cultural upheaval which culminated in the Industrial Revolution. Its birth is to be associated with the transition from a feudal society organised in small self-sufficient units to a much more loosely knit society producing for national and international markets.

3. Security, stability and collectivism. The principal characteristic of feudal society was the stability which it achieved through a highly structured collectivism. The problem of matching scarce resources to man's needs was tackled *locally* and by *collective* decisions, implemented in agriculture through the manorial courts and in industry and trade through the craft and merchant guilds.

In the event of unwise decisions responsibility and resulting hardships were shared collectively. Justice in dealings with other groups was exacted collectively and penalties accepted collectively. The *just wage* and the *just price*, strangely reminiscent of today's prices and incomes policies, were imposed collectively.

The prevailing desire was for the security in life which stems from the certainty that tomorrow will be the same as today. In a spiritual age in which the authority of the Church was absolute hardship in this world would be recompensed in the next.

Hardship there was in abundance and in material terms the age was marked by stagnation.

4. Progress, individualism and *laissez-faire*. The European Renaissance is synonymous with the reawakening of the spirit of enquiry, a questioning of accepted values, a resurgence of individualism. The implications for social organisation were far reaching since feudal institutions were too inflexible to adjust to change. In the towns, where the customs and practices of the guilds appeared to conflict with the individual interests of merchants and craftsmen, they were ignored and individuals prospered. The age of geographical discovery brought in its train an expansion of commerce and still greater prosperity for an emerging middle class of entrepreneurs, who began to organise production to meet increasing demand. Already there could be perceived the separation of the functions of providing capital and labour, the hallmark of capitalism.

A temporary check to the disintegration of collectivist society was made by the state. As the regulatory powers of local institutions declined they were replaced by central government legislation. This process reached its zenith in the reign of Elizabeth I with the establishment of a highly centralised nation state, subject to an absolute monarchy. However, the full flowering of individual freedom, political, spiritual and economic, was not long to be delayed. The conflict of interest erupted in the Civil War of 1688–89, a revolution in a unique sense. Where subsequent revolutions simply substituted one authoritarian caucus for another, on this occasion a whole collectivist ethic was replaced by an unfaltering belief in the right of the individual to free expression, politically, spiritually and economically. The age of *laissez-faire* had dawned.

5. The implications of a market economy. The eighteenth century contained all the ingredients for dramatic change. There existed already a class of wage earners and a class of capital-providing entrepreneurs. The ethic of individual free enterprise was unchallenged and state interference minimal. The need was for technological advance and necessity became the mother of a spate of inventions, which could only be fully utilised in a factory system geared to large-scale production for an expanding market. In the space of a few decades a subsistence economy was transformed into a highly specialised market economy composed of increasingly complex interdependencies. Much had been accomplished in overcoming the fundamental problems of scarcity and how to produce more, but the complexities of the new methods of social organisation themselves raised new problems. *These problems were to become the substance of the new subject of political economy*.

6. A tentative definition. We are now able to see that, while the subject of economics is rooted in the problem of scarcity, the economist only acquires an interest once that problem is set in the context of a particular system. It is, therefore, to be seen as a social or behavioural science concerning itself with all of the implications for the alleviation of scarcity of different methods of organising society.

CLASSICAL MARKET ECONOMICS

7. Adam Smith and the English classical economists. Smith provided the first rationale for a free enterprise economy, in which an optimal matching of available resources to individual wants would be secured through the operation of an "invisible hand", the market mechanism. Collective action through the state would be restricted to the maintenance of internal and external security.

This idea was subsequently explored and developed by the great English classical economists of the nineteenth century. The substance of this line of thinking can be summarised as follows.

(*a*) *The economic problem*. Economics is concerned with the optimal allocation of scarce resources between competing alternatives.

(*b*) *Individual choice*. The order of priority of these alternatives can only be determined with any accuracy by the individual.

(*c*) *The market mechanism*. The market will assure the direction of resources in accordance with this scale of priorities. A high priority will be signalled by a willingness to pay a higher price. In response to the higher price more resources will be drawn into that use. Conversely, a falling price will indicate an over-supply or a lower priority. Resources will now be directed to some other use.

(d) *The market clearing-price.* Assuming there to be no impediment to the market mechanism there would always be a price at which the market would be cleared. Hence there existed no possibility of long-term involuntary unemployment of resources. This proposition was supported by J. B. Say's "law of markets".

8. Say's "law of markets". This law reasoned that the decision of individuals to work and produce is motivated only by the wish to acquire the produce of others. An increase in the output of the individual will generate for him sufficient income to take from the market goods equivalent to those produced by his own efforts.

The fundamental assumption is that all income will be spent upon either consumer goods or capital goods at a rate sufficient to guarantee the full employment of all resources. Resources could remain unemployed in the short run but only because the supply price was too high. In the long run, a fresh equilibrium price established at a lower level would ensure that they were once more fully utilised.

9. Microeconomics and macroeconomics. The traditional aspect of the subject, which has been outlined so far, belongs to the area which the modern economist describes as microeconomics. It attempts to explain the principles which govern the direction of resource use and will, therefore, isolate parts of the economy, one consumer, one firm, one industry, for close analysis.

Distinct from this approach is the attempt to explain the principles which govern the level of resource use in the economy as a whole. This aspect of the subject is referred to as macroeconomics and contributes the most significant element in the *twofold* revolution in economic thinking which occurred in the 1930s. It is to be particularly associated with the writings of John Maynard Keynes, *"the Keynesian revolution"*.

10. Allowing for monopoly influence. Overshadowed by the drastic Keynesian reappraisal of the classical model of the economy, but still of great importance, were the modifications to traditional thinking being made by a number of economists, in particular Edward H. Chamberlin in the USA (*The Theory of Monopolistic Competition*, 1933) and Joan Robinson in England (*The Economics of Imperfect Competition*, 1933).

Implicit in nineteenth-century explanations of the market as the optimal allocator of resources was the concept of "perfect competition". If price were permitted clearly to reflect our changing priorities and productive resources were not impeded in their consequent movement from one use to another, then the economy would remain flexible and capable of satisfying our needs with maximum efficiency. However, no attempt was made to prescribe exactly what conditions "perfect competition" had to fulfil. Once this analysis was made it became clear that in the real world of the twentieth century there was growing monopoly power, exercised not only by the suppliers of end products but also by the suppliers of the factors of production, land, labour and capital. If supply could be artificially restricted in order to secure a higher price and increased monopoly profits then the market was distorted. Price no longer established a natural harmony between the interests of buyers and sellers. Resources were no longer allocated in a way which fully represented the wants of individual consumers and the capacity of individual suppliers.

Recognition that economic activity in the real world took place in a variety of conditions, ranging between the hypothetical extremes of perfect competition and absolute monopoly, led to reformulation of the traditional model of the economy in terms of monopolistic competition by Chamberlin and imperfect competition by Robinson.

THE ECONOMICS OF JOHN KENNETH GALBRAITH

11. The firm's objectives. An even more radical challenge to the traditional view of markets and the behaviour of firms was postulated in the 1960s by John Kenneth Galbraith. In *The New Industrial State*, 1967, Galbraith questions whether the modern industrial firm responds to a market or controls it; whether it is motivated by the desire to maximise profits or whether it has a range of quite different objectives. In the traditional market model the consumer was sovereign, while the pressure of competition obliged the firm to operate with that degree of efficiency consistent with the maximisation of profits. Galbraith argues that in industries where many small firms are producing in highly competitive conditions they are subject to the full authority of the market and will seek only to increase their revenues.

12. Monopoly objectives. Equally, says Galbraith, it has long been assumed that monopolies will behave in a similar way. Why should a monopoly seek to rid itself of the pressures of a competitive market only to settle for less than the maximum possible return?

The answer lies in the pressures which have obliged the large corporation to substitute planning for the market. Rapidly changing and highly specialised technology, with the associated commitment of large sums of capital and extended periods of production time, compel the firm to free itself from the uncertainties of the market. It now seeks to control the prices that it pays for its inputs and which it receives for its outputs as well as taking steps to ensure that buyers take the planned quantities at those prices. In short, instead of being subject to the market, the large corporation has subordinated it to the goals of its planning objectives. Profit maximisation *may* still be a corporate goal but will no longer be enforced by the market while other objectives are likely to be of greater importance.

13. The motivation of senior management. Accepting the separation of ownership and control of the corporation, the profit motive in the conventional view produces a paradox. It is supposed that managers will not seek ruthlessly to reward themselves but to maximise the profits which will accrue to remote and powerless shareholders. Some concession may be made to the view that at the very top the pecuniary interests of managers and owners coincide since higher salaries can be justified by higher corporate earnings. Even this argument dissolves with the rise of "the technostructure".

14. The technostructure. As power passes down the organisation to the scientist, the engineer, the contract negotiator, the sales executive so profit maximisation disappears as the sole obligatory company objective. The members of the technostructure are rewarded to scale while an effective code of behaviour inhibits them from utilising confidential information for their own financial advantage. In short, while they must eschew personal profit the conventional view assumes that they will seek it for others.

15. The same goals for the technostructure, the corporation and society. The goals of the technostructure will be reflected in the goals of the mature corporation, which in turn will be conceded by a society which now makes those goals its own. For example, if a primary objective of the technostructure is autonomy and the level of earnings which sustains it, this will become a corporate goal and one which society will accept and applaud. The relationship will also work in reverse. If society holds rapid technical progress in high regard this goal will be mirrored in the goals of the corporation and of the technostructure.

What is important is an identity of individual, corporate and social purpose. The individual will identify with the goals of the corporation provided that they coincide with some socially laudable objective. There exists no such identity of purpose when the only corporate objective is making money for shareholders, an activity which attracts no great social approval.

Significantly, while some social attitudes originate outside of the technostructure, many simply reflect its personal interests since individuals have a great capacity for endowing their own activities with social value. Company objectives will now be tailored to fit those personal social goals.

16. Survival and growth of sales. These personal goals will manifest themselves in a number of ways. Survival will be the primary objective and therefore the firm will require to maintain a minimum level of profits. This achieved the modern corporation will now seek to expand its sales at the expense of profit.

17. Growth and advertising. The firm wishes to grow and therefore society must be conditioned by advertising to believe that the acquisition of more things is a desirable social objective. The firm, in fact, creates demand for its own products and growth is deified.

Galbraith then comments that Western society already has more things than it knows what to do with.

18. "The scientific and educational estate". Scientific and managerial intelligence are the key resources of the new industrial state. The government supports the system through public provision for education and technological research. In this way material objectives are established and personnel trained to achieve them. This scientific and educational élite thus acquire a certain moral authority and being sufficiently intelligent to see through the cult of growth offer the promise of gradual change to a less philistine style of life.

19. Conclusion. The Galbraithian analysis represents a radical departure from the mainstream of economic thinking. The market exercises authority in only a very limited and diminishing area of the economy. It should therefore be abjured. Real power lies with giant corporations which in fact dictate the path of social and economic development. Observation suggests that this produces a rather unattractive way of life. The implication is clear.

Government, advised by a cultured scientific and educational estate, should play a greater part in planning the way ahead to a better society.

THE RESPONSE TO GALBRAITH

20. General assessment. It is true that conventional theory is insufficiently sophisticated to give a very satisfactory account of the behaviour of today's large corporation. Attempts have been made to provide explanations which could be accommodated within the body of existing theory but none go so far as Galbraith. It is also true that Galbraith's work has attracted a great deal of interest but support for his views has been drawn from the wider public rather than from his professional colleagues.

Professional criticism has come from two main directions.

(*a*) *No systematic economic model.* While there may be important truths in much of what Galbraith says, his various points have not been incorporated in any systematic theory which explains the functioning of the whole economy. Until this happens his insights are unlikely to have any real influence upon the way in which economic problems are handled. At present this seems improbable since in contrast to Smith, Keynes, Friedman and others he has not attracted other economists to form "a school of thought".

(*b*) *Too many dogmatic generalisations.* Many of his hypotheses rest upon sweeping assertions which may be "felt" to be true but remain untested by scientific methods. Attempts have been made to provide such tests with results which have not been favourable to Galbraith's case.

21. The goals of stability and sales maximisation: Demsetz. Professor Harold Demsetz (UCLA) has tested two of Galbraith's central hypotheses on the structure of industry.

(*a*) *"Technostructure orientated firms sacrifice profits to accelerate sales."* Galbraith identifies such firms as those which are capital intensive, heavily advertised, oligopolistic, large and with an orientation towards military production. Demsetz measured the performance of 375 such firms to see if there was evidence of a trade-off of profits against sales. He found no evidence that this was the case.

(*b*) *"Management places stability above profits."* A principal management objective will be to ensure that the firm's plans are not disrupted. Demsetz analysed a sample of thirteen stocks of leading defence contractors. He found that they offered to investors 21 per cent more risk in terms of annual fluctuations in the rate of return to investors than did randomly selected portfolios of thirteen stocks.

22. Planning for a minimum level of profit: McFadzean. Galbraith asserts that the technostructure will simply plan for the minimum level of profit necessary to keep the shareholders pacified.

Professor F. S. McFadzean levels the criticism that "the corporate planners in Galbraith's unreal world start off with a predetermined level of profit to meet the objectives he postulates and presumably juggle with proceeds, volumes, costs and investments to achieve this figure ... it implies a control of events and markets which exists only in a monopoly situation and the imagination of Professor Galbraith".

McFadzean goes on to point out that profits are a residual which no firm can plan with any certainty since all the evidence shows that no firm can ultimately bend the consumer to its will.

23. The technostructure will place its own security above profit maximisation: Solow. Galbraith claims that the shareholder has no power to influence the objectives of the technostructure and that the latter will place its own security above profits.

Professor R. M. Solow argues that this is paradoxical. If managers earn less than is feasible with the resources at their disposal this will have a detrimental effect upon the company's share prices. Lower prices provide an incentive for takeover bids which will displace the existing management. It follows that indirectly shareholders do influence the company's objectives.

24. The mature corporation moulds the consumer to its will: Solow. Fundamental to the Galbraithian thesis is the view that the company through powerful advertising is able to dictate to the consumer.

Professor Solow responds that while much advertising may be thought distasteful or excessive, this is no evidence that the art of salesmanship has freed the large corporation from the need to meet the market test, giving it "decisive influence over the revenue it receives". Galbraith offers no evidence, only assertion.

Accepting that this is a difficult question to resolve it may be equally argued that much competitive advertising is self-cancelling and that much is legitimately informative contributing to competition in the market place.

25. Large corporations do not monopolise the whole economy: Solow. Solow concedes that large corporations may be typical of manufacturing industry but argues that Galbraith underestimates the amount of activity still undertaken by small firms. This is particularly true of trade and services, the sectors which show the greatest growth relative to the whole economy.

Moreover, Professor John Jewkes in *The Sources of Invention* rejects Galbraith's assertion that technological advance depends upon large monopolistic corporations. The evidence shows that much innovation has been carried out by small competitive firms.

26. Conclusions. The Galbraithian controversy has been discussed at some length since it clearly has fundamental implications for economic theory. It must, however, be concluded that without much more research and the production of substantive evidence Galbraith's propositions remain hypothetical. In particular it has to be proved that markets no longer function in the way that main-stream economic thinking has postulated.

THE KEYNESIAN REVOLUTION

27. The depression of the 1930s. In the period 1921–39 only once did the proportion of insured persons unemployed fall below 10 per cent. In two years it was above 20 per cent and the overall average was in excess of 14 per cent. There was immense hardship, apart from which it was estimated that there was an annual loss of potential output of between £400 and £500 million measured at the prices current at that time.

The classical economic model could only explain equilibrium at full employment (*see* 7(*d*), **8** above). It could give no account of the long-term failure to utilise resources.

28. New economic thinking. The attention of economic theorists now shifted from the direction of the demand for resources (microeconomics) to the level of that demand (macroeconomics). It seemed clear to some economists that despite falls in wages, and even if there were no interference in the process of wage bargaining, there would be no inevitable tendency to full employment.

The new macroeconomics was therefore concerned with analysing the relationship between certain variables expressed as aggregates, i.e. the volume of consumer and investment expenditures, the level of national income and employment and the volume of production.

29. John Maynard Keynes. Pre-eminent among the new economic thinkers was Keynes whose analysis is expressed most fully in *The General Theory of Employment, Interest and Money*, 1936.

Focusing upon aggregate demand for goods and services, he suggested that if this were to fall in the short term there would be over-production. As stocks accumulated some people would be thrown out of work. At least initially they would look for work at comparable wages. In the meantime their purchasing power would be reduced and demand would fall still further. They might, in due course, accept work at a lower wage but by this time the continuing fall in demand would have produced a situation in which even this low wage was too high to ensure employment for all. With some unemployment persisting and at a reduced level of activity demand might decline still further producing yet more unemployment.

Before long-run equilibrium was established at a level of wages sufficiently low to guarantee the employment of everybody the economy would have sunk into depression.

30. Key features. Certain features of the Keynesian system are immediately apparent.

(*a*) *Initial impact on output*. The initial effect of a fall in demand would be upon output rather than upon prices. Prices and wages would only begin to fall once it was clear that the decline in demand was more than temporary. The original loss of output and employment would now be magnified as demand continued to decline with an ensuing major recession.

(*b*) *Stickiness of wage rates*. This approach contrasted with the earlier view that the first impact would be upon wages and prices, which at a lower level would remove excess supply from the market.

In the labour market unemployment might in the long run produce competition leading to lower wages and more employment. In the short run determination to find a job at the same wage would in fact lead to a period of zero wages and further falls in demand. It followed that if the decline into depression were to be halted, it was the demand for labour which was crucial.

31. Policy implications. Since the automatic equilibrating function of the market was shown to be inadequate there was a clear

case for government intervention. The shortfall in private sector demand would be compensated by increased public sector
spending.

In the pre-war world, public opinion was not yet prepared to
accept such a dramatic change. *Laissez-faire* economic thinking
was rooted in the view that the state had no part to play in
economic affairs. Central economic planning was essentially
collectivist and socialist.

32. A social and economic watershed. The Second World War
provided the climate for a change of view. For the purpose of
winning a war total planning of the economy was accepted. Would
it not, therefore, be reasonable to accept some degree of central
planning if this led to a fairer, more secure and stable society?

In 1942, the Beveridge Report provided the blueprint for the
Welfare State. Beveridge stressed that any prospect for a comprehensive system of social security founded upon the insurance
principle would have to be underwritten by the certainty of a
continuing high level of employment. The government gave a firm
commitment to this objective in the White Paper, *Employment
Policy*, 1944, and it subsequently became the first priority of all
succeeding governments. The state was now responsible for the
level of economic activity. The age of *laissez-faire* had passed.

33. Economic intervention with social democracy. The Keynesian
analysis appeared to provide a mechanism through which the main
features of the market could be retained while its inadequacies
were compensated by state intervention. In this way it would be
possible to avoid the illiberality of wholly planned economies and
the political totalitarianism which inevitably accompanied them.
Democracy would be preserved.

34. Keynesian policies in practice. Policies designed to sustain
aggregate demand at a level consistent with a high level of employment appeared at first to be remarkably successful. With this
encouragement, the "high level of employment" objective of the
1944 White Paper was now referred to more emphatically as "full
employment". Never defined statistically, in practice it came to
mean 1.2 per cent–2 per cent unemployment. Anything in excess of
2 per cent brought political pressures which required the government to take remedial action.

35. "Stop-go." A new problem emerged. In its anxiety to ensure
that aggregate demand was sustained at an adequate level and

encouraged in this by political pressures to spend more on social measures, the tendency of the government was to over-compensate. In the "go" phase, full employment output was soon achieved. The continued expansion of demand induced inflationary pressure which, in due course, brought imbalance in international payments. To restore the balance it was then necessary to damp down aggregate demand and the economy came to a "stop".

The periodicity of this cycle of events gradually increased along with the level of unemployment experienced in the "stop" phase and the rate of inflation occurring during the "go" phase.

It seemed that the new economic steering mechanism did not function with the precision which had been intended. Indeed for some economists government intervention had itself become a destabilising agent.

36. A new phenomenon. Towards the end of the 1960s there appeared the problem of escalating inflation accompanied by rising unemployment. It was now the new orthodoxy which could no longer explain events, since the theory developed by Keynes's successors postulated a trade-off between inflation and unemployment. When one rose, the other fell.

THE COUNTER-REVOLUTION IN MONETARY THEORY

37. Demand and supply, the short term and the long term. In the short term it is demand which is flexible and subject to instability. It is equally amenable to manipulation. On the other hand supply is inflexible, being dependent upon the availability of productive resources which can only be developed in the long term.

Inasmuch as the Keynesian analysis placed emphasis upon the treatment of unemployment, which resulted from a deficiency of demand, it concerned itself with the short term and tended to neglect the long term. A boost to demand would manifest itself in increased employment and output and hardly at all in prices.

Criticism of this preoccupation with the short term reflects the pre-Keynesian view that, in the long term, variations in demand work chiefly on prices and only indirectly on output. Variations in prices will, however, determine the proportion of productive resources which are employed. On this view the phenomenon of inflation with unemployment is explained. The continued and excessive expansion of demand in the long term results in price inflation rather than increased output. As inflation gathers momentum so the factors of production are priced out of the market and the economy stagnates.

38. The monetarists. It should be remembered that from the outset there were those who contested the validity of Keynes's analysis, in particular his contemporary, Friedrich Hayek (*see also* **40**). It was not, however, until the 1950s that a powerful reaction began to develop in the thinking of the monetarist school of economists which is usually associated with Professor Milton Friedman and the University of Chicago. Their influence has steadily grown.

Their basic contention is that there exists a consistent relationship between the rate of growth of the money supply and the general price level. This in turn will affect the level of employment of resources. Government attempts at short-term "fine tuning" of the economy are self-defeating, since they themselves prove to be the principal source of instability.

Long-term equilibrium will depend, from the side of supply, upon the physical constraints which affect the availability of land, labour and capital. On the side of demand, government should confine its policies to holding monetary growth to a stable rate which would reasonably accommodate any *real* growth in output.

THE AUSTRIANS

39. A challenge to mainstream economic thought. During the 1970s, as Britain's economic problems multiplied, there was increasing popular disenchantment with economics in general, and amongst economists some puzzlement that mainstream thinking, for all its refinements and sophisticated model building, could no longer explain many apparently new phenomena. In this context there has been a resurgence of interest in the Austrian school of economists.

Reappraisal of their work is significant to contemporary thinking in both microeconomics and macroeconomics.

(*a*) *Microeconomics.* In common with mainstream, neo-classical economists they support the market as the most effective co-ordinator of economic plans. They differ in their explanation of how the market process works, preferring a dynamic to a static analysis. They believe that the traditional explanation is both inadequate and inaccurate and has led accordingly to an incorrect diagnosis of market failure. This being the case, twentieth-century intervention by government to compensate for supposed market failure has been misconceived and counter-productive, worsening a situation which the market, unimpeded, would itself have remedied. Some Austrians are therefore led to certain specific policy recommendations in respect of the UK economy of the 1980s (*see* **51** below).

(*b*) *Macroeconomics*. In the neo-Keynesian/monetarist controversy Austrians adopt a monetarist position. They differ from other monetarists in emphasising the *mode* of further monetary injections rather than focusing solely upon the *additions* to the money supply. Further consideration will be given to this variation in IV, **18–26**.

40. The Austrian school of economists. The Austrian school was founded at the University of Vienna by Carl Menger (1840–1921) during the 1870s. Menger's work attracted a number of his contemporaries, most notably Bohm-Bawerk (1851–1914) and Wieser (1851–1926).

The best known of the second generation of Austrians are Ludwig von Mises (1881–1973) and Joseph Schumpeter (1883–1950). The third generation, largely taught by Mises, includes Hayek (b. 1899), Haberler (b. 1901), Machlup (b. 1902) and Rosenstein-Rodan (b. 1902). All four in due course emigrated to the USA where the Austrian school has had its greatest revival.

41. Methodology. Distinctive of the original school was its defence of political economy as a theoretical discipline and its attack on the German historical economists. Until the turn of the century the *Methodenstreit* or "clash over methods" was the main source of controversy amongst the economists. The acceptance of the essential ideas of the Austrian school into mainstream economic thinking led, by the time of Menger's death, to the disappearance of a distinctively Austrian school of thought. However, in one significant respect mainstream economics developed along lines which diverged from those envisaged by Menger. The explanation of the business cycle put forward by Hayek and Mises differed markedly from that offered by Keynes and his associates. It is in this area particularly that most interest has been reawakened, "Austrian" ideas being propagated by Hayek's student Ludwig Lachmann and Mises's students Israel Kirzner and Murray Rothbard. They in turn have been followed by an increasing number of younger scholars teaching in universities in both the USA and the UK.

42. The basis of the Austrian tradition. Menger's thinking is distinguished by the following three characteristics.

(*a*) *Subjectivism.* Contemporaneously, the independently of Jevons and Walras, Menger developed the concept of subjective utility, the view that "value is not a property inherent in goods but constitutes a relationship between an appraising mind and the object appraised" (Lachmann).

(*b*) *The "atomistic" method.* Collective decisions made by the nation are not determined by *one* decision maker but rather by a highly complex collection of *individual* decision makers. It follows that to understand the former one must investigate the processes of the latter. Menger believed that the classical economists had failed to do this and for him the explanation of these phenomena was an inherent part of the substance of economics.

(*c*) *"Organic" and "pragmatic" institutions.* Following from (*b*) above, Menger distinguished between those social and economic structures "pragmatically" created by communal activity, e.g. law, and those "organically" created to promote communal welfare but which are not the result of any explicit communal plan, e.g. markets.

"Language, religion, law, even the state itself, and, to mention a few economic and social phenomena, the phenomena of markets, of competition, of money, and numerous other social structures are already met with in epochs of history where we cannot properly speak of a *purposeful* activity of the community as such, directed at establishing them." (C. Menger, *Problems of Economics and Sociology*, 1883.)

43. Methodological individualism. Menger's atomistic method would today be described as "methodological individualism". This approach explored the assumptions of mainstream, neo-classical economics and finds them inadequate.

The classical theory of general equilibrium in the market (a static concept) makes a number of assumptions, the most unreal of which is *perfect knowledge*. The preferences of consumers at one time and which are clearly known to themselves are by some mechanism collated to form a demand curve. Similarly by some process the individual members of a firm combine to determine and carry out the firm's policy which, collated with the policies of other firms, constitutes the supply curve. From the interaction of the two curves is derived "the equilibrium price" which at *one* time harmonises the interests of buyers and sellers.

Neo-classical economics makes no attempt to explain the processes by which these variable and individual interests are translated into collective choices.

The Austrians would therefore seek to incorporate a number of aspects of human personality, ignored by classical economists, into an explanation of economic behaviour, notably:

(*a*) *the degree of knowledge* of one's own tastes and the opportunities available for satisfying them;

(*b*) *alertness* to new opportunities as they arise;

(*c*) *interpretations* of current events and the reactions of others to those events;

(*d*) *expectations* of future events and the behaviour of others.

The significant feature is that knowledge, alertness, interpretations and expectations of individuals differ and therefore Austrian subjectivism assumes a much wider dimension than the subjectivism of mainstream economics based solely upon *a perfect knowledge of one's own tastes at a given point in time*.

44. Methodological individualism and welfare economics. A "social welfare function" is frequently assumed by many mainstream economists. This concept supposedly embraces the preferences of society as a whole but welfare economics makes no attempt to explain how individual preferences are aggregated to create this function.

Moreover, it is tacitly assumed that once a welfare function has been determined, government policy implements it. No attempt is made to analyse the problems of creating an appropriate framework which ensures that actions taken by organisations are in fact related to the knowledge, preferences, interpretations and expectations of individuals.

Consequently mainstream economics has no adequate explanation of the behaviour of government organisations. Its *normative* prescriptions of what government *should* do, in neglecting to relate "means" and "ends", is, on an Austrian view, naïve.

45. Time and the market process. In mainstream economics, equilibrium in a perfectly competitive market (characterised by perfect knowledge) is achieved at a given point in time. The plans of the individual participants in the market are then fully co-ordinated. The Austrians vary this concept to that of a process which occurs over a *period* of time characterised by a *lack* of knowledge and a consequent *lack* of co-ordination, but also one during which there is the acquisition of new knowledge and *increasing* co-ordination.

The static concepts of economically allocating resources to respond to given tastes, or of demand and supply responding to given prices, are insufficient to encompass the continuing search for new opportunities. This awareness or alertness to the possibility of *improved* opportunities is referred to by some Austrians as *entrepreneurship*.

46. Competition, entrepreneurship and profit. The key to the competitive market process lies in the absence of a perfect knowledge vested equally in all market participants. Different people know different things. The market is the mechanism through which a mass of discrete pieces of information is transmitted, thus co-ordinating economic activity.

In this context the entrepreneur is alert to new information or opportunities not so far grasped by others. Profit is to be seen as the return to this alertness in a market which is not yet fully co-ordinated. When profit opportunities have been exhausted, there is no longer a role for the entrepreneur and the whole system has lost its driving force.

Such an equilibrium is not, however, the nature of the real and *dynamic* world in which there is always uncertainty (imperfect knowledge). All human action therefore contains some element of entrepreneurship.

47. The Austrians and the concept of monopolistic competition. It has already been noted (*see* **10** above) that the classical perfect competition model of the economy was modified in the 1930s to allow for the imperfections of competition.

On an Austrian view these corrections were misconceived since they failed to identify the true weakness of classical theory. Instead of attacking the static equilibrium approach of existing theory they simply substituted *different* equilibrium theories.

For example, Chamberlin, in pursuit of a more realistic market model, focuses upon product differentiation. However, like earlier perfect competition theory his approach assumes that somehow the demand curve is *given*. He does not recognise the trial and error process through which suppliers and consumers seek to discover the products and their variations most suited to the market. The theory of monopolistic competition does not recognise therefore that a major aspect of product differentiation is not a final, fully informed equilibrium choice by consumers but rather the reflection of a continuing process of search for new opportunities.

48. The Austrians and monopoly. Traditional theory assumes that by a deliberate curtailment of supply the monopolist is able to raise his price and secure a monopoly profit. Again, the demand curve is given. For the Austrians, what is important is *how* the monopolist discovers the nature of his demand curve and *why* he is a single producer, unthreatened by potential competitors.

Demand curves are never given but are gradually revealed through the market process of discovering what the customer wants and what he is prepared to pay. This aspect of competition remains unaltered by monopoly.

Moreover, it has been emphasised (Schumpeter) that the fundamental source of competition arises not from producers of the *same* product but from those who produce *new* and *better* products.

This line of thought leads us to ask why a firm is the sole producer. There are a number of answers. Many public enterprises enjoy statutory monopolies. In some cases firms have sole control over a necessary resource and can thus prevent the entry into the market of competitors. In other cases, production is in the hands of one supplier only because others have not seen the activity as profitable or have recognised its profitability only belatedly. The resulting "monopoly profits" are then better described as "entre-preneurial profits", the consequence of grasping an opportunity not recognised by others.

Provided that competitors can enter the market then monopoly is only temporary. Austrians therefore place emphasis upon *freedom of entry* as a necessary and sufficient condition for the operation of the competitive market process.

49. Implications for the economic role of government. Traditional economics argues that in an ideal and perfectly competitive economy resources will be allocated in the most efficient way. In the real world, however, there are frequent cases of market failure, e.g. monopoly, which result in a less than optimal deployment of resources. There are other cases where the market takes no account of social costs, e.g. pollution or unemployment resulting from structural change within the economy. It is the function of the welfare economist to identify these cases and to prescribe remedial government policies. Such "necessary" interventions provide the rationale for a mixed economy.

Characterising this approach, Professor James Meade argues in _The Intelligent Radical's Guide to Economic Policy: the Mixed Economy_ (Allen & Unwin, 1975) that:

> "The intelligent radical starts by advocating the removal of all unnecessary restrictions on the operation of free competitive markets. But he recognises that on the foundations of this market mechanism there must be built a superstructure of governmental intervention and controls. Some of these interventions are needed simply to set a background of conditions in which free competition can work effectively; others are needed to replace entirely the mechanism of competitive markets, where that mechanism cannot be expected to operate effectively; others have an intermediate purpose, namely to modify without replacing the operation of a market mechanism."

In their divergence from mainstream, neo-classical economics Austrians view this approach with some scepticism.

50. The Austrians and welfare economics. For reasons already outlined the Austrians doubt whether the intervention recommended by the welfare economist will ever produce the results intended. In fact, they are likely to be counter-productive, for the following reasons.

(_a_) _Uncertainty and errors._ Welfare economics makes little reference to the uncertainties and errors in the market process. Like all neo-classical economics it views competition as a static equilibrium with _given_ commodities and techniques rather than a dynamic process which furthers the search for _better_ products and _improved_ techniques. The whole system is directed towards the determination of a set of prices which produces the most efficient allocation of resources at one time rather than towards lower prices and greater outputs.

(_b_) _Sources of superior government knowledge?_ Welfare economics does not consider the mechanisms through which government assembles the information necessary for the design and implementation of its plans, and in a way which is superior to the mechanism of the market. This knowledge is not already collected in one place but is dispersed throughout the members of the economy.

(_c_) _The nature of social institutions._ As previously noted (_see_

42(*c*)), the Austrians distinguish between "pragmatic" and "organic" institutions. They believe it necessary to choose the correct balance between the two, to create the appropriate framework of law and government policy within which the organic process can best flourish. They are critical of welfare economics for its lack of recognition of the power of organic institutions and for its almost complete dependence upon "pragmatic" intervention by government to apply direct controls.

51. Dilution of the mixed economy. The views outlined above lead some Austrians to policy recommendations, a number of which would seem startling in the context of mainstream economic thinking but which are nevertheless broadly in line with the stance adopted by the 1979 Conservative Government. A selection of these policy recommendations are summarised below.

(*a*) *On nationalised industries.* Statutory monopolies should be abolished and free entry permitted. Capital should be provided from the market in competition with the private sector. Social obligations should be specified and compensated. Otherwise economic performance should be judged entirely by market criteria.

(*b*) *Indicative planning.* The National Enterprise Board should be abolished with *all* assets sold back to the private sector. Planning agreements should be abandoned.

(*c*) *Competition.* Patents and merger controls should be abolished.

(*d*) *Social costs.* The costs of, for example, pollution should be offset not by government intervention but by the reinforcement of property rights which enable individuals more easily to claim against any infringements.

52. A rationale for Part One. This outline of Austrian economics has been developed in some detail since it is a line of thinking which provides the theoretical basis for much of the contemporary reaction to Keynesianism and interventionism.

The theory of the Keynesian system will be outlined in Chapter II with its implications for government policy explained in Chapter III. Chapter IV points to the crucial difference between monetarists and Keynesians on the role of money in the economy and pursues the criticisms of the Keynesians made by both Friedmanite and Austrian monetarists.

Chapters V and VI examine critically the reliance of Keynesian demand management techniques upon deficit finance and consider the consequences for post-war Britain.

PROGRESS TEST 1

1. List the principal collectivist features of feudal society.   **(3)**
2. What are the characteristics of a free enterprise market economy?   **(5)**
3. What are the principal characteristics of classical economic thinking?   **(7)**
4. Distinguish between microeconomics and macroeconomics. **(9)**
5. What did Joan Robinson and Edward Chamberlin contribute to economic theory?   **(10)**
6. List the principal aspects of Galbraith's *New Industrial State*. **(11–19)**
7. In what general respects may Galbraith be criticised?   **(20)**
8. What is the nature of McFadzean's criticism of Galbraith? **(22)**
9. How does Solow criticise Galbraith?   **(23–25)**
10. What do you understand by "the Keynesian revolution"? **(27–30)**
11. What was the importance for practical policies of Keynesian thinking?   **(31–34)**
12. What do you understand by "stop-go"?   **(35)**
13. Explain the nature of the "counter-revolution in monetary theory".   **(37–38)**
14. In what areas does Austrian thinking differ from mainstream economic analysis?   **(39)**
15. Outline the basis of Austrian economic thought.   **(42)**
16. Elaborate on the concept of "methodological individualism".   **(43–44)**
17. How does "time" affect the concept of equilibrium in the market?   **(45)**
18. Explain the Austrian scepticism of welfare economics. **(49–50)**
19. Indicate some of the areas in which Austrian analysis leads to policy recommendations radically different from those which have been accepted in recent years.   **(51)**

CHAPTER II

The Keynesian System

THE BUSINESS CYCLE

1. A general theory. From one viewpoint the weakness of classical economics was that it was only able to explain the working of the economy in a particular situation, full employment. Keynes provided a "general theory" in the sense that it explained how the economy might function at *any* level of employment. Writing in a time of massive unemployment it was natural that his primary concern should be with this problem. However, it is often forgotten that he provided an explanation of the whole business cycle and had a good deal to say about the problem of over-full employment and inflation.

2. Industrial fluctuations. Variations in the level of economic activity can be observed to occur in different time series and from different causes.

(*a*) *The secular trend*. This is the long-term trend which in Western economies in the nineteenth and twentieth centuries has been one of growth with rising production and consumption.

(*b*) *Seasonal variations*. As the name suggests, for climatic reasons variations occur within the space of one year, e.g. in the building trade.

(*c*) *Erratic fluctuations*. In a wholly unpredictable way variations result from forces external to the economy, e.g. natural catastrophes or political upheavals.

(*d*) *Long waves*. Since 1822 it is possible to define six periods, each averaging twenty-five years' duration, in which the prevailing trends of prosperity and depression alternated.

(*e*) *The business or trade cycle*. Within each long wave there can be discerned between two and a half and three and a half business cycles comprising a regular alternation of prosperity and depression.

Government economic policy in the period 1945–79 aimed to reduce and, hopefully, eliminate cyclical fluctuations, the ultimate objective being a smoothly rising growth curve. The degree of success was to be observed in the less pronounced booms and the less severe depressions, referred to nowadays as "recessions". On the other hand the periodicity of the cycle increased and "stop-go" economic policies became subject to much criticism.

3. Phases of the business cycle. The following four phases may be discerned.

(*a*) *The upswing.* A period of rising economic activity and prosperity. The general price level tends to rise.

(*b*) *The downturn.* The point of crisis at which expansion slows down or ceases.

(*c*) *The downswing.* A period of contraction. The general price level tends to fall.

(*d*) *The upturn.* The point of revival prior to the next upswing.

4. Manifestations of the business cycle. There are three principal criteria by which one may distinguish the phases of the cycle. They are the level of employment, the volume of production and the volume of consumption. At the outset it should be stressed that these indicators need not point in the same direction. If they diverge then the considerations set out below must be set against each other in order to arrive at a conclusion.

5. Level of employment. Because of their far-reaching social and political implications there has been a tendency to accept unemployment figures as the principal if not the only indicator of the phases of the business cycle. The reliability of this indicator must therefore be assessed. It must first be made clear, however, that unemployment springs from a variety of causes.

(*a*) *Seasonal unemployment.* This corresponds to seasonal variations in certain types of business activity.

(*b*) *Frictional unemployment.* This is "short-term" structural unemployment. Within any industry there are always those firms which are contracting while others are expanding. It follows that in the short run there will be unemployment as some men move from one firm to another.

(*c*) *Secular unemployment.* This is "long-term" structural unemployment. In a dynamic society technological change brings new industries while old industries become obsolescent. Unemployment results for those men whose skills are no longer in demand.

(*d*) *Cyclical unemployment.* The figures rise or fall according to the phase of the business cycle.

In the period between the wars the hard core of chronic unemployment was secular in character and associated with the regions in which there had been excessive specialisation in industries such as cotton, coal, iron, steel and heavy engineering. Superimposed was the huge mass of unemployment of cyclical origin. In such a period the economy may move into an upswing while there remains a considerable volume of unemployment for secular, seasonal and frictional reasons.

Moreover, if there is downward pressure on wage rates during the downswing, unemployment figures need not necessarily rise. The same number of men continue to be employed at lower wage levels. This was commonly the case in the nineteenth century and in recent years has manifested itself in trade-union pressure for work sharing as an alternative to redundancies.

On the other hand during an upswing it is possible for the level of unemployment to rise if increased output is due to the improved productivity of labour.

Finally, in utilising this criterion there remains the difficulty of defining full employment as a norm upon which to base policy measures. The choice of figure must ultimately be arbitrary. Judged by government policies in the years 1945–66 it would seem to have been accepted as lying within the range 1.2–1.4 per cent unemployed. There then appeared to be a realisation that such figures were excessively ambitious when the Prime Minister declared in the House of Commons that he did not think the House would find intolerable an unemployment figure of 2.4 per cent.

When in 1972 unemployment exceeded 1 million and even more in 1981 when it topped 2.5 million it seemed that the limits of political tolerance had previously been underestimated. There was also some acceptance that government could not regulate unemployment to the degree that had previously been thought possible. Thus the Prime Minister asserted in 1976 that, "we used to think we could spend our way out of recession. That option is no longer open to us." With this failure of confidence disappeared any clear view of how full employment might de defined.

6. Criticisms of the use of unemployment statistics. In recent years criticism has been directed to the lack of analysis of the unemployment statistics in the returns of the Department of Employment. It is argued that the macroeconomic total of unemployment is a misleading indicator of the phase of the business cycle and therefore an unreliable guide to government in formulating economic policy. Only a microeconomic division of the total by age, duration, sex and other variables can produce a reliable policy guide.

In his research monograph *How Much Unemployment?*, 1972 and his Hobart paper *How Little Unemployment?* (IEA, 1975) John B. Woods argues for a much closer analysis.

7. Distinct indicators for social and economic policy. New data published since 1972 clearly reveals certain features of the labour markets.

(*a*) *Diversity.* There are many markets in labour, not just one. Each displays its own characteristics, e.g. young and old, male and female.

(*b*) *Dynamism.* Even in times of relatively slack demand there is a brisk turnover of labour. This reveals a vital distinction between job changes and the long-term unemployed.

It is therefore argued that a clear distinction should be made between unemployment figures which may provide a guide for social policy and those which indicate how many unemployed are genuinely available for work. The present global figure is of little use as an economic indicator since it takes no account of the different types of unemployment noted in **5** above. Implicit in the official macroeconomic approach is the view that *all* unemployment is of cyclical origin.

8. A new strategic indicator of unemployment. Woods then suggests a new indicator which he defines as "the number in the male labour force aged 25 to 55 without work for more than six months".

His reasons for such a restricted definition are as follows.

(*a*) *Exclusion of those unemployed for under six months.* The issue of P45 forms by the Inland Revenue reveals some 10 million job changes annually. Only about one-third of these jobs are found through job centres and employment offices but even here the turnover is very brisk with each month between 300,000 and 350,000 entering the register and about the same numbers leaving it. The difference between the two flows shows the overall rise or fall.

Those who register fall into two groups, a majority who find work in under two months and the rest who take longer or remain permanently unemployed.

Changes in demand management policy can have no short-run effect. Therefore the short-term unemployed should be excluded from the indicator.

(*b*) *Exclusion of those over 55*. A substantial number of those in the 60–65 group comprise occupational pensioners who register either to receive social security or to have their national insurance contributions credited. This objection was met in April 1981 with scaled reductions of social security entitlements to offset occupational pensions. Effectively, £35 per week marks a ceiling above which there is no social security entitlement.

(*c*) *Exclusion of those under 25*. There are two distinct groups.

(*i*) Adult students: during the 1970s increasing numbers of students registered during vacation in order to qualify for certain social security benefits. This clearly produced temporary distortions in the unemployment figures. The rules have been modified and in 1981 permit students to register without restriction only during the summer vacation. They may then qualify for supplementary benefit, or, if they have paid insurance contributions in the previous year, unemployment benefit.

(*ii*) School-leavers: there are approximately 750,000 school-leavers each year of whom about 500,000 seek work. They present a special problem. They may take a long time to find their first job and even longer to find one that suits them. Initially, they swell the number of job changers disproportionately. However, in the period 1962–72 the median duration of unemployment for boys aged 15–17 was very low at 2–4 weeks. By the end of the 1970s technological change rather than recession had resulted in what will probably be a permanent reduction in the demand for unskilled labour. The problem of school-leavers with no special qualifications is now therefore likely to prove more intractable.

(*d*) *Exclusion of women*. The trend is for women in all age groups to represent a larger proportion of the total work-force. This proportion grew from 25 per cent in 1939 to 37 per cent in 1975. In contrast, male employment has declined not only relatively but, since 1965, absolutely. In the following ten years there was a decline of 800,000 men in employment offset by an increase of 865,000 women.

Moreover, the evidence shows that on average female unemployment for more than six months stands at only 30,000 while female vacancies (when they were still advertised as such) repeatedly exceeded that figure.

The conclusion is that *long-term* unemployment is specifically a male problem.

(*e*) *Other exclusions*. It should also be recognised that a reliable strategic indicator should allow for:

(*i*) long-term unemployment: investigations suggest that there may be in the region of 250,000 people who for physical or psychological reasons are incapable of holding a job;

(*ii*) fraudulent registrations: from successful prosecutions a "guesstimate" of 2 per cent of the total unemployed may be made.

9. Volume of production and consumption. We must next assess the validity of the other two principal indicators of the phase of the business cycle.

(*a*) *Volume of consumption.* It has been observed that during a downswing it is possible for a high level of employment to be maintained at the expense of lower wage rates. However, with lower earnings it is likely that expenditure on consumption will decline and this will be a more reliable index of the state of trade. Even so, it cannot be used in isolation.

(*b*) *Volume of production.* During the downswing the volume of consumption may for a time remain unaffected but expenditure on investment declines. In short, the nation is subsidising its standard of living by consuming capital. Conversely, in an upswing there may be a big increase in capital expenditure while consumption is little affected. The nation is adding to its capital.

10. Policy implications. The aim of macroeconomic policy will be to achieve continuous growth (i.e. eliminate the business cycle) at stable prices and with full employment. If the various manifestations of the business cycle point in the same direction there will be little doubt as to the phase of the cycle and *if* the Keynesian analysis is accepted, a clear indication of the policies to be adopted. Where they diverge the position is less obvious and it will be necessary to balance the evidence and to establish the order of priorities of the three policy objectives.

For example, during 1969 and 1970 the demand for labour was weak and unemployment rose although the volume of production continued marginally to rise. The balance of the evidence indicated that the economy was still in recession but since the policy priority was to counter inflation employment was sacrificed and no stimulus given to demand.

During 1971–72 the unemployment figures continued to rise suggesting that the recession was deepening. Employment now became the first priority and major reflationary measures were undertaken.

NOTE: In line with the criticism that the global unemployment figure has received insufficient analysis and has been incorrectly interpreted, it may be noted that while the *stock* of unemployment rose in 1971–72, from the spring of 1971 more men began to leave the register. From the end of 1971 the notification of vacancies increased. This reflected a new trend which passed unnoticed. Attention was focused upon the stock to the neglect of the underlying flows. This misinterpretation led to policies which were directly responsible for the inflation of 1973–74.

ANALYSIS OF THE CAUSES OF THE BUSINESS CYCLE

11. Business-cycle theories. The causes of the business cycle are complex and it would be idle to claim that any single explanation is adequate or that the same explanation is equally valid for all countries or for every cycle. This is generally recognised by most writers on the subject and differences are usually of emphasis rather than of principle.

There are five groups of theories which may conveniently be placed under the following headings.

(*a*) Psychological theories.
(*b*) Monetary theories.
(*c*) Over-investment theories.
(*d*) Under-consumption theories.
(*e*) Keynesian theory.

It is a merit of the work of Keynes that he gives due consideration to these other theories and having allowed for their validity in certain circumstances goes on to offer his own explanation. We shall for the moment confine our attention to Keynesian theory since this provided the foundation for practical economic policy-making during the period 1945–79.

12. Effective demand, national income and the level of employment. The "General Theory" centres upon the concept of effective demand which comprises total national expenditure upon consumer goods and services and upon capital goods. The crucial thing to remember is that spending generates income and employment while saving does not. What one man spends represents demand for another man's employment and constitutes his income. Expenditure and income are two aspects of the same thing. A third aspect will be the money value of the total volume of production since this equates with both total money expenditure and total money income. Whatever is spent upon production will be distributed in wages, rent, interest and profits.

From these proportions three important conclusions follow, as outlined below.

(a) *The key indicator is the national income figure.* Employment according to Keynes is a function of national income. If income is declining so is employment and vice versa.

NOTE: This is a valid enough assumption in a period of depression. An increase in business activity would be reflected in the use of more labour. The proposition becomes more questionable once a high level of employent has been attained and emphasis is placed upon increasing national income through improved productivity. A post-war phenomenon has been the periodic rise in unemployment at the same time as national income has continued to rise.

(b) *The production of goods and services of a given value generates sufficient income to purchase them in their entirety if we so wish.* However, if we fail to spend the whole of that income then some goods and services will cease to be produced. Income and employment will decline.

(c) *Total effective demand determines the levels of income and employment.* It follows that where the figure of national income shows decline the remedy is to be sought in supporting effective demand.

13. The impact of saving. All income is divided between individuals and institutions in the form of wages, interest, rent and profits.

A part of this income will be devoted to current expenditure upon consumption. The rest will be saved. If a given level of income and employment is to be maintained the *whole* of these savings *must* be devoted to investment, i.e. in the Keynesian sense, expenditure upon capital equipment.

In short, the level of effective demand will be determined by the interaction of the rate of saving and the rate of investment. However, saving and investment are distinct functions governed by different motives and normally carried out by two different groups of people. It would be wholly coincidental if "intentions" to save and invest were to agree. It is essentially because of a discrepancy in these intentions that instability in the level of effective demand arises.

14. The propensity to save. While some savings are corporate and their volume is directly related to a decision to invest, the greater part are the product of decisions by individuals to refrain from current consumption. These decisions are governed by three factors.

(*a*) *Psychological motivation.* A wide variety of personal considerations motivate individual savings, e.g. prudence or the desire to satisfy some ambition. It should be stressed that none of these motives will be in any way related to the investment requirements of the entrepreneur. However, they will be broadly influenced by the prevailing economic climate. Keynes remarked upon "the paradox of thrift". In the downswing of the cycle, a sense of insecurity increases the propensity to save which in itself contributes to the descent into depression. Conversely, during the upswing, while the mood is optimistic, the propensity to save declines, thereby contributing to inflationary pressures.

(*b*) *The rate of interest.* It was assumed by the classical economists that investment and saving would be equated by a fluctuating rate of interest. An increased demand for investment funds by the entrepreneur would be reflected in a higher interest rate. More savings would now be called forth. The evidence of this century suggests that while there is some correlation between the rate of interest and the propensity to save it is not nearly so strong as was once thought.

(*c*) *The level of income.* The principal determinant of the propensity to save will be the level of income. As income rises the marginal propensity to save rises to the point where saving ultimately becomes automatic.

It follows therefore that the marginal propensity to save of the upper-income groups is high and of the lower-income groups low. Conversely, the marginal propensity to consume of the upper-income groups is low and of the lower-income groups high.

If the intention is to regulate total demand by an adjustment of consumer expenditure a redistribution of income may be accomplished in a way which affects the propensities to save and consume.

15. The rate of investment. Investment manifests itself in a demand for new capital goods in either the private or public sector. In the Keynesian sense it does not include the purchase of securities on the Stock Exchange since this normally implies only the transfer of ownership of existing capital.

The rate of investment depends upon the anticipation of business-planners of a profitable return to their outlay. This anticipation is governed by the "marginal efficiency of capital", the phrase Keynes employs to denote the relationship between the prospective yield of one more unit of investment and the rate of interest which must be paid for its use.

In making his assessment of capital's marginal efficiency the planner will take account of certain objective factors, e.g. the size of the existing stock of capital of a particular kind. Nevertheless, however sophisticated his techniques may be his prediction of the future ultimately involves a guess. The problem stems from the unreliability of this guess work. In advanced economies, Keynes asserted, forecasting recurrently erred on the side of pessimism with the result that investment fell short of what would have been justified had the future been more clearly foreseen.

In order to compensate for this repeated shortfall in effective demand there was scope for periodic injections of government expenditure, "pump-priming". While conceding that this expenditure might on occasion be designed to stimulate consumption Keynes argued that in the interest of long-term development it was preferable that it should be expressed in investment.

16. The multiplier. The significance of one unit of investment more or less is amplified when attention is given to the operation of the multiplier.

The investment of a further £100 will certainly increase income and employment in the capital-goods industries, but it will also stimulate the propensity to consume of the income recipients. If it is assumed that one-fifth is saved then £80 will be spent upon increased consumption. Income is now increased in the consumer-goods industries and further stimulus given to consumption. Still assuming a savings factor of one-fifth this will be of the order of £64. The multiplier gradually loses momentum because of the impact of saving until the total addition to effective demand has been £500 and to savings £100.

Seen in terms of the effect upon employment, at an average wage level of £10, the initial investment would give work to ten men. When the multiplier had run its course, employment would be increased by fifty men.

In the same way that the beneficial effect of an extra unit of investment is enhanced by the multiplier, the depressant effect of the withdrawal of investment is equally magnified. In any attempt to stabilise demand timing is therefore of vital importance. A lost unit of investment must be replaced before the multiplier can take effect.

17. Deflationary and inflationary gaps. We are led to conclude at this point that instability in the level of effective demand may be attributed to an apparent disequilibrium between saving and investment.

(*a*) *A deflationary gap* between saving and investment initiates the downswing of the cycle and is magnified by the operation of the multiplier. It may result from:

(*i*) a decline in investment unaccompanied by an increase in consumption;

(*ii*) a decline in consumption unaccompanied by an increase in investment.

Stabilising action calls for the support of effective demand.

(*b*) *An inflationary gap* emerges when the rate of investment exceeds the rate of saving. Total expenditure is now higher than necessary to maintain the economy at the previous level of activity and the cycle has turned into the upswing. It may result from:

(*i*) increased investment unaccompanied by decreased consumption;

(*ii*) increased consumption unaccompanied by decreased investment.

When resources are unemployed, stabilising action may not be required. The tendency for prices to rise consequent upon the increased pressure of demand may be largely offset by the increased flow of goods and services at the higher level of employment. Where resources are already fully employed, price inflation will be avoided only by improved productivity. If this is not forthcoming, stabilising action requires that effective demand should be curbed by restricting either consumption or investment or both.

18. Nature of the disequilibrium of saving and investment. Some economists have adhered to the view that cyclical fluctuations originate in a *real* disequilibrium between saving and investment. Keynes, however, insists that they must equate.

During the upswing the entrepreneur finances his increased investment on credit. At the higher level of income now generated and given a fixed propensity to save, a volume of savings sufficient to cover the increased investment is called forth.

Conversely, during the downswing a lower rate of investment

reduces income. Savings must then be restricted to a level dictated by the rate of investment.

In short the position is not one in which investment waits upon saving. It is the rate of investment itself which determines the ability to save. The two must always equate but may do so at any level of economic activity.

19. Reconciliation of the two views of saving and investment. A reconciliation of the two views of saving and investment has been offered in the following terms. Any given period of production can be viewed from two positions.

(a) *The ex ante position.* At the beginning of any period of production society anticipates a certain level of income and plans consumption, investments and saving in a way which it hopes will fulfil this expectation. Since saving and investment plans are un-coordinated it is unlikely that the two will equate.

(b) *The ex post position.* At the end of a period of production what *in fact* happened can be observed. Expenditure upon consumption and investment generated income sufficient to permit a volume of saving exactly equal to the volume of investment.

In the form of a simple equation:

Consumption expenditure + investment expenditure = National income = consumption expenditure + savings.

It follows that if *ex post* investment (which equals *ex post* saving) differs from *ex ante* saving there is a gap between anticipation and realisation which, if inflationary, moves the economy into the upswing and, if deflationary, moves it into the downswing. The momentum is then increased by the operation of the multiplier.

AN ELABORATION OF THE MACROECONOMIC MODEL

20. The circular flow of income. The real world is of course a good deal more complex than was suggested by the previous simple equation. Figure 1 develops in a rather more elaborate way the central macroeconomic concept of the circular flow of income.

The figure shows two fundamental aspects of the flow which are utilised in the presentation of the national accounts in the annual Blue Book, *National Income and Expenditure.* They are firstly the broad classification into income, production and expenditure accounts and secondly the more detailed division into

FIG. 1 *The circular flow of income*.

...oral accounts. The latter provide an insight into the economic behaviour which may be expected in different sectors, e.g. the spending decisions of households will have a different motivation from those of firms or government.

21. Sectoral relationships. The relationship between the sectors is shown in Fig. 1.

(a) *Distribution of the firm's revenue.* The firm's revenue will be distributed directly to households in wages and salaries, rent and interest. Interest will also be paid to other firms and this will be retained in the productive sector. Revenue may also be allocated to imported goods and services. The residual, profit, will be distributed to households as dividends, to government in tax or to corporate savings.

(b) *Distribution of the household's income.* Household income will be devoted first to consumption. A part of this expenditure will be directed to imports and a part to the payment of expenditure taxes. The remainder will be returned to the productive sector to generate further distributions by the firm.

(c) *Government expenditure, investment and exports.* The productive sector receives further revenue from government expenditure on goods and services, from the spending of firms and financial institutions upon fresh investment and from exports, both visible and invisible.

22. Double counting, leakages and injections. We are now able to see from this analysis that the production, income and expenditure accounts should show the same value after certain complexities have been resolved.

(a) *Double counting.* Firstly, in calculating the value of total production we must avoid the double counting of intermediate (or semi-finished) goods and services and include only the value of the end product. (Hence in Fig. 1 the small circular flow which is confined to the productive sector.) This will be achieved by calculating the value added at each stage.

(b) *Leakages.* Secondly, we must allow for leakages from the system caused by expenditure on imports (both finished and intermediate goods and services) and by the payment of indirect taxes.

(c) *Injections.* Thirdly, we must include injections into the system which result from private investment, total government spending and exports.

Our equation now assumes a rather more detailed form:

$$Y = C + I + G + X - M - T_I$$

where Y is national income/output; C is private consumption; I is private investment; G is government current and capital spending; X is exports; M is total imports; T_I is indirect taxes.

Some further refinement is still necessary. As we have seen, the propensity to save or consume is determined primarily by the level of income but more exactly by the level of *disposable* income after the payment of direct taxes (*see* **14**(*c*) above). We should therefore add a simple consumption function to elaborate the meaning of C:

$$C = b(Y - T_D)$$

where b is the proportion of disposable income spent on consumption and T_D is direct taxes.

We will next note that *all* income is spent on consumption, paid in taxes or saved:

$$Y = T_D + C + S$$

where S is savings. Bearing this equation in mind and remembering our refinement of the consumption function (C) the national income equation may now be expressed as:

$$T_D + C + S = C + I + G + X - M - T_I$$

This equation can be simplified and rearranged as follows:

$$S + T + M = I + G + X$$

where T is total taxation, $T_I + T_D$. The significance of this rearrangement is that we can see quite clearly the sources of leakage from the circular flow of income on the left-hand side of the equation and the sources of injection on the right. The injections will be largely autonomous since they are little affected by the existing level of income. Investment depends upon future predictions of profitability, government expenditure upon current policy, and exports upon overseas demand. In contrast, the leakages are primarily determined by current national income. The higher the income the greater the volume of savings and taxation and the greater the demand for imports.

23. The multiplier and the equation of injections and leakages. From our earlier discussion of the multiplier (*see* **16** above) it will be remembered that the effect of an autonomous injection of fresh expenditure will be magnified in further rounds of increased spending.

With each rise in income, however, there occur leakages in an increased volume of savings, taxes and imports. The situation is only stabilised when total leakages equal the new injection of expenditure. The same will be true when there is an autonomous withdrawal of expenditure.

It follows that if the government is intent upon achieving equilibrium at a high level of income and employment it will seek to influence the autonomous factors in the equation.

This may mean an attempt to stimulate exports (X) through an exchange rate policy which keeps British goods internationally competitive, a feature of the government's strategy for recovery in 1976–77. The emphasis has, however, been upon the manipulation of the factor over which it has closest control, its own expenditure (G), followed by attempts to encourage private investment (I). Since the latter is conditioned by predictions of future consumer demand, consumption (C) has also been regulated.

24. The instruments of control. It was Keynes's view that the most precise control over the various components of aggregate demand could be exercised only through the public finances, i.e. the manipulation of taxation and public expenditure.

Monetary policy, on the other hand, lacked precision and was uncertain in its results.

Lower interest rates might or might not induce more spending. Below a certain level, however, the evidence of the 1930s suggested that it was highly improbable. Moreover, interest rate policy was of little use in guiding spending injections into what might be considered the most appropriate directions and in any case it was likely to have a delayed impact.

In Chapter III we shall consider the part played by the public finances in the management of aggregate demand, returning to the role of money in the Keynesian system in Chapter IV.

PROGRESS TEST 2

1. Point out the main features of five types of industrial fluctuation. **(2)**

2. Distinguish between four types of unemployment. **(5)**

3. What is the essence of John B. Woods's criticism of the use of unemployment statistics? **(6)**

4. Why should there be different indicators for social and economic policy? **(7)**

5. Outline the main features of a more accurate unemployment indicator. **(8)**

6. Explain the importance of the concept of effective demand. **(12)**

7. What determines the propensity to save? **(14)**

8. What governs the rate of investment? **(15)**

9. Explain the operation of the multiplier. **(16)**

10. Reconcile the two interpretations of the relationship between the rates of saving and investment. **(19)**

11. Account for the circular flow of income. **(20)**

12. For what reasons may there be leakages and injections? **(22)**

CHAPTER III

The Management of Demand

A PERSPECTIVE OF PUBLIC FINANCE

1. Objectives. The study of macroeconomics places emphasis upon the use of fiscal policy for the purpose of managing demand. Nevertheless, it should not be forgotten that there are other objectives.

Modern public finance may be said to have three aspects. It is:

(a) *the instrument for the satisfaction of collective wants;*
(b) *an instrument of social policy;*
(c) *an instrument of economic policy.*

2. Satisfaction of collective wants. We should not lose sight of the primary purpose of public finance, which is to raise revenue for expenditure upon collective wants. It has always been considered appropriate that certain services should be provided by collective action in the public sector rather than in response to market forces in the private sector.

In the *laissez-faire* society of the eighteenth century the view was that such services should be limited to external and internal security, i.e. defence and the preservation of law and order. A changing view of society has subsequently brought a gradual extension of the public sector, most dramatically since 1945.

3. Definition of the public sector. In this segment of the economy the production of goods and services depends upon the decision of central or local government. In arriving at a decision, while reference will be made to the cost of production, social objectives will be paramount. Resources will be deployed in a way which would not be achieved by the free operation of the price mechanism, e.g. it is reasonable to assume that a far higher proportion of resources is devoted to education than would be the case if all education were provided by private enterprise.

4. Two types of public expenditure. In the public sector the state commands resources in the following two ways.

(a) *Exhaustive expenditure.* The state directly employs a vast

number of people, e.g. civil servants, teachers, soldiers, etc. Indirectly it employs as many in the private sector in the production
of goods and services for the satisfaction of collective wants, e.g.
defence equipment, schools. Such expenditure is exhaustive in the
sense that resources have been diverted as a result of government
decision from the use which free market forces would have
determined.

(b) *Transfer expenditure.* When income is redistributed from
tax-payer to beneficiary in the form of pensions, child benefit, etc.,
the recipient is free to dispose of his benefits in response to the
pull of market forces.

5. Public enterprise. Since the late nineteenth century local and
central government have extended their economic interests, providing goods and services in response to market forces and sometimes in competition with private enterprise, e.g. water-supplies,
local transport, the BBC. The scope of public enterprise was
greatly expanded after 1945 with the nationalisation of major
industries.

At this point the frontier between public and private enterprise
becomes indistinct. To the extent that public corporations follow
pricing and output policies dictated by the market, their behaviour
parallels that of privately owned companies and they lie *outside*
a strictly defined public sector. To the extent that social and
political considerations determine that they should provide a
service even at the expense of a loss to be shouldered by the taxpayer, they fall *within* the public sector, e.g. the subsidisation of
uneconomic British Rail services.

6. Public revenue. Government has three sources of income from
which it may pay society's collective expenses.

(a) *Taxation.* Taxes are levied upon the income and expenditure
of individuals and corporate bodies in both the private and public
sectors.

(b) *Profits of public enterprise.* While public corporations are not
generally required by their acts of incorporation to do more than
pay their way, occasionally there are trading profits.

(c) *Borrowing.* Until 1945, this source of income was considered
appropriate only in times of national emergency. Sound public
finance required that the Budget should always be balanced. Subsequently it was thought that a deflationary gap could be closed
most effectively by loan-financed public expenditure. Government

borrowing therefore developed as a means of financing both short-term indebtedness on current account and long-term capital investment by public corporations and local authorities.

7. An instrument of social policy. The social objectives of public finance are open to debate and will vary from time to time. A first objective will be the preservation of society and for the exponents of *laissez-faire* philosophy the security of the state was the only legitimate sphere for intervention.

In the nineteenth and twentieth centuries the view gradually developed that society had an obligation to guarantee minimum standards of welfare to all its members. Public finance was then faced with the problem of determining the proportions in which individual contributions should be exacted and benefits allocated. The commonly agreed aim was to secure some reduction in the inequality of income and wealth. The structure of public revenue and expenditure is therefore designed to make a positive contribution to this objective.

8. The principle of progression in taxation. The older view of equity in taxation rested upon the "principle of proportionality". It was argued that if all contributed in the same proportion then income and wealth relationships between individuals remained undisturbed by taxation. When it was appreciated that this approach imposed a greater real burden upon the poor another principle was sought and progression was introduced into the British tax system in the Budget of 1893. Applied first to estate duty it subsequently became a feature of income tax. Progressive taxation requires a more than proportionate contribution from those who are better able to pay.

It will be noted that apart from satisfying modern notions of equity this principle provides a positive instrument for effecting a more equal distribution of income and wealth.

9. Public expenditure. Public expenditure may be classified as follows.

(*a*) *Defence and environmental expenditure*. The benefits of public expenditure upon defence and the maintenance and improvement of the environment by both local and central government are enjoyed equally by all. No attempt is made to equate real net incomes.

(*b*) *Social service expenditure*. It is in the area of social service expenditure that there has been most growth since the war. Under this heading is included outlay upon education, national health, pensions, unemployment insurance, supplementary benefits, etc. While guaranteeing certain benefits to *all* citizens as of right, the intention is nevertheless to concentrate expenditure upon those most in need, i.e. to achieve a more equal distribution of real income.

10. An instrument of economic policy. Public finance may be instrumental in the pursuit of economic policy.

(*a*) *Protection of industry.* Historically, customs duties were viewed not only as the principal source of revenue but also as a means of limiting foreign competition. Only in the mid-nineteenth century did Britain embark upon a period of free trade. In 1932, free trade was abandoned and a protective tariff established. Since 1945, there has been close international co-operation aimed at restoring free trading conditions (*see* X, **19–33**). Nevertheless, in certain conditions a protective customs duty may still be considered legitimate (*see* X, **14–18**).

(*b*) *Support for private enterprise.* Expenditure may be of two types, as follows.

(*i*) Common services: certain services are provided which are of general benefit to all firms, e.g. the Department of Employment, Trade and Industry.

(*ii*) Specific assistance: specific firms or industries may be singled out for support with investment grants and loans on favourable terms.

(*c*) *Development of public enterprise.* In developing a country's economic infrastructure certain industries may be considered so vital that it is felt that their services should be guaranteed by the state and not left to the uncertainties of market forces, e.g. railways, postal services.

(*d*) *Demand management.* It has been explained in II that after 1945 fiscal policy was considered the most powerful instrument for the management of demand. Ideally it would be deployed in a way which secured the optimum utilisation of resources, continuous growth and a stable balance of payments.

11. The reconciliation of objectives. It will be seen from the foregoing discussion that public finance has a variety of objectives which the Chancellor of the Exchequer must reconcile. Of paramount importance will be the need for a structure which encourages the most effective economic performance. Within this framework the detailed pattern of revenue and expenditure will seek to deploy resources between public and private sectors in a way which secures the most rapid attainment of social objectives. It is worth emphasising that, however desirable the social objectives, if the means of achieving them are inappropriate or the pace too fast the subsequent strain upon the economy may make those same objectives unattainable. We shall therefore return to the use of public finance as an instrument of economic policy.

12. Economic policy aims. A system of public finance will seek to manage total effective demand in a way which is conducive to:

(*a*) *full employment;*
(*b*) *growth;*
(*c*) *stable prices and a balance of payments equilibrium.*

In the present imperfect state of economic knowledge it may prove impossible to achieve these objectives simultaneously and socio-political considerations will establish priorities. The record would seem to indicate that during the post-war years the main concern was to stabilise demand at a level consistent with full employment, if necessary at the expense of some inflation and associated balance of payment problems and also at the cost of an unsatisfactory growth rate. A "stop-go" cycle of events emerged. During the upswing unemployment fell towards 1 per cent but demand continued to outstrip full employment output. The subsequent rise in prices and incomes induced an unfavourable balance of payments sufficient to warrant the restriction of demand by fiscal and monetary means and a mild recession ensued.

When unemployment began to rise towards 2 per cent reflationary measures were adopted which moved the economy into the next upswing.

After 1962, emphasis shifted to the management of demand in a way which would produce more rapid growth. The net result was to escalate the rate of inflation and produce more serious balance of payments crises in the middle years of the decade.

The devaluation of 1967 brought a further shift of emphasis. Priority was now given to a restraint of domestic demand sufficient to stabilise prices at a level consistent with a favourable balance of payments at the new rate of exchange. The incoming Conservative Government of 1970, despite a favourable balance of payments, placed still more emphasis upon the need to check inflation as a precondition for the long-run attainment of the other policy objectives.

In 1972, with unemployment rising above 1 million for the first time since the 1930s, the economy was given a massive reflationary stimulus in the hope of inducing a much more rapid growth rate. In recognition of the fact that the upsurge in domestic spending would draw in more imports and bring pressure upon the sterling exchange rate and hence the foreign exchange reserves, the £ was floated (*see* XI, 25(*b*)).

By 1974, with production stagnant and unemployment rising, it was apparent that the increased level of spending was being absorbed almost wholly in a rapidly rising price level. Rather than check spending the Government now relied upon stricter controls over prices and a voluntary incomes policy, the social contract. These measures alone were insufficient to check inflation and the continuing depreciation of sterling. As a condition of a massive loan in the winter of 1976 the International Monetary Fund required assurances that the growth in aggregate demand should be restrained, specifically by reducing the rate of monetary growth and the Government's borrowing requirements which induced it.

During 1976 and 1977, both the Prime Minister and the Chancellor indicated in their public pronouncements their loss of confidence in the ability of government to "fine tune" the economy by Keynesian methods. Nevertheless, a strong stimulus was given to aggregate demand during 1978 in the run up to the general election (*see* V).

The incoming Conservative Government of 1979 indicated its intention to "roll back the frontiers of the state". One aspect of this radical departure was the acceptance of a monetarist rather than a Keynesian explanation of the causes of inflation and unemployment. Implicit was the view that governments in liberal, democratic societies (with no powers to direct resources) were unable to guarantee levels of employment and economic growth. Only an effective functioning market could achieve this. Government should therefore, in principle, restrict itself to creating an appropriate market environment, the main feature of which would be a stable price level based upon careful regulation of the money supply. Within that environment it was hoped that the personal qualities of enterprise, thrift, industry, responsibility and self-reliance would be revived as a basis for economic prosperity and *genuinely* improved standards of social welfare. This would contrast with the spurious "compassion" of a society which had signally failed to produce the wealth necessary for its social objectives. In other words, the "consensus" economic policies which had been adopted by all preceding post-war governments and which had been underwritten by the Keynesian analysis were now abandoned.

Nevertheless, it should be recognised that even though compensatory budgetary policy may be in doubt, such is the present scale of taxation and public spending that they invariably have major implications for the three principal policy aims.

STABILISATION OF DEMAND AT FULL EMPLOYMENT

13. The revenue and expenditure approaches. Total effective demand may be stabilised by varying the structure and volume of taxation or public expenditure. Both approaches will aim to fluence consumption expenditure by altering the propensity to consumer or investment expenditure by affecting the marginal efficiency of capital.

Adopting the revenue approach, taxes may be classified under two headings:

(a) *automatic stabilisers* (*see* **14** below);
(b) *policy-effected stabilisers* (*see* **15** below).

14. Automatic stabilisers. Certain fiscal devices automatically regulate the level of demand without the need for policy decisions. They include the following.

(a) *Unemployment insurance contributions*. In the upswing excess purchasing power is removed and contributions accumulate. Conversely, in the downswing the failure of demand is partially compensated by the payment of benefits.

(b) *Capital depreciation allowances*. Where allowances are based upon "initial" and not "replacement" cost, during the upswing more than true profit is taxed. The opposite is true during the downswing.

(c) *Capital gains taxation*. In an inflationary situation any given rate taxes more than the true gain. During the downswing, if there is a falling price level, then *if* tax is paid it will be on less than the true gain.

Automatic stabilisers have the advantage that they are continuously at work without the need for publicly announced changes in economic policy which in themselves may have an adverse effect upon business confidence. On the other hand they cannot be considered as powerful as decisions to change rates of taxation or to introduce new taxes or delete old ones.

15. Policy-effected stabilisers. It will be generally true that the manipulation of the tax structure is likely to be more effective in closing an inflationary gap than in countering deflation and unemployment. The argument is that higher taxes remove purchasing power which clearly cannot then be utilised. On the other hand while lower rates of tax will increase disposable net incomes there is no certainty of a corresponding rise in demand. The increase may be saved.

Disinflationary taxation may seek to check consumption or investment.

16. Restricting consumption expenditure. Taxes may be varied upon income or expenditure.

(*a*) *Income taxes.* It has been argued that higher rates of income tax are in fact inflationary, since they lead to more militant wage claims which if conceded are reflected in higher prices. For this proposition to be true there is an assumption that the consumer is able to pay the higher price and therefore that credit will always expand ahead of tax liability. It follows that higher income-tax rates should be supported by a sufficiently strict monetary policy if consumption expenditure is to be curbed.

A more widely held view of the effect of high income taxes relates to their possible disincentive influence, which may adversely affect the volume of production. It is argued that the tax structure should encourage earning and saving while penalising spending.

(*b*) *Expenditure taxes.* In practice, most reliance has been placed upon higher expenditure taxes designed to discourage consumption. Much use has been made of the "regulator", the power the Chancellor has to vary the rate of VAT by a maximum of 25 per cent of the rate between Budgets.

The argument against such taxes is that they are regressive. Little account is taken of "ability to pay" and the burden will inevitably fall more heavily upon the lower-income groups.

17. Restricting investment expenditure. Expenditure of any kind represents demand for limited resources. While it is clearly desirable that in the long run adequate resources should be directed to investment it is possible that in the short term investment may exceed the rate which the economy can comfortably sustain. In this case investment allowances may be made less favourable or an investment tax introduced, e.g. in Sweden an arrangement has worked where a tax upon investment was levied during the upswing of the cycle and the proceeds disbursed during the downswing.

18. Reflation. When unemployment figures begin to rise there is invariably political pressure for lower levels of taxation which it is hoped will stimulate demand. It has already been observed that there can be no certainty that an increase in net disposable income will increase the level of demand. Nevertheless, if expenditure taxes on the products of certain key industries are reduced a general expansionary effect will be anticipated provided that demand is elastic, e.g. a reduced purchase tax on motor vehicles may be expected to stimulate demand throughout that industry and also the general level of consumption in the areas in which the industry is located.

Similarly, it may be hoped to induce an "investment-led boom" by lowering the taxation of capital. If net profit margins are widened then not only will investment be encouraged but the liquidity of companies is improved. Funds are available for self-financed expansion.

On the other hand lower levels of direct personal taxation are unlikely to prove very expansionary. While it is possible that greater incentives may now exist the principal benefits will be derived by the upper-income groups who have a high propensity to save. Because of the progression in the tax system relatively little advantage accrues to the lower-income groups who have a high propensity to consume.

19. Varying the level of public expenditure. Variations in taxation depend very largely for their effect upon the uncertain responses of the private sector. A much more positive result may be expected from decisions to increase or diminish public spending.

The following two factors are of importance.

(*a*) *The multiplier.* It should be remembered that the consequence of an addition or a withdrawal of a unit of public investment will be magnified by the operation of the multiplier.

(*b*) *Timing.* Precision in the management of demand depends upon appropriate timing. This implies intervention which forestalls the multiplier. A criticism of the application of these techniques has been that all too frequently government has acted too late, e.g. expansionary measures have been adopted when the economy has already moved into the upswing, thus inducing unwanted inflationary pressures. Certain practical difficulties obstruct the correct timing of intervention, as follows.

(*i*) Delayed information: there is, inevitably, delay in the preparation of statistics upon which policy decisions will be based.

(*ii*) Planning time: a decision having been made there will be an interval before plans to increase or scale down expenditure can be completed.

(*iii*) Implementation of plans: for wholly practical reasons fresh work cannot be started nor existing work stopped without warning.

(*iv*) The operating time of the multiplier: even when the variation in public expenditure has begun to bite there will be a timelag before the impact on demand has worked its way through the whole economy.

Decisions to change the level of public expenditure may be applied through four channels (*see* **20–23** below).

20. Direct central government expenditure. The great expansion of the public sector since the Second World War has made it easier for government to have a direct influence on the rate of investment. All the nationalised industries have investment programmes, the pace of which can be regulated in accordance with the needs of demand management.

21. Local authority expenditure. Since most local authority investment is heavily dependent upon government financial support, it is possible to regulate the rate at which plans for schools, roads, urban renewal, etc., are implemented.

22. Private investment. It may be possible to influence investment decisions in the private sector with the inducement of a system of cash grants. Government agrees to pay in cash a proportion of the total cost of investment. Such a scheme offers the advantage of selectivity both in the industries and in the regions in which the incentives are to apply.

23. Private consumption. Transfer payments in the form of child benefit, pensions and other social security allowances are made to those who may be expected to spend rather than save.

For socio-economic reasons it is unlikely that any attempt would be made to curtail demand (i.e. pursue disinflationary policies) by reducing benefits. On the other hand there may be scope for a more prudent administration of social security in a way which ensures that only those in real need receive benefit.

As a means of providing stimulus for expansion it is certain that the level of consumer demand will be increased by raising benefits and this course of action may be followed if it is not at the expense of the desired rate of investment.

POLICIES FOR ECONOMIC GROWTH

24. Objectives. It has been observed that during the 1960s although the goal of full employment had been achieved there was growing dissatisfaction with the growth rate which had tended to centre upon a figure of about 2 per cent per annum. This compared very unfavourably with most advanced industrial nations and it was felt that the economy should be able to sustain a real expansion of about 4 per cent per annum. Recognition of the greater priority now given to growth policies was implied by the establishment in 1962 of the National Economic Development Council (NEDC) (*see* XIV, **11**(*a*)), the creation of a new Department of Economic Affairs (1964) which placed emphasis upon expansion and the publication in 1965 of a National Plan for growth.

25. Determinants of the growth rate. The rate at which the economy grows depends upon:

    (*a*) *the availability of labour and capital;*
    (*b*) *the efficiency with which labour and capital are utilised.*

Ideally, the structure of public finance will be disposed in a way which is most conducive to improvement under both headings. It should be stressed, however, that in an essentially private-enterprise economy government can only attempt to create the right conditions for expansion. It cannot guarantee that growth occurs.

26. The availability of labour and capital. In the first place the growth rate is governed by the availability of labour and capital of the right quality at the right place at the right time.

    (*a*) *Labour.* Under this heading falls labour of all kinds, skilled and unskilled, managerial and entrepreneurial. Its availability hinges upon the following.

      (*i*) Size and structure of population: absolute size and rate of increase of population together with its distribution between age groups and sexes are factors governing the flow of labour on to the market.

      (*ii*) Geographical and occupational mobility: these are considerations which determine whether labour is of the right kind and in the right place. Implicit is the need for movement not only between occupations or industries or even firms but also between jobs within the same firm, i.e. adaptability to new working methods and procedures.

They are in turn influenced by a country's cultural attitudes and social and economic institutions, e.g. class and sex prejudices, the educational system, the trade-union structure.

(b) *Capital*. The creation of capital equipment of the right kind to assist in further production depends upon the following.

(*i*) Rate of saving: factors governing the rate of saving have alread been considered (*see* II, **14**). However, the saver now requires some inducement to surrender his liquidity by investing in some tangible asset.

(*ii*) Rate of investment (*see* II, **15**): before the entrepreneur will invest he must anticipate sufficient net profit to recompense both himself and those whose savings he utilises.

(*iii*) Research: it should not be forgotten that the purpose of all production is consumption. The creation of capital is not in itself an objective and if it is to assist in satisfying future demand it must be of the right kind. To this end there should be adequate market research to produce a reasonable prediction of demand. Secondly, there should be adequate technological research to ensure that the most productive capital equipment is created.

27. Efficient use of labour and capital. To maximise the productivity of labour and capital it is necessary that they should be both fully employed and combined in the optimum proportion appropriate to any given stage of technology. This accomplished, expansion is then limited by technological and organisational change which permits the progressive substitution of capital for labour. Implicit is the need for flexibility in the deployment of the factors of production.

28. Flexible deployment of labour. Post-war experience suggests that there is a conflict between the objectives of full employment and mobility. When the economy is run at a high level of demand, the balance of industrial power shifts from management to labour. The employee resists change which dislocates his own economic life and which may offer no immediate recompense. He is supported by trade unions which are not disposed to accept redundancies. For the sake of industrial peace the employer continues to use his labour force uneconomically and there is a strong tendency towards overmanning. He is able to hand on higher costs in higher prices since demand continues to be sustained at a sufficiently high level.

29. Flexible deployment of capital. Ideally, it is desirable to have investment which is immediately responsive to the needs of new technologies and new markets. In practice it is very difficult to achieve this sensitivity. Much investment is of a highly specialised nature, large in scale and undertaken well in advance of the demand for the consumer goods at which it is directed. A decision to construct a steel-mill in a particular location cannot be easily reversed although technological or market changes may invalidate the premises upon which the decision was based.

The best that can be said is that sudden and large-scale changes in the direction and volume of investment should be avoided.

30. A tax structure to improve the availability of labour. It may be possible to vary the incidence and the weight of taxation in a way which improves the availability of labour.

(a) *Direct personal taxation.* The disincentive effects of a complicated and steeply progressive system of income tax and surtax have been the subject of recent discussion but the conclusions must remain imprecise. Nevertheless, there is a general assumption that simpler and lower direct taxation will provide an incentive to work harder.

(b) *Indirect taxation.* In general it may be thought that direct taxation which penalises earnings is likely to be more disincentive than indirect taxation whose incidence is upon spending. Moreover, if the incidence of this taxation is upon those luxury goods which are complementary to improved leisure pursuits there may be some incentive to work harder in order to attain them.

31. A public expenditure structure to improve the availability of labour. Public expenditure may be directed in two ways to the improvement of labour's availability.

(a) *Personal direct transfers.* The level of various social security payments may or may not have a direct bearing upon retirements or returns to work. There is a general assumption that they do and governments have periodically attempted administrative adjustments to make the conditions for payment more stringent; e.g. in 1970 the first three days of sickness were disqualified from benefit on the grounds that absenteeism was being encouraged.

(b) *Improvement of the economic infrastructure.* It is from expenditure in this field that the most positive long-term results will be expected although they will not be quantifiable. An effective education service coupled with adequate retraining facilities will improve the quality, the adaptability and the mobility of the labour force. An efficient health service will reduce the number of days lost through sickness and extend the working life of the population. Expenditure upon housing and communications may be expected to improve geographical mobility.

32. A tax structur to improve the availability of capital. The taxation of profits must have regard to the need to leave sufficient incentive to the saver to surrender his liquidity and to the entrepreneur to invest (*see* **26**(*b*)).

(*a*) *Taxation of company profits.* When costs rise more rapidly than the general price level, profits may be squeezed to a degree which is incompatible with the desired rate of investment. Capital cannot be renewed from the reduced volume of retained company profits. There is no incentive to raise fresh equity capital for the purpose of expansion. In such a situation there is a strong argument for the reduction of profits taxation.

Assuming that companies have ample profits they may be induced to reinvest by favourable allowances which can be offset against tax liability, e.g. variable capital depreciation allowances.

(*b*) *Taxation of investment income.* British taxation normally discriminates against distributed profits in the hope that companies will retain a larger proportion in order to finance their own capital requirements. There is further discrimination against dividend income upon which the recipient pays a higher rate than he does on earned income. It may be anticipated that beyond a certain point the incentive to the individual investor is removed and fresh capital will not be forthcoming.

The principal point is that if the net return to risk capital falls below a certain level the willingness to undertake risk upon which change and growth ultimately depend will be inhibited.

33. Public expenditure and the supply of capital. Saving and investment may be encouraged by the following.

(*a*) *Cash grants* to firms on the condition of further investment, e.g. the Investment Incentives scheme of 1966. The objection to this method is that it distorts market forces and may encourage investment which is not genuinely profitable. The scheme was abandoned in 1970.

(*b*) *Support to local authorities* for the purpose of improving the local economic environment which may encourage private investment.

(*c*) *Investment programmes of public corporations*: the government is in a powerful position to force saving and investment by increasing taxation and devoting the proceeds to investment in the nationalised industries.

34. Financial policy and the optimum deployment of labour and capital. It has been observed (*see* **27** above) that the efficient use of labour and capital involves their combination in optimum proportions in the wake of changing technologies and markets. While the principal instrument will be "productivity bargaining" between management and labour, public finance may provide a context which is conducive to such improvements.

(*a*) *Structure of taxation.* The object will be to influence the labour/capital cost ratio in a way which promotes the substitution of capital for labour.

The criticism has been levelled that compared with our European competitors it has been *artificially* cheaper to employ more labour rather than more capital. For example, the proportion of the social insurance contribution borne by the state is considerably higher in the UK than elsewhere. Moreover, food subsidies and the pricing policies of the nationalised industries weighted in favour of the consumer have all tended to relieve the employer of the *full* cost of labour. On the other hand, the taxation of capital in the UK has been severe compared with European countries.

In the middle 1970s the cost ratio further deteriorated. Inflation, incomes policies designed primarily to hold down unemployment together with employment premiums and employment protection legislation all militated in favour of a labour intensive economy.

It will be seen that at least in theory the ratio might be reversed by discriminatory taxation.

(*b*) *Structure of public expenditure.* There are a number of directions in which public funds may be used to secure a better utilisation of labour and capital, including the following.

(*i*) Support for private and municipal house-building programmes may be expected to contribute to labour mobility.

(*ii*) Adequate unemployment benefits when coupled with redundancy payments may relieve the resistance to the redundancies which inevitably follow change.

(*iii*) Education and training when soundly based will improve skills and aptitudes which in turn will increase mobility.

(*iv*) Government-sponsored research and development which encourages selective investment of the most productive kind will also play an important part.

THE STABILISATION OF PRICES

35. The nature of the problem. The stabilisation of prices has been an economic policy objective for the following two main reasons.

(*a*) *Arbitrary redistribution of incomes.* In a period of rapid inflation there is a redistribution of "real" income from those whose money incomes are fixed to those whose money incomes respond to price change; from weak and badly organised labour to strong and militant trade unionists; from lenders to borrowers.

(*b*) *Imbalance in foreign payments.* As inflation progresses export prices lose their competitive edge while the high domestic price level invites an increase in imports. A balance of payments crisis ensues necessitating restrictive policies which retard growth and increase unemployment.

36. A majority view of the causes of inflation. During the 1960s the most widely held view of the cause of inflation rested upon the connection between a high pressure of demand in a tight labour market and rising costs and prices which in turn gave a further twist to the wage/price spiral.

(*a*) *Demand in the labour market.* It was argued by A. W. Phillips that there exists a positive relationship between the rate of change of wages and the demand for labour which in turn is inversely related to the percentage rate of unemployment. It then follows that the rate at which wage rates change will be determined by the unemployment percentage. (*See* IV, **14**.)

(*b*) *Inflated wage costs.* Since wages are a major cost in all forms of production and since all firms in an industry are likely to accede to a wage increase agreed by one there will be a squeeze on profit margins and a strong incentive to raise prices.

(*c*) *Wage/price spiral.* The general rise in prices which was initiated by an excessively low unemployment percentage now gives rise to further wage demands and inflation gathers momentum.

37. Disinflationary policies. If the foregoing explanation of inflation is accepted there are four possible courses of action.

(*a*) *A general restriction of demand* (*see* **38** below).
(*b*) *Regional development* (*see* **39** below).
(*c*) *Structural improvements* (*see* **40** below).
(*d*) *Incomes policy* (*see* **41–43** below).

38. A general restriction of demand. The fiscal measures appropriate to a reduction of the pressure of demand have been considered (*see* **13–23** above). The intention will be to stabilise the economy at a higher level of unemployment.

The following three objections arise.

(*a*) *Social cost.* There are obvious social objections to policies deliberately designed to raise unemployment.

(*b*) *Loss of potential output.* At current prices a rise of 0.2 per cent in the rate of unemployment may be associated with a loss of production of about £1,000 million.

(*c*) *The phenomenon of inflation and rising unemployment.* In the post-war years the fiscal weapon was regularly used to check the rate of inflation and this was generally achieved at about 2 per cent unemployment. However, by 1970, despite severely restrictive taxation the rate of inflation had escalated to $8\frac{1}{2}$ per cent at the same time as unemployment rose to 3 per cent, its highest point since the 1930s. The immediate implication was that to contain inflation by a further restriction of demand would result in unemployment of a wholly unacceptable level.

A more radical view was that the accepted analysis of inflation was invalid. The inflation/unemployment trade-off postulated by Phillips did not occur. Inflation was purely a monetary phenomenon. This explanation will be examined fully in IV.

39. Regional development. The distribution of unemployment is by no means even and many areas of the country, e.g. Merseyside, Cumbria, have figures well above the national average. It is argued that inflation may be relieved by regional policies which increase unemployment in areas where there is excessive demand for labour at the same time as unemployment is decreased in the depressed areas. Thus unemployment is simply "transferred", the national figure remaining the same.

Financial incentives, e.g. favourable tax treatment or discriminatory investment grants, can be built into the fiscal system in an attempt to achieve this objective but the results will be unpredictable.

40. Structural improvements. Inflationary pressures arise from impediments in the functioning of labour markets. Government may assist occupational and geographical mobility with retraining schemes and housing programmes.

More fundamentally, the improvement of industrial relations may ease the problems of damaging and inflationary industrial disputes.

This has been a major theme for some years. In 1969 the Government attempted, without success, to implement the proposals of its White Paper, *In Place of Strife*. These aimed to improve the collective bargaining process in a way which would reduce strike action.

The following Government's Industrial Relations Act of 1971 which had broadly similar objectives was equally unsuccessful, as were the various legislative measures, favourable to the trade unions, which formed a part of the social contract of the mid-1970s.

It is a matter for debate whether trade unions exercise too much or too little power, whether the leadership is more or less militant than the membership, whether they are constrained too much or too little by the law. The conclusions reached will determine the extent to which government may actively contribute to improved industrial relations and the usefulness of this approach in reducing inflationary pressure.

INCOMES POLICY

41. Incomes policy objectives. Incomes policies have been seen variously as short-term expedients for arresting inflation and associated balance of payments problems; as a longer-term method of avoiding inflation at full employment and of achieving a more equitable distribution of income; and more recently as the principal government instrument for checking inflationary wage rises which in a period of monetary restraint would price more men out of work.

42. Chronology of UK incomes policy. There have been six attempts to establish policies in restraint of prices and incomes.

(*a*) *1948.* Following the 1947 balance of payments crisis, the Government applied its remaining wartime powers to check price rises at the same time as it secured the co-operation of the trade unions in postponing wage claims. This policy met with some success until the 1949 devaluation brought inflationary pressures which forced the unions to abandon restraint.

(b) *1956*. The Government asked for a voluntary and temporary "wage pause" but was unsuccessful in gaining union co-operation. An independent and purely advisory body, the Council on Productivity, Prices and Incomes, was then set up but met with little success.

(c) *1961*. A pay pause was initiated, followed in 1962 by the setting up of a National Incomes Commission (NIC) to review pay claims, and the publication of "guiding lights" for wages and salaries. Without union support, the NIC proved uninfluential.

(d) *1964*. A "declaration of intent" on productivity, prices and incomes was signed by employers, unions and the Government as a pre-condition of economic policies which would permit more rapid growth. Finally, the machinery of a full-scale incomes policy was provided in 1965 with the establishment of a National Board for Prices and Incomes (NBPI or PIB) which replaced the NIC and was to review price and pay increases. Its criteria were set out in a White Paper, *Prices and Incomes Policy*. A norm for wage increases was established at $3-3\frac{1}{2}$ per cent. In 1966, statutory effect was given to a six-month wage and price freeze followed by six months of "severe restraint". A return was made to a voluntary policy in 1967. In 1970 the incoming Conservative Government declared its lack of confidence in a formal incomes policy and announced that the PIB would be disbanded.

(e) *1972*. A statutory policy was imposed in November 1972 with an enforced pay standstill. Subsequently a Pay Board and Price Commission were established to apply the rules through the three stages of the Government's policy. Statutory incomes controls were abandoned with the outgoing Conservative Government in 1974.

(f) *1975*. A new "voluntary policy" took the form of the *"social contract"*. The TUC and the Labour Government agreed the broad social and economic policies which were to be pursued. In return the TUC supported a policy limiting pay increases to £6 per week with no increases for those with annual incomes in excess of £8,500. Stage II of the policy was again based upon a flat-rate increase, on this occasion £4 per week. During 1977, after much discussion by the TUC of the need for "an orderly return to free collective bargaining", Stage III emerged as a general indication by the Government that average pay increases should not exceed 10 per cent. In practice this was interpreted as a 10 per cent norm with the Government selectively applying a variety of sanctions to firms exceeding the norm.

The market-orientated 1979 Conservative Government stated quite clearly that incomes policies had no place in its economic philosophy. Nevertheless, like any employer it was obliged to adopt a wage policy in respect of its own employees (*see* **43**(*g*) below). This has been interpreted by some commentators as at least a partial return to an incomes policy.

43. Incomes policy problems. From the preceding account it will be observed that all income policies have been short lived. The evidence points to a number of practical problems.

(*a*) *Do income policies cure inflation?* The prevailing assumption has been that inflation is rooted in rising wage costs induced by running the economy at an unrealistically low level of unemployment. This view is opposed by monetary economists who see rising wages like rising prices as a *symptom* and not a cause of inflation (*see* IV).

(*b*) *Voluntary or statutory?* The trade union movement has not been prepared to accept statutory policies other than for a strictly limited period of time. There is also some suggestion that co-operation in a voluntary policy may be more easily achieved with a Labour rather than Conservative Government.

(*c*) *Voluntary policies.* In the first instance there may be some doubt about a *voluntary* policy which is supported by non-statutory sanctions such as those applied by the government in 1977. Secondly, tripartite agreements between government, TUC and CBI or still more significantly, bipartite agreements between government and TUC would seem to give undue weight to some sectional interest at the expense of others and for this reason may not command the support of the whole country. Thirdly, such agreements disintegrate when the TUC ceases to receive the support of its membership.

(*d*) *Percentage increases.* The experience has been that the declared maximum or average percentage increase has in practice been treated as the minimum which negotiators would accept. This inflexibility has borne heavily upon the very low paid whose *absolute* increases have been correspondingly low.

(*e*) *Flat-rate increases.* Conversely, flat-rate increases erode differentials and reduce incentives. Evidence in 1976–77 suggests that this approach may be a major cause of industrial disputes.

(*f*) *Labour market distortions.* A severe criticism of flat-rate increases is that imperfections in the labour markets are increased. It becomes more difficult for successful, expanding firms to attract the labour they need since they are unable to bid up wages. Labour becomes that much less mobile.

(g) *Public sector pay*. As the most important employer it is of course inevitable that government should have a pay policy in respect of its own employees. With the majority of pay agreements concluded nationally and with increased emphasis upon comparability, awards made in the public sector are clearly of great significance to pay levels in the private sector.

It will be equally true that any acceleration of private sector wage rates will induce pressures in the public sector. Government is therefore obliged to have an interest in the whole spectrum of incomes.

CONCLUSIONS ON DEMAND MANAGEMENT

44. A faulty steering mechanism. It has been observed that during the 1960s the steering mechanism of demand management operated with less and less precision (*see* I, **35–36**). After 1966, the new phenomenon of rising prices and incomes accompanied by increasing unemployment put in doubt the possibility of steering a middle course between too much inflation and too much unemployment, trading one off against the other (*see* IV, **14–17**).

45. Ad hoc interventions. This loss of confidence led in the 1970s to increased reliance upon direct interventions to deal with immediate problems as they arose.

Rising unemployment was checked by subventions for failing firms and industries under the Industry Acts of 1972 and 1975, by employment subsidies, the extension of public ownership, job creation schemes and employment protection legislation.

The strategy for checking inflation rested almost entirely upon phased incomes policy which was accepted with increasing reluctance.

46. Monetarism. The failure of demand management to achieve its goals was from a monetarist point of view entirely predictable (*see* I, **38**). The monetarists' criticism is directed to the role in the economy which Keynesians have assigned to money. This controversy will be examined in IV.

PROGRESS TEST 3

1. In what senses may public finance be employed as an instrument of social policy? **(7, 8, 9)**

2. Point out four areas in which public finance may be employed in support of economic policy. **(10)**

3. At what policy objectives will "demand management" be aimed? **(12)**

4. What do you understand by an "automatic stabiliser"? **(14)**

5. Compare income taxes and expenditure taxes as means of restricting consumption. **(16)**

6. Is it ever justifiable to restrict investment? **(17)**

7. What practical difficulties are encountered in using public expenditure as an instrument of demand management? **(19)**

8. Through which agencies can central government expenditure be channelled? **(20–23)**

9. Analyse the determinants of the economic growth rate. **(25–29)**

10. Compare the effectiveness of direct and indirect taxes as means of improving the availability of labour. **(30)**

11. Suggest how taxes may be varied to improve the flow of capital. **(32)**

12. How might public expenditure improve the rates of saving and investment? **(33)**

13. How might financial policy improve the labour/capital cost ratio? **(34)**

14. Explain the generally held view of the causes of inflation. **(36)**

15. What do you understand by "incomes policy"? **(41)**

16. Do you consider that an incomes policy has any future in the UK? **(43)**

CHAPTER IV

The Role of Money in the Economy

A KEYNESIAN VIEW OF MONEY AND NATIONAL INCOME DETERMINATION

1. A synthesis of the real and monetary worlds. Our account of the Keynesian analysis of national income determination and its implications for public policy has so far neglected the role of money. In fact, a highly important aspect of Keynes's work was to show the impact of financial mechanisms and institutions upon output and employment.

In the classical model of the economy money played a minor role. It was simply a medium of exchange. Production created its own demand for the output and employment of others (*see* I, **8**). *Real* factors determined the level of *real* national income. On the other hand in the world of money, monetary factors determined the general level of prices (*see* **5**).

Keynes attempted a synthesis of the two, making money a central feature of his analysis. For him it was more than a medium of exchange. It was a unique financial asset, the only one with complete liquidity and instant purchasing power. This being the case, significantly it would be held for *precautionary motives*.

2. Transactions money and liquidity or precautionary money. Classical monetary policy centred upon the effect of a moving interest rate which served as a price mechanism. An expansion of the money supply would be consistent with lower interest rates, supply having outstripped existing demand. Cheaper money would in turn encourage businessmen to invest in more capital goods. The higher level of investment would increase national income and employment through the operation of the multiplier (*see* II, **16**).

The implication of this reasoning is that an expansionary monetary policy would lead to growth in income, output and employment. A restrictive policy would have the opposite effect.

Keynesians argued that these predicted results would not necessarily occur. They based their criticism upon a distinction between *transactions money* and *liquidity or precautionary money*.

(*a*) *Transactions money*. This is money in its capacity as a medium of exchange. It is required to conduct everyday business, the amount needed equating with the volume of that business. In other words, it is the national income measured in money terms. We have now to recognise that a monetary expansion which initiates lower interest rates and higher national income necessitates more *transactions* money to finance the increased volume of business. Whether such money is available from a given growth in the supply now depends on the demand for money for liquidity or precautionary purposes.

(*b*) *Liquidity or precautionary money*. A proportion of the total money stock is always required to satisfy the preference in the economy for liquidity. In some part this preference will be determined by the instinctive precaution to have some purchasing power instantly available. For the rest, we shall expect liquidity preference to be geared to the rate of interest. When rates are high liquidity preference will be low, any increase in cash balances being invested in income yielding financial assets. When rates are low the opportunity cost of holding assets in liquid or cash form has been reduced and the risk of holding financial assets of variable value totally eliminated. Liquidity preference consequently increases.

It will now be noted that when liquidity preference is low and excess cash is invested in financial assets, interest rates are driven down. For example, if the market bids up the price of a 5 per cent £100 bond to £200 then the yield falls to £2.50 per £100. If on the other hand liquidity preference is already high then monetary expansion which expresses itself simply in higher cash balances will not reduce interest rates further, since there is no increased demand for financial assets. With interest rates the same the incentive to invest is unaltered. National income does not increase.

This phenomenon was referred to by Keynesians as the *liquidity trap* and explains their belief that monetary policy was incapable of curing a depression. It followed that the thrust of government policy would necessarily depend upon the more direct methods of influencing aggregate demand through the public finances. These were considered in III.

3. Lower interest rates and an adequate money supply. On this analysis monetary policy would still have a subsidiary role. In the first place, low interest rates were desirable both to encourage investment and to minimise the cost of government of sustaining aggregate demand through deficit public finance, i.e. the servicing charge of an expanding national debt.

Secondly, with a low interest rate high national income economy there is a correspondingly high demand for transactions money, less being left for precautionary purposes. Interest rates may, however, fall to a level at which liquidity preference is increased. Some people will wish to exchange financial assets such as bonds for cash. Since the stock of precautionary cash is limited heavy sales will depress capital values, i.e. force up interest rates. At higher rates, investment, national income, employment and the demand for transactions money all decline. Of a given money stock more is now available to satisfy the demand for precautionary purposes. A new equilibrium is established albeit at a lower level of activity. It follows from this argument that attempts to sustain full employment by fiscal methods should be supported by an expansionary monetary policy.

A KEYNESIAN VIEW OF MONEY AND PRICE DETERMINATION

4. Money national income and the price level. In II we examined the factors which determined *real* national income. To this equation we have added the Keynesian explanation of the influence of money and the interest rate. Still adopting the Keynesian analysis we must now explain the determinants of *money* national income. To do so, we should not only understand the factors which determine real income (Q) but also those which govern the *general or average price level* (P). Money national income will then be $P \times Q$.

5. The classical view. The classical explanation of price determination is usually referred to as the *quantity theory of money* expressed in the formula:

$$M \times V = P \times Q$$

where M is the quantity of money, V is the velocity of circulation (the number of times the money stock changes hands), P is the general price level and Q is the *real* national income of goods and services.

It was further postulated that Q would be determined by physical considerations such as the availability of the factors of production and technological efficiency. Velocity was also determined by outside forces in the shape of institutional arrangements, e.g. whether wage payments were made weekly or monthly.

Since V and Q were already determined it followed that movements of P depended upon changes in M. It was the money supply which governed the general price level.

6. Keynesian rejection of quantity theory. Criticism is ultimately aimed at the presumed stability of the velocity of circulation and is based upon the fundamental distinction between transactions money and liquidity money.

Quantity theory is accepted in respect of transactions money. Under a given regime of institutional arrangements this element of the money supply will correspond to money national income, $P \times Q$.

As we have seen, however, the demand for liquidity money varies with the rate of interest. As rates fall so liquidity preference increases and higher cash balances are held. Put another way, the *velocity of circulation of liquidity money varies with the rate of interest.*

It follows that what is true for one aspect of the money stock is relevant to the whole. This view leads to the conclusion that velocity is not a stable factor governed by institutional arrangements alone but that *it is influenced by the rate of interest.*

At this juncture the causal connection between M and P is broken. If interest rates are already low an expansion of the money supply will not express itself in a further reduction. We fall into the liquidity trap and simply add to our cash balances. In short, an increase in M is offset by a decline in V which leaves $P \times Q$ unchanged.

7. An extreme Keynesian view of price determination. The extreme position is one in which the quantity of money is of very little consequence. It may be added that Keynes himself did not subscribe to this view and was fully aware of the effects upon price of monetary expansion once full employment had been achieved.

However, from this extreme position, *money* wages are established by collective bargaining. Simultaneously, the level of employment will have been determined by the size of *real* national income. Real wages, i.e. the share of output accruing to labour, will be in line with labour's marginal productivity. Since money wages *and* real wages are known, we have a fairly good idea of the general level of prices.

Thus, with real national income determined by consumption, investment and government expenditure and prices determined by money wages, money national income will be $P \times Q$.

Money measurements of wages, prices and incomes are thought in any case to be of only minor interest and this analysis gives no attention to any influences which money and prices may themselves exert.

8. The significance of money and prices further developed. Modern monetarists have argued that the Keynesian explanation of equilibrium with low national income and employment depends upon the presence of market imperfections, e.g. the monopoly power of labour unions. Too little attention is paid to the power of flexible prices. If prices and wages were free to move downwards then employment and output would rise.

This claim is disputed by the Keynesians, who argue that their analysis holds good even in a situation in which wages and prices are flexible. A fall in wages and prices will result in a fall in *money* national income. With a given money stock, less is now required for transactions and more is available for liquidity purposes. Some of the extra liquidity money *may* be converted to financial assets, thus increasing capital values and forcing down interest rates. In this case investment will be stimulated and income and employment will rise. *Such a sequence of events will, however, only occur in the absence of the liquidity trap.* In an economy which is already depressed extra liquidity money may be held as cash leaving interest rates unaltered. Flexible market prices are thus no more effective in restoring full employment equilibrium than is monetary policy.

9. A rejoinder. Professor Friedman has responded to this argument by pointing to the work of Professors Pigou and Haberler. The "Pigou effect" describes the way in which the value of money varies in direct proportion to systematic movements in prices and wages. Clearly, if the price level is halved the value of *cash balances* is doubled.

It is then argued that if prices continue to fall a point must ultimately be reached at which the appreciation in the value of cash balances induces holders to increase consumption expenditure.

When this happens, Friedman continues, the liquidity trap is bypassed. Changes in the real quantity of money (purchasing power) directly influence aggregate demand without any dependence upon changes in interest rates.

If it can then be shown that changes in the *nominal* quantity of money govern the price level and hence the purchasing power of money, i.e. the *real* quantity, then it follows that variations in the money stock have a significant bearing upon aggregate demand.

These perceptions provided a starting point for the *counter-revolution in monetary theory*.

A MONETARIST VIEW OF MONEY, PRICES AND NATIONAL INCOME DETERMINATION

10. The price level and money national income are determined by the quantity of money. The modern monetarist position is neatly summarised in the argument developed by Professor Friedman in *The Counter-Revolution in Monetary Theory* (Occasional Paper 33, Institute of Economic Affairs).

(*a*) *A consistent relationship between monetary growth and nominal incomes*. A mass of evidence points to the universal truth of this assertion. Currently, he claims, the time lag between the two is of the order of six to nine months.

(*b*) *Relationship between monetary growth, output and prices*. Initially, the impact of an expansion of the money supply will be absorbed almost wholly in higher output with hardly any effect upon prices. After a *further* six to nine months prices will begin to rise.

(*i*) The *immediate* effect is not upon nominal income but upon liquidity. Cash balances increase relative to other financial assets such as bonds, equities, property. In this assertion, Keynesians and monetarists are in agreement.

(*ii*) Holders of extra cash will now attempt to restore the previous ratio of cash to other assets. For the economy as a whole the attempt will be frustrated since one man's purchase is another man's sale. However, the brisker turnover of financial assets will push up capital values, i.e. drive down interest rates.

(*iii*) Lower interest rates are conducive to increased borrowing and spending both on new assets and on current goods and services. Thus over some six to nine months the effect of monetary expansion has been to increase aggregate demand, nominal incomes, employment and output.

(*iv*) During the same period there has been little change in prices. There are as yet no inflationary expectations and future wages and prices have been set in advance. Subsequently, when entrepreneurs perceive that business remains good they will attempt not only to overcome the physical difficulties of increasing output but also to widen profit margins. Characteristically, the prices of goods and services will therefore respond to an unanticipated rise in nominal demand more rapidly than the prices of the factors of production, e.g. nominal wages. What in fact has happened is that *real* wages paid by employers have fallen and it is this reduction, unperceived by labour, which has made possible the higher level of employment.

(*c*) *The short term and the long term.* Monetarists recognise that in the short term, which may be as long as five to ten years, the overall impact of monetary expansion will be upon money incomes, output and employment. Over a period of decades, however, it is prices which are primarily affected. Expectations are adjusted and labour demands higher money wages to compensate for higher anticipated prices. Increased wage costs now make that expectation a reality.

Since the quantity of money has determined the price of the national output it follows that it has also determined the size of *money* national income.

11. Real factors determine real national income and the level of employment. Professor Friedman's argument continues that in the long term "what happens to the level of output depends upon real factors: the enterprise, ingenuity and industry of the people; the extent of thrift; the structure of industry and government; the relations among nations and so on."

It is these real factors which at any time will determine "the natural level of unemployment". Fundamentally, this level is governed by imperfections in the market, the inability rapidly to redeploy resources to meet changing conditions coupled with the downward inflexibility of wages.

It is impossible to reduce unemployment permanently below this level (which would have been determined in a free market) by either monetary or fiscal stimulus.

12. Implications for public policy. It can be seen from the discussion so far that the differences between Keynesians and monetarists are fundamental. While the former perceive a central stabilising role for fiscal and monetary policy the latter view such attempts at "fine tuning" as being themselves the principal destabilising agents.

(a) *Fiscal policy.* Monetarists consider the measures which were outlined in III as ineffective. If a stimulus to aggregate demand is given through tax financed public spending then there is a corresponding reduction in private sector spending, immediately in consumption or indirectly in savings which would have been lent to other spenders. There is a similar result when public spending is financed by borrowing private savings. Resources are simply transferred from private to public sector use.

"To discover any net effect on total spending, one must go to a more sophisticated level—to differences in the behaviour of the two groups of people or to effects of government borrowing on interest rates. There is no first order effect." (Friedman.)

(b) *Monetary policy.* While recognising the potency of monetary policy, monetarists maintain that too little is known of the *precise* relationship between money and *real* magnitudes such as *real* national income and the level of unemployment for even monetary "fine tuning" to be feasible. The best that can be done is to ensure that variations in the money supply are not themselves the source of instability, e.g. the monetary contractions in the UK, 1925–31 and the USA, 1929–33 which may be seen as the true cause of the slump.

However, nominal magnitudes such as the price level, the money national income and the exchange rate are in principle more amenable to control by the authorities through the money supply. Of these, a stable price level is thought to be of greatest importance since by reducing the risk of forward planning business confidence is increased. Once again, however, the precise relationship between money and prices is ill-understood. The most realistic monetary policy is, therefore, one which prescribes, publicises and adheres to a fixed rate of monetary growth sufficient to accommodate any real economic expansion, e.g. 5 per cent. Long-term price stability would now be assured.

13. Conclusion. In conclusion the fundamental difference between the Keynesian and monetarist approaches should again be stressed. While the former postulates a major role for government in guiding the economy the latter denies the validity of any discretionary macroeconomic policy. A genuine equilibrium will be achieved only through a more perfect functioning of the market.

This conclusion, they say, is based not only upon the logic of their analysis but also upon observation of the inherent instability and structural distortion of economies where discretionary policies have been most widely practised.

This criticism will be developed more fully in the next section with particular reference to the UK economy.

THE PHILLIPS CURVE AND THE INFLATION/ UNEMPLOYMENT TRADE-OFF

14. Steering a middle course. In 1958, Professor A. W. Phillips published the results of extensive research in an essay, "The Relation between Unemployment and the Rate of Change of Money Wages in the United Kingdom, 1861–1957" (*Economica*, Vol. 25, 1958).

He sought to show a regular inverse relationship in which wages rose more rapidly in periods when unemployment was low. Since wages constitute a major element of all costs, when they rose rapidly so would prices.

It followed that a lower rate of inflation could be bought at the expense of a higher level of unemployment and vice versa. Since the Keynesian analysis provided an instrument for determining employment levels it should be possible to steer an acceptable course between the two extremes.

In the early 1960s this thinking was quantified with the suggestion that "full employment" should be reconceived in terms of 2.4 per cent unemployment, approximately twice the previously acceptable figures. With this margin of unused resources we should be able to enjoy a high and stable level of activity without inflation. By 1966, the proposal had been accepted by government.

After 1966 there emerged the new phenomenon of rising unemployment accompanied by escalating inflation. There was now apparently no trade-off. Since it was considered politically impossible deliberately to advocate still higher unemployment as a check to inflation, governments during the following ten years relied even more heavily upon incomes policies in the view that the immediate cause of inflation was wage cost push (*see* III, **41–43**). In contrast, as we have seen, monetarists maintain that "inflation is always and everywhere a monetary phenomenon".

15. The Phillips curve.

FIG. 2 *The Phillips curve.* The curve postulates an inverse relationship between the rate of unemployment and the rate of change of money wages and, hence, prices.

In Fig. 2, E_o is the "natural level of unemployment" consistent with neither upward nor downward pressure on wages and prices. At E_f there is overfull employment inducing upward pressure on wages and prices. At E_u with excessive unemployment wages are falling.

16. The fallacy in the Phillips curve.
Monetarists argue that no economist has ever maintained that demand and supply were functions of *nominal* wages. It is the *real* wage (what the money will buy) which relates to both the demand for and the supply of labour. When the vertical axis is correctly labelled Real Wages (W/P) then the curve tells us nothing of the relationship between the level of unemployment and the rate of change of *money* wages and prices. In other words, it provides no explanation of inflation, the origin of which must be found elsewhere.

Thus, in Fig. 3, at E_o there is equilibrium with neither upward nor downward pressure on *real* wages. *But* that equilibrium will remain undisturbed with money wages and prices separately constant *or* rising at 10 per cent or falling at 10 per cent provided that they both change in the same proportion. It is of course the rise in money wages which is symptomatic of inflation.

Rate of change of
money wages
divided by
Rate of change of
nominal prices
(W/P)

Unemployment

FIG. 3 *The fallacy in the Phillips curve.* The vertical axis now represents real wages (W/P). This curve tells us nothing about the relationship between unemployment and the rate of change of money wages.

The explanation of this simple error, say the monetarists, is to be found in the Keynesian view that increased demand would express itself in increased employment and output. *Prices would remain stable.* It followed therefore that a rise in *money* wages implied an equal rise in real wages.

Phillips himself was in fact being rather more subtle. He was suggesting that an *anticipated* change in money wages would equate with an *anticipated* change in real wages even though that expectation might not be fulfilled.

17. Unemployment cannot be permanently reduced by accepting a higher but stable rate of inflation. From a monetarist standpoint we have established that inflation cannot be checked simply by accepting a higher rate of unemployment. Equally, unemployment cannot be permanently reduced by accepting a higher but *stable* rate of inflation. This aspect of the case is summarised in Fig. 4.

We have shown that monetarists assume that in the long term the main impact of an increase in aggregate demand is upon prices rather than upon employment and output (*see* 10(*c*)). For simplicity, in Fig. 4 it is assumed that there is *no* increase in output.

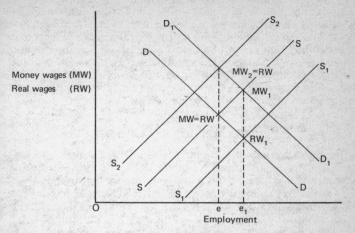

FIG. 4 *Long-term effect of stimulating demand to reduce unemployment.* Employment will be increased only for as long as labour accepts lower real wages.

At O_e employment and money wages (MW) equalling real wages (RW) there is equilibrium without inflation but with ee_1 unemployment, "the natural rate" in monetarist terms.

If it is desired to reduce this unemployment by an orthodox stimulus to aggregate demand, the demand curve (DD) is shifted to the right to D_1D_1. The very short-term effect is the establishment of a new equilibrium at money wages of MW_1 and employment of O_{e1}. Concealed is the fall in real wages to RW_1. While labour was unwilling to accept a lower *money* wage in order to increase employment it has unwittingly accepted a lower *real* wage. The labour supply curve (SS) has in effect moved to the right to S_1S_1 and the true equilibrium lies at RW_1.

The higher level of employment will be sustained only for as long as labour is prepared to accept lower real wages. When expectations adjust to the higher prices associated with higher money wages and no increase in output there will be pressure for still higher money wages to restore living standards. The labour supply curve shifts to the left to S_2S_2 where a fresh equilibrium is established at money wages of MW_2 to equal the original real wage of RW. Unemployment reverts to its "natural" level of ee_1

albeit at a higher level of money wages and prices. A *given* rate of inflation has not sustained the higher level of employment.

The manoeuvre can only be successfully repeated provided that inflation is kept ahead of labour's expectations, i.e. the demand curve is moved to the right more rapidly than the response of the supply curve to the left. This implies a policy of deliberately accelerating inflation since in the long term labour's response to downward pressure on *real* wages becomes increasingly sensitive.

THE AUSTRIAN VARIANT

18. Broad agreement between Friedmanite and Austrian monetarists. The Austrian analysis of the disruptive consequences of monetary and fiscal expansion was put forward by Hayek in 1931. It was largely ignored at that time when the Keynesian technique for curing recession was proving so attractive to academic economists.

The more widely recognised position of the Friedmanite monetarists has already been explained. The Austrians are in broad agreement:

> "The contention that a general rise in prices such as we in the Western world have experienced in recent years is wholly due to, and made possible solely by, an excessive increase in the quantity of money, and that, therefore, governmental monetary policy is wholly responsible for it, is today usually described as the 'monetarist' position. It seems to me in this general form incontrovertible . . ." (*Full Employment at Any Price*, F. A. Hayek, IEA, 1975).

19. The basic difference. Hayek continues: "But in a narrower sense 'monetarist' is today frequently used to describe the expositors of a somewhat mechanical form of the quantity theory of value of money which in my opinion tends to oversimplify the theoretical argument".

Hayek's objection lies in the fact that as a "macro-theory" it considers only the effect upon the *general* price level of changes in the quantity of money. It pays no attention to the structure of *relative* prices.

20. Structural effects of monetary expansion. The central point is that monetary/fiscal expansion does not have a neutral effect upon the *structure* of the economy. The extra money generated in inflation is not scattered evenly across the whole economy as if it had been dropped by a helicopter. It enters through *particular* segments of the economy and consequently affects different areas of activity in different ways.

The initial impact of an increase in aggregate demand is not experienced uniformly across the economy. The *pattern* of demand is distorted to favour the impact sectors and there is consequently a distortion of the natural or market allocation of labour and capital.

21. The effect upon relative prices. The immediate effect of "reflation" is to cause a rise in the price of the outputs of the impact sectors while elsewhere prices remain constant or even fall. When the increased incomes of the impact sectors are spent on the products of other sectors the prices of the latter are brought back into line. In other words the change in relative prices which initially favoured the impact sectors has now been counterbalanced to re-establish the original price relativities. When this occurs there are capital losses in the impact sectors revealing that the reallocation of resources was inappropriate and cannot be sustained.

22. The longer-term consequences of reflation. The tendency is now for the initial impact sectors to contract and for unemployment to rise until redundant labour is reabsorbed into other areas of the economy. Once there has been a full readjustment resources will again be allocated in accordance with the underlying pattern of demand and *unemployment will have been restored to the original or "natural" level.* However, *all* money prices will have risen permanently and during the period of readjustment unemployment will be substantially higher.

23. Permanent monetary/fiscal expansion. When relying upon reflationary demand management techniques the only way in which government can avoid the chain of events indicated above is by deliberately accelerating the rate of inflation in order permanently to distort relative prices and hence the allocation of resources in a way which does not reflect the natural pattern of demand.

24. The impact sectors. The initial beneficiaries of reflation may be intended or unintended by government. Into the latter category fall the property and construction companies who at first benefited from the massive monetary expansion of 1972–73. They were led to over-extend and subsequently collapsed when monetary growth slowed down.

More characteristically, in post-war Britain it has been the public sector which has been repeatedly the beneficiary. Nationalised industries have been heavily subsidised and "lame ducks" rescued and taken into public ownership. An example is the decision in 1971 to invest £3 billion in the British Steel Corporation in order to raise capacity to 36–38 million tonnes by 1980. There followed a distortion in the allocation of resources which today can only be sustained by further vast injections of public money. Similarly, throughout the 1970s and into the 1980s British Leyland has been subsidised at huge cost in the hope that at some time in the future the pattern of demand may conform to the structure of production which has been supported.

Elsewhere, the bureaucracies of central and local government have been the initial beneficiaries of successive attempts to reflate out of recession. It is equally these areas which are most resistant to any attempts to economise in the use of labour. They have consequently been amongst those most heavily criticised for over-manning and low productivity, e.g. direct works departments of local government.

25. The consequences of three decades of Keynesianism. Austrian and Friedmanite monetarists agree that in the short term increases in aggregate demand may produce a temporary increase in employment. In the long term, however, employment can only be maintained at a level higher than the natural or market rate at the expense of accelerating inflation.

Austrians go further. The repeated distortion of relative prices both to sustain ailing industries over a long period and to accelerate out of successive recessions has led to a progressive distortion of the UK economy; an allocation of resources which does not reflect the underlying *pattern* of demand. Further applications of the orthodox Keynesian treatment can only lead to further structural malformation, to hyperinflation and to economic and social breakdown.

26. The cure. Hayek, like other monetarists, is at pains to point out that the remedy for inflation is not a deliberately engineered increase in unemployment. "We do not have the choice between inflation and unemployment, as little as we can choose between overeating and indigestion: though overeating may be very pleasant while it proceeds, the indigestion will follow".

On this analogy, the cure lies in monetary fasting and the final acceptance of a stable diet. The "fasting" will not be painless as it inevitably means a period of rising unemployment, the accumulation of thirty years of "concealed unemployment", before resources can be reallocated in accordance with the processes of the market.

27. Distortion of relative prices, not defective demand, is the source of unemployment. The Austrian criticism of reflationary policies reveals what Hayek considers to be the original source of unemployment: "The correct explanation seems to me to be the existence of discrepancies between the distribution of demand among the different goods and services and the allocation of labour and other resources among the production of those outputs."

These discrepancies are reflected in the distortion of *relative* prices and wages, usually induced by monopolistic or governmental price-fixing. In the context of pre-1939 business cycles Hayek considers that the primary cause was the extension of bank lending to companies during the upswing for investment, resulting in malinvestment in capital goods of longer gestation periods. More fundamentally, in a dynamic market the *pattern* of demand continuously changes in advance of the market intelligence (reflected in relative prices) for a permanent equilibrium co-ordination of demand and supply. When the structure of prices subsequently does change there must be transfers of labour between sectors.

Hayek then argues that although we have a good *qualitative* knowledge of the conditions necessary for "equilibrium" it is impossible *quantitatively* to establish a set of relative prices, deviation from which will result in unemployment. Only the continuing processes of the market can reveal this.

On this view societies which have been preoccupied with "planned" economic solutions to the *social* problem of unemployment have been willing to accept only those theories based upon measurable variables. The "true" explanation is consequently neglected.

PROGRESS TEST 4

1. What did Keynes consider to be the unique feature of money? **(1)**

2. Distinguish between transactions money and liquidity money. **(2)**

3. Explain why interest rates fall when capital values rise. **(2(*b*))**

4. What do you understand by "the liquidity trap"? **(2(b))**

5. Explain the quantity theory of money. **(5)**

6. Why did Keynesians reject quantity theory? **(6)**

7. Why in the Keynesian view will lower wages not necessarily restore full employment equilibrium? **(8)**

8. Explain "the Pigou effect". **(9)**

9. Outline the steps between an increase in the money supply and a rise in the general price level as seen by the monetarists. **(10)**

10. How is real national income determined in the monetarist system? **(11)**

11. What economic policy conclusions will be drawn from monetarist thinking? **(12)**

12. What theoretical reasons would lead us to believe that unemployment cannot be permanently reduced by accepting a higher rate of inflation? **(17)**

13. In what essential respect do Hayekian monetarists differ from Friedmanite monetarists? **(19)**

14. Outline the Austrian explanation of the effects of reflation upon prices and employment. **(21–22)**

15. How does the Austrian analysis undermine orthodox government full employment policy? **(27)**

CHAPTER V

Democracy, Deficit Finance and the Failure of Demand Management

METHODOLOGICAL, POLITICAL AND BUREAUCRATIC ASPECTS

1. The economics of politics. Conventionally, any consideration of politics would lie outside the scope of a textbook on applied economics. However, in post-war Britain a large part of political discussion has centred upon economic problems, which is unsurprising in a country in which approximately one-half of national resources is allocated by political decision rather than by the processes of the market. In the USA over the past ten years, a growing awareness of the extent to which politicians and bureaucrats allocate resources has led to the birth of a new subject, the *economics of politics*, which attempts to apply economic analysis to an understanding of the way in which political decisions are made. While it is not intended to pursue this subject in any detail, it is of practical value to give some general account of the political ethos in which the most influential economic theory of the twentieth century was conceived and applied. These insights will lead to a greater understanding of why the theory, in its application, progressively failed to achieve its intended objectives. This theory was, of course, that of Lord Keynes.

2. Demand management and compensatory finance. As we have seen in II and III, the policy precepts of Keynesian economics purport to be wholly symmetrical. The Budget deficits necessary to counter depression would be offset by Budget surpluses in times when inflation threatened. While the Budget would normally be out of balance in any one fiscal year it would balance over the period of a whole business cycle. This idealised setting rests upon certain defective assumptions about the knowledge of economists and the behaviour of politicians and bureaucrats.

3. The knowledge of economists. Keynes makes the central assumption that economists are capable of possessing sufficient knowledge which, if acted upon, facilitates the co-ordination of economic actions. Hayek's "lost generation of economists" would seem to have been raised in this belief.

In *"The Pretence of Knowledge"*, his Alfred Nobel Memorial Lecture of 1974, Hayek castigated the view that the social sciences could proceed by the same methods as the physical sciences. In the latter it is "generally assumed, probably with good reason, that any important factor which determines the observed events will itself be directly observable and measurable, (while) in the study of such 'essentially complex' phenomena as the market, which depends on the actions of many individuals, all the circumstances that will determine the outcome of a process, *will hardly ever be fully known or measurable.*"

According to Hayek, because of a mistakenly "scientific" (pseudo-scientific) approach to economics there has been a tendency to incorporate into modern theory only those factors which are measurable. Those which are not are ignored as unimportant even though they may be crucial to the *true* theory.

As these assertions relate to the Keynesian analysis: "The correlation between aggregate demand and total employment, for instance, may be only approximate; but as it is the *only* one on which we have quantitative data, it is accepted as the only causal connection which counts." On this view, appearances deceive. A false theory is accepted because there appears to be better "scientific" evidence. The true theory is ignored since it can never be substantiated quantitatively. (Hayek's *"true"* theory is outlined in IV, 27.)

In short, the intelligences of one or a number of economists are incapable of fully grasping the complexity of the infinite number of variables which comprise the market.

4. Keynes's normative assumptions of political conduct. The assumption that "experts could be sufficiently omniscient" fitted well with Keynes's élitist view of how politicians should and would behave. His biographer, Sir Roy Harrod, speaks of "the presuppositions of Harvey Road" (the upper-middle-class location of the Keynes family home in Cambridge).

"We have seen that he (Keynes) was strongly imbued with what I have called the presuppositions of Harvey Road. One of these presuppositions may perhaps be summarised in the idea that the government of Britain was and would continue to be in the hands of an intellectual aristocracy using the methods of persuasion." (*The Life of John Maynard Keynes*, Sir Roy Harrod, Macmillan, 1951.)

In other words, Keynes assumed that his theory would be implemented by "philosopher-kings", who would be advised by experts and would always act impartially in the public interest. He ignored the possibility that in a democratic political setting the dictates of macroeconomic engineering might conflict with the electoral survival of politicians; that there might be political pressures which would render Budget surpluses impossible and Budget deficits untimely and unduly large. He could not anticipate the shift in general beliefs and expectations which was in no small measure the consequence of his own "vision". Once government in Britain had accepted, as it did in 1944 and on the basis of Keynesian thinking, a responsibility for the general economic well-being of the nation, the constraints upon politicians of the pre-Keynesian principle of the balanced Budget were removed. The intended symmetry of Budgets over a business cycle was not achieved. Under the pressures of sectional interests, in a democratic society, the pattern was permanently asymmetrical (*see* **5** below).

5. Political survival in a Keynesian constitutional environment. The nature of "the political market" was fundamentally changed with the abandonment of the principle of the balanced Budget. In the classical setting the political constraint had been the need to balance an expenditure proposal with a taxation proposal. The pressures were now quite different.

(*a*) *Budget surpluses in a democracy.* A surplus requires either an increase in taxation or a reduction in public spending. Individuals, some more than others, are able to perceive in the first case an immediate and direct cost in reduced private consumption and in the second case a direct loss of public goods and services. The indirect benefit of a reduction in the rate of inflation is something which they must *imagine* as a *possibility* for the future and from which they *may* derive some undisclosed personal benefit. In short, there is a reluctance to discount present and certain benefits for future and uncertain gains.

NOTE: After prolonged inflation, in recent years there is some evidence that this outlook may be undergoing change, as is witnessed by the 1979 election of a Conservative Government on the platform of reducing inflation through a *declared* policy of public spending cuts.

(*b*) *Budget deficits in a democracy*. The opposite rule now applies. In the context of government whose responsibility for collective welfare extends to the future as well as the present, there is a disposition to discount that future for present benefits. These are assured whether the deficit is the product of tax cuts which increase private consumption or of increased public spending which expands the consumption of public goods. Some gain more than others *but there are no losers*. The longer-term effect upon inflation again requires an imagination of how great that inflation will be and how much the individual will be affected. Since he has no possible means of calculating the effect the possible consequences are swept aside.

We may conclude therefore that in a political democracy operating under a Keynesian fiscal constitution there is an inbuilt bias towards expanding Budget deficits. We shall see (VI, 5(*c*)) that because of the way monetary institutions operate, Budget deficits are frequently to be equated with an expansion of the money supply and on monetarist analysis this implies a bias towards inflation.

6. The bureaucratic bias towards increased public expenditure. It is not only politicians in a democracy who are likely to be persuaded that public spending, apart from its electoral appeal, is inherently "good" since somehow it must correspond to the "public interest". Public servants of both central and local government must almost inevitably take the same view since therein lies their *raison d'être*.

The mark of success in the spending departments is the expansion of the activities of those departments and the resistance by all means of any attempt to curtail them. Moreover, there is no reason to believe that man's self-interested motives when engaged in private activity should suddenly be transformed into altruism once he becomes a public employee. The record of public sector industrial disputes is self-revealing as is the resistance to the 1979 government's spending cuts. The effectiveness of these cuts is to be seen in an *increase* in real terms in 1979–81 of the order of 3 per cent of Gross Domestic Product.

We shall now relate these insights to the British experience.

THE FISCAL CONSTITUTION BEFORE KEYNES

7. The origins and eighteenth-century growth of the National Debt. The fiscal constitution is that most important part of a country's total political constitution (in Britain's case unwritten) which sets out the rules by which government may tax and spend. In Britain, this aspect of the constitution was for centuries the principal bone of contention between Crown and Parliament. Only when Parliament established its right to vote funds did it finally secure ascendancy over the Crown. The modern National Debt consequently dates from 1694 when the government secured a loan of £1,200,000 from the newly formed Bank of England to finance a war against France. During the following century Britain was at war in every decade and this provides the principal explanation of why by 1815 the Debt had grown to £850 million.

There were, however, other reasons. The House of Commons during this period was ineffective in securing efficient and economical government. The administration of Sir Robert Walpole (1721–42), for example, has been described as "government by corruption". Parliamentary seats were bought and sold, government contracts, sinecures and pensions were distributed as a barely concealed means of bribery, and public spending ran out of control.

There were yet other pressures for fiscal reform. The late eighteenth century saw the emergence of an embryonic party system. By the time of the 1832 Reform Act the Crown was obliged to nominate the majority party as the government. From that time, although theoretically responsible to the Commons, in reality the party of government dominated the Commons who were in no position to exercise an effective brake on public spending.

8. Nineteenth-century fiscal reforms. During the nineteenth century there gradually evolved a set of rules and conventions which governed classical fiscal conduct. They may be summarised as follows.

(*a*) *Standing Order No. 78*. This House of Commons Standing Order dates from 1713. "This House will receive no petition for any sum relating to public service or proceed upon any motion for a grant or charge upon the public revenue whether payable out of the Consolidated Fund or out of money to be provided by Parliament unless recommended from the *Crown*." This precept was subsequently codified in Standing Order No. 82. The power to propose expenditure was therefore vested squarely in HM Government.

(*b*) *Parliament sanctions fiscal measures*. While government may *propose* taxation and expenditures it is Parliament which authorises them.

(*c*) *The House of Commons predominates in fiscal matters.* Following the Parliament Act 1911, it was made clear that matters of spending and taxation were ultimately the prerogative of the Commons and not the Lords.

(*d*) *The Budget statement.* This convention was established in 1861 and required that the government's spending plans should be submitted to Parliament annually, usually in April, in the form of a Budget statement.

(*e*) *"Supply days".* On the days allocated to "supply", the Opposition is free to choose those estimates which will be debated and will do so in order most effectively to challenge ministerial policies.

Alone, these conventions would have been wholly ineffective checks upon excessive public spending and deficit finance within the context of party government. Standing Order No. 78 had been established simply to prevent individual MPs from misappropriating public funds. Similarly the second rule had resulted from the long struggle to eliminate the misappropriations of the Crown. It was virtually useless as a check upon governments which through the party system controlled the majority vote in the Commons. Moreover, the Parliament Act of 1911 removed the possible check of the second chamber upon government budgetary malpractices. Taken in conjunction, conventions (*d*) and (*e*), far from providing a check on government spending, were and are biased in its favour. Debate and voting on the government's spending plans take place in advance of and in isolation from consideration of its plans to raise revenue.

9. The convention of the balanced Budget. In complete contrast to the eighteenth century it became the convention of the nineteenth to balance planned expenditures with adequate revenues, if not in fact to produce a surplus in order to retire existing Debt. This convention was a crucial constitutional innovation designed to keep abreast of the biases of an evolving political system. Without it there existed no effective mechanism for curbing the excessive deficit-financed spending which had been characteristic of the eighteenth and early nineteenth centuries and which was to appear again after 1944.

On this principle and against a background of a century of relative peace the National Debt had by 1914 been reduced to £707 million.

10. Classical economists on the principle of public debt. The principle of the balanced Budget has often been misrepresented as the product of a narrow, Victorian moral code hostile to both borrowing and public spending and with no relevance to modern government. This was not the case. What they sought to remedy was *wasteful* government spending, which, particularly when financed by borrowing, was unrestrained by the existing fiscal constitution.

In certain circumstances, they recognised the necessity for deficit finance, e.g. wars and long-term public investments such as roads and canals. Otherwise the balanced Budget principle was a necessary precaution against the bias of democratic governments to overspend. On the basis of that principle government itself became the best safeguard against wasteful spending since when it had to be financed by increases in taxation there was an immediate *political* cost.

11. The growth of the National Debt, 1914–45. The immensely costly First World War raised the Debt to £7,800 million by 1918. On the basis of the peacetime balanced Budget principle the figure was stabilised between the wars but by 1945 had risen to £23,000 million. Since the greater part of this had been incurred in consequence of wars throughout 250 years of history it is sometimes referred to as the "deadweight Debt" since there are no corresponding, tangible, income-yielding assets.

THE KEYNESIAN FISCAL CONSTITUTION

12. The "Cambridge Circus". Throughout the 1930s, Keynes scorned Gladstonian fiscal principles and argued for deficit-financed public works as a means of relieving unemployment. Initially, he perceived a need to balance the Budget over a period of years but in *The General Theory* appears to have abandoned this constraint. In this respect, he was criticised by some of his contemporaries (e.g. the Oxford economist, Hubert Henderson) for being insufficiently specific on the policy implications of his analysis. It was left to members of the "Cambridge Circus" to develop his ideas (*see* **13–15** below).

13. James Meade. In his *Economic Analysis and Policy*, 1938, Meade provided the details of compensatory finance based upon the Keynesian analysis. Budget deficits in recession would be offset by surpluses in boom, fiscal measures being supported by counter-cyclical monetary policy.

Meade, however, was at pains to point out that there should be no attempt to finance a normal Budget deficit by inflationary means. "For if a government finances a permanent Budget deficit by printing more paper money this must lead to a progressive and inflationary rise in prices."

This is the kind of argument which in recent years has been more readily associated with monetary rather than Keynesian economists. Moreover, at a later date he argued in a similar vein to Friedman that there was in the economy "a standard rate of unemployment" determined by structural factors which influenced the fluidity of the labour markets. If the standard rate were surpassed then government should pursue a contractionary fiscal/monetary policy.

14. Lord Kaldor. In 1944, Kaldor took the view that the immediate post-war problem was likely to be one of inflationary rather than deflationary gaps. The implied Budget surpluses he did not think to be inconsistent with the pursuit of full employment policy. If in the longer term a period of secular stagnation developed as it had between the wars then there might be a need for a steadily rising National Debt to stimulate activity. The rise necessary to sustain full employment, however, would not produce any intolerable increase in the burden of the Debt.

This optimism was matched by the view that "post-war governments will pursue a monetary and wage policy which maintains the prices of final commodities constant". (*Full Employment in a Free Society*, Appendix C, 1944 White Paper.) He considered that a continuously rising price level would prove a threat to long-term economic stability.

15. Hugh Dalton. Originally an academic who was strongly influenced by Keynesian thinking, Dalton was Britain's first post-war Chancellor of the Exchequer (1945–47). He took the view that we should abandon the principle of the balanced Budget but was clear that deficits should not be excessive since the effects of a financial situation apparently out of control could be very damaging. Moreover, in the longer term Budgets must balance since the prospect of a continuing and unlimited increase in Debt was intolerable.

16. Summary. These examples of early Keynesian thinking illustrate its dependence upon the presence of politicians who take a *long-term* view of the public interest, advised by expert, professional economists. Budgets would be balanced over a period of years. Short-run deficits would be modest and carefully managed. There would be no attempt to reduce unemployment below the "standard" or "natural" rate. Long-run monetary and price stability would be maintained.

In the event these expectations were not to be realised.

17. The record. Only in the early 1960s was some attempt made to discover a "natural" rate of unemployment (*see* IV, **14**) and this effort was not pursued (*see* II, **6–8**). There has been no long-term policy of monetary and price stability but a situation in which, for the greater part of the period, the Bank of England attached little importance to the money supply and inflation escalated. There was no long-term offsetting of Budget surpluses against Budget deficits. In the whole post-war period the only surpluses achieved were in 1969 and 1970 and these may be interpreted as the product of the constraints imposed by the International Monetary Fund following the sterling crisis of 1966. On the other hand, there has been no "secular stagnation," as half anticipated by Kaldor, to justify a continuously rising public Debt. Until the oil price explosion of 1973–74 the world economy expanded.

18. The reproductive Debt. Apologists of deficit finance would point to the distinction between "deadweight" and "reproductive" Debt, the latter implying that part of total Debt which represents the nation's investment in publicly owned industry, housing and the general development of the economic infrastructure.

19. "Below the line expenditure." It is certainly true that by the 1950s the Budget Accounts were in some confusion. The concept of an annual Budget had been developed to accommodate the annual current account of government in an age in which public capital spending was minimal.

The post-war expansion of the public sector involved the Exchequer in what was known in the early 1960s as "expenditure below the line" to provide long-term capital for local authorities and nationalised industries and upon which a rate of interest was charged.

A purely *ad hoc* system developed in which current account surpluses were carried forward to the capital account ("below the line"). The investment needs of the public sector were then met and the government was left with a *net borrowing requirement*. In short the Chancellor borrowed from the market on behalf of the whole public sector.

The refinement of accounting procedures which occurred with the institution of the National Loans Fund in 1968 obfuscated rather than answered criticisms of deficit public finance. Current account surpluses were removed to the Fund beyond the control of parliamentary "votes", to be supplemented by the Central Government Borrowing Requirement (CGBR) as a means of accounting for the financial demands of the public sector upon central government. In an attempt to manage aggregate demand Chancellors were, however, obliged to embrace the wider concept of the Public Sector Borrowing Requirement (PSBR) which represented the total requirement of the public sector, from whatever source, and over which government had either direct or indirect control.

The classical objection to potentially wasteful public expenditure in a democratic, party political system is now reinforced. Not only are there constituency pressures for increased and immediate *consumer* benefits, but there also develops an infinitely more powerful lobby for the expansion of sectional *producer* benefits. That section, already in public employment, presses for further public investment and, where its current operations are in deficit, for public subsidy. In 1981, these pressures may be observed in local government from Manchester to the Inner London Boroughs, and in public industry from British Leyland to British Steel.

It may then be added that the supposedly "reproductive" Debt becomes less than that when, as has repeatedly happened, the accounts of public industry are made more respectable by writing off slices of their capital debt to central government. Government loses the interest receipts from "productive" industry but (the taxpayer) continues to pay the charge on its borrowing from the capital market.

20. "A week in politics is a long time" (Sir Harold Wilson). To return to the central theme of this chapter, "the presuppositions of Harvey Road", the idea of strategically minded politicians and advisers acting in concert to secure an objective, long-term "public good" proved to be wholly illusory. The developing democratic politician was a tactician who recognised that political visions could only be realised by politicians *in power*. Long-term economic strategy was consequently sacrificed to short-term political tactics.

In economic terms the Keynesian analysis provided an ideal tool.

It was previously noted (*see* I, **37**) that in the market it is the demand curve which is most amenable to short-term manipulation while the supply curve, governed by physical factors, remains relatively inflexible. Since unemployment was thought to be primarily a consequence of a deficiency in demand it could be remedied by injections of public spending. The illusion of prosperity so induced brought immediate political advantages.

In the long term, monetary economists have argued that continued increases in demand are reflected almost entirely in price inflation which leads to the unemployment of the factors of production (*see* IV, **17**).

Keynes's celebrated dictum that "in the long term we are all dead" was viewed rather cynically by a US Secretary of State who remarked that "in the short term it is Keynes who is dead while the rest of us are left with long term".

21. Attempts to strengthen the British fiscal constitution. The long-term tendency for public expenditure to drift upwards has not gone unnoticed and there has been public concern that more effective control should be exercised. An evaluation of the attempts at greater control will be made in our consideration of the technical aspects of the Debt in VI.

PROGRESS TEST 5

1. Define "the economics of politics". (**1**)

2. On what basis does Hayek criticise the modern economist? (**3**)

3. What do you understand by "the presuppositions of Harvey Road"? (**4**)

4. What process inhibits a Budget surplus in a democratic society? (**5**(*a*))

5. Why may bureaucracy be disposed towards Budget deficits? (**6**)

6. Contrast eighteenth- and nineteenth-century public finance. (**7–9**)

7. What was the "classical" view of deficit finance? (**10**)

8. Outline the views of the original Keynesians on deficit financing. (**12–16**)

9. What in practice was the post-war budgetary experience? (**17**)

10. What post-war development complicated Budget management? (**19**)

CHAPTER VI

Technical Aspects of The National Debt

PRINCIPAL FEATURES OF THE UK NATIONAL DEBT

1. Nature. As observed in the preceding chapter, on occasion government may find it convenient to finance its expenditure by borrowing, normally from its own citizens. It should therefore be noted that while the term "National" Debt is the one in common usage it is misleading since it suggests a debt owed by the nation to the rest of the world. Since the bulk of the Debt is held by UK residents it is more appropriate to think of it as the sum owed by citizens collectively (i.e. the government) to citizens individually, in short the Government Debt.

2. Size and structure. In December of each year, the Bank of England as manager of the Debt, publishes its estimated figures up to the 31st March of that year. At 31st March 1980 the *nominal* total of the National Debt (including foreign currency debt) was £95.6 billion, an increase of £7.8 billion on a year earlier. The bulk of this increase (£7.5 billion) was in market holdings (*see* Table I).

The foreign currency debt comprises direct government borrowing in Europe, post-war reconstruction loans from North America and German assistance with the support costs of BAOR. This amount is normally excluded from conventional Debt analysis.

Of the remaining *sterling* debt, official holdings have a different significance from those of the market which may be analysed as follows:

(*a*) *Funded debt.* Strictly speaking the phrase "funded debt" applies only to those stocks for which no redemption date has been set. The most important example of debt incurred on these terms is 3½ per cent War Loan (1952 or after). The government is under no obligation to repay although it was at liberty to do so at any time after 1952.

Used in the broader sense, the phrase includes dated stock, i.e. all other government and government-guaranteed stocks. They are of varying maturities and are publicly quoted. A single repayment

TABLE I.   *Total official and market holdings of national debt, March 1980*

	£m.	% of market holdings
Official holdings	18,161	
Market holdings		
Sterling marketable debt:		
Government and government guaranteed stocks	60,297	77.9
Treasury bills	2,281	2.9
Sterling non-marketable debt:		
National savings securities	7,902	10.2
Interest free notes due to the IMF and IDA	2,157	2.8
Other	821	1.1
Total	73,458	94.9
Foreign currency debt:		
HMG syndicated credits	1,848	
North American government loans	1,580	
Anglo-German offset agreement	—	
New York bond issue	162	
Other foreign currency bonds	359	
Total	3,949	5.1
Total market holdings	77,407	100.0
Total	95,568	
of which nationalised industries stock guaranteed by government	*254*	

(*Source: BEQB, December 1980.*)

date may be set or there may be two dates, after the earlier of which government can repay if it wishes and on the second of which it must repay.

Prior to the First World War, government borrowed only

TABLE II.   *Sterling marketable and non-marketable debt,*
March 1980

	£m.	% of sterling debt
Marketable debt:		
Funded debt	60,297	82.2
Floating debt	2,281	3.7
Non-marketable debt:		
National savings securities	7,902	10.2
Interest free notes due to the IMF and IDA	2,157	2.8
Other	821	1.1
	73,458	100.0

(*Source: BEQB, December 1980.*)

against undated stock. Subsequently dated stock came to be the principal component of the National Debt.

(*b*) *Floating debt.* Government requires to borrow regularly on a short-term basis in order to accommodate the uneven influx of tax revenue to the fairly even flow of departmental expenditure. This it does by borrowing against Treasury bills which are of two types, "tap" and "tender". Tap bills represent lending by government departments back to the Treasury. Bills payable after ninety-one days are offered for tender every Friday on the London Discount Market.

(*c*) *Non-marketable debt.* The biggest part of non-marketable debt is in the form of securities which are not publicly quoted and which have no redemption date set, although normally the holder is able to claim repayment after giving a period of notice. Included are national savings certificates, defence bonds, premium savings bonds, and the contractual savings schemes of the Department for National Savings and the Trustee Savings Banks.

Other non-marketable-debt instruments include certificates of tax deposit and Ways and Means Advances. The latter item represents the only method by which the Bank of England lends directly to government, lending which is on a very short-term basis (*see* Table II).

3. Distribution of sterling debt ownership. An analysis of ownership gives further insights into the implications of the Debt, providing a basis for examining the extent of the burden placed upon the taxpayer (*see* Table III).

TABLE III.   *Ownership of the national debt,
March 1980 (£m.)*

Official holdings	Public bodies	Banking sector	Other financial institutions	Overseas holders	Other
18,161	4,047	4,271	36,305	8,345	24,133

(*Source: BEQB, December 1980.*)

(*a*) *UK official holdings.* Of the approximate 20 per cent held by government departments or agencies about one-half was attributed to the National Debt Commissioners, who administer the two funds, through which is invested money deposited in the ordinary department of the National Savings Bank and the Trustee Savings Banks as well as the proceeds of national insurance contributions.

More than one-third was held by the Issue Department of the Bank of England as backing for the note issue. The balance was held by the Bank of England banking department, government departments with a temporary cash surplus and the Exchange Equalisation Account. The latter, when it supports the sterling exchange rate by using the hard currency reserves to buy up surplus sterling on the world's exchange markets, invests the proceeds in National Debt.

(*b*) *Public bodies.* A very small amount is held by local authorities and public corporations other than the Bank of England.

(*c*) *Banking sector.* This includes deposit and other banks, the discount market and the National Giro.

(*d*) *Other financial institutions.* This is the most important category of market investors and includes insurance companies, building societies, the investment accounts of the National Savings and Trustee Savings Banks, local authority and other public sector superannuation funds, private sector superannuation funds, investment trusts and unit trusts.

(*e*) *Overseas holders.* There are three elements. The International

Monetary Fund and the International Development Association accounted for £2,157 million due in sterling. This portion is made up primarily of non-interest bearing sterling notes held by the IMF as a counterpart to UK drawings upon the Fund. Secondly, central monetary institutions held £1,989 million. The remainder was held privately.

(*f*) *Other.* Of £24,133 million, individuals and private trusts held £7,132 million, the rest being divided between public trustees, various non-corporate bodies, and industrial and commercial companies.

PRINCIPLES OF DEBT MANAGEMENT

4. The aims of Debt management. The methods by which the National Debt is managed are significant to both the money supply and the level and structure of interest rates. Since these twin aspects of Debt management form the criteria of monetary policy the two are inextricably linked. The links are examined in this section as a prelude to a fuller explanation of monetary policy in IX.

Problems arise from the need to refinance existing Debt as it matures and to finance new Debt when the Central Government Borrowing Requirement (CGBR) is positive and adds to the existing total. Theoretically, Debt can be refinanced from tax receipts when the CGBR is negative but as has been noted (*see* V, **17**) a surplus has only been produced on two occasions since 1945. The Debt has continued to expand thus magnifying both problems.

In this context policy aims will be threefold:

(*a*) regulation of monetary variables in line with current monetary policy (*see* **5**);

(*b*) maintenance of a stable market in Government Debt (*see* **6**);

(*c*) minimising the cost of Debt servicing (*see* **7**).

5. Regulation of monetary variables. In examining the structure and ownership of the Debt in the preceding section it was observed that bonds and Treasury bills are of paramount importance to almost all UK financial institutions. It follows that the amount and type of Government Debt offered for sale on the financial markets will have a major influence on the level and structure of interest rates throughout the economy.

(*a*) *Short-term rates.* Until 1972 all short-term lending rates were geared to Bank Rate. From 1972 when Bank Rate was replaced by minimum lending rate (MLR) until 1978 a formula operated by which the market theoretically determined rates and MLR was geared to the average Treasury bill rate. In practice the authorities were able to influence the outcome by regulating the supply of Treasury bills which dominated the market. Closer, direct control over short-term rates was re-established in May 1978 when MLR was once more administered in the same way as the original Bank Rate (*see* IX, **33**).

(*b*) *Long-term rates*. Gilt-edged securities (i.e. government long-term borrowing) dominate the capital market. When the supply is increased relative to a given demand, capital values will be depressed, i.e. interest rates or *yields* increase, and vice versa.

> EXAMPLE: A nominal £100 at 5 per cent means that the holder will receive a *coupon* of £5 per annum until the debt matures. A sudden increase in the quantity of Debt offered for sale would reduce the price at which the security changed hands on the market. If it fell to £50 the yield would now be 10 per cent per annum and in a competitive market *all* interest rates would now trend upwards.

Furthermore, the relative amounts of short-dated (less than five years), medium-dated (five to fifteen years) and long-dated (over fifteen years) securities affects their *differential* yields and therefore the *structure* of interest rates.

(*c*) *Money supply*. When the government borrows from the banking sector there is a corresponding expansion of the money supply (*see* VIII, **32**(*a*)). Moreover, when that borrowing is short-dated against Treasury bills or stocks which (before long) have less than twelve months to maturity there is an expansion of the volume of reserve assets held by the banking system and upon which they can create further loans to the private sector with a corresponding expansion of the money supply (*see* VIII, **32**(*b*)).

Equally, when government borrows long-term from the non-bank private sector these securities are paid for by transfers from the banks' reserve assets to the Bank of England. Since their liquidity has now been reduced a curb has been placed on their power to make loans and hence expand the money supply (*see* IX, **36**).

It is now apparent that a knowledge of the structure of the Debt and of the possibilities for refinancing existing Debt and financing fresh Debt are fundamental to the conduct of monetary policy.

6. Maintenance of a stable market. With financing problems of
such magnitude the Bank of England (as manager of the National
Debt) has a duty to ensure a stable market and a growing demand
for securities. Rapidly fluctuating interest rates run counter to this
obligation since they increase the possibility of capital losses.
During the 1960s the Bank consequently viewed the stabilisation of
the market as its primary obligation. It adopted a policy of "leaning
into the wind", intervening in the market to moderate short-term
fluctuations in capital values and hence interest rates. While its
intention was not to stabilise long-run prices at any particular level
it may be observed that its preference for holding down interest
rates (when government is the principal borrower in the market)
led to repeated *purchases* rather than *sales* of Debt. These purchases
equated with the injection of new money into the economy.

It should then be stressed that having pursued that preference,
control of the money supply was abandoned. A monopolist (in this
case the sole supplier of new cash) may control supply in which
case price (the interest rate) is determined by demand. Alternatively he may control price, in which case it is now quantity
which is determined by demand. *He cannot control both simultaneously*.

After 1971, a greater concern with the control of the money
supply led to a willingness to see interest rates rise (*see* IX, **34**)
as indeed they did, to historically high levels, by the close of the
1970s. Nevertheless, the Bank of England retains a strong interest
in managing a stable capital market.

On the instructions of the Bank, the Government Broker
buys in stock as it approaches maturity. Without this tactic the
problem of refinancing a large sum which fell due for repayment
on a single day would be insuperable. In replacing this borrowing
the authorities will not suddenly market a large new issue unless
demand is strong. Such action would depress capital values. Rather
is it the case that in the first instance new stocks are taken
up by the Bank of England Issue Department. These issues are then
held on "tap" to be released on to the market as conditions
permit.

7. Minimising the cost of Debt servicing. The servicing charge is
determined by the size of the total Debt and the interest rates
payable on its various components. It must be met from current
taxation or from additional borrowing which imposes certain
"burdens" upon the nation.

THE BURDEN OF THE DEBT

8. Real burden of the external Debt. It has been observed that £8,345 million of the total sterling Debt is held overseas. To the extent that interest payments are made abroad and principal repaid there are implications for the balance of payments. Goods and services must be diverted to foreign use without any compensatory imports. Alternatively, if foreign demand for the debtor nation's goods is inelastic, there will have to be a corresponding reduction in the volume of imports. Either way there will be a real loss to the debtor nation's standard of living.

9. Real burden of the internal Debt. It has been stressed that by far the greater part of the Debt is owned internally. It follows that no increase or decrease in the size of the Debt can make the country as a whole either poorer or richer. Payment of interest or repayment of principal involves simply a transfer from taxpayer to security-holder. To the extent that the debtor (i.e. taxpayer) is worse off, the creditor (i.e. security-holder) is better off.

If all securities were evenly distributed throughout the community and all taxpayers made an equal contribution to the cost of servicing the Debt, the real burden would be nil since for every interest receipt of £1, the recipient would make a tax contribution of £1.

In practice, the ownership of the Debt is not evenly distributed and a real burden arises to the extent that the cost of Debt servicing involves a transfer from taxpayer to security-holder which increases the inequality of incomes. Despite the fact that a broad cross-section of the community may benefit from an interest in that part of the Debt represented by national savings and the holdings of the institutional investors, on balance it is likely that the greater part of the benefits will be directed towards the upper-income groups whose propensity to save will be correspondingly increased. Conversely, as a result of their tax contributions, the propensity to consume of the lower-income groups will be reduced, i.e. they must accept a real cut in living standards.

10. Indirect effects of Debt charges. Annually, substantial sums must be raised in taxation for the purpose of servicing the Debt. The level of this taxation will have implications for the management of the economy as a whole.

(*a*) *Incentives*. It may be argued that the extra volume of taxation can reduce the incentive to work of the taxpayer while that of the security-holder is reduced by his unearned income receipts.

(*b*) *Aggregate demand*. More significantly, redistribution of income will influence both the level of total effective demand and its structure.

(*c*) *Interest rates*. With large sums to borrow from the capital market the Bank must bid up interest rates to attract investors (*see* 5 (*b*) above). The effect is to *"crowd out"* private sector borrowers who are less able to afford high rates. Profitability and hence private investment decline, bankruptcies and *private sector* unemployment increase. This was the course of events from 1979 to 1981 when the Government *nominally* pursued a monetarist economic policy but in practice effected the standard neo neo-Keynesian "credit squeeze" characteristic of the "stop" phase of all post-war business cycles.

(*d*) Sterling exchange rate. The effect of high domestic interest rates is to attract short-term investment funds ("hot money") from overseas. As these funds flow across the exchanges the sterling exchange rate is forced up making UK exports less competitively priced in international markets. Conversely, the effect upon import costs is beneficial. However, domestic producers are now subject to increased foreign competition in home markets.

(*e*) *Inflation*. If these effects upon interest rates are to be avoided the Bank may resort to borrowing from the banking sector. Such borrowing expands the money supply (*see* 5(*c*) above) and on monetarist reasoning is the sole cause of inflation. This is seen to be the explanation of the escalating rate of inflation of the mid-1970s.

In V, 8, some attention was given to the broad principles of budgetary control. These principles will be elaborated and evaluated in the next two sections.

THE NATIONAL DEBT AND THE CONTROL OF PUBLIC EXPENDITURE

11. Consolidated Fund Standing Services and supply services. Each year Parliament reviews certain recurrent items of expenditure but is obliged to sanction them. They are known as the "Consolidated Fund Standing Services" and include interest payments on the National Debt, Royal Household expenses, judges' salaries and post-war credits. These standing commitments are agreed without much discussion by means of a "financial resolution".

All other annual current expenditure comes under the heading of "supply services" and falls into two groups. "Civil supply" comprises eleven classes of expenditure corresponding to the work of different ministries or groups of ministries. Secondly there is the defence budget.

12. Summary of procedure for supply services. Supply services are "voted" annually by the House of Commons. The procedure passes through the following five stages.

(*a*) The spending departments submit estimates of their proposed expenditure to the Treasury which approves, rejects or modifies them.

(*b*) The Crown submits the estimates for the consideration of Parliament.

(*c*) The House of Commons debates the estimates and "votes" sums for agreed purposes.

(*d*) The House authorises drawings upon the Consolidated Fund to meet agreed expenditure.

(*e*) In order to ensure that all drawings are utilised only for agreed purposes an Appropriation Act is passed.

At each stage there is opportunity for control and the whole procedure is underwritten by House of Commons Standing Order No. 78. As noted in V, **8**, the government alone has power to propose expenditure, a factor which militates in favour of coherent financial planning. It follows that the government alone is responsible for the success of the plan to Parliament and the electorate.

13. Treasury control. The spending departments have always viewed the Treasury as a body whose primary concern is to restrain expenditure. The Treasury's authority to do so rests ultimately with the authority of the Chancellor in Cabinet, for it is here that his decisions may be overridden.

Subject to this proviso the Treasury's power is based upon the following two rules.

(*a*) Since 1861, it has been formally agreed that in the light of Standing Order No. 78, proposed departmental expenditure should first be sanctioned by the Treasury. When reviewing the proposals, the Treasury attempts in a common-sense way to produce a balance between competing demands so that the country is given the best value for money.

(*b*) Since 1924 it has been agreed that no proposal for increased expenditure can be circulated in Cabinet without prior discussion with the Treasury.

It can thus be seen that the Treasury is in a very powerful position to exert pressure at the stage when the estimates are first submitted.

14. Parliamentary debate of the estimates. Twenty-nine "supply days" are set aside for discussion of the estimates between February and the end of July. The Opposition is free to choose the estimates which will be debated but will be concerned to challenge the government's overall strategy rather than to achieve detailed economies. In any case, given the scale of expenditure of modern government, the limitations of parliamentary time would not permit detailed consideration on the floor of the House. In July or August an Appropriation Act is passed which authorises the Treasury to make advances to the departments from the Consolidated Fund.

15. Committee on Expenditure. An inter-party committee examines the estimates in more detail than is possible in Parliament, with a view to eliminating waste. Such committees, which have operated since 1921, have performed a useful function in submitting departmental administrations to external criticism, e.g. a Select Committee was responsible for a highly critical examination of Treasury control methods in 1957–58 which led to the Plowden Report on Public Expenditure (*see* **20** below).

If they are to be criticised themselves it is for their lack of financial expertise. They are made up of a cross-section of average backbench MPs who in the course of their enquiries are confronted by highly professional civil servants who are expert in their fields, and who normally may be expected to be concerned with justifying the expenditures of their own departments. The outcome is frequently "no contest".

16. Exchequer and Audit Department Act 1921. This Act requires that each department to which supply grants have been made should prepare "accounts of appropriation" by a given date. The departments and not the Treasury are therefore responsible for their own day-to-day spending but must show that public funds have been utilised only for purposes designated by Parliament.

17. Comptroller and Auditor-General. The appropriation accounts are submitted for auditing to the office of the Comptroller and Auditor-General. The office has a large staff divided into eight divisions, each responsible for auditing the accounts of a group of departments.

Their function is not only to verify the technical accuracy of the accounts but also to look for waste and inefficiency.

18. Public Accounts Committee. The verified accounts are placed before the House of Commons in January and are referred to the Public Accounts Committee. This very powerful body comprises fifteen members with an Opposition MP as chairman. It scrutinises the accounts and publishes a report upon which the Treasury must take action.

19. Conclusion. The administrative machinery described above is a highly sophisticated technical apparatus but one which was developed in a period in which the balanced Budget principle prevailed and in which government spending was confined almost exclusively to a current account amenable to control on an annual basis.

During the 1950s it was recognised, at least in the second respect, that twelve months was far too short a period for the effective planning and control of capital expenditure. For example, expenditure in any one year on building a new hospital had to be viewed in the light of continuing expenditure over a number of years before there was any increase in the supply of medical services.

LONG-RANGE PLANNING AND CONTROL

20. The Plowden Report, 1961. The Plowden Committee was set up to consider appropriate methods for the control of long-term expenditure and also to examine the problem of upward drift in spending. It noted that "the central problem is that of how to bring the growth of public expenditure under better control".

In 1961, the first comprehensive survey was made of the anticipated total of public expenditure in all sectors set against an estimate of the probable growth of national income. At this stage the surveys were forecasts rather than instruments of policy but, from 1965, the Cabinet began to make positive decisions on the portion of anticipated national income to be appropriated for use in the public sector.

The first survey to be published was in 1963 followed by a second in 1966. In 1969, a White Paper, *Public Expenditure 1968–69 to 1973–74*, began a regular annual series of such surveys.

In practice the Treasury maintained that in any five-year

programme the third year was the earliest at which major changes could be made without serious dislocation. Plans for the fourth and fifth years were viewed as provisional.

21. Public Expenditure Survey Committee (PESC). Each summer an interdepartmental committee makes a survey of public expenditure intentions, costed on the basis of the previous year's projections. To this is added the best available estimates of total private sector expenditure and the grand total is set against the anticipated growth of national income. If it exceeds the expected growth rate then the conclusion is that the total claim on real resources is too heavy and there will have to be a cut-back in public expenditure or a general increase in taxation. However, for reasons we have examined, in political terms this is not a very realistic conclusion.

22. Evaluation of the PESC system of control. During the 1960s the inaccuracy of public expenditure surveys stemmed from the recurrent tendency to underestimate costs. From 1963 to 1968 the percentage increase in public expenditure regularly exceeded that which had been planned. Only in 1968–69, and then largely because of the earlier promptings of the IMF, was the annual increase brought under control. The tendency reasserted itself in the 1970s and the actual *increase* in spending has continued to exceed that planned, down to 1981.

The system has a number of defects both of principle and of technique. These are discussed in **23–29** below.

23. Tax implications ignored. The most fundamental weakness is that the system places its emphasis entirely upon the expenditure side. There is an implicit assumption in the way in which the survey operates in practice that planned growth will be financed somehow simply because it *is* planned. One author of the Plowden Report subsequently realised that "in order to get realistic expenditure decisions, governments must argue them, both within themselves and outside, against their tax implications".

Since this is not the case, far from bringing public expenditure under control the system has a bias towards further expenditure growth.

24. Overestimates of GDP. There are strong political incentives to promote over-optimistic estimates of the rate of growth of the Gross Domestic Product. On this basis, public expenditure assumes a smaller proportion of the total. As previously noted, this was true from 1963 to 1968 and certainly again in 1974–75.

25. Underestimates of costs. Similarly, there is an incentive to project a five-year programme as having high costs in the first year which then fall away in subsequent years. As those years in due course become the first year the immediate forecast is revised upwards in contradiction of the earlier projection.

26. Projections of real and not money costs. Under PESC, expenditure has been planned in real and not money terms. The prices used are those prevailing at the time of the survey with an allowance for the relative price effect of anticipated movements of public compared with private sector costs. In other words, in real terms a certain volume of resources has been committed to particular uses regardless of their money costs. When inflation has raised these costs, the Treasury has been obliged to find the extra cash.

27. The illusion of "cuts". When confronted with external pressure for expenditure cuts, e.g. a weakening of the sterling exchange rate, there are strong political pressures upon the spending ministers to attempt to sustain their immediate programmes and to make dramatic announcements of substantial cuts in future years. When the current crisis has passed subsequent surveys reinstate the full programme. For example, the cuts of £1,100 million for 1976–77 announced in the Budget of 1975 were more than reversed in the March 1976 survey.

28. The problem of changed expenditure classifications. An example of this difficulty is found in the change from investment allowances to investment grants in 1966 and back to accelerated capital depreciation allowances in 1970. While grants are classed as expenditure, allowances are treated as offsets against revenue. Although the net effect may be the same, for accounting purposes the abolition of grants reduces public expenditure.

29. Public expenditure not wholly within the control of central government. The Supply Estimates represent only about half of total public expenditure. Local authorities control about a quarter and while central government is in a position to influence their capital expenditure there remains a good deal of autonomy in respect of current expenditure.

CASH LIMITS

30. The crisis of 1976. In 1976, the inflation rate was in double figures, unemployment stood at over 5 per cent, the highest since the 1930s, industrial production was stagnant and there was a balance of payments deficit of almost £1.5 billion. Overseas recognition of the collapse of the Keynesian fiscal constitution was implicit in the terms upon which the International Monetary Fund (IMF) was prepared to grant a standby credit of $3.9 billion in order to avert the collapse of sterling on the foreign exchange markets.

The Public Sector Borrowing Requirement (PSBR) was to be restricted to a maximum of £8.7 billion in 1977–78 and to £8.6 billion in 1978–79. Government expenditure was to be reduced by £1 billion in 1977–78 and £1.5 billion in 1978–79 below the planned figures of the 1976 survey.

In other words, in the absence of an effective internal fiscal constitution, an international monetary authority imposed its own constraints upon the Government's fiscal conduct.

The Government was now obliged to take firm action.

31. Introduction of cash limits. In April 1976, the limits to volume in real terms of the PESC system were supplemented by cash limits upon spending programmes. These limits are determined by converting PESC constant prices to allow for the estimated rate of inflation. If programme costs exceed those planned then there must be a corresponding reduction in volume. The Treasury supposedly was no longer willing to finance an over-run through the submission to Parliament of a Supplementary Estimate.

32. A financial information system. Spending departments make detailed returns to the Treasury within ten days of the end of each month. These are then compared with the planned cash limits on each programme and discrepancies accounted for.

33. Redefinition of government expenditure. By 1976, on the old definition of government expenditure, the public sector was pre-empting 60 per cent of GDP, a figure which Roy Jenkins for one viewed as being incompatible with the survival of a liberal democracy. Moreover, this percentage compared unfavourably with those of other Western countries. The Treasury therefore introduced a change in the definition of government expenditure. As subsequently defined, it excluded the internally financed expenditures of state-owned industries and those interest payments on Government Debt financed by user charges on government sector outputs. The result of this change was to reduce the government's share of GDP to 52 per cent.

34. Evaluation of cash limits. Cash limits remedied the weakness observed in **26** above of calculating programme costs in "funny money" (so described by Samuel Brittan) and restored the need to pay attention to cash costs. (However, it should be noted that about 38 per cent of government expenditure is not subject to cash limits.) The other weaknesses of PESC remain unchanged. Moreover, the effectiveness of limits depends upon the willingness and *ability* of government to impose them. To the extent that PESC now includes a larger contingency reserve upon which it is possible for departments to draw, there is a loophole in the system.

Finally it should be stressed that the modification of the system did nothing whatsoever to remedy the basic flaw in the British fiscal constitution, the *separation, encouraged by the Keynesian approach, of government spending and taxation and of the timing of decisions in these two areas.* The temporary external constraint imposed by the IMF withered as the increasing flow of North Sea oil improved the balance of payments and the possibility of being obliged to ask for further loans receded.

This view would seem to be supported by the events of the late 1970s.

35. Reflation in 1977–78. At the Labour Party Conference of September 1976, the Prime Minister had said that:

"We used to think that you could spend your way out of a recession, and increase employment by cutting taxes and boosting government spending. I tell you, in all candour, that that option no longer exists, and that, in so far as it ever did exist, it only worked by ... injecting bigger doses of inflation into the economy, followed by higher levels of unemployment as the next step. ... That is the history of the past twenty years."

Subsequently, the Treasury observed that "on balance (the IMF imposed measures) would improve prospects for employment" although such a view was in direct contradiction of orthodox Keynesian theory.

Despite these protestations, "the presuppositions of Harvey Road" (*see* **V, 4**) were not about to be fulfilled with a general election rapidly approaching. The autumn of 1978 being considered the most likely date, a policy of reflation was pursued from the mini-Budget of November 1977, with a £1 billion tax cut and increased social expenditure of £1 billion planned for 1978, both to be financed by an increase in the Public Sector Borrowing Requirement.

As had happened with almost every post-war government of either party, the pressures of "the political market" transcended the dictates of sound economic policy.

36. The Conservative Government, 1979. The Government's central election commitment was to a remedy for inflation based upon strict control of the money supply which in turn implied a substantial reduction in the PSBR and hence in the level of public expenditure (*see* **4**(*c*) above). Despite this pledge, during 1979–81 government spending continued to grow in real terms as a proportion of GDP. In the Estimates for 1981–82, the Chancellor encountered strong resistance from the spending ministers to the level of cuts proposed and responded by increasing the level of indirect taxation in his Budget of April 1981. This course provoked a predictable political revolt amongst a number of his backbench MPs whose rural constituencies were said to be especially adversely affected by the steep rise in petrol duty.

As the recession deepened and unemployment rose during its first two years of office, the Government was subjected to demands for "reflation" from within Parliament, from academics, and from the TUC and the CBI, despite the continuing rise in the PSBR and, at least initially, an escalation in the rate of inflation.

On a number of occasions it was suspected that the Government's political resolve was weakening, e.g. the large allocations of public funds to British Leyland and British Steel in 1980–81, and that it was about to make a "U turn".

These more recent developments reinforce the view that whatever the party of government, the political determination to exercise a firm control over public expenditure, in particular that part which is deficit financed, is inevitably undermined by the deficiencies of the present British fiscal constitution.

PROGRESS TEST 6

1. Define the nature of the National Debt.   (**1**)
2. Describe the basic structure of the Debt.   (**2**)
3. Who owns the Debt?   (**3**)
4. What are the basic aims of Debt management?   (**4**)
5. How may interest rates be influenced through Debt management techniques?   (**5**)
6. What are the effects upon the private sector of a large Public Sector Borrowing Requirement?   (**10**(*c*))

7. What is the economic consequence of financing a public sector deficit by borrowing from the banking system? (**10**(*e*))

8. How does Parliament control public expenditure? (**12**)

9. What is the role of the Treasury in controlling public expenditure? (**13**)

10. What is the function of the Committee on Expenditure? (**15**)

11. Who is the Comptroller and Auditor-General? (**17**)

12. What was the conclusion of the Plowden Report? (**20**)

13. What is the Public Expenditure Survey Committee? (**21**)

14. What are the weaknesses of PESC? (**22–29**)

15. How did "cash limits" seek to reinforce the PESC system in 1976? (**31**)

16. Evaluate the effectiveness of "cash limits". (**34**)

17. How may the dictates of "the political market" conflict with those of "the economic market"? (**35**)

PART TWO

THE MONETARY SYSTEM

CHAPTER VII

The Functions, Characteristics and Evolution of Money

THE FUNCTIONS OF MONEY

1. A fully planned economy without money. Provided that society is willing to surrender all individual choice to state planning agencies it is possible to operate an economy without money. This has been demonstrated, for example, in the early days of the Soviet Union. The state determines the relative quantities of different lines of production while distribution is effected by a system of rationing which accords with prevailing notions of social justice. The weakness of such a system lies on the side of distribution once the economy has been raised above subsistence level. What principles of social justice, for example, would govern the allocation of grand pianos or croquet mallets?

2. A free economy without money. In a free economy the only alternative to the use of money is a system of barter such as that which largely prevailed in medieval England. There are, however, three major disadvantages as follows.

(*a*) *Individual wants rarely coincide.* "Rather than there being a coincidence of wants there is likely to be a want of coincidence." It is unlikely that the baker's need for a pair of shoes will be timed to coincide with the shoemaker's need for a loaf of bread.

(*b*) *Adjustment of quantities of goods bartered.* It is unlikely that the shoemaker will want simultaneously the number of loaves of bread for which a pair of shoes would exchange.

(*c*) *Multiple exchange ratios.* It is necessary to establish separate exchange ratios between any one item and all other goods which enter into trade. There is no common denominator.

While barter may work in a simple society, it is clear that it

108

would be inoperable in an advanced industrial economy practising a high degree of specialisation. What now becomes necessary is a "medium of exchange".

3. The functions of money. From the foregoing argument it may be deduced that money has certain functions as follows.

(*a*) *A medium of exchange.* The most important function of money is to serve as the one universally acceptable denominator against which all men are willing to exchange their goods and services. It acts as the lubricant which promotes the smooth functioning of a market economy based upon division of labour not only between trades but also between processes. From this central function of money stem four others.

(*b*) *Extension of individual choice.* The distribution difficulty of the fully planned economy is overcome when the individual works for units of purchasing power which he can use at his discretion.

(*c*) *Standard unit of account.* Money cannot properly be said to be a measure of value since, unlike measures of weight or size, its own value varies. However, it does overcome the difficulty of multiple exchange ratios encountered in the barter system. It is the common denominator to which all trade items may be related.

(*d*) *A store of value.* Individual saving in an economy without money implies the setting aside of goods for future use. The self-evident disadvantage is that many goods are perishable and services cannot be stored. The use of money, however, enables purchasing power to be stored for use at a date determined by the individual.

It should be noted, nevertheless, that money fulfils this function imperfectly inasmuch as its purchasing power varies. The depreciation in the value of money since 1945 is not compensated by the interest paid on bank deposits after allowance has been made for the taxation of unearned income.

(*e*) *A means of deferred payment.* The extent to which money is capable of storing value gives it a final function. It is instrumental to credit transactions. Without money, present borrowing of goods and services would imply repayment in kind. Money enables general purchasing power to be utilised now and repaid later.

It should be noted that inflation will favour the debtor inasmuch as he will repay money whose purchasing power is less. Conversely a deflationary situation will favour the creditor.

THE EVOLUTION AND CHARACTERISTICS OF MONEY

4. Commodity money. The earliest forms of money were commodities held in high regard by the societies which used them.
At first sight it would therefore seem that a prime characteristic
of money is its intrinsic desirability. However, we shall shortly see
that this is not so. Nevertheless, it should be emphasised that a
quality common to all money has been relative scarcity. If the
scarcity is too great, too little value is attached to it for it to continue in this role.

Additionally, early forms of commodity money enjoyed one or
more other advantages, e.g. in the eastern Mediterranean, olive
oil was easily divisible; in western Europe, iron was durable. The
most universally acceptable of all commodity moneys, however,
came to be gold. It had the foregoing qualities and was also port-
able. Second only to gold was silver. Initially, quantities of these
metals were weighed in order to make payment, but from these it
was only a short step to a standard coin of known weight and
fineness guaranteed by the imprint of the state.

5. Paper money. Modern deposit banking began to develop in
Britain for the first time in the sixteenth and seventeenth centuries
in the hands of London goldsmiths. It was their practice to issue
"warehouse receipts" for gold deposited with them and these
receipts circulated freely as money, guaranteed by the good name
of the goldsmith. In the 1680s, Francis Childs is credited with the
introduction of the first true banknotes, receipts for gold but in
standard denominations.

However, paper was seen only as a claim upon real money,
gold, until 1931. The Bank of England's promise to pay the bearer
on demand was a guarantee of immediate convertibility and apart
from two major periods, 1797–1821 and 1914–25, this convertibility was maintained.

During the nineteenth century, it is doubtful, except in periods
of national emergency, whether inconvertible paper money would
have circulated freely. In the periods 1815–21 and 1918–25 there
was considerable public agitation for the restoration of convertibility, but in 1931 the link between paper and gold was finally
severed. Paper appeared for the first time in its own right as true
money. This leads us to an important conclusion about the nature
of money. Its principal characteristic is not its intrinsic desirability

but its "acceptability". Paradoxically, this acceptability can be explained only by a general confidence that everyone will accept it. This confidence will be governed by the degree of political and economic stability. For example, where there is hyperinflation, it is likely that paper money will cease to circulate and there will be a reversion to commodity money. This was partially demonstrated in post-1945 Germany when American cigarettes circulated as money. Our attention is therefore re-directed to the first characteristic of money which has been noted. If it is to be acceptable, there must be a relative scarcity.

6. Limitation of the supply of paper money. When the sixteenth-century goldsmiths first issued receipts for gold deposits there was naturally a strict relationship between the quantity of gold and the paper circulated. However, as public confidence developed in the goldsmith's ability to pay he felt safe in increasing the amount of paper, ensuring only that he maintained an adequate ratio to gold to enable him to meet day-to-day claims for conversion. The danger of this practice was a loss of public confidence which would lead to a run on the bank with all note-holders anxious to convert paper to gold. Many small banks were forced out of business in this way. The 1844 Bank Charter Act aimed to exclude this danger. The sole right of note issue was gradually to be vested in the Bank of England. The Bank was to be permitted a small "fiduciary issue" of £14 million only partially backed by gold. Every note issued in excess of this amount had to be fully covered. England was placed firmly on the gold standard and had in consequence an inflexible money supply.

The Currency and Banknotes Act of 1913 introduced for the first time Treasury notes in denominations of £1 and 10 shillings (50p). (The smallest denomination banknote had been and remained £5.) During the period 1914–18 the Treasury note issue was increased without gold cover and a considerable inflation resulted. Deflationary policies after 1920 sought to restore full convertibility and a large number of Treasury notes were withdrawn. The Gold Standard Act of 1925 established partial convertibility (gold could be purchased from the Issue Department in minimum quantities of 400 Troy ounces) but by 1928 it became apparent that further deflation of the note issue was undesirable. With many Treasury notes still in circulation it was decided to substitute for them £1 and 10 shilling Bank of England notes. This required legislation to permit a corresponding increase in the Bank's fiduciary issue and the Currency and Banknotes Act of 1928 was enacted. The fiduciary issue was established at £260 million but could be increased with Treasury approval over a maximum period of two years. After that the approval of Parliament had to be sought. Subsequently, the Currency and Banknotes Act of 1954 confirmed the general position. The fiduciary issue was set at £1,575 million and could only be increased with Treasury consent and with the ultimate approval of Parliament. In practice such approval has come to be a formality.

NOTE: The legal position governing the note issue is thus determined by the Acts of 1844, 1928 and 1954. The Bank of England retains the power to increase its notes against gold cover but since no notes have been backed in this way since August 1970 this power is of no real significance. In practice, the Bank of England authorities in conjunction with the Treasury determine whether an increase is desirable and parliamentary approval is given automatically.

7. Bank deposit money. (*See also* VIII, **32**.) The final stage in the evolution of money is to be seen in its appearance as a bank deposit, a figure on a ledger which can be transferred through the instrument of the cheque. Cheques were known in seventeenth-century England but their use was given considerable stimulus by the 1844 Bank Charter Act. It will be recalled that this Act rigidly limited the money supply and this in a period of rapid industrial and commercial expansion. Growth might well have been hampered by this restriction had it not been for an increasing willingness to settle business transactions with the cheque.

It should be noted, however, that it is not the cheque itself which is money but the deposit upon which it is drawn. The cheque will of course be valid only if such a deposit exists and the payee may not know this to be the case. Nevertheless, the cheque would appear to be increasingly acceptable, the majority of transactions involving payment of any size being settled in this way. In recent years the banks have attempted to extend their business by popularising current accounts. Many wage and salary payments are made either by cheque or bank transfer while the consumer, assisted by his banker's card (an instrument which certifies any cheque up to the value of £30 or £50), has made ever-greater use of his cheque-book even for relatively small payments. Moreover, the increased use of credit cards, credit accounts and hire-purchase accounts which are settled regularly by cheque or banker's order suggests that cash will continue to play a proportionately smaller part and will finally become the "small change" of the monetary system.

8. The difficulty of a precise definition of the money supply. It has been shown that conventionally money has come to be defined as coin, notes and bank deposits. However, should deposits of *all* types with *all* financial institutions be included within this definition? In recent years there has been a good deal of discussion of this question.

In 1970 the Bank of England concluded that it is possible to select different types of deposits to form various totals which can each be described as the stock of money. "There are, however, no clear rules for deciding which of these totals is most appropriate: there can be alternative definitions of the stock of money, encompassing a wider or narrower set of components." The Bank began with the following three definitions.

(*a*) *M1.* This is the narrow definition consisting of notes and coin in circulation with the public plus sterling sight deposits held by the private sector only.

(*b*) *M2.* This was made up of M1 plus private sector time deposits. It was found not to have real value and was abandoned in 1971.

(*c*) *M3.* This is the widest definition and comprises M2 plus *all* sterling deposits including certificates of deposit held by UK residents in both the public and private sectors together with all deposits held by UK residents in foreign currencies.

In December 1976 a further definition, sterling M3 (£M3), was added. This definition equals M3 *less* the overseas currency deposits of UK residents.

In all definitions, deposits are confined to those made with institutions in the UK banking sector. Table IV gives the totals of the money stock according to the three current definitions.

9. Importance of monetary measurement. Since throughout the Western world it has currently become something of an orthodoxy that control of the money supply is a necessary if not sufficient condition for the control of inflation, it is clearly important that adequate devices are available for monetary measurement. In their absence the following two dangers arise.

TABLE IV. *Money stock, January 1981*

£m.	
M1	29,208
M3	74,370
Sterling M3	67,232

(*Source: BEQB, March 1981.*)

(*a*) Stringent control of an inappropriate aggregate which permits other monies or money substitutes to expand or contract will have unpredictable consequences for the inflation rate.

(*b*) Political support for "reflation" (inflation) is strengthened as it may justifiably be argued that "strict monetary control" has not cured inflation.

DISTORTION OF MONETARY AGGREGATES

10. The problem. Since in practice from 1976 onwards £M3 and M3 have been the principal aggregates upon which monetary policy has been based, it is important to recognise the ways in which they may be distorted and rendered defective. The weaknesses are fivefold (*see* **11–15** below).

11. Exaggerations of monetary growth. This will occur when there are possibilities of "arbitrage" (i.e. the practice of borrowing at one rate and lending at a higher rate) and is known in banking jargon as "round tripping". The common manifestation is when prime borrowers take advantage of their overdraft facilities (which automatically results in an expansion of bank deposit money, *see* VIII, **32**(*b*)) in order to finance the purchase of certificates of deposit (CDs) or time deposits with a higher yield.

12. Exclusion of Treasury bills from monetary aggregates. The liquidity of the economy, i.e. its capacity to revert from financial assets which are "near money" to ready cash, is underestimated in consequence of the process which is known as "soft arbitrage". Because of a differential interest rate yield, non-bank holders switch out of CDs (fixed-rate, fixed-term time deposits with the banks), which are included in the £M3 and M3 definitions, into Treasury bills which are even more liquid ("near money") but which are not so included.

13. Exclusion of building society and National Savings Bank deposits. None of the present statistical indicators of the money stock include building society deposits. It is, however, the case that large numbers of people in Britain prefer to organise their affairs upon a cash basis and that building society deposits provide an attractive alternative to the banks in view of their Saturday opening hours and particularly in times when their net interest rates show an advantage over those of the banks.

Similarly, the National Savings movement issues a variety of deposits or bonds, all of which are extremely liquid but which are not included in any definition of the money supply.

14. Exclusion of unused overdraft facilities. At any one time individuals and institutions have (so far undisclosed) overdraft facilities with their banks which have not been fully utilised but which will only appear in the monetary aggregates when they are drawn upon. However, in principle they are every bit as much a part of the money supply as are bank deposits which remain to be used.

15. Distortion of M3 in consequence of different discretionary decisions. It has already been observed (*see* **10** above) that M3 has been used as the principal indicator of monetary growth. The possible discretionary variants on this definition may, however, lead to very different figures of the money supply which affects the domestic economy.

For example, it would seem reasonable that the foreign currency deposits in the UK of UK residents should be included in M3 since they can easily be converted into sterling balances. Until the end of 1976 this was the position adopted by the Bank of England. However, research into the use of such balances demonstrated that they were rarely spent within the UK economy. Consequently, the concept of £M3 was introduced to exclude these deposits. It should nevertheless be remembered that future research might reveal a changing pattern.

In a similar way, the Bank must use its discretion to decide whether or not to include overseas sterling deposits (currently excluded from both £M3 and M3). On present evidence there would seem to be some reason for *including* them as they appear to be increasingly used for expenditure within the UK.

MONETARY AGGREGATES IN THE USA

16. American practice. In general, monetary policy has received more attention in the USA than in Britain and monetary statistics are much more developed there. Moreover, there is a continuing process as measurement techniques are refined. The intention is not to establish a single "ideal" figure but to provide a range of measurements appropriate to different purposes but which if acted upon together increase the ability of the authorities to control *those assets with the attributes of money.*

NOTE: In this connection, Hayek has commented that it is a pity that we treat the word "money" as a noun. "... it would be more helpful for the explanation of monetary phenomena if 'money' were an adjective describing a property which different things could possess to different degrees." (*Denationalisation of Money*, F. A. Hayek, IEA, 1976.)

American practice has contrasted with that of the Bank of England which has so far concentrated upon the refinement of *one* definition (M3) and in so doing has prejudged technical questions upon which there may be disagreement among experts.

17. Range of US monetary aggregates. Currently, the Federal Reserve publishes eight expanding totals, M1 to M7 plus a definition known as *bank credit proxy* which includes total member bank deposits subject to reserve requirements plus Euro-dollar borrowings, loans sold to bank related institutions and certain other non-deposit items.

Of particular interest are the American definitions of M2 and M3.

(*a*) *M2*. Averages of daily figures for M1 (notes, coin and sight deposits) plus savings deposits, time deposits open account and time certificates of deposit *other than* negotiable CDs of over $100,000 of large weekly reporting banks.

(*b*) *M3*. M2 plus the average of beginning and end-of-month deposits of mutual savings banks, savings and loan shares and credit union shares. (These items represent savings outside the banking system.)

These two definitions deliberately omit large certificates of deposit and therefore avoid the distortions resulting from "round tripping" (*see* **11** above). On the other hand, M3 and M5 (M5 = M3 plus large negotiable CDs) are sufficiently wide definitions to avoid the distortions of "soft arbitrage"—switching between different classes of institution (*see* **12** above).

18. Speed in publishing US monetary statistics. A further contrast between American and British practice is the speed and frequency with which US statistics are published. The Federal Reserve issues weekly totals for M1 to M5 which show the position for the week ended on Wednesday of the previous week.

This almost instantaneous provision of data is of great assistance to the monetary authorities. In Britain there is less frequency and greater delay. Figures for two aggregates only are published on the twentieth of each month and refer to the middle of the previous month.

19. American monetary "targets". The range of US monetary statistics assists in the formulation of monetary policy. The Federal Reserve sets out to hold four aggregates (M1, M2, M3 and bank credit proxy) within target ranges selected every quarter for the year ahead. This approach makes it possible to allow for the effects of distortion upon any one measure through the selection of its target and through the emphasis given to it in relation to the other measures.

20. Conclusion and rationale for Part Two. This outline of American practice suggests that the Bank of England has some way to go in the development of the monetary statistics necessary for the effective control of the "money supply".

Chapter VIII examines the nature of and the relationships between the major financial institutions and has the central purpose of demonstrating their role in the creation of "money".

Chapter IX then considers the part played by the Bank of England, particularly in respect of its obligation to devise and implement monetary policy.

PROGRESS TEST 7

1. Why may money be viewed as essential to an advanced economy? **(1–3)**

2. Explain why "acceptability" is the most important characteristic of money. **(5)**

3. What legislation today limits the quantity of banknotes? **(6)**

4. What was the significance of the Bank Charter Act 1844? **(6)**

5. How did the Bank Charter Act stimulate the use of the cheque? **(7)**

6. What is "bank deposit money"? **(7)**

7. Compare the relative importance of banknotes and bank deposit money. **(7)**

8. Give three statistical definitions of the money stock. **(8)**

9. Why is it important to have adequate devices for measuring the money supply? **(9)**

10. What do you understand by "round tripping"? **(11)**

11. Explain "soft arbitrage". **(12)**

12. Why may the existence of building societies distort monetary statistics? **(13)**

13. How may different discretionary decisions affect the M3 aggregate? **(15)**

14. How does American practice differ from that of the UK in its approach to the measurement of monetary aggregates? **(16–19)**

CHAPTER VIII

The Commercial Banks

STRUCTURE OF BRITISH BANKING

1. Classification. Over the past 400 years the British banking system has developed as one of the most highly specialised financial centres in the world. It has created a complex and sophisticated market for both short-term and long-term finance on an international scale, a business which is of value not only to Britain as a source of overseas earnings but also to overseas countries as a source of investment funds and trade credit. The system may be classified under six main headings.

(*a*) *The central bank.* At the centre of the system stands the Bank of England. It fulfils a unique role to which attention is given in the following chapter.

(*b*) *The commercial banks.* These are sometimes referred to as the "joint-stock banks". They are for the most part limited liability companies, subject to the appropriate company law and operated for the profit of their shareholders. They include:

(*i*) the London clearing banks;

(*ii*) the Scottish and Northern Irish banks;

(*iii*) British overseas and foreign banks with London offices.

(*c*) *The discount houses.* The London Discount Market Association comprises eleven houses. They have a specialised function in the provision of short-term finance.

(*d*) *The merchant banks.* Used loosely, this term is often applied to a variety of financial institutions. In a specific sense it includes the following.

(*i*) Accepting houses: their basic business is the "acceptance credit" through which a considerable part of Britain's overseas trade is financed.

(*ii*) Issuing houses: they are concerned with raising credit for borrowers at home and abroad and, where appropriate, organising a market in bonds and shares against which funds are raised.

(*e*) *The savings banks.* Independently operated savings banks where small savings could be deposited to earn a rate of interest arose in Britain in the early nineteenth century. To afford greater security to depositors, legislation in 1817 brought them under the supervision of the National Debt Commissioners. Management remained in the hands of local trustees—hence Trustee Savings Banks.

In order to bring savings facilities within reach of the whole community legislation in 1861 led to the foundation of the Post Office Savings Bank, now known as the National Savings Bank.

(*f*) *The National Giro*. The National Giro was set up in 1969 in the belief that by providing facilities for current account payments it would very quickly be in a position to compete on even terms with the commercial banks.

2. Evolution of the London clearing banks. It has been observed that in Britain the first indigenous banking was developed in the sixteenth and seventeenth centuries by goldsmiths who issued paper money against the security of gold deposits (*see* VII, 5). They also established rudimentary current accounts and cheque and bill-discounting facilities. An Act of 1707 imposed certain legal restrictions which delayed the development of joint-stock banking in England except for the Bank of England itself. Scotland did not suffer this legal impediment and joint-stock banking developed on a sound basis at an earlier date.

The result was a system of banking based upon private partnership which persisted until 1826. In that year the County Bankers Act permitted the formation of joint-stock banks *with* note-issuing powers outside a sixty-five mile radius of London. In 1833 a further Act allowed joint-stock banks *without* note-issuing powers within that radius. The Bank Charter Act of 1844 denied all new banks the power to issue notes but the development of the cheque diminished the significance of this restriction. An Act of 1862 extended the privilege of limited liability to banking companies and the last obstacle to the growth of large-scale joint-stock banking was removed.

The following sixty years were a period of expansion, takeovers and amalgamations in which was established a national system of branch banking. In 1919, the formation of the British Bankers' Association promoted consultation and co-operation between its fifty-six members. Included in this membership were fourteen English, five Scottish and three Northern Ireland commercial banks.

A large part of British banking business is concentrated in the six members of the London Bankers' Clearing House (*see* 7). Until 1968 there were eleven which included Midland Bank Ltd.; Barclays Bank Ltd.; Lloyds Bank Ltd.; Westminster Bank Ltd.; National Provincial Bank Ltd.; District Bank Ltd.; Martins Bank

Ltd.; Williams Deacon's Bank Ltd.; National Bank Ltd.; Coutts & Co. and Glyn Mills & Co. Mergers have caused the gradual loss of a separate identity of Martins following its fusion with Barclays and of District following its amalgamation with National Provincial and Westminster to form the National Westminster. Williams Deacon's merged with Glyn Mills to form Williams and Glyn's.

3. Scottish banks. Scottish banking business is concentrated in four banks with head offices and some 1,700 branches in Scotland. These banks retain the power of note issue which, apart from a small fiduciary issue, is made against the cover of Bank of England notes. The advantage is largely a matter of advertisement.

4. Northern Irish banks. There are three native banks with head offices and some 500 branches in Northern Ireland. Like the Scottish banks they issue their own notes. Additionally, a number of other banks with head offices in Dublin, Cork and London have branches in Northern Ireland.

5. British overseas banks. There are thirty-two members of the British Overseas Banks Association with head offices in London or the Commonwealth and branches overseas. The Association comprises four groups: African, Australasian, Canadian and Eastern. They act as exchange-dealers and finance monetary transactions between Britain and these areas and between third parties. They also employ funds in London primarily in the money market. They therefore provide a mechanism whereby British short-term investment funds can be rapidly employed in all parts of the world and conversely foreign funds employed in Britain. The bulk of their London deposit liabilities do in fact originate overseas.

6. Foreign banks. By far the most important are the American banks which owing to increased US investment in Europe have experienced a dramatic expansion of their business. At the end of 1980 deposits totalled £64,084 million of which £8,639 million were in sterling. In a similar way other foreign banks by virtue of their trading connections and special knowledge are able to provide for their own nationals a unique service in London. In 1981 their total deposits amounted to £110,460 million of which £9,883 million were denominated in sterling.

A number of these banks fulfil all the functions of the domestic banks but by unwritten agreement do not attempt to compete with them.

7. Functions of the clearing banks. The description "London clearing banks" is applied to the six members of the London Bankers' Clearing House, the place where their representatives meet to settle inter-bank indebtedness. These banks account for the greater part of the normal commercial banking business of England and Wales although in the last decade there has been a considerable expansion of the business of the non-clearing banks.

8. Deposits. The basic clearing bank service from which all others stem is the provision of facilities for current and time deposit accounts.

(*a*) *Current accounts.* In February 1981 current accounts totalled £16,193 million covering personal and business deposits. The banks are enabled to exercise their principal function, the transfer of money, through the use of the current account in conjunction with the following.

(*i*) The cheque system: a cheque is an instruction to a bank to make payment of a specified sum to a third party.

(*ii*) Bank Giro credit: the expense of separate cheques and postages can be avoided by the completion of Bank Giro credit forms in favour of a number of payees and payment to the bank of the total amount either in cash or with a single cheque.

(*iii*) The standing order: this method of money transfer is designed for regular payments of fixed amount, e.g. mortgage or hire-purchase instalments. It is a standing instruction to the bank to pay a certain sum regularly upon a specified date.

(*iv*) Direct debit: a second method of automatic payment is the direct debit which differs from the standing order in which the "payer" gives his bank the necessary standing instruction. In this case it is the "payee" who originates the payment.

(*b*) *Deposit accounts and certificates of deposit.* In February 1981 they totalled £26,053 million. They differ from current accounts in the following two respects.

(*i*) These accounts yield interest.

(*ii*) Funds may be withdrawn only after an agreed period of notice has been given. In practice there is often flexibility in the application of this rule.

9. Advances. The second most important banking service and the one which is most profitable to the banks themselves is the provision of personal and business overdraft facilities against security. This security may take the form of something tangible and marketable, e.g. share certificates, savings certificates, title-deeds, insurance policies. Sometimes the proven integrity, business ability and prospects of the borrower are sufficient.

Rates of interest until September 1971 were geared to a formula, normally a fixed margin above Bank Rate subject to a minimum. The majority of customers paid 1 to 2 per cent above Bank Rate, the biggest and most creditworthy about $\frac{1}{2}$ per cent. Since 1971 the banks have pursued independent policies in respect of interest rates.

The provision of working capital for industry and commerce is based upon the assumption that the loan will be self-liquidating, i.e. as the firm's income grows, so it is enabled to repay the loan which has made its activities possible. Traditionally, the banks have financed agriculture with short-term advances of a seasonal nature. In industry, banks may be prepared to make longer-term loans for, say, two to three years for the purchase of machinery and buildings. In commerce there has been in the last decade a considerable expansion in the finance of export contracts.

Advances in February 1981 stood at £29,646 million.

10. Security facilities. Bank strong-rooms are available to customers for the safe-keeping of valuables and night-safe facilities allow customers to deposit money overnight after banking hours for payment into their accounts the following morning.

11. Investment-advice and services. Banks will give advice on the investment of savings and through their own stockbrokers will make purchases and sales, their charges being paid out of the normal broking commission. Arrangements can be made for dividends to be paid directly into bank accounts or for the banks to detach coupons from bearer bonds and present them for payment. They will also act for their customers in applying for allotments arising from fresh capital issues and pay calls as they are made.

12. Income tax services. Most banks will advise or undertake to act on behalf of individuals in the preparation of income-tax returns, the checking of coding and notices of assessments and the making of claims for tax overpaid.

13. Executor and trustee services. Most banks have either an executor and trustee department or an affiliated company to deal with this branch of business. A bank may be nominated as an executor and, if necessary, a trustee of an estate after death. The advantages are professional expertise in handling a variety of assets, complete impartiality and continuity of administration.

14. Foreign travel. The banks will provide their customers with foreign currency, travellers' cheques which can be encashed at corresponding banks overseas or, for larger sums, letters of credit, any part of which the traveller can draw upon as required.

15. Remitting money abroad. Individuals may remit money abroad by two methods.

(*a*) *Bank draft.* This is a banker's cheque, often expressed in sterling but made payable in a foreign currency. The customer pays his bank in sterling at the current rate of exchange. The cheque will be honoured upon presentation at the foreign bank.

(*b*) *Cable transfer.* A credit is cabled by the payer's bank to the payee's bank.

16. Export finance. The larger commercial banks have special departments which specialise in the finance of foreign trade. They are assisted by banks affiliated to them overseas, or alternatively have arrangements with foreign banks which act as correspondents.

In the seller's market of the immediate post-war years international indebtedness was often settled on the basis of "cash on delivery" or even "cash with order". Increasing competition between the industrial nations has meant that price and quality are not always the deciding factors. The credit terms which the exporter is able to offer will often be decisive in winning an order. The banks have been encouraged, even in periods of domestic credit restraint, to afford short-, medium-, and longer-term export finance.

17. Short-term finance. The most usual method of settlement for exported goods is the "bill of exchange". The exporter draws a bill on the overseas buyer, attaches shipping documents to it and hands it to his own bank for collection. The documents are then forwarded to a bank in the buyer's country and handed over against payment or acceptance, the proceeds then being transmitted to the exporter through the two banks. The bill may be payable at sight or at a fixed future date, normally a maximum of six months forward. In the latter case the drawee "accepts" the bill, i.e. agrees to pay when the bill is due. In both cases, however, the exporter must wait before the proceeds are credited to his account. The banks can help either by purchasing the bill or by making an advance against its security, the exporter's working capital thereby being immediately received. An interest charge and a collection commission are charged.

Bank finance is given against approved bills, approval being contingent upon:

(*a*) the financial standing of the drawee;

(*b*) absence of restrictions upon money transfers from the country in which payment is to be made;

(*c*) the bill having a maximum of six months to run to maturity.

If the above conditions are not satisfied the banks may still provide finance if the Export Credits Guarantee Department provides suitable cover.

18. Export Credits Guarantee Department (ECGD). This department of the Department of Trade provides extensive insurance cover against the risk of default by the foreign buyer whether his failure to pay results from insolvency or delay or from the political risk of exchange control restrictions being imposed in the buyer's country. The Department operates on commercial principles and charges an insurance premium.

19. Medium-term finance. This is offered by the banks to assist exporters in granting credit terms in excess of two years. Terms for each transaction are calculated on an individual basis but all are subject to the availability of ECGD cover.

20. Long-term finance. This is available from individual banks or banks in consortium for sums in excess of £2 million where repayment is spread over five to fifteen years. Such a loan would again be underwritten by the ECGD. The unusual feature of such long-term finance is that it is provided by the banks direct to the overseas buyer. The British exporter can therefore be paid on a cash basis.

21. The economic importance of bank lending. It should be stressed that, while the wide range of financial services described are of great importance to the smooth running of the economy, it is bank lending which is of central interest to economists because of its implications for the money supply.

THE STRUCTURE OF LONDON CLEARING BANK LOANS

22. London clearing banks, a composite balance sheet. Examination of the liabilities side of the balance sheet shown in Table V gives a clear picture of the stucture of and the limitations placed upon bank lending.

The principal items in the balance sheet will now be selected for explanation and comment.

23. Sterling deposits. Sight deposits are the current accounts upon

TABLE V. *London Clearing Banks: a composite balance sheet, February, 1981* (£m.)

Liabilities		
Sterling deposits		
Sight deposits		16,193
Other		26,053
	Total	42,246
Other currency deposits		12,882
Sterling assets		
Notes and coin		874
Reserve assets		
Balances with the Bank of England		579
Money at call		1,780
UK and Northern Ireland Treasury bills		150
Other bills		935
British government stocks up to one year		383
	Total	3,827
Special and supplementary deposits		—
Market loans other than reserve assets		7,059
Bills other than reserve assets		62
Advances		
United Kingdom		26,877
Overseas		2,769
Investments		
British government stocks over one year and undated		1,866
Other		1,716
Other currency assets		
Market loans and advances		12,810
Bills		29
Investments		510
Sterling and other currencies miscellaneous assets		6,690
Acceptances		621

(*Source: BEQB, March 1981.*)

which cheques may be drawn and which form the kernel of the money supply, M1 (*see* **32** below). The other deposits are time deposits upon which interest is paid and which may also be included in the sterling M3 definition of the money stock.

24. The 12½ per cent reserve ratio. In determining the level of their lending, banks must steer a middle course between two conflicting considerations. On the one hand, they wish to maximise loans in order to increase their revenue. On the other hand, they must maintain a sufficient reserve of cash or liquid assets readily convertible to cash in order to meet day-to-day withdrawals.

Until 1971, the London clearing banks voluntarily observed two rules, an 8 per cent cash ratio and a 28 per cent liquidity ratio of total liquid assets to deposit liabilities.

In 1971, the Bank of England imposed a uniform and obligatory rule for *all* deposit banks. It established a minimum reserve ratio of 12½ per cent, *eligible reserve assets* to *eligible deposit liabilities*. (*See also* IX, **39–42** for current changes.)

25. Eligible liabilities. These are defined as the *sterling* deposit liabilities of the banking system with the exception of those deposits originally made for a minimum period of two years. Added to this are net liabilities in currencies other than sterling.

26. Eligible reserve assets. These are more strictly defined than the previous and looser concept of liquid assets. However, they share the characteristic that if they are not cash already they can be readily converted to cash on the financial markets.

(*a*) *Balances with the Bank of England.* All the clearing banks maintain accounts at the Bank of England. There is an informal arrangement that these balances will not be allowed to fall below 1½ per cent of eligible liabilities. Note that cash in bank tills no longer counts as a reserve asset.

(*b*) *Money at call.* This is very short money advanced primarily to the London discount houses (*see* **36, 37** below).

(*c*) *Treasury bills.* (*See also* VI, **2**(*b*).) The banks can improve their cash position by running down their Treasury bill holdings or may sell them outright on the London discount market.

(*d*) *Other bills.* These are commercial and local authority bills representing short-term lending. The former may be treated as reserve assets *up to a maximum of 2 per cent of total eligible liabilities*. Like Treasury bills they may be sold on the discount market.

(e) *British government stocks up to one year.* Again the banks may reduce their holdings as stocks mature or they may sell them on the discount market.

(*See also* IX **39–42** for current changes.)

27. Special and supplementary deposits. Special deposits appeared in the balance sheet for the first time in 1960. The Bank of England has the power to call upon the banks to deposit a specified sum in cash, thus reducing bank liquidity and the power to expand credit (*see* **32** below). Interest is paid at current Treasury bill rate.

Supplementary special deposits were introduced in 1973 (*see* IX, **37**). When banks do not succeed in restraining the growth of deposits ("bank deposit money") in line with current guidelines they are "fined" by being required to make cash deposits with the Bank at zero interest.

28. Market loans and bills other than reserve assets. These items comprise loans to other banks and to the private and public sectors in forms which do not qualify them as eligible reserve assets.

29. Investments. These are made up almost wholly of British government securities, some Commonwealth government and local authority bonds and some fixed interest securities of public companies. All of these securities are marketable and therefore in one sense liquid. However, they are illiquid to the extent that sale on the stock exchange before maturity may involve a capital loss. The bankers' portfolios are so arranged that a proportion of their investment matures each year and the greater part of it within ten years.

The banks do not aim to maintain any fixed percentage of investments, this being the residual item after the demand for advances, the most lucrative asset, has been satisfied.

30. Advances. These assets are the most illiquid, the most risky and the most profitable. A fairly substantial proportion of overdrafts may in normal circumstances be for personal or professional purposes but by far the greater part are for business purposes.

THE CLEARING BANKS AND THE SUPPLY OF MONEY

31. Significance of the London clearing banks. The difficulties of a precise definition of the money stock have already been observed (*see* VII, **8–15**). However, if the sterling M3 definition is adopted, in February 1981 the supply of money amounted to £67,232 million. Of this £9,943 million comprised notes and coin in circulation with the public. At the same time the eligible liabilities of the London clearing banks stood at £42,246 million, the principal constitutent of the money supply.

32. The creation of bank deposit money. To a very small extent new deposits are created when notes are deposited at the banks rather than remaining in circulation. *The greater part of the new deposits are, however, created at the initiative of the banks themselves.* This occurs whenever a bank makes a loan. Loans may be made to the public or the private sector.

(*a*) *The public sector.* Loans to government, whether in the form of purchases of securities or Treasury bills or in advances to the discount houses for the financing of Treasury bills, will all result in the creation of fresh deposits immediately the proceeds are spent; e.g. government funds raised in this way may be used to pay a civil engineer for road construction work. They then appear as an addition to his bank account.

(*b*) *The private sector.* Similarly, advances to private customers or purchases of commercial bills result in an expansion of deposits when the proceeds are spent.

It will be noted that in neither case do the banks hand out notes over the counter. If they purchase bills or securities they do so with a cheque drawn upon themselves. If they grant an overdraft, the borrower uses his cheque-book to make payments from an account which now shows a debit balance. The banks can create deposits in this way up to the point where their reserve assets bear a minimum $12\frac{1}{2}$ per cent ratio to eligible deposit liabilities, (or whatever other ratio that prudent banking or monetary controls currently dictate).

EXAMPLE:

Liabilities Deposits	Assets Reserve assets	Investment & advances
£50	£12.50	£37.50

In this position the banks are considerably "under-lent" since they are holding a reserve ration of 25 per cent. They have capacity to increase their lending under the heading of investments and advances.

Deposits	Reserve assets	Investment & advances
£100	£12.50	£87.50

In the second position more "deposit or ledger money" has been created and deposit liabilities have risen to £100. The banks are now said to be "fully lent", since their reserves bear the minimum $12\frac{1}{2}$ per cent ratio to deposit liabilities.

33. Restriction upon the creation of deposits. The clearing banks do not have unlimited power to create money as has been demonstrated in the preceding example. The reserve assets rule imposes one restriction. Other limitations arise from the availability of collateral security, the necessity for all banks to observe a common lending policy and, most important of all, the controls which are imposed by monetary policy (*see* IX, **32–42**).

34. Availability of collateral security. For a loan transaction to be completed it is necessary for the borrower to provide satisfactory security to the banker. Share certificates, insurance policies and title-deeds are examples of such security although in practice there may be some flexibility in what individual bankers accept. However, since collateral securities are themselves limited in supply, this limitation must exercise some restrictive effect upon the creation of deposits.

35. A common lending policy. The banks must move broadly in line in determining the level at which they will lend. Since there are now four big banks the probability is that three-quarters of any loans made by one will be expressed in fresh deposits for customers of the other three and only one-quarter as fresh deposits for its own customers. If all four banks are lending at the same rate, then their deposits will grow in line and their interindebtedness at the clearing house will roughly cancel out.

If, however, one bank adopts a more liberal lending policy than the others it will find that its cash balances at the Bank of England are gradually depleted as it settles its greater indebtedness with the other banks. In order to maintain its liquidity it must now drop back into line and restrict its lending.

THE LONDON DISCOUNT MARKET

36. Composition. The market comprises eleven discount houses which form the London Discount Market Association, together with a number of other firms which are not members and whose discounting operations form only a part of their total business.

37. The role of the discount houses. Essentially they are intermediaries in the provision of short-term finance standing between original lenders and ultimate borrowers, between banks with cash shortages and those with surpluses and between the commercial banks and the Bank of England.

(*a*) *Original lenders and ultimate borrowers.* The houses borrow from a variety of sources but primarily the commercial banks and for the most part *at call*, i.e. very short term.

In general the banks have favoured this arrangement since it provides them with an asset which yields interest and yet is highly liquid. Loans can be recalled immediately.

The ability of the houses to repay is underwritten by the Bank of England. Since 1829 they have enjoyed the *unique* right to borrow or to rediscount certain securities at the Bank. The securities which the Bank of England currently deems acceptable for this purpose are today's *eligible reserve assets.* At the Bank they must pay MLR, the only institutions which ever do so.

The funds which the houses borrow from the banks are then used to discount (at a higher interest rate than that paid) a number of instruments including Treasury, local authority and commercial bills and short-dated government stocks. In other words the houses are making short-term loans to finance trade and to meet the needs of central and local government.

(*b*) *Banks with shortages and banks with surpluses.* When a bank with a cash shortage recalls money from the market, before resorting to the Bank of England where they are obliged to pay the penally high minimum lending rate, the houses will attempt to make good the repaid loan by borrowing from a bank with a cash surplus.

(*c*) *Commercial banks and the Bank of England.* Since 1825, the banks have never found themselves in a position where they have been obliged to borrow from the Bank of England. They have been able to maintain adequate cash reserves by the mechanism described in (*b*) above.

Finally, it should be stated that the market plays a central role in the application of monetary policy. This will be considered in IX.

THE SECONDARY BANKING SYSTEM

38. Primary and secondary banks. During the past decade there has been a spectacular expansion of the UK banking system in a way which makes it convenient to draw a distinction between primary and secondary banks.

The primary banks are those whose *central* role is the operation of the economy's money transmission service. They comprise the London, Scottish and Northern Ireland clearing banks, the Banking Department of the Bank of England, the discount houses and the National Giro.

The secondary banks include the accepting houses, other British banks, foreign banks in the UK and consortium banks. While their assets structure has some similarity to that of the primary banks, their liabilities are very different. They are made up almost entirely of term deposits, the bulk of which are denominated in foreign currencies. In other words their deposit liabilities do not form a part of the UK payments mechanism.

A further distinction is the size of deposit acceptable to secondary banks (£50,000–£100,000 minimum) and the relatively small number of accounts compared to the primary banks.

In **39–42** below the characteristics of the various segments of the secondary banking system are examined, as well as the factors which have led to the dramatic growth of recent years.

39. Merchant banking. A concept difficult to define, the original merchant banks (accepting houses) were merchants turned bankers who utilised their knowledge of the creditworthiness of their overseas trade customers to underwrite (for a commission) bills of exchange on their behalf. These "guaranteed" bills could then be readily discounted on the London Discount Market.

The status of a merchant bank is usually judged by whether it is a member of the Accepting Huses Committee. There are at present seventeen members, names which most people would associate with merchant banking, e.g. Kleinwort Benson, Schroders, Hambros, Lazard Brothers and N. M. Rothschild.

Their fortunes have varied and their interests diversified but a major impetus was given to their activities with the birth of the Eurocurrency markets (*see* **49–54**) which many of them were instrumental in developing in London.

The merchant banker is once again to be found arranging finance for international trade, foreign governments and international projects, as well as for domestic borrowers.

40. British overseas banks. A product of the British Empire, these banks had head offices in London, following and encouraging trade by providing banking services to British communities across the world through a network of branches which today exceeds 5,000.

As Commonwealth countries gained their independence, on occasion there was outright nationalisation of branches or ownership and direction had to be shared. These events coincided with the rise of the Eurodollar market and it was natural that the overseas banks should diversify into these activities while attempting to retain as much of their traditional business as circumstances permitted.

The big names in this group are Standard Chartered, Grindlays Bank Group. Barclays Bank International and Lloyds Bank International.

41. Foreign banks. At the end of the Second World War there were only about eighty foreign banks with London offices. They shared with British banks the traditional function of financing trade through "the bill on London", specifically trade with their own countries. This function remains but has been vastly supplemented as a result of the rise of the Eurodollar market, the growing needs of multinational corporations and the establishment of the Common Market. The consequence is that today there are well in excess of 300 foreign banks in the City of London, of which sixty-five are American, more than in New York.

In the 1950s, British secondary banks began to look for foreign currency, particularly dollars (subsequently known as Eurodollars) to finance trade and various investment projects throughout the world. The US banks already in London were the first to realise that they could share in this new business and were encouraged to do so by the fact that US currency regulations prevented these activities at home. Moreover, the ability of the US banks to tap the new London market arose at a time when multinationals were looking for a foothold in the newly formed Common Market and required appropriate finance. Eventually, no major US bank could afford not to have a London office.

42. Consortium banks. The growth of the Eurocurrency markets prompted other developments. Some foreign banks, lacking sufficient resources and expertise, joined with others to form consortium banks for the purpose of financing large projects in particular regions through the medium of the Euromarkets.

On occasion London clearing banks were drawn into consortia, e.g. Midland and International Banks (Midland), Orion (National Westminster) and European Banking Corporation (Midland).

THE PARALLEL MONEY MARKETS

43. The "classical" money market. Until about fifteen years ago the London money market comprised the set of relationships between the clearing banks, the discount houses and the Bank of England, to which reference has already been made (*see* **37** above). Subsequently, the dramatic expansion of the secondary banking sector was accompanied by an equally rapid development of new markets in money.

44. The interbank market. The equalising function between banks with shortages and banks with surpluses traditionally performed by the discount houses (*see* **37**(*b*)) was now overtaken by the growing practice of borrowing directly surpluses from *non-clearing banks* of which there was now a much greater number. In due course this market was extended to include all the clearers. The emergence of sterling money-brokers specialising as intermediaries between banks marked the start of this new interbank market.

In this way, the "classical" money market was expanded to embrace new sources of money. Nevertheless, despite the scale of the total market (approximately one-fifth of all UK bank deposits are interbank deposits) the banking system can still encounter deficits on a day-to-day basis. The discount houses' access to the Bank of England therefore remains important as the ultimate channel for extra funds (*see* **37**(*b*) and (*c*)) and consequently as a means of moulding monetary policy.

45. Markets in certificates of deposit (CDs). The establishment of an interbank market led naturally to the introduction of certificates of deposit as an option to an interbank deposit and as an outlet for non-bank funds.

There is an advantage to a depositor when, in agreeing to lend a fixed sum, at a fixed interest rate for a fixed period of time, he can do so against a negotiable instrument such as a CD. The discount Houses not only hold CDs on their own behalf but also make a secondary market for the convenience of others.

Bank of England permissven for dollar CDs in the UK in 1966. On the basis of this experience a sterling market was opened in October 1968. They are currently issued by the secondary banks and the clearing banks.

46. Local authority market. Other circumstances led to the development of still further markets in money. During the 1950s local authority borrowers were under restraints imposed by the Public Works Loans Board, at that time the chief source of public funds. After 1955, they had to meet a greater proportion of their borrowing requirements from the market.

As we have seen, the funds were available, particularly in Eurodollars which could be switched to sterling but also from the growing number of secondary banks with spare deposits and from insurance companies and pension funds with money to lend.

Specialist brokers therefore emerged to bring borrowers and lenders together in a new market.

47. Market deposits for finance houses. Instalment credit companies traditionally financed a large part of their business by bidding for public deposits. The growth of their business from the 1950s increased their demand for funds and coincided with the development of the secondary banks. A new market began to develop in large deposits, not only from the banks but also later from industrial companies and other financial institutions.

48. Implications for the structure of clearing bank balance sheets. During the past ten years the development of the secondary banking system and the wholesale money markets, the increasing degree of competition for deposits following *Competition and Credit Control* in 1971 (*see* IX, **33**), and the effects of inflation upon operational costs and upon the disposition of depositors to prefer interest-bearing deposits to current accounts, have all brought pressures to bear upon the clearers which have led to a continuing change in the structure of their balance sheets.

A most important category of deposit is the sight deposit (current account) but in order to collect and increase this business across the country, particularly in the face of more intensive competition, it has been necessary for each of the clearers to expand and maintain their branch banking networks. While traditionally current accounts are thought to have an "endowment" element (i.e. the banks have had free use of such deposits) the costs of collecting and operating them are now estimated to be equal to a 7–7½ per cent interest rate. Therefore, in seeking to extend their lending business the clearing banks have found it feasible to bid for deposits in the wholesale money markets. The fact that these are for fixed terms has enabled the banks to lengthen the period of their own lending. This development has matched the needs of many of their customers. The short-term overdraft facility, subject to instant cancellation, now looms less large in relation to fixed, medium-term lending to industry and commerce.

THE EUROMARKETS

49. Nature of Eurocurrencies. The Euromarkets deal in very many currencies, e.g. Eurodollars, Euromarks and Eurosterling. These currencies have one thing in common. They are held by banks, corporations or individuals, *outside their country of origin*. They are then on-lent, providing credit to borrowers world wide. Dealing is not restricted to European financial centres, and in recent years Nassau, Cayman, Bahrein, Tokyo, Hong Kong and Singapore have gained in importance. London, however, remains the paramount location for this huge and expanding pool of international credit.

50. Birth of the Eurodollar. In 1958, for the first time since the war, the leading European currencies together with the Japanese yen joined the dollar in gaining a measure of freedom from exchange controls and becoming convertible to other currencies. At the same time US international payments moved into deficit, particularly with Europe, reflecting the recovery of the European economies from the effects of war. It therefore happened that surplus dollars became available (and concentrated in European hands) at the same time that currencies were permitted to move more freely across frontiers. This flow of dollars was swelled by the profits of US companies abroad who for tax reasons did not wish to repatriate them.

London's secondary banks were not slow to seize the opportunity of securing these Eurodollars for fixed terms at competitive interest rates in order to on-lend them to their global contacts. London continues as the prime centre, the market having subsequently been extended to include deposits of all the world's major currencies.

NOTE: The inward and outward flow of Eurocurrencies does not affect the sterling exchange rate *unless* the UK public or private sectors borrow from the market and switch into sterling. In this respect the London market is as isolated from the UK economy as it would be were it located in the Bahamas.

51. Period of loans and deposits. Originally a short-term market which enabled deposits to be used for periods of three to six months, new techniques were evolved which enabled loans to be "rolled over" (renewed) and, later, offered at floating interest rates adjusted on a six-month basis to the current Eurocurrency rate. This flexibility of interest rates enabled banks to meet the growing demand for large syndicated loans for longer periods. The market for such loans is essentially made up of other banks acting as intermediaries for their customers. These Euroloans contrast with Eurobonds (*see* **52** below).

Deposits in the Euromarkets are made by wealthy individuals, industrial corporations and central banks, but most important of all by *other commercial banks*. They may be made for periods ranging from "overnight" to five years but are usually for one year. These interbank deposits attract current interest rates with the six-month rate being adopted as the basis for LIBOR (the London Interbank Offered Rate). The interest rate on Euroloans is then geared to LIBOR according to the term and the risk of the loan.

52. Eurobonds. Just as the modern Eurocurrency serves the same purpose (on a much vaster scale) as did sterling as an "international currency" in the nineteenth century, so the modern Eurobond is the equivalent of the foreign bonds issued by foreign governments in European financial centres during the same period. Such loans continued to be made, primarily on the New York market, after 1945. The imposition of various restrictions on this market during the early 1960s coupled with the new convertibility of European currencies encouraged the world's international banks largely centred upon London to develop fund-raising activities in Europe.

The principal characteristics of Eurobonds are that they are fixed-term loans (usually 5–15 years) at fixed interest rates, the whole sum being drawn at once. The bond issue will be managed by one bank but underwritten by anything up to 100. The bonds are sold world wide to individual and institutional investors. They are usually denominated in US dollars, German marks, Swiss francs or Japanese yen.

53. Evaluation of the Euromarkets. These developments have produced their advantages and potential dangers to the stability of the world monetary system. The advantages are outlined below while the dangers are discussed in **54**.

(*a*) It will be observed that the spectacular expansion of the world economy during the 1950s and 1960s would have been stifled without access to adequate sources of finance.

(*b*) National Treasuries and central banks have been able to secure advantages from the markets. When, in 1958, US foreign payments moved into deficit, the Americans were quick to recognise that dollars absorbed by the new Euromarkets could not be presented for conversion to gold at the New York Federal Reserve. Their central reserves were thus protected. Some countries, e.g. Italy and Belgium, when experiencing exchange rate crises found it convenient to borrow from the market to support their exchange rates. Other countries like Japan with continuing payments surpluses were able to avoid unwelcome revaluations by *lending* surplus dollars to the market. With the oil price crisis after 1973–74, many governments with huge payments deficits resorted to the market as an alternative to borrowing from the International Monetary Fund whose lending terms were very restrictive. Britain was an early beneficiary with large-scale borrowing by government, public corporations and local authorities. Subsequently, Eurocurrency borrowing has been dominated by the developing countries and the Soviet bloc.

(*c*) It will be noticed that London's position as an international financial centre with vast overseas earnings was preserved by the evolution of Eurocurrencies at a time when sterling which had originally performed these functions was losing its attraction.

54. The dangers. The increasing complexity of the relationships which have developed within the financial system have posed new problems for the monetary authorities.

(*a*) *"Hot money" flows.* On occasion the fear has been expressed that the ever-increasing volume of "hot money" flowing across the exchanges in search of preferential interest rates may have a highly destabilising effect upon exchange rates.

(*b*) *Pyramiding of credit.* Less commonly heard at present is the fear that the pyramiding of credit upon credit which would seem to be possible in the Euromarkets may spiral out of control with inflationary results. This argument is, however, offset by the recognition that the whole process still depends ultimately upon the cash and liquidity ratios imposed by individual monetary authorities.

(c) *Bank failures*. The danger here is that a bank failure in one country may, through its Euromarket connections, have a ripple effect which brings down other banks throughout the international system. To deal with this problem, central bankers jointly established the Committee on Banking Regulations and Supervisory Practices to ensure that *all* banks and their subsidiaries would fall under someone's jurisdiction and supervision.

(d) *Large national borrowings*. A possible threat to the system arises from the size and quality of government borrowings from the market, particularly those of developing countries. In the first place, individual bankers are being asked to assess the creditworthiness of nations. Secondly, instead of spreading risk evenly across a wide range of borrowers, national loans mean a much greater concentration of risk.

PROGRESS TEST 8

1. What types of bank are found in the UK? **(1)**

2. What do you understand by the expression "clearing banks"? **(2)**

3. Explain the principal function of the British overseas banks. **(5)**

4. Point out the most striking feature of the US banks in London. **(6)**

5. List the principal services provided by the commercial banks. **(8–20)**

6. Why is the banks' interest in export finance of especial economic significance? **(16)**

7. Explain the function of the Export Credits Guarantee Department. **(18)**

8. List the assets of the London clearing banks and compare their importance in the balance sheet. **(22)**

9. Explain the importance of the reserve ratio. **(24)**

10. Why are advances the asset of greatest interest to the banks? **(30)**

11. Explain the way in which the banks themselves are able to create both their own assets and their own liabilities. **(32)**

12. Why are the banks unable to expand their assets and liabilities without limit? **(33–35)**

13. In what sense is the London Discount Market an intermediary between the Bank of England and the commercial banks? **(37)**

14. Distinguish between primary and secondary banks. **(38)**

15. What is a "merchant bank"? **(39)**

16. What are the British overseas banks? **(40)**

17. Why are there so many foreign banks in London? **(41)**

18. What is a consortium bank? **(42)**

19. Explain the nature of the interbank market. **(44)**

20. What is a CD? **(45)**

21. What has brought about major changes in the structure of clearing bank balance sheets? **(48)**

22. Define a Eurocurrency. **(49)**

23. Who are the depositors on the Euromarkets? **(51)**

24. What is LIBOR? **(51)**

25. What are the characteristics of Eurobond? **(52)**

26. Explain the advantages which have been derived from the presence of the Euromarkets. **(53)**

27. What dangers may arise from Euromarket developments? **(54)**

CHAPTER IX

The Bank of England

HISTORY

1. Foundation. The Governor and Company of the Bank of England was incorporated in 1694 by an Act of Parliament which granted a Royal Charter. It was the result of pressure in the city for a larger institution which could offer greater security and lower interest rates than the existing private banks. The privilege of a Royal Charter was offered in return for a loan to the government of £1,200,000 against an annuity of £100,000.

2. The early work of the Bank. In the eighteenth century, the Bank accepted deposits and made advances against security. It discounted approved bills of exchange and later undertook the circulation of Exchequer bills and the issue of government securities. In 1751 it took over the management of the National Debt.

3. The Bank Charter Act 1844. The unique position of the Bank was advanced a stage further by this Act which decreed that no new banks would have the power to issue notes while existing banks would have this power curtailed. The result was that in due course the Bank of England became the only note-issuing bank in England and Wales. The Act also granted a fiduciary issue to the Bank, all notes in excess of which had to be backed by gold.

It was also established that the Bank should be divided into two departments, the Issue Department and the Banking Department, the objective being to enable the same institution to carry out the duties of a central note-issuing authority at the same time as it engaged in normal commercial banking. The two functions did not prove to be entirely complementary with the result that commercial activities have almost completely disappeared, being gradually replaced by central banking functions.

4. Growth of central banking functions. The establishment of the Exchange Equalisation Account in 1932 following the departure from the gold standard, the introduction of exchange control in 1939 and the great increase in government expenditure throughout this century all added to the special responsibilities of the

Bank. The position was formally acknowledged in 1946 with the Act of nationalisation.

5. The Bank of England Act 1946. The Bank was taken out of private ownership and the capital stock vested in the Treasury. Power was expressly given to the Treasury to issue such directives to the Bank as seemed to accord with the public interest. In fact there has never been occasion to use this power since the Bank has simply continued its pre-nationalisation practice of meeting the government's requirements in respect of monetary policy without resort to statutory intervention.

The Radcliffe Committee found that the Bank remained a separate entity but that through a number of committees continuous consultation with the Treasury was maintained, views and advice being exchanged and policy determined. It is this series of liaison bodies that we refer to as "the monetary authorities".

ADMINISTRATION OF THE BANK

6. The Court of Directors. The Crown appoints a governor, deputy governor and sixteen directors to the Court which controls the Bank. There may be four working or executive directors with the remainder in a part-time capacity drawn from banking, commerce, shipping, industry and the trade unions.

7. The committees. The policy body which examines the work of all the other committees is the Committee of Treasury made up of seven members of the Court including the governor and deputy governor.

The other standing committees are as follows.

(a) *The Debden Committee* which supervises the Bank printing works at Debden.

(b) *The Audit Committee.*

(c) *The Committee to Consider the Securities of Certain Funds* which supervises the investment of the Banking Department.

(d) *The Committee on Bank Premises.*

(e) *The Staff Committee.*

(f) *The Charitable Appeals Committee.*

(g) *The Committee on Permanent Control of Expenditure.*

8. The departments. There are eight departments each subdivided into a number of offices covering various aspects of the Bank's work.

(*a*) *The Accountant's Department* maintains registers of stock on behalf of the UK government, Commonwealth governments, nationalised industries and some local authorities, and issues dividend warrants.

(*b*) *The Cashier's Department* deals with the note issue, the Exchange Equalisation Account, and all banking operations. Under the last heading come dealings with the discount market and in securities.

(*c*) *The Economic Intelligence Department* is concerned with collating and interpreting financial and economic information.

(*d*) *The Overseas Department* is responsible for relations with foreign central banks and international financial bodies.

(*e*) *The Audit Department.*

(*f*) *The Secretary's Department.*

(*g*) *The Establishment Department.*

(*h*) *The Printing Works.*

THE BANK RETURN

9. Significance. Like the balance sheet of the commercial banks the Bank Return gives an insight into the operations of the Bank of England. For accounting purposes the twofold division into Issue Department and Banking Department has continued to be observed since 1844.

10. Issue Department (selected items), March 1981.

TABLE VI. *Bank return, Issue Department*

Liabilities		Assets	
Notes issued:	£m.		£m.
In circulation	10,236	Government securities	5,720
In Banking Department	14	Other securities	4,530
Total	10,250	Total	10,250

(*Source: BEQB, March 1981.*)

11. Issue Department liabilities. It will be observed that liabilities consist entirely of notes, either in circulation or in reserve with the Banking Department.

12. Issue Department assets. Assets are made up of the following.

(*a*) *Government securities.* This is by far the most important group of assets and any increase in the note issue implies an equivalent increase in government securities. This is to say that whenever the note issue is expanded the Issue Department receives interest-bearing securities in exchange.

(*b*) *Other securities.* Included in this category are certain eligible bills and coin other than gold coin.

NOTE: It will be seen that the note issue is almost entirely fiduciary.

13. Banking Department (selected items), March 1981.

TABLE VII.   *Bank return, Banking Department*

Liabilities	£m.	Assets	£m.
Deposits:		Government securities	454
Public	40	Advances and other	
Bankers	568	accounts	1,022
Reserves and other		Premises, equipment and	
accounts	1,341	other securities	474
Special	—	Notes and coin	14
		Total	£1,964

(*Source: BEQB, March 1981.*)

14. Public deposits. These are the balances of the branches of government and include the accounts of the Exchequer, the Paymaster-General, the Revenue Departments, the National Debt Commissioners and the National and Trustee Savings Banks.

It will be noted that the balance is relatively small. This is deliberately so since the accumulation of large public deposits in consequence, say, of substantial tax payments would correspondingly reduce bankers' deposits.

The reverse would be true when government is making payments to society. Alternating shortages and excesses of cash would cause wide fluctuations in the short-term rate of interest and since the government is the largest short-term borrower it desires an orderly and stable money market (*see* **25** below).

15. Bankers' deposits. The Bank of England is the bankers' bank and stands in much the same relationship to the clearing banks as the latter do to their customers. The clearing banks are enabled to make payments to each other or to the Exchequer by cheques drawn on their accounts and they can draw out the notes and coin that they require.

(a) *The clearing*. Net indebtedness between banks which can be settled only in cash is regulated through an adjustment in the bankers' balances at the Bank of England. Settlement at local clearings is carried out through the provincial branches of the Bank of England.

(b) *Cash and coin*. In the same way that the individual may draw notes or coin from his bank so the clearing banks can draw upon their accounts at the Bank of England. At holiday-times when the public's demand for cash rises, the banks are able to meet requirements by drawing upon these balances.

NOTE: We shall see later that bankers' deposits are important to the implementation of monetary policy. In the same way that the banks are able to vary the volume of their total deposits the Bank of England is in a position to vary the volume of bankers' deposits and therefore, at least theoretically, the credit which is related to them.

16. Reserves and other accounts. These include unallocated profits together with the accounts of overseas central banks maintained in London to assist in settling trade indebtedness, accounts of overseas governments and the few remaining private accounts. The Bank of England does not compete with the commercial banks and will not therefore accept fresh private business. However, a number of old-established firms continue to enjoy the banking facilities which they have always had.

17. Special deposits. This item corresponds to the asset which appears in the combined balance sheet of the commercial banks. It has been noted that the banks can be called upon to deposit a percentage of their own total deposits with the Bank of England as a means of reducing their liquidity and hence restricting their power to create deposits.

18. Government securities. Included here are Treasury bills and longer-dated securities (bonds) and Ways and Means Advances to the Exchequer to cover a temporary need for funds. This occurs normally when at the end of the day the Exchequer balances are run down and the government needs to borrow only until the following day. Since July 1971, Treasury bills discounted for customers appear under this heading.

19. Advances and other accounts. These fall into two groups.

(*a*) *Private customers.* Advances on private accounts.

(*b*) *Discount market.* The Bank discounts bills for the discount market and also makes advances against bills as collateral security. In so doing it carries out its function as "lender of last resort". If for any reason the commercial banks recall money from the market (money at call and short notice) the discount houses in order to meet their obligations may now be "forced into the Bank" to borrow at minimum lending rate. Since this rate is in excess of discount rates they are put under penalty and there will be a restriction of business until the market can get out of the Bank.

If the Bank wishes to avoid this situation it will operate "at the back door", acquiring bills approaching maturity from the commercial banks and enabling them again to increase their lending to the discount houses.

These operations are vital to the control of the monetary system and further consideration will be given to them (*see* **35** below).

20. Premises, equipment and other securities. These are non non-government securities and include commercial bills acquired from time to time in order to test their quality and discourage the circulation of bills of which the Bank does not approve. Also included are shares and debentures in certain institutions established in the 1930s to stimulate industrial activity and in the 1940s to promote post-war industrial and commercial reconstruction. Since July 1971, premises and equipment have been added to this heading.

21. Notes and coin. It will be observed that this item is insufficient to cover the total balances of the commercial banks held with the Bank of England. If therefore there is an unduly high demand for cash by the banks consequent upon an increased demand by the general public the Bank of England's reserves will be depleted. If it falls below a certain level, the machinery will be set in motion for an increase in the fiduciary issue (*see* VII, **6**). This level is known as the "proportion", the ratio between cash reserves and total assets, and is somewhat similar to the cash ratio of the commercial banks.

THE BANK OF ENGLAND'S DOMESTIC BUSINESS

22. The bankers' bank. It has been noted that the commercial bankers maintain cash balances with the Bank of England in order to facilitate the operation of the clearing and from which they replenish their supplies of notes and coin.

Beyond routine banking business exists a close relationship maintained by constant contacts through organisations such as the Committee of London Clearing Bankers and the British Bankers' Association. There are regular meetings between the governor and deputy governor of the Bank and the chairman and deputy chairman of the Committee of London Clearing Bankers as well as meetings at a lower level between bank executives and Bank of England senior officials. Both operational and policy matters are discussed. In this way the Bank becomes the channel of communication between government and the banking system and the means whereby the Chancellor can make his wishes known without resort to the statutory powers which exist but which have never been used.

The Bank of England Act 1946 gave power to the Bank to request information from and make recommendations to bankers. If authorised by the Treasury it also empowered the Bank to issue directions to any banker for the purpose of securing that effect is given to any such request or recommendation. The evidence would, however, seem to cast doubt upon the effectiveness of this clause.

23. Banker to the discount houses. The eleven discount houses which make up the London Discount Market Association all maintain working balances at the Bank but unlike the clearing banks enjoy the unique privilege of being allowed to borrow. Each house maintains a Loan Account at the Discount Office of the Bank of England where, if it is unable to meet its commitmets, it can always raise cash either by rediscounting approved bills or by borrowing against eligible security. The Bank, however, dictates its own terms, specifically with reference to the interest charged which is known as "minimum lending rate". Since this is in excess of "Treasury bill rate" (the rate at which the market discounts Treasury bills) and well in excess of "money rate" (the rate at which the market borrows from the clearing banks to finance its operations), the discount houses will use the Bank only as "the lender of last resort".

Nevertheless, this borrowing facility is vital to the functioning of the monetary system. The clearing banks are enabled to maintain minimal cash reserves in the certain knowledge that when necessary money can be recalled from the discount houses which in turn will always be able to repay by resorting to the Bank of England.

24. Banker to the government. The Bank's unique position among financial institutions stems from its historic relationship with government.

Of first importance is the Exchequer account, the government's central bank balance which together with certain subsidiary accounts is held at the Bank of England. The Bank also arranges to meet the government's borrowing requirements either through Ways and Means Advances or through short-term securities (Treasury bills) and long-term bonds whether for cash or conversion.

25. Treasury bills. The Treasury offers a certain quantity of Treasury bills for sale by tender every Friday. These bills are normally for ninety-one days and do not yield any set rate of interest. Instead, offers are made at a price less than redemption value, i.e. the bills are discounted. It is the Bank of England which opens the tenders, makes the allotments, issues the bills and credits the proceeds to the Exchequer account. Bills are allotted to the highest bidders among applications from the discount houses, the Bank of England itself, acting on behalf of foreign central banks, the London branches of overseas banks, and British banks acting on behalf of institutional investors. (By agreement with the discount houses the clearing banks do not compete on their own behalf at the weekly tender but make their purchases of bills from the discount houses after the bills have run at least a week.)

The Bank of England also pays bills as they mature.

It has been observed earlier (*see* **14** above) that the Bank seeks to avoid alternating shortages and excesses of cash in the money market which would cause fluctuations in short-term interest rates. To this end it operates almost daily in the market, putting cash out by buying Treasury bills or taking cash in by selling. This is one aspect of the Bank's "open market operations" and is carried out through a firm of discount brokers known as "the special buyer". The Bank does not itself deal directly with the market.

26. Issues of stock. The Bank also carries out continuous open market operations in long-term securities. It advises the government on new issues and conversions, publishes prospectuses, receives applications and allots the bonds.

On the day that a new issue is made, it is not anticipated that the public will take up the whole amount. Arrangements are therefore made for the balance to be bought by the "departments", which effectively means the Issue Department of the Bank. These bonds are then gradually released to the market through the "government broker", a firm of stockbrokers acting on behalf of the Bank.

The Bank is also a regular buyer of the stock which next matures so that on the redemption date the number of bonds remaining in the hands of the public is considerably reduced.

It therefore follows that whether the Bank is releasing a new issue or redeeming or refinancing existing debt, cash movements between the public and private sectors are smoothed out over a period of months.

Through these open market operations the Bank seeks to establish an orderly gilt-edged market which is consistent with the wise management of the National Debt. If security prices are falling (i.e. interest rates rising) the Bank may intervene more actively as a buyer in order to check the trend. Similarly, as a seller, if the Bank has always "on tap" at least one medium- and one long-dated stock, the rate at which it releases them to the market will have a major influence upon the price and therefore the yield of gilt-edged securities.

THE BANK OF ENGLAND'S EXTERNAL BUSINESS

27. Four tasks. There are four tasks which the Bank must perform in its dealings outside the UK.

(a) The operation of the Exchange Equalisation Account.
(b) The management of foreign exchange control.
(c) Monetary relations with foreign central banks.
(d) Participation in international financial institutions.

28. The Exchange Equalisation Account. After the gold standard was abandoned in 1931 there no longer existed a common denominator which would automatically relate the exchange values of two paper currencies. In order to avoid the fluctuations which would have resulted from the determination of exchange rates solely by market forces the Finance Act of 1932 set up the Exchange Equalisation Account. Gold was transferred from the Issue Department and these funds, placed under the control of the Treasury, were to be utilised in stabilising the foreign exchange markets.

An excess supply of sterling which resulted in a depreciation in its exchange value was checked by the purchase of sterling with gold or foreign currencies. Conversely, an appreciation in the exchange rate was checked by the sale of sterling for gold or foreign currencies.

In 1939, the balance of the gold held by the Issue Department was transferred to the Account which ever since has been the sole depository of the nation's gold and foreign currency reserves.

The Finance Act of 1946 widened the scope of the Account to include the conservation or disposition in the national interest of the means of making payments abroad.

The Bank of England manages the Account in accordance with the terms of Britain's membership of the International Monetary Fund.

NOTE: When the Bank enters the foreign exchange markets to buy sterling with gold or foreign currencies the proceeds are lent to the Exchequer against "tap" Treasury bills. Conversely, when sterling is sold it becomes necessary to call in loans, with the result that the Exchequer has to borrow from other sources.

29. Foreign exchange control. Exchange control was introduced in 1939 and given a peacetime form in the Exchange Control Act of 1947. The Treasury was given extensive powers of control over the conversion of sterling to foreign currencies and over the disposal of the foreign currency receipts of UK residents.

Control policy varies and is agreed between the Treasury and the Bank of England and administered by the latter.

Some 250 banks have been appointed authorised dealers in foreign exchange and they are allowed a certain latitude according to the policy in force to deal freely with applications for foreign currencies.

30. Foreign central banks. The Bank of England provides banking services, e.g. the management of sterling holdings, for many foreign central banks. These banks provide reciprocal services.

In recent years this relationship has developed beyond a narrow banking connection to the point where there are regular exchanges of views and information. The link is especially strong with the US Federal Reserve System, the Bank of Canada and the European central banks.

31. International financial institutions. The Bank of England takes an active part in the work of a number of international bodies and in some cases provides the representative of the UK.

(*a*) *Bank for International Settlements.* The Bank of England as the country's central bank is a member in its own right. Since the war, the BIS has been primarily concerned with the acceptance from European central banks of short-term deposits of gold and dollars and the granting of short-term credits.

(*b*) *The International Monetary Fund* (*see* XII, **31–41**). The Bank works in conjunction with the Treasury in making preparations for IMF proceedings.

The Bank also makes a substantial contribution to the work of:

(*c*) *the International Bank for Reconstruction and Development* (*see* XII, **54**);

(*d*) *the Organisation for Economic Co-operation and Development* (*see* X, **35**).

THE BANK OF ENGLAND AND THE IMPLEMENTATION OF MONETARY POLICY

32. Traditional monetary policy. It has been observed previously (*see* IV, **2**) that classical monetary policy centred upon the regulatory effect of moving interest rates upon the demand for and the supply of credit. In practice, this had meant variations in Bank Rate which were "made effective" by supporting operations in government debt.

During the 1930s the power of monetary policy to achieve its objectives was questioned (*see* IV, **2**(*b*)) and Bank Rate remained static from 1931 to 1951. When in 1951 monetary policy was re-activated experiments were made with additional weapons of credit control. By 1971, methods had been evolved which placed the twin instruments of Bank Rate and open market operations in a different perspective.

33. The Bank of England's minimum lending rate (MLR). In the course of some 250 years traditional Bank Rate had acquired a number of functions.

(a) *The "prime rate"*. It was the rate to which bank deposit and lending rates were directly linked.

(b) *An indicator of the Chancellor's intentions*. Particularly during the 1960s, variations in the rate were viewed as a signal of the government's assessment of the state of the economy and of future economic policy. From an international standpoint, if for some reason short-term foreign funds were being switched out of sterling investment bringing pressure on the exchange rate then it was hoped that a more attractive interest rate would encourage their retention. Additionally, it indicated to foreign sterling holders and to businessmen at home that the government intended to take a firm hold on inflationary pressures. This, it was reasoned, would improve confidence.

(c) *The minimum lending rate to the discount houses*. Most significantly, Bank Rate was defined as the minimum rate at which the Bank of England would rediscount eligible securities for the discount houses. In the event that the houses were obliged to repay money at call borrowed from the banks they would be "forced into the Bank of England" where they would pay a rate of interest in excess of the rates at which they were discounting. In short, they now made a loss. It followed that if Bank Rate rose bill rates would not lag far behind.

By 1972 these functions had been largely overtaken by events. The implementation in 1971 of the Bank's proposals for *Competition and Credit Control* led to the commercial banks adopting their own independent base rates to which their other rates were now linked.

Secondly, while from an external point of view Bank Rate was still important in checking the outflow of "hot money", as an economic signal it was increasingly displaced by explicit government statements. The third and most important function was proving on occasion to be ineffective. During 1972, there developed a situation in which the market could *theoretically* borrow at Bank Rate, a supposedly penal rate, while the *actual* market rate for money lay above. Moreover, the Bank had developed techniques for influencing bill rates *directly* (*see* 35).

Consequently, on 9th October 1972, Bank Rate was replaced by *minimum lending rate*, defined as the minimum rate at which the Bank would rediscount securities for the discount houses. It differed in being the product rather than the cause of market rates and was calculated by taking the last Treasury bill rate, adding $\frac{1}{2}$ per cent and rounding up to the nearest quarter point.

In practice market forces induced repeated shifts in MLR which often conflicted with the interest rates desired by the authorities. On such occasions the Bank suspended the formula and dictated MLR as it had done with Bank Rate. The position was regularised on 25th May 1978 when the Bank announced that henceforth it would once again administer the rate (still called MLR) every Thursday.

34. Open market operations in gilt-edged securities. It should first be noted that in its operations in the gilt-edged market, the Bank may find that its monetary policy objectives conflict with those of its Debt management policy. For example, if the Bank finds it necessary to borrow large sums of money by the sale of gilts, this will depress capital values and force up interest rates (*see* IV, 2(*b*)). High interest rates may not be appropriate to current monetary policy. Equally, it may be the case that the Bank places the desirability of Debt servicing at low interest rates above the need for high interest rates called for by monetary policy. During the 1960s this proved in fact to be the case. The Bank gave preference to its Debt management responsibilities and was consequently inhibited in using market operations for monetary purposes.

In 1971, the Bank indicated its willingness to see interest rates rise. Priority would now be given to monetary objectives and open market operations in gilts conducted in the traditional way.

When the Bank goes to the open market to purchase government securities from the general public it must pay with cheques drawn upon itself. When these cheques are paid into the commercial banks, the Bank of England will have an adverse balance at the Clearing House. This can be settled only by crediting the cash balances of the commercial banks, i.e. bankers' deposits will increase. We have seen that these deposits are treated as part of banks' reserve assets. Since these have now been enlarged the banks will be able to pursue a more liberal lending policy and deposits will grow.

Conversely, when the Bank enters the market to sell, cheques drawn on the commercial banks in favour of the Bank of England will result in a reduction of bankers' deposits and a curtailment of their ability to lend. The immediate effect will be the recall of money from the discount market in order to make good cash balances. The discount houses will now be compelled to borrow from the Bank of England where minimum lending rate is now made effective. Since the houses are making a loss on this borrowing they will be obliged to curtail their lending in order to repay as soon as possible. Credit will be scarce and consequently dear.

35. Open market operations in Treasury bills. The Bank may also operate in the market in Treasury bills in a way which can influence short-term interest rates directly.

On the assumption that the Bank has some flexibility in borrowing internally, i.e. from government departments, it may regulate the supply of bills to the market in a way which will produce the interest rates which it desires. Not only is this possible at the Friday tender but also in the type of day-to-day dealings on the market in which the Bank has engaged since 1971. Whereas previously it had agreed not to try to influence rates in this way subsequently it has done so.

It should also be noted that Treasury bills are one of the reserve assets upon which the banking system can base the expansion of credit. It follows that one aspect of monetary policy will be the regulation of the supply of these assets, since the greater the proportion of short-term government borrowing the more liquid the banking system and the greater the danger of an inflationary monetary expansion. During the 1970s there was in fact a considerable expansion of the Treasury bill issue.

One way of dealing with this excessive liquidity was by calls for special deposits.

36. Special deposits. The scheme was first introduced in 1960. From time to time the banks may still be called upon to make special deposits with the Bank of England. They are calculated as a percentage of total bank deposits, cannot be treated as part of the cash balances (and hence reserve assets) but do yield interest, in normal circumstances the current Treasury bill rate.

The object of the special deposit scheme was to restrict the liquidity of the banks, thereby putting a brake upon lending where the traditional instruments of monetary policy had failed.

The evidence of the 1960s suggests that this scheme did not prove as effective as had been hoped. Nevertheless, it was retained in the new monetary policy of 1971.

37. Supplementary special deposits. The basis of the 1971 policy was a strictly defined and universally applicable reserve ratio against which open market operations and the special deposits scheme could be used to contain bank liquidity. With the power to create credit limited, flexible interest rates could now be left to regulate the demand for money and its allocation between different uses.

The policy did not have the potency which had been expected. The banks found it possible by a variety of means to "manufacture" their own reserve assets and thus their capacity for creating credit.

The existing instruments were therefore augmented in 1973 with a *supplementary special deposit scheme* (*"the corset"*). The scheme was suspended in 1975 and reinstated in November 1976.

The approach was different in that an attempt was made to regulate the liabilities side of the balance sheet directly rather than bringing pressure to bear upon bank assets. These liabilities of course represented "bank deposit money" (*see* VIII, **32**).

The banks were obliged to restrain the rate of growth of their *Interest Bearing Eligible Liabilities* (IBELs) to a specified percentage. If they exceeded this rate they were "fined" by being required to deposit up to 50 per cent of the excess growth in cash at zero interest.

Even this approach was not without its difficulties. By, for example, offering more free services, banks could persuade their customers away from deposit accounts and into current accounts which were not subject to the same constraints. Equally, they could direct such deposits into other interest-bearing financial assets such as Treasury bills and short-dated local government securities.

38. Problems of current monetary policy. A number of problems emerge from our discussion of money so far.

(*a*) *Should the thrust of monetary policy rest upon the control of the money supply or the manipulation of interest rates?* It has been observed that traditional monetary policy rested upon the power of a moving Bank Rate to regulate monetary demand. Modern monetarists assert that this is to approach the problem from the wrong direction. It is impossible to peg interest rates at a level different from "the natural rate" for the same reasons that it is impossible to peg the level of unemployment at anything other than the natural or market rate. This rate will be determined by the demand for loans and the availability of credit, which when granted generates an expansion of "bank deposit money". If emphasis is placed upon the supply side, upon control of the availability of credit, then the interest rate will be the product of monetary policy rather than its principal criterion.

(*b*) *What is money?* If it is conceded that emphasis should be placed upon controlling the rate of growth of the money supply, there remains the problem of a precise definition of money (*see* VII, **8**).

(*c*) *Debt management and the interest rate.* When a restrictive monetary policy results in rising interest rates this conflicts with the Bank's concern to minimise the cost of government borrowing.

(*d*) *International capital flows.* Short-term foreign investment capital ("hot money") is sensitive to differences in interest rates in the world's financial centres. Domestic rates must therefore be broadly in line with international rates if destabilising "hot money" flows are to be avoided.

(*e*) *Should there be a discretionary monetary policy?* It was shown in IV, **12**(*b*) that monetarists argue that so little is known of the precise relationship between the rate of monetary growth and aggregate demand that no attempt should be made at "fine tuning the economy".

(*f*) *Which instruments of control are effective?* Our experience of monetary policy since 1951 shows that there are major difficulties in prescribing effective instruments of monetary control (*see* **32–37** above).

MONETARY POLICY IN TRANSITION

39. Monetary Control, March 1980 Green Paper. Recognition of the problems outlined above, in particular **38**(*a*), (*b*) and (*f*), led to the publication in March 1980 of a government Green Paper followed by a number of Bank discussion papers which considered several possible modifications to the existing techniques of monetary control.

The areas in which tentative changes were being put into effect in the Spring of 1981 were as follows:

(*a*) monetary base control;
(*b*) market operations in bills (*see also* **35**);
(*c*) liquidity requirements for the banks.

40. Monetary base control. The discussion papers focused upon the possibilities of developing techniques for controlling the monetary base, thus reflecting the Bank's increasing interest in methods for *directly* regulating monetary expansion. The monetary base is seen as the ultimate foundation upon which all credit is created. It is not, however, a simple concept to define.

In a statistical note published in March 1981, the Bank suggested that "... in general terms the monetary base comprises some or all of the liabilities of the monetary authorities". There may, however, be some disagreement as to which liabilities to include. The narrow view would comprise only banks' till money and balances with the Bank of England. A broader definition would extend to notes and coin in circulation with the general public. The broadest definition of all would include other deposits, in particular public deposits (*see* Tables VI and VII).

In December 1980, the Bank was considering two types of proposal for the operation of a monetary base system:

"(*a*) non-mandatory systems in which banks are free to choose the amount of cash balances which they hold at the Bank of England; and

(*b*) mandatory systems in which banks are required to hold a specified proportion of their liabilities as cash balances at the Bank of England" (BEQB, December 1980).

During the inter-war years a mandatory 10 per cent cash ratio had been observed. This was followed by an 8 per cent ratio after 1945 and a $1\frac{1}{2}$ per cent ratio from 1971.

By March 1981, a tentative compromise solution was adopted. It was decided that "recognised banks and licensed deposit-taking institutions ... will be *required* to hold cash balances on *special, non-operational, non-interest-bearing accounts with the Bank*."

The figure proposed was $\frac{1}{2}$ per cent of eligible liabilities. In addition the London clearing banks would maintain sufficient *operational* balances for clearing purposes. Other banks would also continue to maintain such balances as are appropriate to their business.

41. Market operations in bills. The Bank has indicated the changes which will be developed in its interventions in the money markets.

(*a*) *Emphasis on open market operations.* The intention is to influence short-term interest rates through its own sales and purchases on the market rather than through "forcing the market into the Bank" as "lender of last resort" to pay minimum lending rate. It was agreed to continue these operations in the bill markets and primarily through the existing intermediaries (the London Discount Market Association) rather than in the interbank market.

(*b*) *An unpublished band of interest rates.* The operational aim

is to keep short-term rates within an unpublished band consistent
with current monetary objectives. As lender of last resort to the
discount houses, the Bank will normally charge a rate above
market rates but within the unpublished band. At "an appropriate
stage" the Bank may cease to announce a minimum lending rate.
Such arrangements should allow market factors a greater role in
determining short-term rates.

(*c*) *Offsetting cash flows.* The Bank's market operations will be
broadly intended to offset destabilising daily cash flows through
the clearing between the Bank and the money market.

42. Liquidity requirements of the banks. By December 1980, the
Bank had determined that: "Once consultations with the banking
system regarding adequate holdings of liquid assets have been
completed and *appropriate norms* agreed, the reserve asset ratio
will be abolished". A step in this direction was taken on 2nd
January 1981 with a reduction from $12\frac{1}{2}$ to 10 per cent.

Two problems then remain to be resolved, and discussions with
the banking system are continuing. Firstly, in exercising its supervisory role, the Bank recognises that for prudential purposes it
is necessary for individual banks to maintain sufficient high quality
liquid assets in relation to their deposit liabilities. While prudent
ratios may vary from bank to bank and are a matter for
management, the Bank hopes that in due course it will be possible
to establish a common measure.

Secondly, in implementing monetary policy, as we have seen the
Bank intends to lean more heavily upon its open market operations
in bills. This means that there remains a need for bill markets of
adequate size to provide the paper in which the Bank's operations
are conducted. Once the reserve ratio is abolished it is not possible
to predict exactly how the banks will adjust the quantity and
composition of their liquid assets nor the effect upon "money at
call" placed with the discount houses who are the main market
makers in bills.

To deal with this problem, adequate paper will be provided
through the expansion of the commercial bill market. A number
of "acceptors" whose bills have not hitherto been treated as
"eligible" will now be so included. To guarantee an adequate flow
of funds to the discount houses to cover this business it is suggested
that a minimum level of "secured funds" from the banks should
be agreed, at least as an interim measure.

PROGRESS TEST 9

1. Why may the Bank of England be described as a "central bank"? **(1–5)**

2. Describe the organisation of the Bank.   **(6–8)**

3. What is the nature of the assets which back the note issue? **(12)**

4. Why are public deposits at the Bank surprisingly small? **(14)**

5. What essential purpose do bankers' deposits serve?   **(15)**

6. What are "special deposits"?   **(17)**

7. Explain the phrase "lender of last resort".   **(19)**

8. What is the "proportion"?   **(21)**

9. List the three key rates of interest in the money market. **(23)**

10. How are Treasury bills issued?   **(25)**

11. Who is the "special buyer"?   **(25)**

12. How does the Bank attempt to establish an orderly gilt-edged market?   **(26)**

13. What is the Exchange Equalisation Account?   **(28)**

14. Define minimum lending rate.   **(33)**

15. Explain the use of open market operations in making minimum lending rate effective.   **(34)**

16. What problem inhibits the Bank in employing open market operations to pursue its monetary policy?   **(34)**

17. How effective has the special deposit scheme been?   **(36)**

18. Explain the operation of the supplementary special deposit scheme.   **(37)**

19. Outline the principal problem areas of modern monetary policy.   **(38)**

20. In which main areas of monetary control techniques are changes occurring in 1981?   **(39)**

21. What do you understand by "the monetary base"?   **(40)**

22. Outline the Bank's views on the liquidity requirements of banks.   **(42)**

PART THREE

INTERNATIONAL TRADE AND PAYMENTS

CHAPTER X

The Liberalisation of World Trade

THE THEORETICAL CASE FOR FREE TRADE

1. The theory of comparative costs. The gains to be derived from international trade are explained by the theory of comparative costs. This theory is best developed in stages, the first of which is the proposition that the immediate cause of international trade lies in absolute differences between domestic and foreign prices.

2. Absolute differences in international prices. Given a rate of exchange between the currencies of two countries it is possible to make direct price comparisons. When price differences exceed transportation costs between these countries it is clearly profitable for them to engage in trade. However, this is not the end of the argument, for we must now discover the reason for these price differences.

3. Absolute differences in international costs. International price differences imply absolute international differences in production costs since long-run prices, whatever the degree of competition or monopoly, must at least cover long-run costs.

So far the theory seems to make the obvious suggestion that trade between two countries will be profitable when each specialises in the production of those goods for which it has the lowest costs of production. This is not the whole story, however, for trade may still take place in two commodities between two countries and to their mutual benefit even when one country has an absolute advantage in the production of both goods provided that each country has dissimilar cost ratios. This proposition is the core of the theory of comparative cost.

4. Dissimilar cost ratios. The principle may be illustrated by two simple arithmetical examples. Assume in each case trade between two countries only, the USA and the UK, and in only two goods, wheat and textiles.

EXAMPLE 1: *The USA having lower production costs in wheat, the UK in textiles.*

Let us assume that in the USA 10 units of resources (land, labour and capital) will produce either 10 tonnes of wheat or 5 metres of cloth and that in the UK 10 units of resources will produce either 10 metres of cloth or 5 tonnes of wheat. While in this example neither country has an absolute advantage in the production of both goods each has a comparative advantage in the production of one.

If we further assume that the USA has 300 resource units and the UK 200 and that each divides its production evenly between wheat and textiles, total output will be as follows:

TABLE VIII.   *Example of production figures before trade*

	Resource units	Metres of cloth	Tonnes of wheat
USA	300	75	150
UK	200	100	50
Total	500	175	200

Let each country now specialise completely in that commodity in which it enjoys a comparative advantage and the result will be as follows:

TABLE IX.   *Production figures after specialisation*

	Resource units	Metres of cloth	Tonnes of wheat
USA	300	—	300
UK	200	200	—
Total	500	200	300

As a result of specialisation, the total output of the two countries has been maximised and trade will take place to their mutual advantage at any exchange rate within the limits determined by their respective cost ratios, i.e. 5 metres of cloth: 10 tonnes of wheat and 5 tonnes of wheat: 10 metres of cloth. At the limits trade may still take place although all the benefit will be enjoyed by one or the other country.

EXAMPLE 2: *The USA having lower production costs in both wheat and textiles.*

More significantly trade may still be mutually advantageous even though the USA has an absolute advantage in the production of both wheat and textiles.

Let us now assume that in the USA 10 units of resources will produce 10 tonnes of wheat or 9 metres of cloth and that in the UK the same quantity of resources will yield only 4 tonnes of wheat or 8 metres of cloth. Again assuming the USA to have 300 resource units and the UK 200, each dividing their resources equally between the two goods, the result will be as follows:

TABLE X.   *Production figures before trade,*
one country having an absolute advantage

	Resource units	Metres of cloth	Tonnes of wheat
USA	300	135	150
UK	200	80	40
Total	500	215	190

If there is now complete specialisation in the products for which each has a comparative advantage the result will be:

TABLE XI.   *Production figures after trade, each*
country having a comparative advantage

	Resource units	Metres of cloth	Tonnes of wheat
USA	300	—	300
UK	200	160	—
Total	500	160	300

The effect of complete specialisation has been a substantial increase in total wheat production but a fall in the production of cloth. The UK even when devoting all its resources to this activity is unable to achieve the previous figures. For this reason specialisation in the USA will not be complete and resources will still be directed to cloth production:

TABLE XII.   *Production figures increased even with incomplete specialisation*

	Resource units	Metres of cloth	Tonnes of wheat
USA	300	81	210
UK	200	160	—
Total	500	241	210

Let us assume that 30 per cent of her resources are so used. In this position total output of both cloth and wheat has been increased as a result of specialisation. Again, at any exchange rate within the limits set by their respective cost ratios each is able to enjoy a higher consumption of both cloth and wheat.

5. Significance of comparative costs. From the foregoing discussion it will be seen that it is differences in "comparative" not "absolute" costs which provide the basis for international trade and that impediments to such trade serve to restrict the growth of total output and rising world living standards.

However, the benefits of increased world output will not be evenly distributed between countries but will depend upon "the terms of trade."

6. The terms of trade. The terms of trade between two countries are dictated by the elasticity of each country's demand for imports relative to the elasticity of the supply of the other country's exports.

In Table IX above if US demand for textiles is relatively stronger than the UK demand for wheat then the terms of trade will move in favour of the UK. A world price for wheat will be established at an exchange ratio approximating to 10 tonnes of wheat: 5 metres of cloth. If the terms of trade move against the UK the world price of textiles is falling and the new exchange ratio will be closer to 5 tonnes of wheat: 10 metres of cloth.

In the inter-war period the terms of trade moved against the primary producing countries in favour of the manufacturing countries since the world price of raw materials and foodstuffs fell more steeply than the world price of manufactures. To this extent the hardships of industrial depression were somewhat mitigated. After 1945 the sharp upturn in the demand of the manufacturing countries for raw materials moved the terms of trade in favour of the primary producers, until 1955. Thereafter, the movement was again generally in favour of the industrial countries.

THE EMPIRICAL ARGUMENT FOR FREE TRADE

7. Great Britain and her free traders. At the close of the Napoleonic Wars British commerce lay strangled by a complex web of import and export duties. Almost every item which entered into trade was subject to taxes upon which government depended for the greater part of its revenue.

On the other hand British industry had no rival anywhere else in the world and felt in no need of protective customs duties. Rapid industrialisation had built up enormous production potential which required the safety-valve of wider overseas markets. It was argued that lower import duties would reduce the price of food and raw materials. The result would be lower wage and production costs. Moreover, if Britain led the way in lowering duties the foreigner might be induced to follow.

The consequence of these pressures was the great British free trade movement beginning in the 1820s when Huskisson initiated a reduction of duties. The process was continued by Peel and completed by Gladstone. By the 1860s all protective duties had been abolished. There remained only a few "countervailing customs duties" (i.e. duties on imports which correspond to internal excise duties).

8. The results of free trade. The full effects of free trading policies can be observed in the extremely rapid expansion of British overseas trade in the years 1850–70. (It should, however, be noted that there also existed other favourable circumstances.)

APPROXIMATE VALUE OF EXPORTS (£m.)

1850	1854	1860	1870
71	97	135	250

Moreover, as had been hoped, other European nations began to emulate Britain's example in reducing tariffs (e.g. Holland, Portugal, Switzerland, Germany, Austria and most notably France as a result of the Cobden Commercial Treaty, 1860).

The last quarter of the century, although a period of depression and falling prices, saw a continued expansion in the volume of British exports.

9. Reaction to free trade. Until 1870 the strength of her industry enabled Britain to enjoy a virtual monopoly of exported manufactures throughout the world. Thereafter, her competitors began to gather strength, their developing industry increasingly sheltered by rising tariffs. In 1880 Germany raised duties and was shortly followed by France. In 1890 the effects of the McKinley Tariff in the USA were especially severe for UK exports. The Dingley Tariff of 1897 finally committed the USA to a policy of protection and in 1902 Germany followed suit.

At this stage it may be argued that protection was invaluable to the newly developing industrial countries since it assisted them to narrow Britain's lead and, in some industries, to overhaul her. In any event the total volume of world trade continued to expand and by 1914 there had developed an intricate pattern of international specialisation.

10. Economic nationalism, 1920–39. After a short-lived boom the world economy sank into depression. Four years of war had disrupted the pattern of international trade. Old customers had turned to alternative suppliers or had developed domestic sources. Throughout the industrial world unemployment figures rose and international payments were unbalanced. In the prevailing climate of political and economic uncertainty nations everywhere sought self-sufficiency. Reverting to an earlier ideal they believed that only in economic independence could national security be achieved. This thinking made itself manifest in high protective tariffs which aimed hopefully to conserve the domestic market for domestic industry, thus guaranteeing some measure of employment.

11. The consequences for international trade. Attempts by one country to penalise the exports of another could only lead to retaliatory action, to the detriment of both. The volume of world trade therefore shrank. The decline was accelerated by the practice, adopted increasingly after the 1929–31 slump, of bilateral trading agreements which replaced the normal multilateral basis of world trade and payments. (Bilateral trade requires each country to balance its payments separately with all its trading partners. The total volume is therefore dictated by the country with the lower imports. Multilateral trade enables a country with a deficit in one part of the world to finance it with a surplus earned elsewhere. Total trade is maximised.)

12. Britain's return to protection. While Britain remained wedded to the ideal of free trade long after her competitors had taken refuge in protection the slump brought some of her major industries to the verge of collapse. Under mounting pressure from manufacturers the government agreed to afford a degree of protection to the home market and in 1932 the Import Duties Act was passed. Free trade was now a dead letter.

13. Conclusion. In international economic relationships as in domestic affairs, the Second World War provided a radically new approach. It was appreciated that there would need to be a high degree of co-operation between nations if the pre-war stagnation of world trade was not to be repeated.

The objective was to be a balanced expansion of international trade which would lead to rising world living standards. Instrumental to this ultimate goal would be three subsidiary aims:

(*a*) the gradual reduction and final abolition of protective duties and quotas throughout the world (*see* **19–32** below);

(*b*) international co-operation to improve the means of financing world trade (*see* XII, **31–41**);

(*c*) the promotion of investment by the advanced countries in the developing countries in order that the latter might play a fuller part in an expanding world economy (*see* XII, **53–56**).

While it is true to say that the validity of the general principle of free trade has now been universally accepted there remain certain reservations.

THE CASE FOR PROTECTION

14. Political and strategic reasons. Government economic policies are by no means based solely upon objective economic considerations. Political or social pressures may be such that a government finds itself impelled to afford protection to a particular sector of the economy. In the USA powerful sectional interests have frequently been successful in persuading government in this way to reduce the intensity of foreign competition.

Again, for strategic reasons a country may feel it necessary to develop domestic sources of supply if it believes that complete dependence upon an overseas source may leave it exposed to unwelcome foreign pressures.

In a more extreme way, when there exists the possibility of military confrontation there will be no inclination to assist the opponent's economy by engaging in trade, e.g. until June 1971 there was a complete embargo by the USA on all trade with China.

In short there may be, at least in the short term, a perfectly valid case for restricting foreign trade based upon factors which override purely economic considerations.

15. Assistance for infant industries. Possibly the only sound economic argument in favour of protection is that which claims that it is necessary to give short-term assistance to new industry in order that it may establish itself.

This argument will be particularly valid where there is initially an investment of a high proportion of capital. At first output will be small and unit costs very high. As output expands and the economies of scale are enjoyed, so unit costs fall and the industry becomes more internationally competitive. At this stage it is then desirable that the protective duty should be removed and that the industry should stand on its own feet. The difficulty is that once interests have become entrenched there is likely to be considerable resistance to the removal of the duty.

Moreover, there is always a considerable possibility that an industry will be encouraged which has no real chance of survival in competitive conditions.

16. Correction of the balance of payments. It may be argued that where there is an adverse balance of payments it is legitimate to restrict the volume of imports and to encourage domestic import-displacing industry. However, pre-war experience suggests that such action invites retaliation from the country against whose exports there is discrimination. The problem then escalates.

The General Agreement on Tariffs and Trade (*see* **24**(*b*) below) exceptionally permits this practice but only after the fullest international consultation.

17. Protection against "dumping". It may occur that a foreign producer is able to practise "discriminating monopoly". He produces on a large scale in order to gain the advantage of low unit costs but restricts supply to his home market in order to secure a high price. He then disposes of the surplus overseas at very low prices, if necessary below total unit cost. The British steel market was opposed to such "unfair competition" from the German steel cartel in the 1920s producing, inevitably, a demand for protection which was finally acceded to in 1932.

18. Protection of vested interests. In old-established industries there may be built up a vast stock of fixed capital which will seem of great value to the owners but may in due course become obsolescent. Similarly, the workers in these industries will acquire specialist skills, in which they too have a vested interest.

If such an industry is now faced with a new foreign competitor whose production costs and selling prices are infinitely lower there will be a demand for protection against "unfair" foreign competition. Such was the appeal of the Lancashire cotton industry when faced with competition from Japan and Hong Kong where wage rates were relatively much lower.

A too simplistic economic answer to such an appeal would be that cheap imports could only be of benefit to the UK economy as a whole and that it would be better to divert the factors of production currently devoted to cotton manufacture to some other activity commanding a higher return. However, factors of production in the form of mills, textile machinery, skilled spinners and weavers are relatively immobile. They cannot suddenly be translated into, for example, a motor assembly plant.

Thus, if the running down of an industry is generally agreed to be desirable it may also be conceded that in the short term a degree of protection is necessary to ease the difficulties of reallocating resources.

THE GENERAL AGREEMENT ON TARIFFS AND TRADE (GATT)

19. The goal of global multilateral trade. It has been observed that during the Second World War a good deal of thought was directed towards the creation of a liberal, multilateral system of world trade. Close co-operation was envisaged in the field of international trade relations, payments and investment. Wartime planning produced the most striking results in respect of payments and investment with the setting up of the International Monetary Fund and the International Bank for Reconstruction and Development. Co-operation in respect of trade was somewhat delayed.

After the war, it quickly became apparent that the original objective was overly ambitious and, faced with Communist expansion, attention was concentrated upon promoting European co-operation and reconstruction to meet this threat. In the 1950s and 1960s therefore the most notable achievements in liberalising trade have been regional in nature and have been centred upon Europe.

20. The abortive International Trade Organisation (ITO). The end of excessively ambitious international planning was marked by the failure of the US Congress in 1950 to ratify the treaty setting up an International Trade Organisation. The ITO Charter had been signed by fifty-four countries in March 1948 and covered a very wide range of topics including not only trade but also employment, cartels, economic development and state trading.

The failure of the ITO might have signalled the end of any global attack on tariffs but for the almost accidental birth of GATT.

21. Nature of GATT. In 1947 an international conference met in Geneva to consider a draft charter for ITO. As a sign of good faith the USA also engaged immediately in negotiations with twenty-two other countries which resulted in commitments on 45,000 different rates of duty embodied within principles laid down by a "General Agreement on Tariffs and Trade". On 1st January 1948, GATT began its life when eight of the contracting countries made effective the concessions negotiated in Geneva. At this stage GATT was viewed simply as a provisional arrangement which would lapse once the ITO was established. In the event it has remained the principal instrument for achieving tariff reductions on a global scale.

It should be noted that technically GATT, unlike the IMF or the IBRD, is not an organisation but a treaty and that the signatories are not strictly speaking "members" but "contracting parties". However, it does have a permanent secretariat located in Switzerland and since 1953 an informal court to consider disputes.

22. The basic principles of GATT. The Agreement comprises thirty-eight Articles and many annexes and schedules covering the thousands of concessions which have subsequently been negotiated.

There are, however, four basic principles as follows.

(*a*) *Most favoured nation treatment* (*mfn*). This first rule requires that any concession made to one signatory must be made equally to all.

(*b*) *A binding commitment* to observe all concessions already negotiated.

(*c*) *A general prohibition against quantitative restrictions* (quotas).

(*d*) *Developing countries.* Special provisions in respect of the trade of the developing countries.

Articles not concerned with these general principles relate to exceptions to the rules and to other commercial measures whose effect may be to impede trade.

23. Tariff obligations. The signatories are obliged to accord mfn treatment to each other in respect of duties, customs regulations and internal taxes and regulations.

The exceptions to this general rule are:

(*a*) *an existing well-known tariff preference*, e.g. Commonwealth preference;

(*b*) *a full customs union or a free trade area*, e.g. EEC, EFTA.

Once negotiated, concessions must be observed except where it can be demonstrated that as a result imports have risen so steeply as to constitute a threat to domestic producers.

24. Quantitative restrictions. While there is a general prohibition against quota restrictions, among the several exceptions to the rule the four most important are in respect of the following.

(*a*) *Agriculture.* Quotas may be imposed upon agricultural imports when it can be shown that they are necessary for the implementation of government policies on marketing and production control.

(*b*) *Balance of payments.* When a country's monetary reserves are in jeopardy quotas may be applied but may be continued only in close consultation with the other signatories.

(*c*) *National security.* Trade may be directly controlled when national security is at issue.

(*d*) *Developing countries.* Developing countries are permitted to impose non-discriminatory import restrictions as a means of fostering infant industry.

In all cases where quotas are permitted they must be applied in accordance with the mfn principle.

25. Specific measures to assist developing countries. A new Part IV headed "Trade and Development" was added to the Agreement in 1965 and comprises three Articles which oblige the advanced countries:

(*a*) *to give high priority to the reduction and elimination of restrictions on those goods which are of especial interest to the developing countries;*

(*b*) *to refrain from introducing all new restrictions on such products;*

(*c*) *to give favourable internal tax treatment to the primary products of the developing countries.*

The developing countries are equally obliged under Part IV to take similar action in respect of the trade of those countries less developed than themselves.

26. Operational procedures. The signatories of GATT meet annually and also at special tariff conferences. Between meetings an Intersessional Committee prepares agendas while working parties report on specific topics. The existence of a permanent secretariat adds continually to the work of GATT and enables it to behave more like genuine international organisations.

The work falls into three categories:

(*a*) the elimination of quota restrictions;

(*b*) the regulation of disputes;

(*c*) the reduction of tariffs.

27. Elimination of quota restrictions. For as long as a chronic imbalance remained in payments between the USA and the rest of the world the majority of signatories took advantage of the balance of payments exception to the general prohibition of quotas. In 1958, the USA for the first time moved into deficit and the Western European countries were able both to restore the convertibility of currencies and the following year at the Tokyo session of GATT to reaffirm their intention to abandon the balance of payments escape clause as soon as possible. Subsequently, all the major trading nations gave up the quantitative restrictions which had been justified on these grounds.

The remaining major problems in this area related to restrictions upon agricultural products in which progress has been disappointingly slow.

Countries which still make use of the balance of payments exception are required to hold periodical consultations with GATT as a means of exerting pressure upon them. Discussions are also mandatory when new restrictions are to be imposed.

NOTE: When in 1964 Britain imposed a 15 per cent import surcharge as a measure to correct the balance of payments the rules were violated since although it is permissible to employ quantitative restrictions for this purpose an increased tariff may not be so employed. In consultation with GATT considerable pressure was exerted for the early removal of this surcharge.

28. Regulation of disputes. It is in this little publicised area that GATT has enjoyed some of its most notable successes. Previously trade disputes often went unresolved for many years, souring international relations and normally ending in success for the stronger party.

GATT has improved matters by providing a world forum before which grievances can be aired and also a formal complaints procedure. Many disputes have been resolved bilaterally, probably assisted by the knowledge that GATT stands in the background, e.g. the UK Government was persuaded to repeal a restriction upon the manufacture of pure Virginia cigarettes when the USA protested that this violated the General Agreement.

If the dispute is not settled by the parties concerned an appeal may be made to the collective membership. A report is drafted and recommendations made. If these recommendations are not observed the complainant country may be authorised to suspend certain of its trade obligations to the other country *but* only to a degree which will not escalate the dispute, e.g. the 1962 "chicken war". The EEC increased rates of duty on poultry imports which were mainly from the USA. The dispute was unresolved and upon appeal to GATT it was calculated that US exports had suffered by $26 million in 1963. The USA was then authorised to reduce concessions to EEC by an amount which would have a similar effect on the Community's trade. Duties were raised on brandy, trucks and other imports by an amount which affected EEC trade by a sum estimated at $25.4 million.

Although in this case the dispute was not settled the main point is that retaliation was limited and there was no further escalation of the problem.

29. Reduction of tariffs. The major achievement of GATT has been a series of six tariff conferences (the last being the "Kennedy Round"), at which reductions have been effected on more than 60,000 rates of duty covering more than half the world's trade.

In each new agreement the mfn principle is applied. Before each conference the participants prepare a list of products on which they are prepared to negotiate. Countries are then paired on the "chief supplier" principle, i.e. one country negotiates on those products which are chiefly supplied by a second country. The negotiations result in a large number of bilateral agreements which are then incorporated in a single muster agreement to which each country appends a signature. All the signatories then enjoy all the concessions which have been made at that conference. A set of bilateral agreements have been in this way made multilateral in effect.

The advantage of this system lies primarily in the time saved and difficulties avoided were a similar volume of concessions to be negotiated independently by separate trade agreements. Moreover, conferences provide an atmosphere in which countries are disposed to be generous since while negotiating they know that they are about to receive many more benefits from other negotiations taking place concurrently.

30. The Kennedy Round. As duties have been lowered negotiations have become tougher and more protracted, the Kennedy Round lasting from May 1964 to June 1967. At this conference the procedure was somewhat different. Instead of negotiations being based upon specific products it was felt that more rapid progress would be made by linear reductions of all national tariffs with minimal lists of excepted goods. In the case of the USA the Administration had authority to halve the tariff with only ten excepted products and to abolish all duties which did not exceed 5 per cent. The results although not as spectacular as had been hoped were nevertheless most notable.

The major industrial countries reduced tariffs on imports valued at $26 billion in 1964. Some 70 per cent of the reductions were of the order of 50 per cent or more. In the UK cuts on industrial imports averaged 38 per cent. The major benefits to UK exports have resulted from the reductions made by the EEC,

USA and Japan while the same countries have been the principal beneficiaries of the UK cuts.

Although progress at this conference was essentially limited to manufactured goods and to tariff restrictions on trade, it is generally agreed that both the scope and scale of the cuts achieved were infinitely more significant than those resulting from any previous negotiations and that for many manufactured products duties will cease to be a restriction to trade.

31. The Tokyo Round. A ministerial meeting of GATT was held in Tokyo in September 1973 and attended by eighty-three contracting members. They formally launched international negotiations intended to produce agreement on a new set of general tariff cuts and reductions in other barriers to world trad.

That little progress has subsequently been made is in no small part due to the effect upon world trading arrangements of the instability of exchange rates throughout the 1970s (*see* XII, **42–48**).

32. Appraisal of GATT. In the first place it must be acknowledged that GATT has provided a context for orderly international trade negotiations without historical parallel. In its thirty years of existence it has achieved a massive reduction of the obstacles to trade throughout the world.

On the other hand its success has been largely confined to trade in manufactured goods. Relatively little progress has been made in respect of agricultural products. This failure has given rise to some scepticism in the developing countries and the likelihood of continuing pressure through UNCTAD for the revision of GATT's rules in a way more favourable to those countries.

NOTE: United Nations Conference on Trade and Development (UNCTAD), first convened in 1964, is supposed to meet every three years.

33. Organisation for Trade Co-operation (OTC). A weakness of the GATT arrangements is that they are provisional and may be dissolved at any time. An attempt to rectify this difficulty was made in 1955 when the signatories negotiated an Organisation for Trade Co-operation, which was to be a permanent world organisation to administer GATT. Due to the opposition of protectionist interests, primarily in the USA, this agreement has never been ratified.

EUROPEAN ECONOMIC COMMUNITY (EEC)

34. Organisation for European Economic Co-operation (OEEC).
OEEC was established in 1948 and comprised sixteen countries.
Its initial task was the administration of Marshall Aid (American
assistance to Europe) in the Joint European Recovery Programme.
It then developed as an organisation for general economic co-
operation whose major achievement lay in the progressive
removal of quantitative restrictions upon European trade assisted
by a system of multilateral payments, the European Payments
Union. (When in 1958 ten European countries adopted global
convertibility of their currencies on current account, the EPU
lost its function and was brought to a close.)

**35. Organisation for Economic Co-operation and Development
(OECD).** By the close of the 1950s Europe had made considerable
progress in the liberalisation of trade and payments, but simultaneously increasing economic interdependence between Europe
and North America had brought the need for fresh forms of co-
operation. Therefore, in 1961, OEEC was replaced by OECD. (To
OEEC's membership of Austria, Belgium, Denmark, France, Germany, Greece, Iceland, Ireland, Italy, Luxembourg, the Nether-
lands, Norway, Portugal, Sweden, Switzerland, Turkey and the
UK were added Canada, Spain and the USA and, in 1965, Japan.)

Through a series of committees OECD seeks to promote co-
operation in a wide variety of economic fields and aims at the
development of the whole free world. In this respect it is more
outward looking than OEEC which was concerned only with the
development of Europe.

36. European Coal and Steel Community. In the early 1950s strong
arguments were being advanced in Europe for much closer economic integration than was possible under the auspices of OEEC.
If Europe was to compete with the continental economies of the
USA and the Soviet Union then industrial rationalism was necessary across frontiers. A single mass European market would enable
the economies of scale to be exploited to the full.

The first fruit of this thinking was the establishment in 1952 of
the European Coal and Steel Community (ECSC). All restrictions
on trade in coal, steel and iron-ore between Belgium, the Nether-
lands, Luxembourg, France, Germany and Italy were abolished
while a common tariff on these commodities was adopted against
countries outside the group.

37. Treaty establishing the European Economic Community (Treaty of Rome), 1957. In 1955, the members of the ECSC decided to enlarge the scope of their agreement to cover the whole of their economies. Negotiations led to the signing of the Treaty of Rome on 25th March 1957 and its implementation from 1st January 1958. (Simultaneously a separate treaty set up a European Atomic Energy Community, Euratom.)

The treaty is a complex document comprising more than 200 Articles. The objectives may be classified in the following way.

(*a*) *The creation of a full customs union* with free trade in industrial and agricultural products (*see* **38–39** below).

(*b*) *The creation of a common market in labour, enterprise and capital* (*see* **40** below). The free movement of people, businesses, and capital.

(*c*) *The ultimate integration of national economies into a single European economy* (*see* **41** below).

(*d*) *Political union* (*see* **42** below).

38. A full customs union. There are two aspects to the creation of a full customs union: firstly, the abolition of all restrictions upon trade within the group and, secondly, the adoption by the union of a common external tariff and commercial policy.

The treaty envisaged a transitional period of between twelve and fifteen years. In the event progress was more rapid than anticipated and all tariff and quota restrictions (other than in exceptional circumstances) were finally abolished on 1st July 1968.

While the establishment of free trade in industrial products had brought rapid benefits and raised relatively few problems, free trade in agricultural products presented many more difficulties.

39. A common agricultural policy (CAP). The basic problem derives from a technological revolution in European farming methods which is rapidly raising productivity, tending to depress prices and cause vast numbers of farmers to leave the land. Already the Community is fully self-sufficient in pork, sugar, potatoes, vegetables, milk and butter and almost self-sufficient in cheese, poultry, veal, beef, wheat and feed grains. On occasion the output of some commodities outstrips demand. The difficulty has therefore been to establish free trade in these goods and at the same time secure the economic position of the Community's farmers.

The structure of the common agricultural policy is based upon the following four factors.

(a) *Target price*. This is the base price established by reference to the region of the Community with the least adequate supplies. Subsidies are then paid as necessary to enable farmers to achieve the target price.

(b) *Intervention price*. This is the guaranteed minimum selling price at which the Community will purchase all surpluses. It stands at a given percentage below target price.

(c) *Threshold price*. This provides the basis for calculating the variable import levy. Having allowed for the transportation and marketing costs of imports it is the price necessary to bring the price of these imports into line with the target price. In short, imports from outside the Community are not permitted to compete with any price advantage.

(d) *Variable import levy*. This is constantly recalculated and is equivalent to the difference between the world price of the commodity and the Community's threshold price.

EXAMPLE:

	Per tonne of wheat	
	$	$
Target price		96.00
Intervention price		88.00
Threshold price		
Target price	96.00	
Less Marketing/transport costs	4.00	92.00
Variable import levy		
Threshold price	92.00	
Less World price	56.00	36.00

Two important aspects of this policy should be noted. In the first place the Community operates no production controls to eliminate possible surpluses. Secondly, the variable import levy serves to make countries outside the Community the residual suppliers of those products which the Community cannot itself produce in their entirety.

40. A common market in labour, capital and enterprise. Already free movement of individuals in search of work is permitted within the EEC and social legislation and labour law are being harmonised so that all workers enjoy the same rights and protection.

Firms also are able to move freely, to expand throughout the union or to participate in mergers. Progress is also being made on the elimination of restrictions which impede the rationalisation of service industries, insurance, banking, law and medicine.

41. The full integration of national economies. Free trade is only the first step in the creation of a wholly effective customs union. Beyond this lies the harmonisation of many aspects of the social and economic life of the uniting countries. It is necessary to develop a common approach to monopolies and mergers, transportation and energy, fiscal and monetary policy, prices and incomes and social security services to name but a few areas in which differences must be eliminated.

The progress made by the EEC in this direction has been quite substantial in those matters specifically covered by the Treaty of Rome but hesitant in matters dependent upon negotiation by the Council of Ministers. The field in which least success has been achieved is that of monetary and fiscal policy since these are subjects which lie at the heart of national sovereignty. Integration here seems to depend upon simultaneous progress towards some form of political union.

42. Political union. Since the Second World War many Europeans have seen political union as the ultimate goal. Early attempts to achieve this objective directly were too ambitious and attention therefore turned to economic union as a first step.

In 1961 the six countries reaffirmed that the ultimate objective of the EEC was to achieve a formal political union. However, a gulf has remained between the French concept of a loose confederation of sovereign states and the broadly agreed aim of the remaining five of a supranational federal government. At the present time therefore political integration would seem to be a distant, if desirable goal.

43. EEC institutions. There are four basic institutions.

(*a*) *The Commission.* This represents the Community itself as distinct from the member states. It is a fourteen-member executive body (following the accession of Greece in January 1981), the larger countries, i.e. the UK, France, West Germany and Italy, appointing two Commissioners, and the remaining countries appointing one. Each Commissioner has a specific portfolio, and the Commission administers Community policies and proposes fresh ones to the Council of Ministers.

(*b*) *The European Council.* The Council comprises the Heads of State of the ten member countries. It makes the final decision on policy proposals made by the Commission and it is therefore through this instrument that national governments are able to influence the evolution of the Community.

(c) *Court of Justice.* The Court is the sole arbiter of the legality of actions taken by the Commission and the Council and its decisions have the force of law throughout the Community.

(d) *European Parliament.* This body has little real power save for its right to remove the Commission upon a vote of censure.

BRITAIN AND THE EUROPEAN COMMUNITIES

44. European Free Trade Area (EFTA). In the mid-1950s Britain was unprepared for obligations as far reaching as those implied by the Rome Treaty. Her trade was global rather than focused upon Europe and the Community's common external tariff seemed to threaten old-established relations, particularly those with the Commonwealth. Moreover, the implications of political union seemed unacceptable to a country which had never really visualised itself as an integral part of Europe.

Britain therefore engaged in negotiations to establish a broad free trading area based upon the membership of OEEC and of which the newly established EEC would be a part. This attempt broke down in 1958, whereupon attention was directed to securing the co-operation of other European countries. In 1960 the Stockholm Convention set up the European Free Trade Area comprising the UK, Norway, Sweden, Denmark, Portugal, Switzerland and Austria.

The main provision was that tariff and quantitative restrictions upon trade in industrial products should be progressively removed. This differed from the EEC arrangements in that there was no provision for a common external tariff. Each member was completely free to determine its own trade policies with the rest of the world.

45. UK applications to join the EEC. By the early 1960s opinion in Britain was beginning to shift. The rapid economic expansion in Europe resulting from the creation of the EEC could now be observed. Moreover, despite the growing obstacle of the Community's common external tariff this was the segment of the UK's overseas trade which was expanding most rapidly.

Consequently, in 1961 Britain opened negotiations to enter the Community. This was followed in 1962 by the remaining members of EFTA expressing a willingness to join or become associate members. In 1963 negotiations were abruptly halted when France unilaterally vetoed British entry.

In May 1967, a second application for full membership was lodged. In December of the same year the Council of Ministers failed to reach unanimous agreement on the British application which was nevertheless kept on record and reconsidered over the following two years. Finally, at the end of 1969 it was agreed to open negotiations with the UK and other candidate countries as soon as the necessary preparatory work could be completed.

46. The basis of the UK application. The reasons for the UK's application and the basic issues for negotiation are to be found in a 1967 White Paper (Cmnd. 3269) and in a statement by the Foreign Secretary on 4th July 1967.

(*a*) *From the economic point of view* the White Paper spoke of "the long-term potential for Europe, and therefore for Britain, of the creation of a single market of approaching 300 million people with all the scope and incentive which this will provide for British industry, and of the enormous possibilities which an integrated strategy for technology on a truly continental scale, can create."

(*b*) *From the political point of view* the White Paper pointed out that whatever the economic arguments "the Government's purpose derives above all from our recognition that Europe is now faced with the opportunity of a great move forward in political unity and that we can—and indeed we must—play our full part in it ... Together we can ensure that Europe plays in world affairs the part which the Europe of today is not at present playing."

(*c*) *The fundamental issues for negotiation* were said by the Foreign Secretary to include the inequitable burden upon Britain of the EEC's existing financial arrangements for agriculture; the need for a transitional period; the need to make provision for the interests of the developing countries particularly those dependent on the Commonwealth Sugar Agreement; and the need to make provision for New Zealand's dairy products.

47. Accession and renegotiation. On 1st January 1973, the UK acceded to the Treaty of Rome and was joined by Denmark and Eire. "The Six" became "the Nine".

There were, however, many in both the Labour and Conservative Parties who were not sympathetic to membership. They continued to stress what they believed to be the economic disadvantages to Britain, particularly the ultimate loss of independence to manage the economy with purely national objectives.

The incoming Labour Government therefore undertook to re-negotiate the terms of British membership. Four basic reasons were advanced.

(a) *The burden of the Community budget.* It was argued that Britain enjoyed only 14 per cent of the Community's Gross Domestic Product but contributed 24 per cent of the budget. When the negotiations were concluded at a summit meeting in Dublin in March 1975, this problem had been remedied with a new mechanism which automatically corrected "disproportionate contributions".

(b) *The common agricultural policy was particularly onerous for Britain.* It was made clear that Britain was making no attempt to change the terms of the Treaty of Rome, only to improve the application of certain clauses. The CAP, it was said, limited access to world markets and encouraged the production of surpluses, particularly in respect of certain products such as beef and butter. It kept selling prices unnecessarily high and was too inflexible since it did not differentiate in its treatment of the problems of different areas of the Community.

Some concessions were made to the British point of view.

(c) *The constraints upon trade relations with the Commonwealth and the Third World.* The common tariff had an adverse effect upon trade in agricultural products which was in the interests neither of the producing countries nor of the consuming countries in the EEC. Little progress seems ever to have been made in dealing with this complaint, except in respect of the spcific case of New Zealand. At the conclusion of Britain's five-year transitional period at the end of 1977 concessions were made for the access of New Zealand dairy produce for a three-year period.

(d) *Regional policy.* Britain argued for a measure of independence which would otherwise have been denied, in dealing with her severe regional problems by a variety of methods which amounted to subsidisation. This implied "unfair competition" with parallel industries in Europe. Advantage has been taken of the concessions which were made.

The Government considered that the renegotiations had been successful and recommended that the UK's membership of the EEC should continue.

48. The referendum. During 1975 a powerful campaign was mounted by the supporters and the opponents of British membership to determine finally whether the UK should remain in the Community. A referendum in June produced an overwhelming response in favour.

A NOTE ON THE EUROPEAN COMMUNITY
IN THE 1980s

49. An evaluation of current progress. For all of the members, the twenty-three years of the Community's existence have seen a continuing and still unresolved battle between national and "European" interests.

On the credit side, an EEC citizen has the right to live and work anywhere in the Community and his social security rights are transferable. Theoretically, manufacturers and agricultural produce can move freely across frontiers. The reality is rather different since there has been only limited progress in the harmonisation of fiscal systems, much less tax rates, e.g. VAT rates differ, rising to 33.3 per cent in France. Taxes on alcohol, cigarettes and other items vary and customs posts remain. Moreover, non-tariff obstacles to trade are not infrequently created, e.g. the British ban on French milk on health grounds; the German ban on British beer since it does not meet certain German criteria; the French ban on British lamb without any supportable grounds.

The feature of the Community which continues to be most heavily criticised is the Common Agricultural Policy. Agricultural surpluses are rising at a rate which by universal agreement the Community cannot afford. Member governments, however, are in no mood for major reforms and the most that can be hoped for is modification of the system.

In short, after almost two decades during which the basic objectives of the Treaty of Rome were achieved, by the early 1970s the European momentum had slowed down. Britain joined at what may now be considered the worst possible time. In 1973, European economies were beginning to stagnate after years of uninterrupted growth and inflation was rising.

50. Britain's continuing complaints. The major irritants continue to be a CAP expressly designed for Continental interests and the inequity of Britain's contribution to the Community budget. Following much negotiation, in May 1980 the net contribution for that year after deduction of regional grants, refunds and other rebates amounted to £371.5 million, a cut of 8 per cent. However, the struggle over the appropriate share for the future is far from resolved.

Additionally, "harmonisation" has led to a growing volume of complaints about the excessive bureaucracy of the Brussels administration. The attempts to devise European definitions and standards for manufactured and agricultural products have encountered severe criticism from politicians, trade unions and trade associations. The EEC answers these criticisms by pointing out that the purpose of "harmonisation" is to remove non-tariff barriers to trade.

51. Political opposition to EEC membership. On other than economic grounds, opposition to EEC membership continues to be spread across the two major political parties. Many find the surrender of any aspect of national sovereignty to be unacceptable. The Labour Party National Conference, 1980, declared that without substantial renegotiation of the Treaty of Rome (which in practice the EEC would not countenance) a future Labour Government would take Britain out of the Community. This would seem a logical position to adopt by a Party now committed to a very high degree of central economic planning and Government intervention which would be emasculated by EEC membership.

Others view this prospect with alarm and further, consider that any attempt to extricate Britain from the economic relationships with Europe already established would be potentially catastrophic.

52. Enlargement of the Community. In 1978 membership applications were made by Greece, Spain and Portugal. Greece signed a treaty of accession in May 1979 with effect from January 1981. Negotiations with Spain and Portugal continue with some opposition from France's agricultural interests.

PROGRESS TEST 10

1. Explain the theory of comparative costs. **(1–5)**
2. What do you understand by "the terms of trade"? **(6)**
3. What benefit did the UK derive from free trade in the nineteenth century? **(8)**
4. Explain the phrase "economic nationalism". **(10)**
5. What effect did the economic nationalism of the 1930s have upon international trade? **(11)**

6. List the reasons which might validly be offered in support of protection. **(14–18)**

7. What was the ITO? **(20)**

8. Single out the main features of GATT. **(22)**

9. What is the mfn principle? **(22(a))**

10. What exceptions are there to the general prohibition of quotas? **(24)**

11. Give an example of GATT's success in reducing the strain of international trade disputes. **(28)**

12. Outline the results of the Kennedy Round. **(30)**

13. What is the Tokyo round? **(31)**

14. Describe the evolution of OECD. **(34–35)**

15. What are the main features of the Treaty of Rome? **(37)**

16. Distinguish between a customs union and a free trade area. **(38, 44)**

17. Describe the operation of the CAP. **(39)**

18. What are the main institutions of the EEC? **(43)**

19. What was the Stockholm Convention? **(44)**

20. Outline the basis of Britain's renegotiation of EEC membership. **(47)**

21. Summarise the reasons for continuing opposition in Britain to EEC membership. **(49–51)**

CHAPTER XI

The UK Balance of Payments

THE BALANCE OF PAYMENTS ACCOUNTS

1. Concept of the balance of payments. The balance of payments accounts of the UK include all transactions between UK residents and non-residents, transactions being registered when the ownership of goods or assets changes or when services are rendered.

The accounts are set out in sterling values although clearly every transaction involves a foreign currency. Conversions are made simply by applying current rates of exchange.

The term "UK residents" includes all individuals residing permanently in the UK, business undertakings located in the UK (but excluding their foreign branches) and UK central and local government authorities and agencies.

At the outset, the point should be stressed that international payments must balance. For any deficit resulting from an adverse trading balance there must be a compensatory monetary movement, i.e. a running down of national reserves, or alternatively an increase in overseas borrowing.

2. Compilation of the accounts. The accounts are to be found in a number of official publications. In the spring of each year, a White Paper gives *Preliminary Estimates* for the preceding year. These figures are finalised in a Pink Book, *United Kingdom Balance of Payments Accounts*, which appears in the autumn. Estimates of the current position are published in *Economic Trends* and in the *Bank of England Quarterly Bulletin*.

The concept that international payments must balance can be demonstrated through a presentation based upon five major headings (*see* Table XIII).

(*a*) *Current account.*
(*b*) *Investment and other capital flows.*
(*c*) *Balancing item.*
(*d*) *Balance for official financing.*
(*e*) *Official financing.*

TABLE XIII. Summary balance of payments, 1974–79 (£m.)

	1974	1975	1976	1977	1978	1979
Current account						
Visible trade	−5,194	−3,203	−3,571	−2,279	−1,546	−3,404
Invisibles	+1,657	+1,556	+2,344	+1,995	+2,166	+1,541
Current balance	−3,537	−1,647	−1,227	−284	+620	−1,863
Currency flow and official financing						
Current balance	−3,537	−1,647	−1,227	−284	+620	−1,863
Investment and other capital flows	+1,684	+203	−2,819	+4,460	−3,518	+1,170
Balancing item	+282	−21	+418	+3,186	+1,772	+2,403
Balance for official financing	−1,646	−1,465	−3,628	+7,362	−1,126	+1,710
Allocation of special drawing rights	—	—	—	—	—	+195
Total	−1,646	−1,465	−3,628	+7,362	−1,126	+1,905
Financed as follows						
Net transactions with overseas monetary authorities	—	—	+984	+1,113	−1,016	−596
HM Government borrowing	+644	+423	—	+871	+191	—
Public sector under ECS borrowing	+1,107	+387	+1,791	+242	−378	−250
Official reserves (drawings on +/additions to −)	−105	+655	+853	−9,588	+2,329	−1,059
Total official financing	+1,646	+1,465	+3,628	−7,362	+1,126	−1,905

3. Current account. The current account comprises two main categories, as follows.

(*a*) *Visible trade*. The principal payments and receipts are in respect of imported and exported goods. *The Overseas Trade Statis Statistics of the United Kingdom* provide the basis for the balance of payments figures subject to certain adjustments in respect of valuation and coverage. The most important adjustment is the deduction of freight and insurance from the valuation of imports since these values appear elsewhere under the heading of "Invisible trade".

(*b*) *Invisible trade*. This includes the following.

(*i*) Government: all UK government current expenditure and receipts not appropriate to visible or other invisible trade transactions.

(*ii*) Transport—shipping: UK payments and receipts in respect of freight, time charter hire, port disbursements and passage money.

(*iii*) Transport—civil aviation: receipts in respect of all non-resident transactions with British airlines and payments in respect of resident transactions with overseas airlines.

(*iv*) Travel: all personal expenditure by UK residents abroad and by non-residents in the UK.

(*v*) Other services: among miscellaneous service transactions are included receipts and payments for financial services, royalties, commissions and education.

(*vi*) Interest profits and dividends: all investment income remitted from and to the UK in respect of profits and dividends together with profits remitted or retained for reinvestment. In the public sector are balanced payments and receipts on inter-government loans and on the debit side payments on overseas holdings of the UK government, local authority and public corporation securities together with the interest due on official currency liabilities.

(*vii*) Private transfers: remittance to and from the UK of migrants' funds, gifts and legacies.

4. Investment and other capital flows. These fall under the following headings.

(*a*) *Official long-term capital*. Inter-government loans by the UK and repaid to the UK and to the UK and repaid by the UK together with subscriptions to certain international organisations, e.g. International Development Association.

(b) *Overseas investment in UK public sector.* UK government stocks, local authority securities and mortgages, public corporation issues and borrowing by public corporations and local authorities from foreign banks.

(c) *Overseas investment in UK private sector.* Direct investments by foreign companies with UK branches and portfolio investment in UK company shares.

(d) *UK private investment overseas.* Both direct and portfolio investment.

(e) *Overseas currency borrowing or lending (net) by UK banks.*

(f) *Import credits excluding trade credit between related firms.*

(g) *Export credits excluding trade credit between related firms.*

(h) *Overseas exchange reserves in sterling.*

(i) *Other external banking and money market liabilities in sterling.*

(j) *Other short-term flows.*

5. The balancing item. This is the amount necessary to arrive at a balance and represents the net total of errors and omissions throughout the accounts.

The value of the balancing item will be such that total payments will equal total receipts for the balance of payments considered in its entirety. When the item is positive, if we assume the figure for total investments and other capital flows to be correct, an unrecorded net export is signified. If we regard the current account as correct an unrecorded net reduction in assets has occurred (i.e. UK foreign assets have diminished or foreign UK assets increased). The opposite conclusions will apply when the balancing item is negative.

In the short term the item is more likely to be the product of unrecorded capital flows but in the longer term is not amenable to reliable analysis.

6. Balance for official financing. This is the net currency flow resulting from all external transactions. It includes the current balance, total investment and capital flows and the balancing item.

7. Official financing. This means increases or decreases in the country's reserves or official borrowing drawn or repaid. They reflect the total currency flow together with the allocation of Special Drawing Rights and the payment of gold subscriptions to the International Monetary Fund.

When the total currency flow is positive, i.e. in favour of the UK, there will be a corresponding increase in the reserves or net repayments of overseas borrowing or a combination of both.

This heading covers the balance of loan transactions with the IMF and other overseas monetary authorities and the drawings on or additions to the official reserves.

8. Relationship of current account and investment and capital flows. It has been observed that the accounts as a whole must balance. If, however, we consider the current account alone it is highly unlikely that in practice a balance will be struck. When payments exceed receipts a current account deficit has arisen and when receipts exceed payments there is a current account surplus.

An immediate conclusion might be that investment and capital flows will be induced by the result achieved in the current account. A deficit may be financed by short- or long-term borrowing which implies a corresponding charge upon the investment and capital-flow sector of the accounts. Similarly, a current account surplus implies a corresponding outward capital flow.

However, it would be erroneous to assume that investment and capital flows are determined solely in this way since many capital transactions occur quite independently and without any reference to the current account balance, e.g. a government decision to grant an overseas loan. In simple terms, a decision to invest overseas does not take account of whether the country has earned a sufficient surplus on its current account to finance that investment. It may occur that even with a current deficit there is still a substantial outward movement of investment capital which will add further to the total deficit. This was notably the case in 1964 when a capital account deficit of £370 million was added to a current deficit of £399 million.

When this is the case the total deficit (or surplus) will be matched by a change in the reserves or in short-term borrowing from the IMF and foreign central banks. This change appears under the heading of "Official financing".

ANALYSIS OF THE ACCOUNTS

9. Current account, 1966–79. In only very few years since the eighteenth century has the visible trade balance been positive but this has normally been compensated by a surplus on invisible trade to give an overall surplus on current account.

TABLE XIV. *Current account, 1966–79 (£m.)*

	1966	1968	1970	1972	1974	1976	1979
Visible trade							
Exports (fob)	5,182	6,273	7,885	9,449	16,538	25,416	40,689
Imports (fob)	5,255	6,916	7,882	10,151	21,732	28,987	44,093
Visible balance	−73	−643	+3	−702	−5,194	−3,571	−3,404
Invisibles							
Government services and transfers (net)	−470	−466	−480	−561	−858	−1,546	−2,874
Private services and transfers (net)	+209	+478	+576	+835	+1,209	+2,581	+4,126
Interest, profits and dividends:							
Public sector	−160	−235	−264	−143	−355	−652	−473
Private sector	+549	+560	+796	+677	+1,661	+1,961	+762
Invisible balance	+128	+337	+628	+808	+1,657	+2,344	+1,541
Current balance	+55	−306	+631	+106	−3,537	−1,227	−1,863

(*Source: UK Balance of Payments Accounts, 1980.*)

On the invisible account the recurrent deficit in the public sector in respect of services, transfers and interest payments is usually outweighed by the surplus enjoyed in the private sector (*see* Table XIV).

10. Trends in visible trade. In the period 1913–45 the volume of British exports declined irregularly and over the whole period 1913–79 increased by only about 35 per cent. (At current values the increase was sixfold.) The visible trade account remained in deficit and its traditional relationship to the invisible account was unchanged (*see* Table XV).

TABLE XV. *Visible and invisible balances, selected periods 1913–79*

	Visibles	Invisibles		Visibles	Invisibles
1913	−134	+340	1964	−537	+138
1927–29	−373	+480	1967	−552	+255
1937–38	−388	+355	1976	−3,571	+2,344
1952–54	−242	+384	1979	−3,404	+1,541

(*Sources: Abstract of British Historical Statistics* (*CUP, 1962*); *UK Balance of Payments* (*HMSO*).)

The second trend which we may note is in respect of the UK's share of world export trade in manufactures (which account for about 85 per cent of our visible exports). The decline which had originated in the 1870s but was interrupted in the period 1939–50 continued during the 1950s. In the middle of that decade the UK's share of world markets stood at about 20 per cent. By the late 1960s it had fallen to 11 per cent and continued to decline in the 1970s. The immediate explanation of the decline since 1950 lies in the economic recovery from a standing start of the industrial nations of the world, particularly Germany and Japan, and their subsequent growth rates which greatly exceeded that of the UK. A lower growth is not of itself particularly significant but taken in conjunction with the UK's recurrent difficulties on current account requires some explanation upon which to base remedial policies.

Certain factors bear upon Britain's competitiveness in international trade and clearly play their part in explaining the post-1955 decline in her share of world markets.

11. Competitive factors in international trade. In the first place it may be noted that during the 1950s and 1960s UK prices rose on average twice as fast as those of our major industrial competitors. Until the 1967 devaluation this was clearly a factor which served to diminish the international competitiveness of British goods. The extent to which uncompetitive prices may be viewed as the cause of Britain's declining share of world markets depends upon assumptions made about the elasticity of demand for exports. Early econometric studies suggested that relative prices were comparatively unimportant. Later studies, however, conclude that the elasticity of demand is much greater than was originally believed. At present, the view generally held is that while price is one very important factor there are others.

There then emerges a list of criticisms which have periodically been aimed at British exporters since the nineteenth century.

(*a*) *Absence of aggressive marketing.*

(*b*) *Failure to research effectively the requirements of local markets.*

(*c*) *Unwillingness to vary basic designs to cater for local tastes.*

(*d*) *Poor after-sales services.*

(*e*) *Poor quality.*

(*f*) *Uncompetitive credit terms.*

(*g*) *Deliveries—long dated, unreliable and late.*

The validity of these criticisms is not amenable to testing by econometric techniques but it is generally agreed that they exert considerable influence.

Finally it must be recognised that the volume of exports depends not only upon the conditions of demand but also upon the conditions of supply. If the economy is being run at a high level of demand then exports are likely to be diverted to home consumption, attracted by the easier market conditions. Manufacturers require more than the assurance of politicians that "exporting is fun".

12. Imports. The visible trade balance depends of course not only upon the receipts from exports but also upon the cost of imports. first observation therefore is that when aggregate domestic demand is managed at a high level not only are exports diverted to home consumption but an increase in the volume of imports is also encouraged.

Comparison of the rate of increase of imports and exports during the 1960s at first sight seems reassuring (*see* Table XVI).

It will be observed that with the exceptions of the years

1963–64, 1966–67 and 1967–68, the value of exports grew more rapidly than the value of imports. The figures, however, disguise

TABLE XVI.   *Annual increase in imports/exports, 1961–70 (£m.)*

	Imports	Exports		Imports	Exports
1961–62	53	102	1966–67	419	− 60
1962–63	272	293	1967–68	1,242	1,151
1963–64	641	184	1968–69	286	788
1964–65	46	311	1969–70	680	824
1965–66	206	405			

(*Source: UK Balance of Payments.*)

the fact that the volume of imports was growing more rapidly than the volume of exports. This discrepancy between the value and volume growth rate of imports and exports was explained by a continuing movement of the terms of trade in favour of the UK.

Secondly, it will be noticed that from 1961 to the crisis year of 1964 and again from 1964 to the devaluation year of 1967 the rate of increase of imports far exceeded the rate of increase of exports. Subsequently, imports responded to devaluation in 1968–69 but the trend was re-established in 1969–70 with imports expanding at a far more rapid rate than exports.

It is accepted that since the UK is highly dependent upon imported foods and raw materials economic expansion will be related to an increase in such imports. However, since 1950 the growth rate of these items has diminished relative to the growth rate of imported manufactures.

TABLE XVII.   *Annual increase in imports/exports, 1971–79 (£m.)*

	1971–72	1972–73	1973–74	1974–75	1975–76	1978–79
Imports	1,370	4,317	7,264	932	6,323	7,476
Exports	588	2,666	4,423	2,923	5,955	5,618

(*Source: UK Balance of Payments.*)

Table XVII shows that the more rapid growth of imports over exports continued into the 1970s. In the middle years of the period this could be attributed to the reflationary stimulus of 1972–73 aimed at inducing more rapid growth. The substantial rise in the value of both imports and exports in 1973–74 was in part the consequence of the downward float of the sterling exchange rate. The huge increase in the value of imports was, however, primarily due to the 25 per cent deterioration in Britain's terms of trade during the period 1971–74. A simultaneous boom in Japan, Western Europe and the USA sharply increased world demand for foodstuffs and primary products and prices accelerated. It was, however, the fourfold increase in the price of oil between 1973 and 1974 which made the biggest impact, placing an additional £2,000 million upon Britain's import bill. The fall in the rate of increase of both imports and exports in 1974–75 is evidence of the effect of world recession upon international trade, while recovery is reflected in the turnround of the figures for 1975–76. It will be observed that in that year exports were beginning to close up on imports. This more optimistic trend was continued throughout 1977. The subsequent reversal of this trend in 1978–79 may be attributed to the pre-election boost to consumer spending which attracted more imports and the reappearance of inflationary pressure which, coupled with a rising sterling exchange rate, militated against exports.

13. Invisible trade. Examination of current account transactions shown in Table XIV reveals the importance of invisible trade to the balance of payments. This has long been the position. In the 1930s net earnings on invisible account paid for approximately one-third of UK visible imports. At the outbreak of war invisible receipts stood at 44 per cent of total receipts while payments represented 18 per cent of total payments.

In the immediate post-war years the relative importance of invisibles declined but by the late 1960s had been restored to the position where they produced 38 per cent of total export earnings and accounted for 32 per cent of total payments. Since the invisible account consistently produced a surplus it is clear that it made a major contribution to the current account surpluses of the 1950s and to a reduction of the deficits in the 1960s and 1970s.

14. Private services and transfers. The accounts show the following five categories.

(*a*) *Transport: shipping.* The post-war period saw a continuous deterioration in this account with deficits being returned in the 1960s. The trend was reversed in 1967 only to reverse into deficit again in 1970. During the 1970s it hovered around the break-even point. The sums involved are by far the largest items in the invisible accounts but the net flows are relatively small. A number of factors bear upon the UK's weakened position as a maritime power, including the following.

(*i*) Unfair competition from countries which subsidise their shipping lines for strategic or prestige reasons.

(*ii*) The rapid increase in world tonnage. Britain's share shows a relative decline.

(*iii*) Imports are carried increasingly in foreign ships and since these tend to be bulk cargoes the freight charges are higher than the export cargoes carried in British ships.

(*b*) *Transport: civil aviation.* In the past decade both sides of the account have grown quite rapidly but in step, to give a consistent and stable small surplus.

(*c*) *Travel.* Historically, this part of the accounts always showed a fairly substantial deficit and it would seem that until recent years Britain did not view the tourist industry as a potential major exporter. During the 1960s a surplus emerged which expanded dramatically until 1977. Subsequently, inflation has caused some decline.

(*d*) *Other services.* This category is a major contributor to the net surplus and includes a variety of items such as banking and financial services, royalties, commissions and education.

(*e*) *Private transfers.* This category normally shows a deficit which has ranged from a low point of £14 million in 1963 to a high point of £96 million in 1968. In 1970 the figure was £72 million. Subsequently, higher figures reflect inflation.

15. Interest, profits and dividends: private sector. Prior to 1914 Britain was the world's principal overseas investor, the income from her investments making an ever-growing contribution to the total of invisible exports. In the inter-war period the rate of investment slackened and during the Second World War a substantial portion of her holdings were liquidated to finance imports.

After the war investment abroad was resumed with cumulative benefits for the balance of payments since the net surplus on this item currently makes one of the biggest contributions to the total surplus on the invisible account (*see* Table XVIII).

There is, however, one important new feature in the accounts of the 1960s and 1970s. During this period the rate of foreign investment in the UK has grown substantially with a correspond-

TABLE XVIII. *Interest, profits and dividends:
private sector net surpluses, 1968–79*

1968	1969	1970	1971	1972	1973	1974	1975	1976	1977	1978	1979
560	793	796	709	677	1,523	1,661	1,417	1,961	761	1,094	782

ing rise on the debit side of the account. Until 1968 the rate of growth of debits in fact exceeded that of credits. This clearly has significance for exchange-control restrictions upon outward capital movements which, while they may be justifiable in the short run to correct an adverse balance of payments, in the long run must serve to erode the net surpluses on profits and dividends.

16. Interest, profits and dividends: public sector. Substantial deficits under this heading constitute a major offset to the surpluses in the private sector (*see* Table XIX).

TABLE XIX. *Interest, profits and dividends:
public sector net deficits, 1971–79 (£m.)*

1971	1972	1973	1974	1975	1976	1977	1978	1979
−204	−143	−200	−355	−517	−652	−715	−574	−473

Very large debit items arise in respect of overseas holdings of UK government securities, interest paid on official currency liabilities and charges paid on IMF drawings.

17. Investment and other capital flows. The twelve items which make up investment and other capital flows are shown in Table XX.

(*a*) *Official long-term capital.* Lending, chiefly at favourable rates to developing countries, continued to exceed repayments at a stable level.

(*b*) *Public sector.* This item excludes foreign currency borrowing by the public sector under the exchange cover scheme whereby government guarantees the loan at an agreed rate of exchange. Such borrowing is shown as a financing item.

(*c*) *Private sector.* Overseas investment in British industry continued at high levels totalling £18,186 million for the period.

(*d*) *UK private investment overseas.* Overseas investment showed a sharp upturn in 1976 and throughout the period amounted to £21,790 million.

(e) *Overseas currency borrowing and lending*. UK banks provide a source of international investment finance for both domestic and overseas residents. The decline in the figures in the mid-1970s and again towards the end of the period in some measure reflects world recession.

(f) *Exchange reserves in sterling*. These are "the sterling balances" representing the extent to which certain overseas countries prefer to invest a portion of their central monetary reserves and trading balances in income-yielding financial assets. A comparison of the two items reveals the preference for short-term investments in banking and money market liabilities. The alternations between large sums flowing in (+) and flowing out (−) demonstrate the volatility of the market.

(g) *Import and export credit*. An import credit is the equivalent of an overseas exporter making an investment in the UK. Conversely, an export credit represents a new overseas investment for the UK. The rapid expansion of export credits throughout the period will be noted.

18. Total currency flow and official financing. When the balances on current and investment and other capital flow accounts are totalled and adjusted by means of the balancing item, a figure for the total currency flow for the year is established. To this is added any allocation of Special Drawing Rights by the IMF.

If the final figure is negative, official financing will involve overseas borrowing or drawing upon the reserves. When the figure is positive as it was in 1971 official financing implies a repayment of existing short-term loans from foreign central banks and the IMF or an addition to the reserves.

EQUILIBRIUM IN THE BALANCE OF PAYMENTS

19. The concept of equlibrium. While international payments must always balance they need not necessarily be in equilibrium. By "long-term equilibrium" is understood a situation in which, at any given rate of exchange, the average current account surplus taken over a period of years is sufficient to finance all net external capital transactions (investment, foreign aid and debt repayment) together with any necessary expansion of official reserves to cover increased liabilities. Further, this equilibrium will be genuine only when it

TABLE XX.   *Investment and other capital flows, 1971–77 (£m.)*

	1971	1973	1975	1976	1977	1978	1979
Investment and other capital flows							
Official long-term capital	−274	−254	−288	−158	−139	−336	−384
Overseas investment in the UK:							
Public sector	+107	+175	+43	+203	+2,182	−99	+900
Private sector	+1,052	+1,652	+1,719	+2,051	+3,188	+2,640	+2,833
UK private investment overseas	−836	−1,848	−1,383	−2,154	−2,222	−4,414	−6,401
Overseas currency borrowing or lending (net) by UK banks to finance:							
UK investment overseas	+280	+595	+320	+165	+550	+835	−470
Other transactions	+191	−70	−85	−271	−181	−1,271	+2,043
Exchange reserves in sterling							
British government stocks	+55	+74	+7	+14	+5	−115	+247
Banking and money market liabilities	+658	+87	−624	−1,421	−24	−4	+518
Other external banking and money market liabilities in sterling	+709	−7	+550	+255	+1,481	+293	+2,590
Import credit	+54	+349	+224	+242	+297	+349	−133
Export credit	−287	−552	−570	−1,178	−638	−839	−710
Other short-term flows	+107	−152	+290	−567	+141	−557	+97
Total investment and other capital flows	+1,816	+49	+203	−2,819	+4,640	−3,518	+1,130

(*Source: UK Balance of Payments Accounts, 1980.*)

has been achieved without recourse to the management of domestic demand at a level inconsistent with full employment and without dependence upon trade and payment restrictions inconsistent with a country's obligations to GATT and the IMF.

It should be stressed that disequilibrium will occur not only when a country consistently experiences an adverse balance of payments but also when it recurrently produces large surpluses, as has repeatedly been the case in post-war Germany.

20. Disequilibrium in the UK balance of payments: the origin. While the UK balance of payments was never very strong during the 1950s it has been argued that the year 1958–59 marked a positive turning-point after which there was a steady deterioration until 1967, significant of a fundamental disequilibrium.

Throughout the 1950s there had been a gradual reduction of the restrictions upon foreign trade and payments which during and immediately after the war had served to limit the volume of imports and restrict the export of capital. In this way the balance of payments had been protected. In 1958 sterling was made freely convertible to gold or dollars for all non-resident holders in respect of current account transactions. In 1958–59 the residual import restrictions which had been designed to conserve foreign exchange were finally removed. Apart from a normal customs tariff which had in any case been lowered as a result of GATT the UK had now adopted a comparatively liberal system of trade and payments. It was now inevitable that in any expansionary phase, with domestic demand running at a higher level, imports would boom. In the event between 1956 and 1960 total imports rose by 23 per cent and manufactures upon which restrictions had been most stringent by some 56 per cent.

21. Disequilibrium, 1961–64. It has been observed (*see* III, **12**) that during the 1950s the major goal of government economic policy had been full employment but that in the 1960s attention became increasingly directed to more rapid growth. Whereas in the preceding period (1956–60) the annual average growth of Gross Domestic Product was only 2.4 per cent, in the period 1961–64 it increased to 3.6 per cent. With demand now functioning at a higher level the balance of payments was subjected to stress and two sterling crises (in 1961 and 1964) resulted.

As a result of the expansion of imports the visible trade balance worsened in 1961 to £153 million, recovered marginally in 1962 and 1963 with figures of −£104 million and −£80 million, only to plummet in 1964 to −£537 million. On the invisible account moreover the government deficit was increasing more rapidly than the private-sector surplus, while one aspect of the latter was in fact declining. The net surplus on private services fell from £230 million in 1962 to £177 million in 1963 and £167 million in 1964.

While a net capital inflow relieved the pressure in 1961, subsequent capital account deficits of £98 million in 1962, £148 million in 1963 and £370 million in 1964 were clearly not being financed from the current balance. The cumulative deficit over the period on current and capital account was £740 million, largely financed by massive borrowing from the IMF and a depletion of the reserves by £327 million.

22. Disequilibrium, 1965–67. In this period the balance of payments and the preservation of the exchange rate of sterling became a major target of economic policy. Stringent demand management slowed the growth rate to an average of 1.6 per cent per annum, initially with some result. The visible trade deficit shrank to £237 million in 1965 and £73 million in 1966, only to rocket to £552 million in 1967. The surplus on the invisible account could not match these figures. In fact the net yield from invisibles fell in 1966 by £32 million owing primarily to a substantial rise in the government account deficit and a fall in the net surplus from profits and dividends.

The result was that although the current account deficit was reduced to £77 million in 1965 and converted to a surplus of £55 million in 1966, in 1967 a deficit of £297 million was returned. It is perfectly clear that the current account was not able to support the net outward flow of investment which totalled £462 million.

If a comparison is made with the preceding period in terms of the old "basic balance" (i.e. current account plus capital account), the cumulative deficit, ignoring the balancing item, had deteriorated from £740 million to £781 million despite government remedial policies. The position was further aggravated by a diminution of the sterling balances over the period by £431 million, and by other adverse monetary movements.

Official financing during this time amounted net to £165 million drawn from the IMF, £1,095 million borrowed from other monetary authorities, £165 million drawn from the reserves and £520 million transferred to the reserves upon the liquidation of the US dollar portfolio.

23. Deflation or devaluation. From the foregoing discussion it would seem conclusive that a fundamental disequilibrium existed in the UK balance of payments from 1959 to 1967. In this situation the balance may be rectified by operating on either of the following.

(*a*) *The current account.* Broadly the intention will be to make domestic prices more internationally competitive either by deflation or by devaluation. (Detailed consideration will be given to this subject in the following chapter.)

(*b*) *Investment and other capital flows.* Exchange control restrictions upon capital movements may be tightened.

In the event devaluation was forced upon the government in November 1967 and although this was no voluntary act of policy it was hoped that it would provide in the long run the solution for the hitherto intractable balance of payments problem.

24. Impact of devaluation on the balance of payments. The immediate consequence of devaluation is to raise the price of a given quantity of imports and reduce the receipts from a given quantity of exports. It was not therefore surprising that in 1968 the current balance worsened to £306 million. The "basic balance", however, improved from the 1967 deficit of £418 million to £387 million primarily because of a net inflow of official long-term capital and an increase in overseas investment in the UK public sector.

By 1969 the visible trade balance was responding to devaluation, exports expanding by £788 million and imports by £286 million, to reduce the deficit to £141 million. In 1970 exports continued their sharp upward trend, growing by £824 million while imports disappointingly also rose sharply by £680 million. The result was a highly unusual surplus on visible trade, albeit of only £3 million.

The surplus on invisibles also improved dramatically, having more than doubled from £255 million in 1967 to £628 million in 1970.

The net result was an improvement in the current balance to a surplus of £631 million and in the "basic balance" to a surplus of £338 million in 1970. Short-term capital movements were also especially favourable to the UK balance of payments in 1970, adding a further £161 million to the surplus.

The total currency inflow produced in the years of surplus, 1969 and 1970, amounted to £2,163 million. From this position the authorities were enabled to repay £164 million of IMF drawings and £1,830 million of foreign central bank borrowing and also to add £169 million to the reserves.

25. Deterioration in the balance of payments, 1971–74. The deterioration in the current account from a surplus of £1,058 million in 1971 to a deficit of £3,537 million in 1974 was unprecedented both in speed and scale. The 1974 current deficit in fact amounted to almost 5 per cent of national income, about £1.50 per week per inhabitant. There were three basic reasons.

(*a*) *Stimulus to aggregate demand.* With unemployment exceeding one million for the first time since the 1930s, the government felt impelled to reflate the economy and pursue growth policies as the first priority. It recognised that an inevitable consequence would be some imbalance in international payments but hoped to offset this by permitting the sterling exchange rate to float downwards. This hope was not fulfilled. There was a big upsurge in imports and exports were diverted to the home market.

(*b*) *The downward float of sterling.* The immediate effect of a depreciated exchange rate is to raise the cost of imports. Only in the longer term when industry has had time to increase output will exports respond to the price advantage which they now enjoy in overseas markets. However, if domestic inflation keeps pace with the rate of depreciation in the exchange rate this price advantage never materialises. This proved to be the case.

(*c*) *Adverse terms of trade.* The terms of trade signify a ratio between the export prices of one country relative to the export prices of another. During the early 1970s the terms of trade moved strongly in favour of the primary producing countries (*see* **12** above).

26. Improvement from 1974 to 1977. Between 1974 and 1976 the current account gradually improved from a deficit of £3,537 million to one of £1,227 million. However, inflation continued at very high levels and the lack of foreign confidence in the ability of the UK government to gain control of the situation was reflected in capital outflows of £2,819 million in 1976, primarily short-term deposits in the UK money market. The government was consequently left with a total deficit of £3,628 million to finance by borrowing from the IMF and other central monetary institutions.

As a condition of a further loan to finance the prospective 1977 deficit the IMF insisted upon strict control of the UK Public Sector Borrowing Requirement, the expansion of domestic credit and the rate of growth of the money supply. Implied was some belief in a monetary explanation of UK inflation.

In 1977, the economy responded to these measures with a gradual reduction in the rate of inflation. The current balance showed substantial improvement moving to a surplus of £399 million for the third quarter of the year. Significantly, this figure incorporated an improvement in the visible balance from a deficit of £930 million in the first quarter to one of only £50 million in the third quarter.

27. Uneven improvement, 1978–80. The stringent economic policies of 1976–77 were rewarded in 1978 with a reduction in the visible deficit from £2,279 million to £1,546 million while the invisibles balance improved from a surplus of £1,995 million to one of £2,166 million. The net result was a payments *surplus* on current account of £620 million.

More relaxed pre-election policies in 1978 doubled the visible deficit in 1979 to £3,404 million, imports having risen by £7,476 million against an increase of only £5,618 million for exports. Meanwhile the invisibles surplus deteriorated to £1,541 million to yield a current account *deficit* of £1,863 million. This position was, however, more than offset by net inward movements on capital account which produced an overall payments surplus of £1,905 million. These movements are to be explained primarily by the attractiveness of sterling as an investment currency, backed by North Sea oil reserves and yielding relatively high interest rates.

These attractions have been reinforced by the central commitment of the 1979 Government to countering inflation, thus improving the world's assessment of sterling's future stability. However, it should be remembered that overall payments surpluses which are chiefly attributable to inward capital flows tend to conceal the underlying weakness of the UK economy on the visibles account.

PROGRESS TEST 11

1. Why must international payments always balance?   **(1)**
2. List the main items in the current account.   **(3)**
3. What is the significance of the "balancing item"?   **(5)**
4. What does a positive total currency flow indicate?   **(7)**
5. How do current account items relate to investment and capital flows?   **(8)**

6. Describe the general trend in the visible trade balance in the twentieth century. **(10)**

7. What criticisms have been levelled at British exporters in this century? **(11)**

8. Explain the significance of import trends in the 1960s. **(12)**

9. Explain the importance of invisible trade to the UK balance of payments. **(13)**

10. Compare the relative importance of the various items on the invisible account which fall under the heading "private services and transfers". **(14)**

11. What is the significance of restrictions upon outward capital movements for the balance of invisible trade? **(15)**

12. Compare the importance of "official long-term capital" with the other items which appear under the heading "Investment and other capital flows". **(17)**

13. Explain the concept of "equilibrium" in the balance of payments. **(19)**

14. What was the source of disequilibrium in the UK balance of payments at the end of the 1950s? **(20)**

15. Account for the 1964 sterling crisis. **(21)**

16. What were the effects of the 1967 devaluation upon the balance of payments? **(24)**

17. Explain the deterioration in the balance of payments in 1971–74. **(25)**

18. What brought about an improvement in 1974–77? **(26)**

CHAPTER XII

Foreign Exchange

THE DETERMINATION OF FOREIGN EXCHANGE RATES

1. The rate of exchange. The rate of exchange may be defined as the domestic money price of foreign currency purchased on the foreign exchange market. The rate varies daily and is derived from the domestic price quoted for bankers' bills of exchange transmitted by cable, the quickest means of international payment. This establishes the "base" rate. Other slower means of international payment, bankers' sight and time bills and trade sight and time bills, are carried by airmail and sell at a discount from the base rate to take account of differing liquidity and risk factors.

In this way a pattern of exchange rates is established all of which are geared to the base rate which may be taken as the "key" rate of exchange.

Movements in the rates of exchange depend upon the structure of the foreign exchange market (*see* **2, 3, 4** below).

2. Variable exchange rates. In this situation exchange rates may be completely free to move in response to market forces. Such a foreign exchange system in fact approximates to the classical notion of perfect competition since any given foreign currency is a homogeneous product and the market comprises many buyers and sellers none of whom is able individually to influence the final price.

The demand for foreign currency originates in the debit items in the balance of payments while the supply derives from the credit items. It therefore follows that when demand increases relative to supply the price of foreign currency is forced upward, i.e. the exchange rate moves against the home country. The opposite will be the case when supply exceeds demand.

3. Stable exchange rate systems. Exchange rates have in practice rarely been left free to be determined by demand and supply. Stabilisation has been achieved in two ways.

(*a*) *Passive stabilisation.* This system is exemplified by the "gold standard" which functioned throughout the greater part of the nineteenth century and with interruptions to the 1930s. A country observes a full gold standard when its monetary unit is defined in terms of a fixed weight of gold, when the monetary authorities are prepared to buy and sell gold freely at this fixed ratio and when there are no restrictions placed upon the free international movement of gold.

In the situation where a number of countries observe this standard their currencies are linked by a common denominator and must therefore always exchange at this fixed rate.

(*b*) *Active stabilisation.* A genuine international gold standard has not functioned since the 1930s. Subsequently, foreign exchange markets have either been controlled directly or stabilised by official intervention. Intervention requires that the monetary authorities should have at their disposal both supplies of the domestic currency and reserves of gold and convertible foreign currencies. When the flow of domestic currency on to the world's foreign exchange markets is excessive the reserves are used to buy up the surplus in order to support the price (i.e. exchange rate) at the fixed level. Similarly, when the domestic currency is in *short* supply on the exchange markets the tendency for its price to rise will be forestalled when the monetary authorities sell domestic currency against gold or foreign currency.

4. Exchange control. In neither of the two preceding systems is any restriction placed upon private transactions in foreign exchange. Where the foreign exchange market is fully controlled all foreign currency earnings must be sold to the control authority at a given exchange rate and all purchases made from the authority at a given rate.

The supply of foreign currency earnings (i.e. the credit items in the balance of payments) is largely outside the control of the exchange authority except to the extent that exports or foreign loans can be encouraged. Supply is therefore taken as fixed and the authority turns its attention to restricting demand, usually by a system of licensed imports. Licences are allocated to individuals in a way which restricts the total volume of imports, and hence the demand for foreign exchange, to a level which equates with the supply of foreign currency earnings.

5. Balance of payments disequilibrium and foreign exchange rates.

When there exists a fundamental disequilibrium in the balance of payments the effect upon exchange rates varies with the nature of the foreign exchange market.

(a) *Freely fluctuating rates.* When there is a recurrent deficit disequilibrium, there will be a continuing deterioration in the rate of exchange. Conversely, with a surplus disequilibrium the exchange rate will appreciate.

(b) *Stable rates.* Whether the rates of exchange are stabilised actively or passively the results will be the same. With a deficit disequilibrium there will be a continuing diminution in the reserves and/or an accumulation of foreign debt. A surplus disequilibrium will produce additions to the reserves and/or a reduction of foreign debt.

(c) *Exchange control.* The existence of exchange control is itself evidence of a "suppressed" disequilibrium. Were the demand for foreign currency free to rise the result would be an exchange rate lower than the one which currently pertains.

We shall now examine in some detail the adjustment of international payments disequilibrium under different systems of foreign exchange, making special reference to the historical experience of the UK.

ADJUSTMENT OF PAYMENTS DISEQUILIBRIUM IN A PASSIVE STABLE RATE SYSTEM

6. The classical theory of adjustment. The oldest theory of international payments adjustment was propounded by the eighteenth-century writer David Hulme and refined by the British classical economists of the nineteenth century. It hinges on the concept of "the price-specie flow mechanism". An inflow of gold resulting from an excess of exports over imports will increase the domestic money supply and raise home prices. Conversely, the outflow of gold from abroad will reduce the foreign money supply and foreign prices. The response will be an expansion of imports and a reduction of exports to the point where international payments are automatically brought into equilibrium.

7. The gold standard. Prior to 1914 and during the second half of the 1920s the pound sterling was defined as 113 grains of gold and the US dollar as 23.22 grains. Since the pound therefore represented 4.8665 times as much gold as the dollar, the so-called "mint parity" of the two currencies was £1:$4.8665. Any holder of 113 grains of gold could freely acquire £1 or $4.8665 from the UK or US monetary authorities respectively or alternatively exchange these sums against 113 grains of gold.

Any tendency for the exchange rate to move away from the mint parity was checked when importers, rather than accept an unfavourable rate, would withdraw and export gold in payment. However, a marginal movement of the exchange rate was possible within the limits set by the "gold points".

(a) *The gold export point* by adding the cost of freight, insurance and handling to the mint parity rate of exchange established the effective rate above which it paid the importer to make payment in gold.

(b) *The gold import point* by similarly subtracting shipment from the mint parity rate of exchange established the lowest rate which the foreign importer would accept rather than make payment in gold.

It therefore follows that on the gold standard any disequilibrium in international payments was compensated by gold movements which left the exchange rate undisturbed within the range of the two gold points.

8. Restoration of equilibrium. A gold standard implies a stringent control over a country's money supply. The 1844 Bank Charter Act permitted a small fiduciary issue in Britain but required that every other banknote should have full gold cover (*see* IX, **3**).

Given an unfavourable balance of payments and a movement of the exchange rate to the gold export point, bullion now flowed out of the country. It followed that the volume of currency had now to be curtailed and the banking system was compelled to follow a policy of deflation. Bank Rate was raised and the Bank of England engaged in open market operations to reduce the cash reserves of the commercial banks which, in turn, were obliged to restrict credit in order to maintain their cash ratio (*see* IX, **35**). In short, there was a contraction of the money supply in terms of both cash and bank deposits.

It was argued that these deflationary policies produced a decline in the domestic price level which encouraged exports and discouraged imports. Equilibrium in the balance of payments was restored automatically, albeit at the expense of a deflation over which there was no control.

Given a favourable balance of payments and an inflow of gold the course of events was reversed.

9. Advantages and disadvantages of the gold standard. Assuming the foregoing explanation to be an accurate account of the sequence of events on an international gold standard, certain advantages and disadvantages are apparent.

(*a*) *Advantages.* Internally it is impossible for inflation to be excessive since the money supply is strictly controlled. The domestic price level must therefore in the long run remain internationally competitive and the balance of payments can be left to adjust itself automatically.

(*b*) *Disadvantages.* Economic expansion may be impeded by a too inflexible and arbitrary restriction of the supply of money and credit. Moreover, the inevitable deflation or inflation which must accompany an outward or inward gold flow may be wholly at odds with internal economic needs, e.g. deflation in a situation of high unemployment.

By the 1930s a considerable body of opinion was disposed against a wholly arbitrary system in which gold was the master and a country was robbed of control over its economic fortunes.

10. The validity of the price-specie flow mechanism. Two main criticisms emerge which reduce the validity of the theory as conceived by the classical economists.

(*a*) *Quantity theory of money criticism.* The quantity theory assumes that a change in the money supply will bring about a proportionate change in the price level. However, the effect of a change depends upon the extent to which the volume of spending responds. A decrease in the quantity of money may be compensated by an increase in its velocity of circulation and vice versa. Therefore there can be no direct or certain response from prices to any given change in the money supply.

(*b*) *No allowance for income changes.* In the classical theory of perfect competition and continuing full employment there could be no change in spending which did not simultaneously produce a corresponding change in both prices and incomes. The classical economists saw that deflation (reduced spending) subsequent to an adverse balance of payments reduced the purchasing power (i.e. income) of the deficit country since exports were now made at lower prices. However, the view was that the reduction of income was the incidental accompaniment of the reduction in prices, the latter being the key to international payments adjustment. It was not seen that there could be an autonomous change in income unrelated to price change which would itself contribute to adjustment.

11. Income change and the balance of payments. Modern theory places a great deal of emphasis upon the notion that income changes play a major role in the long-run adjustment of international payments.

Where there exists a recurrent disequilibrium at stable exchange rates and the deficit country is forced to deflate, prices may or may not respond. What is certain is that at lower levels of spending national income will decline, thus inducing a fall in home consumption. The volume of imports will be reduced and goods released from home use for export.

At the same time the income of the surplus country will be inflated with unpredictable consequences for the price level. However, at the higher income level further imports will be attracted and exports diverted to home use.

Nevertheless, it is to be expected that at the same time prices will be falling in the deficit country and rising in the surplus country.

The two sets of circumstances will combine to reduce both deficit and surplus and establish an equilibrium.

12. Variations on the gold standard. In 1914 the gold standard was suspended but fixed rates of exchange maintained. After the war exchange rates between many currencies were permitted to fluctuate and settle at whatever level the market determined. In the resulting chaos many monetary authorites were convinced of the desirability of a return to the gold standard. This course was followed by Austria (1922), Germany (1924), Britain (1925) and France (1928).

(*a*) *The gold bullion standard.* Britain did not readopt a full gold standard as it had functioned before 1914. It was more a gold bullion standard. Bank of England paper was convertible but only into gold bars in minimum quantities of 400 ounces, about £1,560. While gold was once more used in settlement of international payments it was no longer circulated internally.

(*b*) *The gold exchange standard.* This technique enables a country to link its currency to gold without in fact holding gold reserves of its own. Instead, it holds its reserves in the currency of a country observing the gold standard and thus enjoys the advantage of interest receipts on these deposits.

13. Abandonment of the gold standard. For a number of reasons the world was obliged to abandon an international gold standard in the years between 1931 and 1936.

(*a*) *Failure to observe gold standard obligations.* It has been noted that an automatic consequence of payments disequilibrium will be a degree of inflation in the surplus country and of deflation in the deficit country. During the period of the restored gold standard no country was prepared fully to accept these consequences. In deficit countries such as the UK it would have been necessary to permit severe deflation even in the prevailing conditions of industrial depression and rising unemployment. In surplus countries such as the USA which was receiving huge quantities of gold there was an unwillingness to accept an inflation which might jeopardise exports. The inward flow of gold was therefore stabilised.

(*b*) *"Hot money."* Before 1914 most capital movements were for the purpose of long-term investment. After the war a huge volume of short-term money shifted from one country to another in search of refuge from depreciation. These movements added instability to the balance of international payments.

(*c*) *Overvaluation of sterling.* In 1925 the mint parity of sterling was re-established at its 1914 level. In view of the great inflation which had occurred in Britain during the war this rate clearly overvalued the pound. The degree of deflation required to reduce the UK price level to a point which made the exchange rate realistic proved impossible of attainment. There followed inevitably a fundamental disequilibrium in the balance of payments which produced a steady drain upon the gold reserves. Following an adverse balance of £100 million, Britain in 1931 was compelled to leave the gold standard. Since sterling was a key reserve and trading currency other countries were obliged to follow suit.

EXCHANGE-CONTROL SYSTEMS

14. Origins. Exchange controls were first adopted by many governments during the First World War as a means of safeguarding those imports vital to the economy. After the war controls were abandoned until the international financial crisis of 1931. Failure of confidence in the ability of one nation after another to honour its short-term international obligations led to massive withdrawals of funds from these countries which were checked only by the reimposition of exchange controls.

In due course confidence in sterling was affected but instead of adopting controls the UK reacted first by abandoning the gold standard and allowing the pound to depreciate and then, in 1932, stabilising at a lower parity with the aid of the Exchange Equalisation Account.

By 1935 a clear pattern had emerged in which Germany and the countries of south-east Europe together with Brazil, Argentina and Chile practised stringent exchange controls. The currencies of the rest of the world remained freely convertible.

15. Extension of exchange controls. During the Second World War tight controls were imposed by all countries. After the war while other direct economic controls were dismantled exchange control was retained. By 1958 there were only eleven fully convertible currencies. After 1958 a general easing of international payment difficulties enabled many more countries to revert either to full or to partial convertibility. While it is true that exchange controls have not yet been completely eliminated they no longer have the restrictive effect on trade and payments that they had during the post-war years. The exception is in the case of some developing countries where they are used as a major instrument of economic policy.

16. Purposes of an exchange-control system. An exchange-control system will have one or more of the following purposes.

(*a*) *Correction of a balance of payments disequilibrium.* Since 1945, exchange controls have been, and still are, imposed to correct a disequilibrium which springs from massive capital outflows. For example, half the 1964 UK deficit sprang from capital account transactions and controls over these were subsequently tightened.

Current account deficits may be corrected in this way where countries are unwilling to deflate or devalue. However, after 1958, all the world's major trading nations agreed to abandon controls over current account transactions.

(*b*) *Instrument of economic planning.* We have seen in Part One that in private-enterprise economies governments seek to implement national economic plans by indirect methods, notably fiscal and monetary policy. Since the achievement of objectives such as full employment or more rapid growth may set up inflationary pressures which induce a balance of payments disequilibrium, exchange controls may be adopted as a short-term planning expedient.

(c) *Source of revenue*. In this case the exchange-control authority arbitrarily sets the price at which it will purchase foreign exchange below that at which it will sell, thus leaving itself a profit margin. Today this objective is mainly restricted to the developing countries.

(d) *Protection*. Like a customs tariff exchange controls may be used to protect domestic industry.

17. Types of system. Exchange-control systems may vary considerably in detail but all will fall into one or other of two categories.

(a) *Single-rate systems*. The exchange-control authority has the sole right to buy and sell foreign currency but does so at one official rate. In this case the price mechanism plays no part in allocating currency between competing importers. The system must therefore be supported by import licences which determine who shall be entitled to foreign currency.

(b) *Multi-rate systems*. There is one official buying rate and one or more selling rates. In this case the price mechanism serves partially to allocate the supply of foreign currency and there need be less reliance on supporting trade controls.

18. Disadvantage of exchange control. The major criticism of any system of exchange control is that by rendering a currency inconvertible it disrupts multilateral settlements which enable a country to offset a deficit in one sector of its trading with a surplus earned elsewhere.

Let us suppose that Peru has traditionally a deficit in its trade with Chile, which has normally been financed by a surplus in its trade with the USA, i.e. dollar earnings have been converted to Chilean pesos. If the USA now adopts exchange control which makes the dollar inconvertible then Peru must balance its payments bilaterally with Chile.

To do so it must reduce its imports (probably by adopting its own exchange controls) to the detriment of Chile and itself. Peru is still left with dollars which can only be utilised in the USA for the purchase of imports which it might otherwise not wish to take.

In short, the volume of world trade is reduced and the natural pattern distorted. The advantages of international specialisation are lost.

ADJUSTMENT OF PAYMENTS DISEQUILIBRIUM IN VARIABLE EXCHANGE RATE SYSTEMS

19. Variants. Variable exchange rate systems may be of many types ranging from a position in which the rate is determined solely by market forces to the other extreme of an "adjustable peg". The operation of the latter is exemplified by the UK Exchange Equalisation Account and has been described earlier under the heading of "active stabilisation" (*see* **3**(*b*)). (The adjustable peg may be considered a variant of either the stable or fluctuating rate systems since it combines both principles.)

Between the two extremes lie a number of *floating rate* systems which display varying degrees of flexibility. However, all the variants share the common principle that the exchange rate moves continuously or occasionally.

20. Adjustment through freely fluctuating exchange rates. When the exchange rate is permitted to move freely and without limit the risk of foreign exchange dealing is intensified. Dealers are unwilling to hold bills of exchange and therefore when exporters supply them in exchange for domestic cash they must be sold immediately to importers who wish to make payment in foreign currency.

An increase in the supply of foreign bills will force down their price (i.e. improve the rate of exchange) until there is an increase in demand from importers wishing to settle accounts abroad. If this demand continues to increase the price of bills of exchange will be forced up (i.e. the exchange rate deteriorates). In this way imports and exports continuously offset each other at varying exchange ratios. There can consequently be no disequilibrium in the balance of payments and therefore no need for compensatory short-term capital movements. It follows that gold and foreign currency reserves are not required.

21. Adjustment of disequilibrium in an adjustable-peg system. This is the system to which the major trading nations of the world adhered from 1945 to 1972. In the short run exchange rates are pegged and adjustment takes place as in a stable rate system. In the long run adjustment is assisted by planned and limited variations in the exchange rate.

In the case of a recurrent deficit disequilibrium a planned

devaluation will be effected and in the case of a surplus disequilibrium there will be a planned revaluation.

The problem then arises of selecting the right exchange rate to establish equilibrium. One solution is to allow the market temporary freedom to establish a rate in response to the forces of demand and supply. This was done in the UK in 1931 and to a limited degree in Germany in 1971. Equilibrium achieved, the rate is then stabilised. However, this approach is seldom favoured since it unleashes the possibility of large speculative capital movements out of a currency which is depreciating or into a currency which is appreciating. These movements will only serve to exacerbate the disequilibrium.

It is possible nevertheless to make a theoretical approach to the problem through the "Doctrine of Purchasing Power Parity".

22. Doctrine of purchasing power parity. In the 1920s Gustav Cassel argued that the equilibrium rate of exchange between two currencies should reflect the ratio between their respective domestic purchasing powers. For example, if the purchasing power of $1 in the USA is a half of the purchasing power of £1 in the UK, the equilibrium rate of exchange is $2:£1.

Unfortunately, this theoretical approach is beset with difficulties as follows.

(a) *Problem of comparing purchasing power.* It is clearly difficult if not impossible to compare the purchasing power of, say, the pound sterling and the Congolese franc when assortments of goods are purchased in the two countries.

(b) *Inadequate coverage.* The theory in any case only utilises the merchandise price level to determine purchasing power parities, thus excluding the service and capital transactions which also influence the exchange rate.

(c) *Autonomous influences on the rate of exchange.* It is possible that a change in a buyer's tastes or income may act independently upon the exchange rate without any change in comparative price levels.

We may conclude therefore that while this theory is useful in drawing attention to the effect upon the exchanges of differing national rates of inflation or deflation it is of little value in determining an equilibrium rate of exchange.

23. Determining the equilibrium rate in practice. In the absence of any accurate technique reliance has to be placed upon a mixture of economic analysis and guesswork. The test of a genuine new equilibrium rate is whether it reverses those tendencies which have produced a disequilibrium in the first place. In the case of a deficit disequilibrium economic analysis will attempt to establish the degree of devaluation necessary to improve the balance of individual items in the accounts. For example, an assessment of demand and supply elasticities of imports and exports must be made in order to predict the response of these items to a given depreciation in the exchange rate.

24. The effectiveness of devaluation. The effectiveness of devaluation in remedying a fundamental payments disequilibrium depends upon the relative elasticities of demand and supply in respect of foreign exchange. If both are highly elastic then the new more unfavourable exchange rate will induce a greatly increased supply of foreign exchange at the same time as demand is greatly curtailed. The devaluation will have been extremely effective. The opposite will be the case when elasticities are low and a much greater devaluation may be necessary to eliminate even a small deficit.

25. Elasticity of demand for foreign exchange. This depends primarily upon the elasticity of domestic demand for imports. Elasticity will tend to be high where luxury consumer goods and expensive capital equipment constitute a large part of total imports and low when foodstuffs, raw materials and semi-manufactures are the principal elements. The ease of substitution of home home-produced goods for imports will also affect the degree of elasticity.

When import supply is wholly elastic (i.e. when the supply can be varied at constant price) then the elasticity of demand for imports wholly determines the elasticity of demand for foreign exchange.

In this case, when the elasticity of demand for imports is greater than zero, devaluation will produce a reduction in the volume of imports and consequently of the demand for foreign exchange. From the side of demand devaluation has proved effective.

26. Elasticity of supply of foreign exchange. The principal determining factor is the elasticity of foreign demand for domestic exports. When export supply is perfectly elastic, i.e. the domestic price remains unchanged after devaluation, then the elasticity of demand for exports wholly determines foreign exchange supply elasticity.

When export demand elasticity has a value of 1 (unit elasticity) a 10 per cent devaluation will produce a 10 per cent increase in the volume of exports and total foreign exchange receipts will therefore remain constant, i.e. the supply elasticity of exchange is zero and the effect of devaluation is zero.

When export demand elasticity has a value greater than 1, a 10 per cent devaluation will produce an increase in the volume of exports in excess of 10 per cent and total foreign exchange receipts will be enlarged, i.e. the supply elasticity of foreign exchange is greater than zero and devaluation will have been effective.

When export demand elasticity has a value below one then a 10 per cent devaluation will not be matched by an equivalent increase in the volume of imports and total foreign exchange receipts will decline. The deficit has been enlarged.

27. Import and export supply elasticities. In the preceding two paragraphs it was assumed that the supply of imports and exports was wholly elastic, i.e. that the "foreign currency" price of imports and the "domestic" price of exports remained unchanged after devaluation. In that case the demand elasticities for imports and exports were the sole determinants of the effectiveness of devaluation. Allowance must now be made for this unrealistic assumption.

In the extreme (and hypothetical) case of perfectly inelastic supply of both imports and exports, by definition there can be no variation in the quantity supplied. A 10 per cent devaluation can have no effect upon the volume of domestic exports but domestic prices will be forced up by 10 per cent as foreign buyers compete to retain their share of the fixed supply. Similarly, foreign exporters, unable to curtail their output, will compete to retain their market in the devaluing country by cutting their prices by 10 per cent. The effect of devaluation is therefore neutral.

On the other hand when the supply elasticity of imports is high then devaluation will have the effect of increasing domestic import prices and it may be expected that imports will contract provided that import demand elasticity is also high.

When the supply elasticity of exports is high then exports will expand at lower foreign exchange prices provided that export demand elasticity is also high.

On the other hand when demand elasticities are low it is preferable that supply elasticities should also be low since the lack of any great response to devaluation in the demand for imports and exports will be compensated by a relatively small fall in foreign exchange export prices and a relatively small rise in domestic import prices.

28. The theoretical case for freely fluctuating rates. The argument in favour of fluctuating exchange rates derives largely from observation of the drawbacks inherent in exchange rates which are too inflexible. When rates are pegged it is expected that a deficit will be adjusted by a deflationary movement of domestic incomes and prices and that, hopefully, output and employment will be undisturbed by lower price and wage levels. In practice oligopolistic industries and powerful trade unions are able to resist the downward pressure on prices and wages, so that the reduced expenditure engendered by deflation manifests itself in declining output and rising unemployment. Since governments are committed to both growth and full employment they are likely to frustrate deflation by adopting compensatory fiscal and monetary policies. The balance of payments therefore remains in deficit disequilibrium.

Within these limiting circumstances it is unlikely that long-run adjustment can be achieved in a stable rate system without recourse to direct controls on trade and payments. Since these run counter to the world's declared intention to liberalise trade and payments the only alternative is to adopt a system of fluctuating exchange rates. Governments are then free to pursue their own policies for growth and full employment in the knowledge that the external balance of payments is self-regulating.

29. The case against fluctuating rates. Criticism of fluctuating rates is again based upon observation of the difficulties which arose during the early 1920s and again in the 1930s when fixed exchange rates were abandoned. These were periods of great uncertainty which saw violent movements in the exchanges accompanied by massive flows of speculative capital (hot money) and deleterious effects upon trade.

This argument is countered by the suggestion that it confuses cause with effect, that violent exchange rate fluctuations were a product of an instability which sprang from other deep-rooted causes.

A further standard argument against a fluctuating rate system is that it increases the risks of (and therefore deters) international trade. Apart from accepting the normal business risks of their own trade, importers and exporters must also accept the risk of adverse movements in the exchanges.

Against this argument it is claimed that the development of forward exchange markets which may be associated with a fluctuating rate system enables the trader to hedge foreign exchange risks.

Finally, it is claimed that a stable rate system enforces a monetary discipline which makes hyperinflation impossible. On the other hand, it is argued, a fluctuating rate system leaves a country permanently exposed to this danger.

30. The case for and against an adjustable-peg system. It has already been noted that this was the system, sponsored by the International Monetary Fund, through which the world's major trading nations sought to achieve international payments equilibrium.

The intention is to enjoy the combined advantages of stable and fluctuating rate systems while eliminating their disadvantages. Short-term stability is achieved by supporting operations on the exchange markets, in the case of the UK, through the medium of the Exchange Equalisation Account. If in the long term a fundamental surplus or deficit disequilibrium develops at the existing exchange rate, then provision is made for an adjustment upward or downward to a new peg.

In practice the weakness of this system proved twofold. In the first place there is the difficulty of determining the appropriate degree of rate variation (*see* **16–18** above). Secondly, for political and prestige reasons, and in the case of a key currency country such as the UK because of the implications for overseas holders of sterling, a decision to devalue is likely to be postponed in the hope that internal economic measures will rectify the disequilibrium. In the event the decision is likely to be put off until overseas credit is exhausted and the reserves are disappearing. At this point it becomes universally apparent that devaluation is imminent with a resulting capital flight which puts the reserves under further pressure and makes devaluation inevitable. Such proved to be the case in the UK devaluation of 1967.

INTERNATIONAL MONETARY FUND (IMF)

31. Objectives. The Articles of Agreement of the International Monetary Fund (IMF) were signed at a 1944 conference in Bretton Woods, New Hampshire, by forty-four nations. The agreement was implemented in March 1947.

The five objectives set out in Article I are as follows.

(*a*) *International monetary co-operation*, through a permanent institution.

(*b*) *Balanced expansion of world trade*. This is the key objective since the other purposes are means to this end.

(*c*) *Exchange stability*. The maintenance of orderly exchange relations and the avoidance of competitive devaluations.

(*d*) *Multilateral payments*. The elimination of exchange restrictions and the promotion of multilateral payments on current account.

(*e*) *Short-term credit*. In order to add confidence to trading relations, the provision of short-term credit in the event of a temporary balance of payments disequilibrium experienced by a member.

32. The IMF's resources and their significance. There are today more than 100 members each of which contributes to the IMF a quota, calculated in US dollars and related to its GNP. Of this quota 25 per cent was paid in gold (the gold tranche) and the remainder in its own currency (but *see* **48**(*b*)).

The size of the quota is important in that it determines:

(*a*) *the voting power* of each member's Executive Director;
(*b*) *the extent of a member's drawing rights*.

33. Drawing rights. Technically the IMF does not grant loans but authorises a member to purchase with its own currency the currency of another member, i.e. it has the right to draw foreign currency from the Fund subject to certain conditions. These stipulate that the Fund must not previously have declared the desired currency to be scarce nor the drawer to be ineligible and that drawings should not exceed 25 per cent of a member's quota in any one year or a total of 20 per cent. It follows that as a member exercises its drawing rights so the Fund's holding of that country's currency rises. It can be seen therefore that strictly this is not a loan although the drawing country is expected to redeem the Fund's excess holding of its currency in gold or other acceptable currency normally within three to five years.

It should be stressed therefore that the Fund provides only short-term finance to enable a country to meet a temporary disequilibrium in its payments. The Fund's resources must continue to rotate if they are to carry out their function as an international reserve.

34. The Bretton Woods exchange rate policy. Upon joining a member declared a par value for its currency in terms of the US dollar.

All exchange transactions with other members were then carried out within 1 per cent of this parity (*see* **44**(*c*) below). If a member wished to vary this rate it could do so only after consultation with the IMF and then only to correct a fundamental disequilibrium in its payments.

In this way the IMF rules sought to ensure short-term stability of the exchanges which allowed for long-term adjustments, i.e. this was an adjustable-peg system.

35. Prohibition of exchange control. Article VIII prohibits the application of exchange-control restrictions on current account transactions. On the other hand Article VI permits controls over capital movements.

There are two exceptions to the general prohibition, as follows.

(*a*) *Scarce currencies.* If the Fund is unable to supply a particular currency and has declared it to be scarce then controls may be imposed on transactions in that currency. This was the case with the US dollar until 1958 owing to a continuing US surplus disequilibrium.

(*b*) *Existing controls may be retained.* Article XIV permits a country to retain controls over current account payments which existed when it became a member. This was viewed simply as a post-war transitional measure but in the event it was not until 1961 that Western Europe was able to adopt Article VIII. Where advantage is still taken of Article XIV members are obliged to consult annually with the IMF in order to justify the continued retention of controls.

36. Appraisal of the IMF's operations. From the foregoing discussion it can be seen that the IMF has aimed to promote the expansion of world trade by improving the means for international settlement in two ways:

(*a*) stabilising the foreign exchange markets;
(*b*) providing short-term compensatory finance.

37. Stabilising the foreign exchange markets. The intention at Bretton Woods was to establish a system which combined the advantages of a gold standard with those of a fluctuating rate system. What was desired in the exchanges was short-run stability with long-run flexibility since it was considered inevitable that periodically there would have to be a realignment of exchange rates. A devaluation or revaluation would, however, be carried out in an orderly way and only after international consultation.

In the event until 1971 the goal of stability was achieved but at the expense of an almost total inflexibility of the exchanges in the long run. For a variety of reasons governments proved unwilling to depart from a rate of exchange once it had been established. The result was continuing disequilibrium in the payments of a number of countries over protracted periods, e.g. the UK 1959–67, the USA 1958–71.

38. Short-term compensatory finance. In this respect the intention was to guarantee the convertibility of currencies by supporting national reserves with the resources of the IMF. A country with a deficit disequilibrium would be able to obtain short-term finance while it adopted remedial internal policies which would not include resort to exchange control. However, such an objective would only be achieved in a world in which there was a substantial degree of equilibrium overall and no persistent maladjustments such as the dollar shortage. For this reason throughout the 1950s the world was compelled to rely upon exchange controls, and only when the USA moved into deficit did it become possible to achieve convertibility. At the same time the Fund's reserves began to be employed in the way which had been anticipated.

However, the return to convertibility brought another problem, the massive movement of speculative capital between the world's financial centres which has had a highly unstabilising effect upon the balance of international payments. This factor placed the Fund's resources under strain and led to the "General Arrangements to Borrow".

39. General Arrangements to Borrow (GAB). Since 1962 the IMF resources have had support from the "Group of Ten" (EEC (the original Six), USA, UK, Sweden and Japan).

Additionally, there have been developed "swap arrangements" between central banks whereby each agrees to make balances available to the others for specified periods of time. In the late 1960s the UK made much use of these facilities.

40. World liquidity problem. Apart from the strain placed upon national reserves and the resources of the Fund by speculative capital movements, it became increasingly clear in the 1960s that the rapid expansion of world trade called for additions to the international money supply. Throughout the post-war period there had been a steady decline in the ratio of official reserves of gold and foreign exchange to world imports from about 80 per cent in the late 1940s to about 30 per cent at the end of the 1960s. This decline was partially offset by the conditional reserves of the IMF drawing rights, the GAB and the swap arrangements. However, since the last two devices were purely *ad hoc* measures it was felt there should be a more positive and formal attempt to raise the level of international reserves. Consequently, in April 1968, the IMF published its plan for "Special Drawing Rights".

41. Special Drawing Rights (SDRs). The simplest way to envisage the scheme is to see the SDRs as "international paper money" which all countries will accept in settlement of debt.

Technically they take the form of an automatic right to receive foreign currency by transferring one's SDRs to another country designated by the Fund. The basic obligation of each member is to provide his own currency upon the Fund's request up to a total of three times his own allocation of SDRs.

There is a very broad requirement for drawing countries to reconstitute their position but the repayment terms are very liberal. In due course this requirement may well be reconsidered.

From the activation of the scheme in 1970 until 1981 there have been two series of annual allocations. The first, of SDR 9.3 billion, took place between 1970 and 1972; the second, SDR 12 billion, started in 1979 and was completed in January 1981. During the whole period, SDRs have been used in transactions amounting to SDR 33 billion.

(*a*) *The principal reserve asset.* On 1st April 1978, the second amendment to the Articles of Agreement of the IMF was implemented. This has the objective of substituting SDRs for gold as the principal reserve asset in the international monetary system.

(*b*) *Valuation.* Since July 1974 the value of the SDR has been determined by the "standard basket" method, one SDR being equal to the sum of specified quantities of certain major currencies. From 1974 to 1980, sixteen currencies were included in the "basket". On 1st January 1981, this was reduced to five, with new weightings: US dollar (42 per cent); Deutschmark (19 per cent); French franc (13 per cent); Japanese yen (13 per cent); £ sterling (13 per cent).

On these weightings the currency amounts in the basket were fixed on 31st December 1980: US dollar (0.54); Deutschmark (0.46); French franc (0.74); Japanese yen (34.00); £ sterling (0.071).

The value of the SDR is then calculated daily by the IMF in terms of the US dollar, using noon, middle-market rates in London for the dollar (i.e. 0.54 cents) against the fixed quantities of the four other currencies.

In the light of the considerable volatility of exchange rates in recent years and the progressive demonetisation of gold, the SDR is assuming increasing importance as an international unit of account by official organisations and in the financial markets.

NOTE: In connection with the fears in the 1960s of an inadequacy of world liquidity, it will be observed that the development of the Euromarkets has done much to solve this problem (*see* VIII, **49–54**).

THE FOREIGN EXCHANGE CRISIS OF 1971

42. Persistent US disequilibrium. It has previously been noted that in 1958 the US balance of payments moved into a deficit which has subsequently remained unchanged, primarily because of overseas military and aid commitments. For the post-war dollar shortage there was consequently substituted a dollar glut which periodically expressed itself in pressure on the dollar exchange rate. In due course this situation led the USA in 1968 to restrict the convertibility of dollars into gold. Gold from the reserves would now be sold at the official price of $35 only *to central banks*. Parallel to this official gold market there developed a free market with a substantially higher price which gave a truer reflection of the dollar's real international value.

43. Dollar crisis, 1971. In August large sales of surplus dollars by European central banks produced such a heavy drain of US gold reserves that convertibility was now *entirely* suspended. Pressure on dollar exchange rates throughout the world then caused the emergency closure of exchange markets. When dealings were resumed the price of the dollar in terms of all other major currencies had fallen substantially away from the previous parities.

The US monetary authorities were then subjected to considerable pressure from their world trading partners to accept an *official* devaluation against gold in order that markets might be quickly stabilised. Rather than accept a course of action which would depreciate the dollar uniformly against *all* other countries, the US authorities preferred that certain of her major trade competitors, notably Japan and the West European nations, should *revalue* individually and in varying degrees against the dollar. This solution was not acceptable to those countries since they feared that such revaluations might weaken the competitiveness of their export prices and so have adverse effects upon their trade.

In this impasse exchange rates were permitted to float with central banks intervening only to forestall an excessive appreciation of their own currencies. The USA meanwhile took action to protect her balance of payments by imposing a 10 per cent import surcharge. Over the following four months fears were expressed that possible retaliatory trade and currency restrictions coupled with the existing exchange rate instability were leading to a downturn in trade and conceivably a world depression.

44. Group of Ten meeting, December 1971. After long preliminary negotiations the finance ministers of the Group of Ten met in late December at the Smithsonian Institute, Washington and arrived at a *temporary* solution to which the IMF gave its support. This subsequently became known as the Smithsonian agreement. The compromise involved the following.

(*a*) *Concessions by the USA.* The USA agreed to devalue gold from \$35 per fine ounce to \$38, i.e. a devaluation of 8.57 per cent. Since the dollar remained wholly inconvertible the measurement against gold had only numerical significance. Gold provided a useful yardstick. At the same time the import surcharge was abandoned.

(*b*) *Concessions by the Group of Ten.* The other members of the Group of Ten agreed to revalue against the dollar by varying amounts. At one end of the scale the Japanese yen and the Deutschmark appreciated by 16.9 and 13.5 per cent respectively. At the other extreme, Italy and Sweden appreciated by only 7.5 per cent. Roughly in the middle, the UK and France revalued by 8.57 per cent, precisely the same as the increase in the dollar price of gold; i.e. while revaluing against the dollar they maintained their existing parities with gold.

(*c*) *Wider margins.* To give the exchanges greater flexibility and monetary authorities a stronger position in dealing with speculative capital flows, dealing margins were widened to $2\frac{1}{4}$ per cent. The implication for sterling with a new parity of \$2.60 was an obligation on the UK monetary authorities to support the rate of exchange within the limits of \$2.54 and \$2.66.

What could be observed in these arrangements was the first

realignment of *all* exchange rates since the Bretton Woods agreement in 1944.

45. The Group of Ten communiqué. The opinion was widely held that the situation had been retrieved only at the eleventh hour and then only temporarily. In their communiqué, the finance ministers therefore agreed that discussions should be promptly undertaken, particularly within the context of the IMF, to consider more permanent arrangements for the reform of the international monetary system. It was agreed to direct attention to the appropriate monetary means of stabilising exchange rates and ensuring convertibility: to the proper role of gold, of reserve currencies and of special drawing rights; to the permissible margin of fluctuation on either side of agreed parities and to other means of establishing flexibility; and to measures appropriate to dealing with the movement of short-term capital.

It therefore transpired that the weakness of the Bretton Woods agreement led ultimately to a world monetary crisis which was temporarily resolved only by long and patient multilateral negotiation.

MANAGED FLOATING

46. Breakdown of the Smithsonian agreement. The attempt to re-instate an adjustable-peg system was sustained for only a few months. During 1972, one country after another broke away to apply a number of variations on floating rates.

The first few years of floating proved moderately successful even though the system was completely contrary to that which the IMF had considered essential to world monetary stability. In due course the new arrangements came to be seen as a permanent feature of the international monetary system and at the Jamaica conference of the IMF in 1976 were legalised in an amendment to the Articles of Agreement.

47. A managed float. Theoretically, a floating exchange rate should produce equilibrium in the international balance of payments. However, unless there is a high elasticity of demand for imports and exports the adjustment process may be protracted. During this period there is no guarantee that surpluses or deficits will be offset by capital flows.

Accordingly, *managed* floating has been generally accepted. Governments attempt to limit the severity of exchange rate movements through central bank intervention in the market.

In the UK, intervention has taken three forms. Central monetary reserves are used to make sales or purchases at spot (present) rates, thus artificially influencing those rates. Secondly, the authorities may operate in the forward market to influence the future spot value. This may serve to deter speculation against the currency. Thirdly, changes in domestic interest rates may influence short-term capital movements across the exchanges.

48. Evaluation of the system. There are three main features.

(*a*) *Method of adjustment.* This mechanism provides for the longer-term adjustment of payments disequilibrium. Moreover, the burden of adjustment is not placed exclusively upon the surplus or deficit countries but is shared. It may also be thought that floating rates are less amenable to speculative pressures on currencies which previously had difficulty in adhering to pegged rates.

(*b*) *Liquidity.* In the first place, with no requirement to support a fixed rate of exchange, there is less need for international liquidity. However, the development of the Eurocurrency markets has increased the availability of liquid funds so that it becomes relatively easy for countries to borrow (outside the constraints of the IMF) should they wish to intervene on the exchanges. In short, the constraints of fixed rates upon inflationary domestic policies have been reduced.

Floating rates have also served to advance the demonetisation of gold as a source of international liquidity since it could no longer be the ultimate *numeraire* (i.e. acceptable international currency to which national currencies are related at a fixed rate) in which exchange values are expressed. This process went further at the 1976 conference when it was agreed that the IMF should sell one-third of its gold holdings and no longer require members to pay a quarter of their quota (or quota increase) in gold. Foreign currencies or SDRs may now be used for this purpose.

(*c*) *International co-operation.* The abandonment of the fixed rules established at Bretton Woods has reduced the need for formal co-operation. There is now more flexibility but accompanying dangers should countries engage in competitive depreciation of their currencies in order to maintain the competitiveness of their own exports. This was a common practice in the 1930s.

MONETARY UNION

49. The Werner Report, 1970. The report proposed the following stages by which European monetary union could be achieved as an instrument for the more rapid attainment of the political and economic objectives of the EEC:

(*a*) a progressive reduction in the margins within which member currencies would be permitted to fluctuate against each other;

(*b*) the pooling of foreign exchange reserves;

(*c*) ultimate elimination of margins and the creation of a single common currency;

(*d*) the establishment of a single central bank.

The adoption in principle of the report in 1971 coincided with the dollar crisis and the Smithsonian agreement. The new IMF arrangements which permitted exchange rate movements of $2\frac{1}{4}$ per cent either side of parity conflicted with the report's first objective of reducing such fluctuations between its members. Consequently, the "snake in the tunnel" system was devised.

50. The "snake in the tunnel". Member countries agreed to contain exchange rate movements between their currencies within a narrow band of $2\frac{1}{4}$ per cent (the "snake"). At the same time, these currencies would move together as a bloc within the wider band of $4\frac{1}{2}$ per cent permitted by the Smithsonian arrangements (the "tunnel").

The scheme was implemented in 1972 with the six original EEC members, Eire, Denmark and, for a short time, the UK participating. The abandonment of the Smithsonian agreement in 1972–1973 removed the "tunnel" leaving the "snake" to float against the currencies of the rest of the world.

For some countries, adherence to the "snake" proved difficult in the context of differing national rates of inflation and the instability of international payments and exchange rates induced by the oil crisis and the onset of world recession. It appeared that the Werner plan would have to be abandoned.

51. Bremen conference, 1978. A fresh initiative was taken at a summit conference of the heads of the nine EEC governments held in Bremen in July 1978. A fresh plan was outlined to promote closer monetary co-operation.

52. European Monetary System (EMS). The system began to

operate in March 1979 and included all EEC members with the exception of the UK. Central banks were required to operate in accordance with the following two principles.

(a) *A "parity grid"*. In a similar way to the "snake", the exchange rates of member currencies were permitted a maximum movement against each other of $2\frac{1}{4}$ per cent.

(b) *The European Currency Unit divergence indicator*. The European Currency Unit (ECU) is based upon a "basket" of EEC currencies (including sterling) weighted in accordance with their relative importance to EEC output. The ECU is then used as a base for calculating the central rate for each currency. A maximum percentage deviation is allotted to each currency. At this point remedial action by national governments is expected.

The adoption of the two principles was a compromise made in the interests of weaker members. Their objection to the "parity grid" alone, as to the "snake", was that the burden of adjustment was carried solely by the weaker, deficit nations. The inclusion of the ECU divergence indicator facilitates some sharing of the burden. When weaker currencies depreciate so does the value of the ECU. Stronger countries are then obliged to take action to prevent their currencies rising above their permitted deviation.

THE WORLD BANK GROUP

53. Objectives. It has been noted that the ultimate purpose of the IMF is the promotion of international trade as a means of raising world living standards. Similarly, the World Bank Group which is concerned with increasing the flow of investment in the developing countries may be said to have the same objectives. The more rapidly the economies of the developing countries expand the fuller the part they can play in international trade.

54. International Bank for Reconstruction and Development (IBRD). Basically this is an international investment bank financed by the developed nations and which makes loans to governments for approved projects for periods up to thirty-five years at the substantial interest rate of $5\frac{1}{2}$ per cent.

A criticism of IBRD has been that the debt service burden at this rate of interest has grown so rapidly that during the 1960s it was absorbing 10 per cent of the export income of the developing countries, thus jeopardising their economic programmes.

55. International Development Association (IDA). This organisation is also financed by the governments of the developed countries. It was set up because of the inability of some developing countries either to qualify projects for IBRD support or to meet the high interest charges. The loan terms are liberal with easily staged repayments and no interest other than a $\frac{3}{4}$–1 per cent service charge.

56. International Finance Corporation (IFC). Unlike IBRD and IDA, the IFC which was set up in 1956 does not make loans to governments. Along with private investors it participates in private industrial enterprises.

PROGRESS TEST 12

1. Explain how a rate of exchange is reached. **(1)**

2. What do you understand by a variable exchange rate system? **(2)**

3. Explain how an exchange rate may be actively stabilised. **(3(b))**

4. What do you understand by "exchange control"? **(4)**

5. Where exchange rates are stabilised, what will be the effects of a payments disequilibrium? **(5(b))**

6. Explain the price-specie flow mechanism. **(6)**

7. What were the main features of the gold standard? **(7)**

8. How was equilibrium supposedly restored on a full gold standard? **(8)**

9. What were the main disadvantages of the gold standard? **(9(b))**

10. Criticise the concept of the price-specie flow mechanism. **(10)**

11. What is the significance of changes in income to the balance of payments? **(11)**

12. Explain one of the variations to the full gold standard. **(12)**

13. Why was the gold standard abandoned? **(13)**

14. What are the purposes of an exchange-control system? **(16)**

15. What are the disadvantages of exchange control? **(18)**

16. Define an "adjustable peg". **(21)**

17. What are the shortcomings of the theory of purchasing power parity? **(22)**

18. Upon what factors does a successful devaluation depend? **(24–27)**

19. Compare the main arguments for and against fluctuating exchange rates. **(28, 29)**

20. Appraise the case for an adjustable-peg system. **(30)**

21. List the objectives of the IMF. **(31)**

22. What are "drawing rights"? **(33)**

23. What policy does the IMF pursue in respect of exchange control? **(35)**

24. Assess the success of the IMF's operations. **(36–38)**

25. Explain the nature of the world liquidity problem. **(40)**

26. What are "Special Drawing Rights"? **(41)**

27. What was the Smithsonian Agreement? **(44)**

28. What do you understand by "managed floating"? **(47)**

29. What are the principal features of the present exchange rate system? **(48)**

30. Outline the proposals of the Werner Report. **(49)**

31. Explain the operation of "the snake in the tunnel". **(50)**

32. List the features of the European Monetary System. **(52)**

33. Which institutions fall within the World Bank Group? **(53–56)**

34. What are the objectives of the World Bank Group? **(53–56)**

PART FOUR

GOVERNMENT AND INDUSTRY

CHAPTER XIII

Industrial Structure

PROBLEMS OF DEFINITION

1. Introduction. The final part of this book is concerned with government involvement in industry, for even a *laissez-faire* inspired government cannot divorce itself from direct contact with a nation's industrial affairs.

Involvement can occur at several policy levels: size (monopolies and mergers), overseas aspects (multinationals and the EEC), location (regional aid), ownership change (nationalisation), the fostering of new technology (National Enterprise Board), or the establishment of social responsibilities (equal opportunities legislation).

Governments will seek by compulsion, persuasion or incentive to improve the nation's industrial structure, although rigorous and calculable definitions of improvement are seldom offered.

This chapter offers an organisational and economic framework within which to evaluate a government's attempts to modify the country's industrial structure.

2. What is a firm? This appears to be a trite question until it is realised that the local corner newsagent, the main street dry cleaner and Unilevers are all called firms in common language, yet their size, their methods of organisatio and their economic impact are so widely disparate that a unique definition seems impracticable.

Economic theory defines a firm as a mechanism for transferring imputs into outputs and it assumes a single decision-making process undertaken by an entrepreneur. The economist then assumes the firm's sole aim is to maximise prfit and he studies the price/output policies of the firm under various types of competition. The theoretical economist is not concerned with the internal organisational workings of a firm important though they are for decision-making.

Applied economists accept the first part of the definition (inputs into outputs) but they must also study the ownership control problem because of its impact on policy-making (*see* **4–9**), and they question the aims of the company (*see* **10–14**) and its pursuit of efficiency (*see* **15–18**). Problems of size variation (*see* **19–20**) are also of importance.

The widening of the economists' interests in the firm should be of use to governments as they chase the dream of the perfect industrial structure.

3. What is an industry? An industry is equally difficult to define, e.g. is chocolate making a self-contained industry or part of the confectionary industry or even the food industry? This definitional problem might appear to be pure semantics but in monopoly studies firms are said to dominate a market or industry. Obviously in this case some degree of definitional accuracy is required.

Statistically, the government has designated twenty-five Industrial Orders under the British Standard Industrial Classification (BSIC), e.g. V is Metal Manufacture, VIII is Vehicles and X is Textiles. The Orders are then subdivided into small industries and eventually into products.

For example:

Order — Electrical goods industry
Industry — Domestic and electrical appliances
Product — Electrical cookers, refrigerators

OWNERSHIP, CONTROL AND POWER

4. Introduction. Four potential power elements can be delineated in a firm: shareholders, directors, management and workers. The traditional simple idea was that the shareholders (the owners) elected directors (the controllers), who appointed managers to run the day-to-day business; the workers were merely a human resource input. In a small firm the ownership and control factor would be amalgamated in the owner's hands.

However, today the interrelationship of the four is infinitely more complex in any firm above a small to medium size. The changes have arisen because society's perception of the status or role of each partner has altered and society in general has developed a more participatory philosophy of life.

5. Shareholders. The traditional shareholder was an individual with a big or small stake in one firm who really believed that he could influence the company via the annual general meeting when the directors were elected. Today the major shareholders are the institutions, e.g. pension funds and insurance companies, who hold 40–45 per cent of all British private equity. How and to what purpose they exercise this considerable power is a matter of some controversy.

On paper they should be able to pressurise firms to act in an efficient manner because this will benefit their investment, but the institutions have a paranoiac fear of publicly arguing with management because of the effect on share prices, therefore any pressure for good or bad is exerted behind the scenes. Some union leaders would like a voice in the distribution of institutional funds allegedly to increase levels of industrial investment but they refuse to discuss by what criteria the investment would be made.

6. Directors. In practice directors are no longer beholden to the shareholders' meeting because, through the use of proxy votes and the institutional votes, directors have become self-perpetuating, changes usually only occurring through boardroom arguments and divisions.

. Today the main debate revolves around the role of the non-executive directors. Many years ago most boards would have non-executive members but from the 1950s fashion changed, it was felt that directors of this type were for decorative purposes and many companies switched to full-time executive directors. Now doubt is creeping in, particularly with so many poor industrial performances and company scandals. Current opinion again favours non-executive directors but to have a watch-dog role. This belief extends to a suggestion that Britain should copy German and some USA companies in having an executive board and a supervisory board, the latter representing shareholder, worker and financial interests.

7. Management. The role of managers has not changed but there has been a marked reappraisal of the power of that role. Many organisational students, Galbraith in particular (see I, **11–19**), believe that management forms cliques and by controlling information flows to directors and workers it can effectively direct the running of the company to safeguard its own interests. Interestingly, East-European commentators have noted the phenomena in socialist industries. Galbraith has named this new power base the techno-structure. Its influence will depend on the level of management under discussion and the executive power of the directors.

8. Workers. Workers now have far more legal rights, e.g. in relation to security of employment and trade union activity, but the main new interest is worker involvement in policy-making. Many ideas are canvassed, worker directors, worker co-operatives, consultative committees to name but a few. Evaluation of the various methods is outside the scope of this book but any discussion about mergers, nationalisation and restructuring must recognise that a worker's labour gives him some rights in the policy-making processes of his firm.

9. Conclusion. The control problem of the modern firm becomes even more complicated because some critics feel it ought to be accountable to the public at large, either through some form of government representation or by allowing consumers a voice in company affairs. (*See* **13**.)

Clearly the last decades of the twentieth century will see a significant change in the real concept of a firm, but it is very easy for opponents of the traditional firm to become obsessed with ownership and control problems and totally ignore the purposes and efficiency problems which are at the heart of industrial success.

AIMS OF A FIRM

10. Profit maximisation. Standard economic theory of the firm assumes that the sole aim is to maximise profits and all decision taking is geared to that end. Laymen also suggest that a business is trying to make as much money as possible. These views are over-simplified and ignore the intricate workings of the modern company. The concept of profit maximisation, apart from the problem of measuring profit (*see* **16**), is difficult to interpret in a meaningful practical way. (*See also* I, **20–26**.)

11. Problems of profit maximisation.

(*a*) The premise is based on a marginal analysis whereas firms tend to use average precepts, e.g. a firm has far more knowledge of average rather than marginal costs, thus the company has no precise guide to decisions which will maximise profits.

(b) A company might not know if it was maximising profits because it has always to make a choice between different policy options. Suppose it chooses policy A, then, with hindsight, it realises policy B or C might have produced better profit figures, yet history cannot be reversed. As information costs are not negligible the firm never acts on anything approaching perfect knowledge, thus it may never know whether it is achieving maximum profits.

(c) The time scale of profit making is an important consideration. It is possible to make large-scale, short-period profits but in so doing damage the long-term health of the company. Similarly firms often accept short-run losses to build up business.

(d) The assumption of profit maximisation ignores the fact that a business organisation is made up of individuals often coalescing into groups motivated by a whole range of objectives, psychological, social as well as economic (see 12(d)), and the objectives of these groups are not necessarily profit orientated.

12. Alternative aims. There is an ever increasing research literature on business aims other than profit maximisation. Below are brief sketches of the major schools of opinion with their protagonists' names in brackets.

(a) *Managerial discretion (Williamson)*. Management will always seek profit to satisfy the shareholders but it also has its own needs, e.g. status from empire building or non-taxable perks, all of which are costs charged out of profits. Williamson suggests this idea is more applicable to large organisation management which may be remote from day-to-day money-making decisions.

(b) *Sales revenue maximisation (Baumol)*. Sales maximisation is good for the morale of workers, customers and financiers so the company tries to maximise sales within the constraint of adequate profits.

(c) *Managerial growth (Maris)*. The company is a bureaucratic structure whose performance will be judged on growth and security. Management feels its prestige will arise out of company growth; being a big company manager creates its own status.

(d) *Behavioural theory (Cyert and March)*. A company is a human organisation with a wide range of goals, expectations and choices overladen with uncertainties. Therefore any decision will

be a compromise between a coalition of interests; that such decisions should produce profit maximisation seems unlikely.

(*e*) *X-theory of inefficiency* (*Leibenstein*). A firm is split between
the utility functions of its various human components and unless
there is a policing system, e.g. intense competition or profit sharing, inefficiencies will creep into the company as its members
seek their own objectives. For example, a company in a monopolistic position may settle for a quiet life without too many
pressures.

In general the common thread of the new thinking is that if a firm
seeks satisfactory levels of profit to stay in business then its
various levels of organisation pursue their own objectives.

13. Social role. The discussion on aims has so far assumed the
firm to be self-contained but in fact it operates in the community.
Should its aims therefore contain obligations to the people at
large? Types of question involved here are: What costs should a
company incur to avoid pollution? Should it employ certain
numbers of handicapped people? Should it create jobs for the
young unemployed? What are its attitudes to women and coloured
people?

Critics of the profit motive suggest that companies ought to
produce 'social accounts' wherein the costs and benefits to society
of their economic activities would be listed and if possible
measured.

While not going this far, many companies have become sensitive
to the social implications of their business policies, although
any definition of social good must be subjective (*see* E. J.
Morgan, "Social Responsibility and Private Enterprise", *National
Westminster Bank Review*, May 1977).

14. Private and public ownership. The tangled arguments on company aims have assumed private ownership but the modern firm
may be sustained by government money or it may be nationalised. Nearly two generations of nationalisation in practice have
failed to unravel the aims of a nationalised organisation (*see* XVIII,
22–29) so the chances of solving the aims problem of a half-
government-owned company seem remote.

The basic dilemma is the role of profit (*see* **15**) and its relations
to social need. Some people try to find a middle road by asking
companies to act in the national interest but this is surely a subjective nebulous idea unless a country is at total war. Ultimately

a country's industrial organisations must make efficient use (*see below*) of the nation's scarce resources.

COMPANY EFFICIENCY

15. Profits. In Western societies and increasingly in Marxist controlled countries profit (surplus for Marxists) is used as an efficiency test but paragraphs **16–21** will show that this relationship can have pitfalls and that efficiency is itself a difficult concept to measure in practical terms.

Profits have four functions.

(*a*) They are a source of funds for investment. (In Britain approximately 75 per cent of investment comes from undistributed profits.)

(*b*) They act as an incentive to undertake business risks. Individuals are willing to run the risk of supplying goods and services because they hope to make a profit.

(*c*) They are an allocative device because· past profits or the chance of future ones attract resources into a business.

(*d*) They serve as a test of efficiency in the sense that companies making large profits are thought to be efficient. This can be a narrow view of efficiency and the point is taken up in **17**.

Profits have a vital role to play and no economy can organise itself without the pursuit of profits. Critics of profits confuse the making of them, which is a necessity, with the distribution and ownership of them, which is a socio-political question.

16. Problems of defining profits. No effort was made to define profits in **15** and apart from accountants and enlightened economists few people realise what an elusive concept it is. Conventionally, profit is defined as the difference between total revenue and total costs. This is accurate but ignores huge difficulties of defining revenues and costs and in particular such terms as asset and stock valuation and depreciation.

Currently there is heated debate on how to allow for the impact of inflation on asset valuation because different accounting methods can produce totally different profit figures. In 1975 companies were showing profit on paper, yet in practice, in terms of liquidity, were near bankruptcy. In 1977 a leading motor manufacturer using one accounting method showed profits of £59 million, and using another method produced profits of £7 million.

XIII. INDUSTRIAL STRUCTURE

Profits will always be used as a guide to economic performance but blind faith should never be put in a single set of profit figures.

17. Profits and efficiency. Bearing in mind the possible problems outlined in **16**, profits can be used as efficiency criteria. As an absolute figure, e.g. last year Company X made £100,000 profits, they are valueless but must be expressed as a percentage, usually of capital or possibly turnover. (Retailers may consider profit in relation to selling space.)

If a company has a return on capital of x per cent, how is this to be judged good or bad? Possible criteria include the following.

(*a*) Does x per cent attract new investors?
(*b*) Is it sufficient for internal resource growth?
(*c*) How does it compare with similarly situated companies?
(*d*) How does it compare with previous performance? This can be a dubious argument because there is a hidden implication that x should always be increasing, which is an impossible business situation.

When all these questions have been answered one final question must be asked. In what circumstances were the profits made? Did they arise out of a monopolistic situation? Were they the result of government subsidy or protection? If the answers are "yes" then how efficient was the company? Given the ambivalences surrounding the use of profits to test business efficiency there is always a search for alternative criteria.

18. Alternative efficiency tests. Because the financial measurement of efficiency is so fraught with accounting difficulties there has always been a desire to find more precise measurements based on the relationship between factor inputs and output. Even here there are measurement problems. For example, the input labour will vary tremendously as to effort, skill and attitudes and it is arguable how accurately wages measure these variations. In addition, nobody can evaluate the exact interdependence of capital, labour and management in producing a given output.

The most common form of this method is "technical efficiency" when a firm tries to operate at the lowest possible average cost, thereby producing a given output with the least possible input or alternatively maximising the output from a fixed input.

The company's efficiency might also be judged by its innovating record measured through its ability to produce new goods or better production methods. "Better" is, of course, a subjective word because the new idea might, for example, lay off many people thus causing social hardship. Obviously efficiency is impossible to measure precisely, but that is no excuse for attacking the pursuit of efficiency because all societies are faced with the reality of scarce resources and they must devise systems of using the resources effectively. That is the true meaning of efficiency; it does not represent an economic attack on human dignity as some critics suggest.

19. Business size and efficiency. Private companies have grown enormously over the last fifty years (*see* XV) and the justification for the growth has usually been to achieve efficiency through scale economies. Since 1950 governments have vastly increased their involvement with industry, and again have often justified their actions by the desire to obtain scale economies. This argument stretches through most of the remaining chapters of the book—is it therefore a valid argument?

Scale economies simply mean that as a firm expands output its costs do not rise in the same proportion, therefore costs per unit fall. The saving arises because bigger companies have cost advantages (scale economies) in finance, labour, management, technology and resource purchase. Traditionally, Henry Ford was the industrialist who first stumbled on the idea with the mass production of his Model-T.

The situation is shown diagrammatically in Fig. 5.

The crucial question for industrialists and policy makers is where does the point OA (minimum average cost) occur because afterwards costs rise through scale diseconomies (market saturation, rising labour costs, management difficulties)?

Industries have argued that the cost curve is very elongated, almost L-shaped (*see* Fig. 6), and that therefore it makes sense for companies to grow almost indefinitely. However, recent research is showing disturbing facts which seriously question the policy of recklessly pursuing the goal of size to achieve scale economies.

20. Doubts on size and efficiency. Efficiency arguments based on scale economies are very difficult to prove because it is so difficult to measure economies of scale. There can be different definitions of average costs, outputs are seldom homogeneous and cost variations can be realistically attributed to factors other than size. So great are the problems that many studies merely investigate

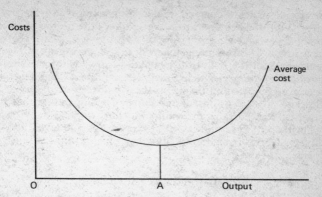

FIG. 5   *Average total cost curve.* Traditionally, the curve is considered to be saucer-shaped.

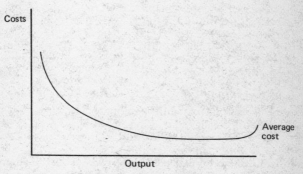

FIG. 6   *An L-shaped average total cost curve.* The curve continues to decline over a very substantial output.

production inputs and outputs. This is an engineering approach
and ignores the vital elements of administration, marketing and
transport. (*See* C. A. Smith, *Readings on the Theory of the Firm*,
Penguin.)

These statistical problems have not deterred people from making
a generalised correlation between size and efficiency but even this
relationship is severely questioned by reports ranging from ten-year

academic studies to congressional investigations of conglomerates (*see* XV, **16**). Time and again the results show no link between profitability and size of business. The obstacle facing the big company is the traditional diseconomy of management. Management expertise seems to disintegrate as companies grow. Indeed most large companies acknowledge the problem and react by decentralising decision taking, as they want their managers to be closer to grass roots output and money-making and not become involved with bureaucratic empire building (*see* **12**(*a*)).

Sociologists have shown that humans react more favourably to the small firm ambience and this has obvious implications for problems of size and efficiency.

21. Summary. Industrial efficiency is the moonbeam chased by all governments but few of them show awareness of the need to define efficiency concepts before coherent policies can be formulated.

In many ways the simplest and perhaps the best efficiency test links profit and returns on capital (*see* Table XXI).

TABLE XXI. *Top ten efficiency table (gross profit/net capital ratio), 1970–79*

1. Kwik Save	6. Alfred Dunhill
2. Coral Leisure	7. Bambers Stores
3. Electro Components	8. Mothercare
4. M.F.I. Furniture	9. Allied Colloids
5. Comet Radiovision	10. Dale Electric

(*Source: Management Today, February 1980.*)

PRESENT INDUSTRIAL STRUCTURE

22. A mixed industrial structure. Britain has a mixed industrial structure involving both the private and public sector.

The private sector operates exclusively with marketable goods for which output costs must be met by product sales revenue. The public sector is involved with marketable goods via the nationalised industries but it also produces non-market goods, e.g. health and education, for which costs are met out of taxation. By the 1980s Britain's non-market sector accounted for approximately 43 per cent of the Gross Domestic Product.

Within the private sector, compared to our competitors, Britain has a higher level of oligopolistic concentration, a higher degree of conglomerate diversification (*see* XV, **16**), and a smaller small company segment. Our market structures stretch from near perfect commodity markets to the single supplier market, e.g. coal.

Moving into the last decades of the century, Britain, together with the older industrial nations, is suffering from the erosion of its manufacturing base as the steel, textile, shipbuilding, and even car and other consumer durable industries suffer from general depression in the West and intense competition from industry in the Far East. The older nations must guard their affluence via the new electronic and sophisticated service industries.

This switch can be seen in the British Business Profitability League 1979 (*Management Today*, October 1980) where the "top ten" is dominated by six distribution and two electronic companies, while RACAL, the electronics company, was the fastest growing company by stock market value in 1979 (*Management Today*, June 1980).

23. Galbraith thesis. J. K. Galbraith the American economist has long argued that the traditional market classification (ranging from perfect, through imperfect and oligopolistic, to single supplier) does not represent a realistic picture of Western economies. He suggests two categories as follows.

(*a*) *Market economy*. Many small firms exist in a variety of industries but their work is unplanned and they seldom have long production runs. They have little power (except perhaps in small geographical areas) over prices, their consumers or the government.

(*b*) *Planned economy*. Most industries are dominated by big companies with huge, expensive technology. Because of the big financial involvement the firms must try to dictate to the consumer over prices, quantities and qualities of output. To help their domination they are closely involved with the government at many levels of management.

Critics of Galbraith say he ignores the interdependence of big and small firms for subcontract work and that he overemphasises the power of big companies to manipulate demand. Business history reveals some terrible demand miscalculations and also shows a surprising fluidity in the rise and fall of big companies.

However, Galbraith does well to highlight the changing pattern of industrial structure and to show how it differs from the traditional economic textbook. These new perspectives are especially valuable in dealing with monopoly and merger problems.

24. Private industry and government. As the remaining chapters show, industry and government are now entangled so remorselessly that it is pointless to argue for an economy with a total private industrial sector.

Four examples of the involvement are given below.

(*a*) The impact of government policies on industry, e.g. transport policy on civil engineers and car producers.

(*b*) The government as buyer and seller, e.g. defence contracts, nationalised industries.

(*c*) The impact of big firm policies on the economy, e.g. petrol, chemicals and drugs.

(*d*) Government use of subsidies and taxes for social purposes.

Governments are going to involve themselves with industry but what criteria have they for their interventionist policies?

GUIDELINES FOR GOVERNMENT POLICY ON INDUSTRIAL STRUCTURE

25. Basic situation. Despite Galbraith (*see* **23**) all firms operate in fairly uncontrolled markets and if government is dissatisfied with private industry, the analysis must be within three elements of the market, viz. market structure, conduct and performance.

R. T. Nelson summarised the areas of investigation in the diagram reproduced in Fig. 7 (R. T. Nelson, "Industrial Economics", *Economics*, Summer 1974).

The arrows between the market boxes indicate the common belief about the causal relations but research evidence suggests the relationship is not so obvious, e.g. changes in market performance could alter structures, performance now could vary conduct in the future. Despite these reservations the basic premise is that governments will be trying to influence activities within the boxes because they believe the current market situation is:

(*a*) not producing economic effectiveness;

(*b*) not reflecting the community's social values and desires.

Economics via welfare theory offers guidelines to the government, but non-market believers put their trust in civil servants pursuing the national interest as the basis for governments altering the industrial structure.

FIG. 7   *An analysis of the functioning of a market.* The diagram suggests causal relationships within the market.

26. Welfare theory. This paragraph is a very simple interpretation of a most complex piece of theory which centres on a concept called the Pareto Optimum. This optimum is achieved when it is impossible to devise a policy which makes one person "better off" without making someone else "worse off". Better and worse imply higher and lower levels of satisfaction. Should the Pareto Optimum be realised then an optimum allocation of resources will be achieved.

As an example consider the following. (Assume a two-product model economy.)

		Marginal			
		Cost			
	Price	*(MC)*		*Price*	*MC*
Cars	£2,000	£1,500	Washing		
			Machines	£200	£300
	Price $>$ MC			Price $<$ MC	

i.e. the utility to the consumer (measured by price) exceeds the value of the productive resources utilised.

i.e. the utility to the consumer is less than the value of productive resources utilised.

In this situation it would benefit the consumers to switch resources from washing machine manufacturing to car producing.

For example, switch £1,500 of resources.

Benefits — consumer gains an extra £2,000 of cars

Losses — consumer loses $\dfrac{£(1,500 \times 200)}{300}$

$= £1,000$ of machines

∴ Benefits are greater than losses.

This movement of resources will continue until price = MC

For example:

	Price	*MC*		*Price*	*MC*
Cars	£1,500	£1,500	Washing		
			Machines	£300	£300

Now a £1,500 switch produces a gain of £1,500 value of cars but a loss of £1,500 of machines, so no consumer gain would materialise.

The main lesson is that at the optimum position the value of each good to society must equal the costs incurred by society in producing the good. This position is the price = marginal cost equilibrium position of perfect competition and is an argument for allocating resources by encouraging a perfect market situation to exist.

27. Criticisms of welfare analysis. The major pragmatic criticisms of welfare theory concepts are as follows.

(*a*) The theory tends to concentrate on private costs and benefits while ignoring social costs and benefits which are called externalities. For example, a firm working in a market situation may create pollution which affects the community outside the immediate market environment. It is therefore argued that market price does not reflect a true social valuation.

(b) Given the presence of almost immovable monopolistic elements, e.g. large companies or unions with a closed shop policy, in the modern market situation no government is in a position to pursue policies based on the existence of a perfect market.

28. Consequence of criticism. Because of the above doubts the modern policy maker has tended to wander along two avenues of thought.

(a) *Market improvement ideas.* This means attacking the social and economic defects of the market system through the use of, for example, subsidies, taxation and anti-monopoly policies. Such policies still leave choice decisions in the grip of the consumer and producer.

(b) *Market replacement ideas.* Examples here are the education and health services and nationalisation as originally conceived in its socialist pristineness. In this case, choice is much more in the hands of the bureaucrats.

The latter idea has grown remarkably in the last twenty years and has become quite fashionable because its supporters believe something called social justice will thus be achieved.

29. Criticism of market replacement ideas. These beliefs, now the conventional wisdom, are in fact under severe intellectual attack. Three major protagonists are A. Downs, *An Economic Theory of Democracy*, Harper, New York 1957; W. A. Niskanen, *Bureaucracy and Representative Government*, Aldine Atherton, 1971; and S. Brittan, "Government and the Market Economy", *Hobart Papers*, Institute of Economic Affairs, 1971.

The basic attack centres on the belief that bureaucrats and planners are men without sordid human motivation, who have divine insights into the needs of other men and can allocate resources to satisfy these needs apparently without any allocative criteria. The critics suggest bureaucratic organisations are human maximisers (like producers and consumers) and they seek to maximise their budgets because herein lies the path to bureaucratic satisfactions, e.g. good salaries, promotion, job security and prestige. Politicians also act in the same way to maximise votes. Thus a bureaucracy perhaps allied to a production interest can convince a government that a certain policy is a vote winner, but to believe or prove that the policy makes economic sense in terms of resource allocation is another matter altogether.

Indeed it is a mystery to economists why the anti-market forces place such faith in the bureaucratic decision maker, for the latter needs the combined talents of a Benedictine monk and Einstein to justify the faith placed in him.

30. Conclusion. This chapter has shown the difficulties of searching for a perfect industrial structure—the rest of the chapters study governments making this search. In evaluating government actions and the advice given to governments, it will benefit readers to refer back to this chapter to establish whether decisions are being taken for identifiable economic and social ends or merely for short-term political gain.

PROGRESS TEST 13

1. Describe the difficulties in defining a firm. **(2)**
2. What is the British Standard Industrial Classification? **(3)**
3. Explain a techno-structure. **(7)**
4. Discuss the problems of using profit maximisation as the single goal of a firm. **(11)**
5. What is meant by the behavioural theory of the firm? **(12)**
6. What are social accounts? **(13)**
7. Outline the functions of profit. **(15)**
8. Explain what is meant by scale economies. **(19)**
9. Suggest two criticisms of Galbraith's view of the modern economy. **(23)**
10. What is the Pareto Optimum? **(26)**
11. Explain a "market replacement" policy. **(28)**

CHAPTER XIV

General Government Policy Towards Industry

PHILOSOPHY OF RELATIONSHIP

1. Aim of study. Governments have always wanted to tinker with the trade and industry of their country, e.g. in the nineteenth century the early railways were restricted by governments in their pricing policies, but the extent of this involvement has changed radically in this century.

Until 1914, conventional wisdom believed in the virtue of comparatively unfettered industrial growth and change, but the depression which followed the First World War initiated a more positive government role in industrial life. An even more commanding position for the government developed during the Second World War and from then onwards an active governmental policy became politically acceptable not only in macroeconomic affairs (*see* I, **27–36**) but also in the microeconomic world of industrial structure and performance. However, in the late 1970s and early 1980s several countries (including Britain) elected governments committed to reducing the level of their economic activity particularly in the industrial field.

This chapter examines the philosophies behind the various shifts in government industrial policies.

2. *Laissez-faire* attitudes. The vast majority of nineteenth-century thinkers believed that national economic and social benefits would be maximised through the summation of the efforts of each individual consumer and producer working unrestrictedly towards his own aims within the parameters of the economic laws of supply and demand. Economic theorists of the time believed that the laws would work most effectively within a perfectly competitive framework which (*see* E. Seddon, *Economics of Public Finance*, Macdonald & Evans) would produce the most efficient allocation of resources and the maximisation of consumer satisfaction.

These beliefs encouraged governments to refrain from intervening in economic life unless they were trying to prevent groups of individuals co-operating to restrain trade. However, although the nineteenth century saw a great growth in economic prosperity there were periods of economic depression and many people lived in conditions of considerable human squalor, so doubts were raised about the validity of the *laissez-faire* principles as a method of improving man's material well-being.

3. Decline in *laissez-faire* attitudes. The twentieth century has seen an almost total absence of people who believe in a complete *laissez-faire* economy. Three historical developments have moulded this change.

(*a*) *Change in the role of government.* It is clear that the aims of different individuals and organisations are not necessarily complementary, that they are more likely to conflict. Thus the government must create an environment in which the individual can pursue his own interest but only at the limited expense of others. Originally this doctrine was applied via the law to general human conduct but the last hundred years has seen it applied to the clash of economic interests.

(*b*) *Growth of industrial organisations.* Advances in technology with the required huge financial commitment plus the growth of markets based on rising living standards and mass communications has produced large-scale business organisations straddling international boundaries (*see* XVII). Allied with these phenomena, labour has become organised on a large scale at least at the national level. Economic policies based on a perfect competition analysis will therefore have difficulty in relating to the existing world.

(*c*) *Growth of socialist thought.* Through the nineteenth century many men, the most significant being Marx, argued that there were no naturalistic laws of economics and that man's problems arose out of the private ownership of resources which caused men to compete rather than co-operate with each other. Consequently the allocation of resources could be undertaken in a just fashion by rational decisions owing nothing to the laws of supply and demand; the achievement of such a society would also bring human harmony. The emotional appeal of such reasoning was obvious and its adherents argued that the state should be the neutral holder of the nation's resources, allocating them in the most beneficial fashion. This philosophy was the necessary underpinning to justify the increasing interventionist role of government.

4. Corporate/socialist capitalism. The growth of mass markets and large-scale organisation plus the apparent needs of technology produced very big organisations heavily dependent on easy access to capital. This development was also fostered in the 1960s by a belief in a relationship between size and efficiency. (*See* XIII, **19–20**.)

These tendencies were clear in both Western liberal economies and the totalitarian Socialist countries. In the West there grew up close ties between big business, government and the unions. Industrial policies seemed to evolve from endless tripartite discussions, and decision taking became a bureaucratic rather than an entrepreneurial activity.

Critics argued that the industrial system was becoming a facet of a corporate state. Of course the bureaucratic nature of this development was also akin to the industrial organisation (minus the unions) in the Socialist states. Both systems stifled initiative and hindered dynamic economic change.

5. Return of market forces. By the late 1970s, the world's nations, whatever their political creed, were suffering from a mix of economic problems:

(*a*) long-lasting intransigent inflation rates;

(*b*) rising, possibly irreversible, unemployment rates;

(*c*) a diminution of fuel supplies producing a severe rise in prices;

(*d*) a considerable slowing down of economic growth rates;

(*e*) great uncertainties about the future impact of technology.

In addition the advanced Western countries found their basic manufacturing industries under severe attack from Far Eastern countries.

Many of these economic problems were attributed to excessive government spending (*see* VI, **20–35**), the expansion of government involvement with industry, and a lack of flexibility and dynamism within the bureaucracies of government, industry and the unions.

All countries were facing rapidly changing economic circumstances producing a need for a fast response in the reallocation of resources. Suddenly the market system with its reallocative device, the price mechanism, regained its attractions. Economists urged politicians to move from the Keynesian concentration on the demand side (*see* II) to the supply side of the economy, i.e. the efficient production of goods and services. These new ideas became known as supply side economic policies. Emphasis was placed on improving the efficient working of product and labour

markets and on the release of entrepreneurial talents within a
nation's industries. Implicit in these ideas was a belief in the
value of small organisations. Such a rationale together with an
effective monetary policy (*see* IX, **39–42**) is supposed to produce
a vibrant industrial base operating in a non-inflationary environment to create economic growth and expanding employment
opportunities.

6. Government attitudes to industry. Within the last ten to fifteen
years governments have faced a rapidly changing world (*see* **5**)
without the comforting security of precise, relevant economic
precepts to guide them through the jungle of their industrial
problems (hence the psychological appeal of the price mechanism).
All British governments have believed that industrial inadequacies,
however defined, have been a root cause of the country's economic
decline. Various ideological responses to the problem invariably
give way to a pragmatic approach which often creates inconsist-
encies (various governments have encouraged mergers and concurrently attacked monopolies).

These contradictions arise from a basic ignorance of the macro-
relationships within the industrial structure. The following are some
of the problems that need to be explored.

(*a*) Is there a correlation between organisational size and efficiency?

(*b*) What are the causal connections between investment, technology and growth?

(*c*) Can good management be precisely identified, defined and
trained?

(*d*) What are the relative economic/social costs of unemployment
and overmanning?

Industrial difficulties must also be a function of a country's
history as expressed in its social and cultural structures, e.g. the
impact of history and education on management and union attitudes.

Somewhat inevitably governments of all political hues arrive at
industrial policies which lack internal consistency and economic
rationale and which deviate from the government's alleged philosophy.

7. Basic problem of government intervention. Government has
always created a legal framework in which industry must exist and
although there is some resentment at the extension of the legal

aspects, particularly in employment areas, the real problem and controversy arise when governments become financially involved with private industry.

The government usually justifies its monetary help on the basis of national interest while critics of the aid argue that it is wasteful to subsidise inefficient companies which cannot work using normal financial channels.

National interest can be interpreted from three viewpoints.

(*a*) Political, e.g. defence.
(*b*) Economic, e.g. technology, balance of payments.
(*c*) Social, e.g. unemployment, environment.

Unfortunately, these aims can conflict, e.g. technology creates unemployment, nuclear fuels may cause a health hazard, therefore government help to a firm for one reason can create other problems. There is also the danger that ailing companies regard government as an all-the-year-round Father Christmas.

A further serious worry is the control the government is able to exercise once it has dispensed the taxpayers' money to industry, because many companies which have received financial assistance prosper for a while but then their managerial and financial inadequacies seem to recur.

8. Future developments. The remainder of the century, after decades of stability and economic progress, may mark a turning-point in man's history as the alternative economic strategies for solving the world's problems become seemingly irrelevant.

A reasonable scenario suggests that by the year 2000, the basic twentieth-century concepts of large-scale production, the work ethic and unlimited economic growth will be meaningless and the then industrial structure may not be within today's intellectual comprehension.

AN OUTLINE OF BRITISH GOVERNMENT INTERVENTIONISM

9. Controls. The government exercises control over the industrial sector by the use of rationing, licensing quotas and price fixing; it hopes to allocate resources through bureaucratic decision to achieve some defined need.

After 1945, the consequences of the war created severe shortages and the Labour administration had to rely on the old wartime controls, but by the end of the decade the controls seemed to exist for doctrinaire reasons and both consumers and producers felt trapped and without incentive.

The incoming Conservative Government of 1951 embarked on a policy of dismantling the controls. They were helped by an expansion of world trade and a severe fall in commodity prices which allowed British industry to prosper.

Yet by the late 1950s there was growing evidence that Britain was slipping behind her European rivals in the prosperity race. Strangely the British government looked at France which had been experimenting with economic planning (rather than Germany which was still very market orientated) and decided that Britain ought to indulge in economic planning.

Curiously it was a Conservative Government which introduced this new facet of interventionism.

10. Planning. Economic planning might take two forms as follows.

(*a*) *Imperative planning.* This involves government control of output decisions of the private sector. Indeed it is questionable whether a private sector could exist in this situation.

(*b*) *Indicative planning.* This is planning by consent and was the basis of the French experience (*see* **9**). Government and industry co-operate in deciding how best to utilise resources to attain agreed goals which are usually expressed in percentage increases in output. It is also hoped the planning produces mutual respect and understanding between both partners (three partners if industry is subdivided between management and labour).

11. British planning. Planning in Britain was pioneered by the Conservative Government in the early 1960s and was taken up by the Wilson administration from 1964.

(*a*) *Conservative contribution.* In 1962 the National Economic Development Council (NEDC) was formed and is still in being. It consists of the following two parts.

(*i*) Top Council: representatives are from both sides of industry and the government. The Chairman is the Prime Minister or the Chancellor.

(*ii*) The Office: this is a body of economic and industrial experts led by a Director-General to carry out day-to-day research and suggest economic strategies for consideration by the Council.

NEDC's terms of reference were to examine the economic performance of the nation and to identify the obstacles to achieving faster rates of economic growth. In 1963 NEDC produced a plan based on the reports from a cross-section of seventeen industries. The plan assessed the sectoral implications of a 4 per cent rate of growth up to 1965 and stressed the need for greater training facilities and improvements in labour mobility. However, these ideas were never formulated into a coherent plan and NEDC has scarcely been more than a talking shop and an intelligent pressure group.

(b) *Labour contribution.* Theoretically it would seem that a Labour Government would favour planning as a major economic tool but in practice this has not been the case. George Brown in 1965 produced a plan which was no more than a series of economic aspirations and consequently it had no effect. The Government also formed NEDC working parties for the major industries to highlight the strengths and weaknesses of the industries. These were christened little Neddies.

12. Problems of planning.

(a) There is insufficient theoretical or statistical evidence to suggest how the economic variables, macro or micro, interact to produce economic success or failure. It is very difficult to dis-aggregate the economy in order to see how the total economy works.

(b) Only France has had a coinciding of prosperity and planning and it is too simplistic to accept that this shows a certain causal relationship. The Socialist countries using imperative planning (*see* 10(a)) have had no great economic success relative to the West.

- (c) Indicative planning (*see* 10(b)) depends on very full and free co-operation between government and industry but in Britain the confidence for such co-operation never appears to exist.

13. Labour institutions for intervention.
Labour politicians have always favoured the use of specialist bodies to foster the restructuring of industry with the goal of improving industrial performance. Such a policy is repellent to Conservative administrators. Two bodies have been created by Labour Governments, the Industrial Reorganisation Corporation (*see* 14) and the National Enterprise Board (*see* 15).

14. Industrial Reorganisation Corporation (IRC).
Established in 1967, its major function was the restructuring of industry with special stress on improving the quality of management. With capital of £150 million, the IRC either took a shareholding and tried to pressurise management into reform, or financed mergers

between the efficient and the inefficient. However, it was not expected to bail out dying companies.

In four years the IRC was involved in ninety projects ranging from motor cars to fishing and like any investing institution it had successes and failures.

The 1970 Conservative Government, which was committed to market forces (at least for two years), killed off the IRC in 1971.

15. National Enterprise Board (NEB), 1976. This was a very similar concept to the IRC but operating on a bigger scale. The NEB was envisaged as an amalgam of a merchant bank and a holding company. With an original capital allocation of £1,000 million, its brief was to:

(*a*) promote the restructuring of industry;
(*b*) establish, maintain and develop vital industrial undertakings;
(*c*) promote industrial democracy;
(*d*) extend public ownership into profitable manufacturing enterprises.

By 1979 its portfolio of interventions was very wide. Besides huge investments in British Leyland and Rolls-Royce (Aero-Engines), it was involved in industries ranging from computers and medical supplies to clock making and office equipment.

Although in the first year of operation the NEB obtained a return of 11.8 per cent on its investment, many of its clients soon became entangled in the growing recession.

The new Conservative Government disapproved of the whole rationale of the NEB and immediately reduced its role to promoting technology, encouraging investment in Northern England, and helping small companies. By 1981, the Department of Industry had assumed responsibility for Rolls-Royce; British Leyland ignored the NEB and dealt directly with government; and some big companies were sold off, e.g. Ferranti, while others went into liquidation, e.g. Alfred Herbert. The NEB's interests were therefore reduced to a small group of firms concentrated in computers, office equipment and microchip technology (but with some oddities, e.g. private medicine).

The area of microchip technology was very difficult as the Government was most uncertain how to utilise the NEB's involvement with their chip technology company Inmos which was supposed to be Britain's contribution on the frontiers of the new technical knowledge.

16. Industrial strategy. The 1974 Labour Government became convinced that an overall policy strategy was required to overcome the country's industrial woes. The basic features of these problems were considered to be as follows.

(*a*) Too many resources had been transferred from the wealth-creating marketable goods, e.g. manufacturing, to the non-wealth-creating public sector, e.g. health and education.

(*b*) Resource allocation decisions were moving from economic to political groups.

(*c*) British industry, relative to its competitors, suffered from low productivity.

The Government's strategy evolved from the 1975 Industry Act which gave birth to the NEB (*see* **15**) plus planning and information agreements. These agreements were designed to encourage companies to divulge a range of basic commercial facts pertaining to their long-term plans so that both government and unions could co-operate in the business planning exercise. The concept never developed as the vast majority of companies sheltered behind the accepted need for commercial confidentiality.

The Government also established thirty-nine Sector Working Parties (SWPs) on which representatives of both sides of industry in selected sectors were to study current structures and performance and suggest areas of improvement especially in terms of technology, exports and import substitution. Excellent analytical reports were produced but no mechanism existed for implementing the suggestions without excessive, hence unacceptable, dictatorial directives from Whitehall. Cynics might suggest that the SWPs are another fine example of the British preference for debate rather than action.

17. Non-intervention policies. The Conservative Government elected in May 1979 came to office with economic policies based on monetarism (*see* VI, **35**) and supply side economics. They wanted to disentangle government from industry by:

(*a*) curbing inflation and hoping to produce growth which would stimulate industry;

(*b*) privatising parts of the nationalised industries by selling assets to the private sector;

(*c*) making the nationalised industries more commercially vigorous;

(*d*) reducing the activities of the National Enterprise Board;
(*e*) encouraging the growth of small businesses.

By the middle of 1981, the Government was submerged beneath its monetary policies and world recession both of which severely damaged the fabric of British industry. However, despite its basic philosophies the Government continued to pour money into loss-making organisations such as British Leyland, Harland and Woolf, British Steel and the National Coal Board. As with all British governments it became difficult to identify and understand the theory and practice of industrial policies.

18. Conclusions. Since 1945 British governments have tried every variation of industrial policy short of total socialism or *laissez-faire* yet the underlying weaknesses of low productivity, profits and pay remain. Disturbingly, British industry appears ill-equipped to use or benefit significantly from the new technological revolution.

Possibly these problems require not the selection of correct economic policies but the changing of attitudes. The following are some of the questions that need to be answered.

(*a*) Do the British people have different work/leisure prefer-ences from other nations?

(*b*) Does British society offer a higher status to the values of bureaucrats than those of the entrepreneur?

(*c*) Is the us/them conflict an inherent part of British life?

If the premise about attitudes is correct, then solutions will be long in coming and outside immediate government control.

PROGRESS TEST 14

1. Describe the basis of a *laissez-faire* economic policy. **(2)**
2. Account for the development of large-scale business organ-isations. **(3)**
3. What is a "corporate state"? **(4)**
4. Why has there been a resurgence of interest in the use of market forces? **(5)**
5. How might a country's history contribute to its industrial problems? **(6)**
6. Give examples of economic controls. **(9)**
7. What is meant by indicative planning? **(10)**
8. Outline the major functions of IRC and NEB. **(14–15)**

9. Explain the basic industrial problems of Britain as seen by the 1974 Labour Government.   **(16)**

10. What was the basic industrial policy of the 1979 Conservative administration?   **(17)**

CHAPTER XV

Size and Monopolies

THE GROWTH IN INDUSTRIAL SIZE

1. Introduction. Within the last seventy years, big companies have taken over an ever increasing share of industrial output in all Western nations. In Britain, for example, the largest hundred companies in 1909 produced 16 per cent of manufacturing output; by the late 1970s the figure was well over 40 per cent.

This development has worried all nations for the growth and potential domination of big companies implies a concentration of economic power in a few hands, hands possibly beyond the control of democratic processes.

This chapter investigates the growth in and problems of industrial size and then examines its competitive impact. Subsequent chapters look at the problems associated with mergers (*see* XVI) and the growth of industrial giants across international boundaries (*see* XVII).

The reasons for the growth in industrial size are discussed in **2–9** below.

2. Mass markets. The size and geographical spread of markets has increased considerably in the last hundred years. Reasons for this are:

(*a*) population growth giving potentially more customers;

(*b*) improved transport facilities which speeds up distribution;

(*c*) world-wide radio and television which have narrowed cultural and social differences and eased the marketing of standardised products.

3. International competition. Because of the last point a nation's idustries are competing at an international level and there is a belief that only big companies can do this successfully. This view has influenced the government's thinking on mergers. (*See* XVI, **7, 24**.)

4. Economies of scale. Economies of scale were explained in XIII, **19**. Despite the difficulties of measuring them and the growing suspicion that the optimal scale of production is lower than exists in big companies, the lure of the synergy principle $(2 + 2 = 5)$ in terms of production costs has ensured that companies will grow.

5. Diversification. No company, because of demand fluctuation, can afford to be a single product firm, therefore companies have always wanted to diversify into new product markets. The easiest way of diversifying is to buy up a company in the new market and this policy is bound to produce larger companies.

6. Product development. The industrial world is increasingly based on science and technology and as products develop and improve (often in hope rather than fulfilment) a big and costly research injection is required. The development can be so costly that only a big firm can undertake it.

7. Capital intensive industries. Many industries by their nature need huge capital equipment, e.g. fuel and energy, rail and air transport, car and aircraft manufacturing, so these industries will inevitably be dominated by big companies.

8. Managerial politics. It is suggested in XIII, **12**(*c*) that managerial status can be measured by organisational size. This point can be linked to the psychology of managers who tend to be power seekers. Consequently the managerial ethic will respond favourably to the pursuit of company growth.

9. Size begets size. The previous reasons will cause companies to become bigger. If they then wish to expand and merge, the merger is between much larger units than was the case twenty-five years ago and so growth becomes an accelerating process.

SMALL COMPANIES

10. Survival of small companies. Despite the previous arguments, the small firm (usually defined as employing fewer than 200) still dominates in terms of numbers all Western economies. Indeed American research (*The Economist*, 26th January 1980) suggests that small companies may be the major source for the generation of new employment as big companies switch to ever more capital intensive forms of production.

11. Reasons for survival. Small firms flourish under the following conditions:

(*a*) a clearly identified small market, e.g. property repairs;
(*b*) specialist, quality, non-standardised products;
(*c*) geographical areas with a small labour pool;
(*d*) the development of a new idea.

The small company can also offer good relationships with its customers and work-force thus creating a harmonious business environment.

GROWTH METHODS

12. Introduction. Most big business organisations have grown by acquisition and various types of organisation have developed for controlling these empires. The major classifications are given below.

13. Integration. This can be of two types.

(*a*) *Vertical.* To turn raw materials into finished products requires a chain of productive processes with different companies providing one process or link in the chain. Vertical integration occurs when a firm reaches forward or back in the chain to take over a customer or a supplier. They do this to guarantee supplies or to have more control over outlets. This method is now practised on a widespread scale; well-known examples occur in the beer, oil, building, clothing and shoe industries.

(*b*) *Horizontal.* In this method companies at the same level in the productive chain come together basically to cut down competition and reduce distribution costs. Again, it is a common form of organisation with obvious examples over the years in the motor, hotel, entertainment, brewing, biscuit and confectionery industries.

14. Interlocking directorates. Several companies appear to exist independently but in fact their boards of directors overlap considerably in membership so the company policies will have a coherent thrust. This organisational type is difficult to identify, but the best known example exists in the South African diamond industry.

15. Holding company. This is a method of holding together a business empire. A company is set up merely to be a significant shareholder in a collection of other firms and the controlling interest of the holding company is the real power behind all the other firms. It is a common device (look at the stock exchange quotations to see the word "holdings" after a company's name).

Unilever is so organised and the massive British Shoe Corporation is in a business empire controlled by Sears Holdings. The National Enterprise Board (*see* XIV, **15**(*b*)) acted as a government holding company to organise those companies with a large involvement of government money.

16. Conglomerate. This is an American word to describe a business empire based on financial and managerial expertise rather than production and marketing needs. The empire will consist of a range of companies operating in a random non-competing and non-complementary series of industries. The controlling company will have (or think it has) financial and managerial skills which it injects into ailing or under-valued companies hoping to revitalise the firms; for whose gain is questionable.

Conglomerate economic performance is now under a cloud of suspicion in America and although the species is rare in Britain one of the few examples, Slater Walker, did not inspire confidence.

Conglomerates raise anxieties for the following reasons.

(*a*) A big financial unit buying into a new market could narrow the chances of other possible entrants.

(*b*) The centre of the conglomerate may use cross-subsidisation policies (*see* **44**) or in the multinational sense doubtful transfer pricing policies.

(*c*) They may lack financial soundness. In the USA, congressional investigators found that growth was often based on the issue of endless new shares and true shares and true financial returns were locked in a tangle of balance sheets.

(*d*) If the conglomerates are successful they represent a source of considerable economic power, the analysis of which is outside conventional economic theory.

FEARS OF INDUSTRIAL SIZE

17. Introduction. As **2–9** suggested the growth of company size seems inevitable and it is also inevitable in society that any power centre which grows quickly will arouse fear and suspicion. The following sections outline these fears, concentrating finally on fear of monopoly for this way is capable of economic evaluation, whereas the other misgivings have a socio-political basis.

18. Social and economic power. As companies grow their power to influence the community through investment, pricing and employment policies correspondingly grows, but paradoxically the men who make the policy decisions become obscure, lost in the web of their bureaucratic empires and responsible to nobody.

Fears also exist that big companies become bureaucratised and lose the incentive to take the risk of exploiting new ideas; this is scarcely the recipe for economic change and growth which requires the gifts of entrepreneurship (small firms have largely pioneered microchip technology). Their power, in other words, freezes the economy.

19. Social purpose of industry. This argument was mentioned in XIII, **13**. The worry is whether the potential economic advantages of size are outweighed by social costs. For example, does work on large-scale production units debilitate the human personality; does the vastness of large-scale business empires reduce human dignity? These questions are of course not confined to business, they must be asked of any large-scale organisation, such as schools, local government or hospitals. Alternatively, it can be argued that only big companies can afford to employ handicapped people, sponsor sport and fund educational institutions; so big companies make a more positive contribution to life in general than do small companies.

The social purpose of industry is a vital and fascinating question but cannot be answered in an economic context.

MONOPOLIES

20. What is a monopoly? The word monopoly has provoked fear almost throughout the history of mankind but it is most difficult to define the word for practical economic and legislative purposes. Theoretically a perfect monopolist would be a producer facing a totally inelastic demand curve being able to charge any price he wished, but this is too unrealistic and better definitions are required.

21. A single producer. A monopolist has been defined as the single producer of a good in a market. However, this definition has two weaknesses.

(a) *Branding*. A branded good is made by one firm but brands compete, e.g. only G. & J. Greenall make "Vladivar" vodka, but they are not a monopoly because they sell their product in a highly competitive market.

(b) *Overlapping markets*. Only British Rail provide a train market but that market is a part of the bigger transport market which is fiercely competitive.

22. A lack of substitutes. A firm producing a good for which there is no close substitute is in a monopolistic position. In practice this market situation seldom exists unless the producer has control over a basic raw material, exclusive patent rights or legal protection. The Post Office is a legally protected monopoly although Conservatives wish to relax this protection (*see* XVIII, **28**).

23. Market concentration. Given the definitional problems many economists and legislators have tried to define monopoly power through concentration ratios, i.e. what share of output, sales or assets in an industry is in the hands of a given number of companies (five companies are often used in this exercise). It is best to use output or sales share figures because share of assets will vary with the capital intensive nature of the industry (*see* Table XXII).

The use of concentration ratios appears to give a degree of precision to monopoly definition but there are many difficulties.

(*a*) How are the boundaries of the market defined, e.g. are boiled sweets in the same or a different market from bars of chocolate and mints? To what extent does an industry differ from a market?

(*b*) How are multi-brand firms to be treated? Distillers Co. Ltd. has about 80 per cent of the whisky market but it produces a variety of whisky brands all with their own brand-loyal customers. If Distillers allows the separate whisky producers a large degree of marketing freedom, is it a competitive or monopolistic market?

(*c*) There can be significant variations in concentration ratios between area, national, regional and international markets, e.g. two firms could dominate the Scottish market but their impact would be slight on the British market and even less in Europe. Another aspect of this problem is how to allow for import shares in the home market.

(*d*) There is evidence that concentration ratios increase with the age of an industry and also with lack of growth in a market. Therefore competition is seemingly a natural element associated with new, dynamic and growing industries.

The value of concentration ratios is a matter of dispute. "It has not been established that there is a unique correlation between the degree of concentration and either the degree of discretion available to the firm, the types of business practices pursued or the

TABLE XXII.   *Concentration ratios in Britain above 50 per cent, 1971*

Order	Industry	Number of products analysed	Sales concentration 5 largest companies
III	Food, drink, tobacco	12	57
V	Chemicals	14	64
VI	Metal manufacturers	3	61
IX	Electrical engineering	8	63
XI	Vehicles	4	73
XVI	Bricks, glass, pottery, cement	5	53

(*Source: 1971 Census of Production.*)

character of the economic effects." (J. F. Pickering, *Industrial Structure and Market Conduct*, Martin Robertson, p. 21.)

24. Market domination. A simplified view of concentration is to try to assess one company's share of a market, given the problems of defining market (*see* **23**(*a*)), and then arbitrarily to select a figure of domination. British policy used to use 33⅓ per cent, but now it uses 25 per cent (*see* **53**(*a*)).

25. Size. A common fault is to equate company size and monopoly. Marxists are very guilty of this sloppy thinking. Big companies usually operate in highly competitive markets whereas smaller companies may dominate their own smaller market; the classic monopolist is the village shop in the remote village, with almost unlimited power to fix prices.

26. Summary. A precise definition of a monopoly is not feasible, so anti-monopoly legislators will construct an arbitrary definition. They must then balance the arguments for and against monopolies.

ARGUMENTS AGAINST MONOPOLIES

27. Higher prices. A monopolistic market price may be greater than the competitive market price because the lack of substitutes (*see* **22**) gives the producer a more inelastic demand. Economic theory also indicates that a monopolist's price is greater than marginal cost (*see* Fig. 8) which also has implications for resource allocation (*see* XIII, **26**).

28. Inefficient resource allocation. Economic theory argues that the most efficient resource allocation occurs under conditions of perfect competition, where price = marginal cost and all factors are paid the value of their marginal product (*see* XIII, **26**). It is argued in **27** that monopoly prices are above marginal cost and that the inelastic demand in the product market increases trade union power over wages in the labour market. (J. D. S. Appleton, *Labour Economics*, Macdonald & Evans, p. 13.)

Applied economists (e.g. Leibenstein "Allocative Efficiency v. X-efficiency", *American Economic Review*, vol. 56, 1966) also argue that lack of competitive pressure reduces the incentive on companies to use their resources in the most efficient manner.

29. Restriction of choice. The consumer is forced to buy from the monopolist and he has no adequate redress if his purchase is unsatisfactory. The ultimate power of the buyer is to take his custom elsewhere without undue cost.

30. Lack of innovation. If a company has little competition there is no incentive to improve its product, its efficiency or indeed any aspect of its business behaviour. Should these attitudes grow and prevail in an economy stagnation must be the final result. All nations which have enjoyed industrial success at any moment of history have done so on the bedrock of innovation.

31. Political domination. In a small country or a particular region of a bigger country one company can monopolise the area's economic life, e.g. the American Sugar Corporation in pre-Castro Cuba. A major part of the resources flow into the company eventually allowing it to dominate the economic, social and political life of the area.

ARGUMENTS IN FAVOUR OF MONOPOLY

32. Benefits from economies of scale. If the benefits accrue in accordance with theory (*see* XIII, **19**) then costs should be lower and consumers will gain via lower prices.

Many cases exist, e.g. cars and television sets, where volume production has lowered prices, but we lack knowledge of any correlation between optimum production levels and market shares, i.e. at what level of output do economies come into play?

33. Costs of innovation. The American economist Schumpeter has argued that the accelerating dominance of science and technology in industry was bound to increase the costs of innovation to a level where only market-dominating firms could afford research and development.

This argument has been used by governments to justify nationalisation in certain cases (steel and aircraft) and also the formation of big units in private industry (computers and cars).

34. Stabilising economic force. Any economy is subject to short-term economic fluctuations and companies in highly competitive situations operating possibly with low profit margins are liable to go bankrupt with consequent waste of resources. The company in a monopolistic position is less prone to violent demand fluctuations and can offer greater security to the work-force and shareholders.

35. Costs of competition. Because of traditional economic theory, competition has been elevated to the position of an absolute good but in fact competition can incur considerable costs as follows.

(*a*) *Cut-price wars*. In the short period consumers gain from price wars but ultimately they lead to quality reductions, low profits and investments and the driving out of companies, all situations which ultimately work against the consumer.

(*b*) *Marketing costs*. A fiercely competitive market is bound to increase marketing costs as firms fight for their share of the market. At worst marketing costs may become the largest single cost element for some products, e.g. with certain drugs and cosmetics marketing accounts for 30–45 per cent of total costs.

36. Summary. The problem of dealing sensibly with monopolies is underlined by the contradictory nature of the traditional arguments for and against. One school of opinion suggests the need to concentrate on the behaviour of monopolists—do they in fact operate restrictive practices which would seriously affect consumer freedom?

EXAMPLES OF RESTRICTIVE PRACTICES

37. Resale price maintenance. Manufacturers force retailers, through threats of withdrawing supplies, to charge a standard price for a commodity thus effectively restricting price competition in the retail trade. This practice was banned in Britain in 1964 except for the sale of books (*see* **62**).

38. Full line forcing. A manufacturer insists that the retailer takes all his product lines and not just those which the retailer feels are good sellers.

39. Exclusive dealings. A group of manufacturers or a single monopolist ensures its products are only handled by specific outlets, thus a consumer's choice is restricted. The petrol and beer industries use this practice although in these cases most customers have easy access to a range of outlets. The main fear of exclusive dealings is that they restrict freedom of entry to a market and this is an essential condition of competition (*see* **54**(*b*)).

40. Import restrictions. A market dominator in country A agrees not to export to country B if a firm in the latter country offers a reciprocal agreement. In the past Swedish and British match manufacturers have used the system.

41. Restrictive tendering. In certain industries, e.g. civil engineering, the customer orders his product by asking suppliers to submit a tender for the work. It is not unknown for the market leaders to agree privately who will do the work and then fix the tender to ensure their desires are met. More sophisticated methods can be devised and the customer finds difficulty in proving that his true choice is being restricted.

42. Price fixing. The dominating firms in the market agree to charge the same prices perhaps only lowering them to drive out newcomers. Open price fixing is usually illegal but it is easy to have informal price agreements (*see* **61**(*b*)).

43. Aggregated rebates. Rebates are given to a customer who remains loyal to the producer. This practice may seem innocuous but the period of expected loyalty may stretch over a number of years; thus newcomers would have to offer almost non-profitable terms to gain a foothold in the market. This method is fairly common in the shipping industry.

44. Cross-subsidisation. A company with products in many markets may use the profits from a monopolised market to subsidise its goods in another market, to drive out competition and create a second monopoly. It may also use profits from an established product to subsidise negative cost flows from products in the early stages of their life cycle.

45. Arguments for restrictive practices. Conventionally restrictive practices are condemned for restricting customer choice and protecting the inefficient producer, but companies can defend these practices on the following grounds.

(*a*) Price cutting can create long-term costs in the effects on profits and investment (*see* **35**(*a*)).

(*b*) The practices stabilise the business environment and create confidence which leads to more investment.

(*c*) Pooling of technical agreements cuts down on costs of research and information.

PROBLEMS OF FRAMING MONOPOLY LEGISLATION

46. What is competition? Anti-monopoly legislation is trying to increase the competitive nature of markets but competition is itself a vague concept. Economic theory concentrates on price competition but in the growing number of oligopolistic markets (markets containing a few big companies actively competing with each other) excessive price competition is frowned on because if one company cuts prices significantly, the others will have to follow, no extra sales will accrue and thus revenue and profit will fall. Oligopolists prefer administered prices which is a polite way of saying unofficial price fixing.

These companies compete via their commodity, its use and design and through promotional schemes. Even in the retail trade where price competition is obviously present it is uncertain if customer loyalty is just a function of price or whether other variables, e.g. shop amenities, are important.

47. Multi-product firms. Today many companies supply a variety of products to a vast complex of markets and any one firm may be faced with the total textbook range of competitive situations. Satisfactory analysis requires knowledge of the company's policy in each market, e.g. How are overhead costs allocated in the market prices? Is there cross-subsidisation of prices (*see* **44**)? If the products come from individual units within a big company, what freedom of policy decisions exists in the units?

48. Home and international competition. Many companies operate in home and world markets. They may argue that a secure monopolistic domestic market gives them the confidence to attack the export trade. A similar argument implies that only big companies can effectively compete internationally (*see* 3). Governments will be torn between protecting the home consumer from monopoly and encouraging exports.

49. Distinction between economies of scale and market domination. Most companies claim that big market shares enable them to reap the economies of scale, but seldom is this claim quantified. Investigators of this argument must ask the following type of question.

(*a*) Are the economies in one plant or through the whole company?

(*b*) Are the economies technical, financial or administrative?

(*c*) What market share is necessary to achieve these economies?

(*d*) Are the economies producing lower costs and prices?

50. Guidelines for companies. In controlling monopolies, governments have to choose between a pragmatic approach, which is non-judicial, and a legalistic approach. The first method treats every monopolistic situation on its merits. This seems equitable but companies claim they are unsure which commercial policies will prove acceptable. They may be tempted to restrict competition if government policy seems indecisive.

A legal approach clarifies the situation for a company but an inflexible legal attitude to market domination might not be in the public interest for, as 32–35 indicated, benefits can arise from monopolistic situations.

51. Use of economic criteria. The economic textbook approach to monopolies would be to judge them on the basis of the allocation and efficient use of resources. These criteria obviously should not be ignored but their use does pose problems.

The resource allocation analysis contrasts perfect competition and monopoly but in practice the competitive situation is difficult to define (*see* 46). Efficient use of resources is similarly difficult to evaluate (*see* XIII, 15–20). Governments may also turn a blind eye to the economic deficiences of a specific monopoly for political (e.g. defence needs) or social (e.g. employment) reasons.

52. Alternative methods of attack. Bearing the above problems in mind, anti-monopoly legislation can take the following forms.

(*a*) *Regulation of structures.* The government is concerned with the size of companies supplying a market. It will try to prevent any firm or group of firms obtaining more than a specific share of the market. This method requires information on concentration ratios (*see* **23**) and is the backbone of American monopoly control.

(*b*) *Regulation of behaviour*. A monopolist offends by using restrictive practices (*see* **37–44**) and governments will try to attack these practices. This approach has formed part of the British legislation (*see* **57–61**).

(*c*) *Regulation of performance*. Theory argues that the monopolist will operate inefficiently and that therefore his performance must be monitored. The obvious criteria are price/cost relationships, profit levels, innovation record and ability to meet demand. Unfortunately it is difficult to define acceptable levels of performance, e.g. what is a satisfactory level of innovation? Supposing profit levels are higher in a monopolistic as opposed to a competitive market; is this a result of market domination or greater efficiency? The British Monopolies Commission (*see* **53**) has concentrated on studying performance in monopolistic situations.

THE MONOPOLIES AND RESTRICTIVE PRACTICES (INJURY AND CONTROL) ACT 1948

53. Monopolies Commission. The 1948 Act established a Commission to investigate monopolised markets which were referred to it by the government. The criteria for investigation were as follows.

(*a*) A third of output is produced by a single firm or more than two companies working together (now 25 per cent of output).

(*b*) Firms in the industry are deliberately trying to restrict competition.

The Commission tries to establish the presence of restrictive practices and then to evaluate whether this behaviour is in the public interest. It also studies the economic performance of the companies under review.

A report with recommendations is submitted to the Department of Trade and to Parliament but only the government can take action (usually it quietly suggests to the firm that different behaviour would be appreciated); in this respect the Commission is powerless.

54. Established principles. Although essentially pragmatic the Commission's work has evolved definite strands of thought.

(*a*) The most damaging result of restricting competition is a reduction in incentives to innovate.

(*b*) Freedom of entry is the essential condition of competition. This view supports the exhaustive research done by the American economist, Bain.

(*c*) Very high profits and return on capital are probably indications of a lack of competition, although a Monopolies Commission report on the pet food industry said the average capital return of 46.7 per cent (national manufacturing average 16.2 per cent) achieved by Pedigree Ltd. was the result of efficiency rather than market domination and high prices.

(*d*) More intensive competition is likely to be oligopolistic (*see* **46**), therefore company size and market shares may be an irrelevant measure of monopoly. In the detergent market two companies, Unilever and Procter & Gamble, dominate to the extent of 45 per cent market share each, yet the market is extremely competitive.

55. Achievements. During its long existence the Commission has investigated many industries, e.g. electric light bulbs, dental goods, detergents, glass making, photographic films, brewing, cellulosic fibres, matches, car accessories, breakfast cereals, frozen foods, tobacco, petrol, infant milk foods and pet foods.

The Commission can scarcely claim to have made significant changes in the competitive structures of British industry and it has often been criticised (*see* **56**). Nevertheless its reports have been very informative and they revealed the horrific depth of restrictive practices. The early findings were so bleak that they prompted the government to formulate the tougher legislation of the 1956 Act (*see* **57**).

56. Criticisms of Monopolies Commission. Criticisms have included the following.

(*a*) *The body lacks power*. Very few recommendations have been enforced by the government and the force of bad publicity has been a seven-day wonder, so Imperial Tobacco still control Gallagher and film distribution is still dominated by Rank and ABC.

(*b*) *When the Commission's suggestions are followed quaint results can follow*. Kodak cut their prices and nearly drove their main competitor out of business; the detergent companies produced with little advertising a new low priced product whose sales were very low.

(*c*) *The Commission was too slow*. Up to 1965 this was a valid criticism, some reports taking up to four years to be completed. Since then the staff has been increased and the time taken has been cut down to about two years.

(*d*) *Is the impact of the Commission worth the cost?* The cost of the reports may be considerable if the Commission's research costs are added to the time and effort needed by companies to prepare their submission. Unilever complained that it spent many thousands of pounds to show the efficiency of its Birds Eye division; a proof accepted by the Commission thus causing Unilever to wonder about the point of the operation.

Even if the Commission attacks a company's behaviour and performance little is achieved in improving the competitive nature of a market and only a great optimist would suggest the Commission has had a significant influence on British competitive structures.

The validity of this criticism is confirmed by the need to introduce the 1956 legislation.

THE RESTRICTIVE TRADE PRACTICES ACT 1956

57. Introduction. The Act was the outcome of the 1955 Collective Discrimination Report which revealed that restrictive practices were rife in at least eighty industries and the practices were against the public interest for they frustrated the innovators and created very rigid markets. A tougher body than the Monopolies Commission was required.

58. Main principles. The Act created two new institutions.

(*a*) *Registrar of Restrictive Practices.* The office registered any agreements between two or more companies which placed restrictions on the price of goods supplied, the conditions of sale, the quantity of goods produced and the category of person supplied.

The Registrar codified the agreements and if companies wished to maintain their agreements they justified them to the Court of Restrictive Practices (*see* **64**(*a*)).

(*b*) *The Court of Restrictive Practices.* This is a proper legally organised court although the judge has lay advisers and the defendants are assumed guilty, i.e. they have to show their practices are in the public interest. This term is so vague that the Act laid down "gateways" or arguments which must be used in the defence submission (*see* **59**).

59. Gateways. The defences laid down in the Act are as follows.

(*a*) The restriction protects the public from danger in the sale or installation of the good.

(*b*) The removal of the restriction would deny the public specific and substantial benefits.

(*c*) The restriction helps the participants to secure fair terms for the supply of goods from firms who are dominant suppliers.

(*d*) The restriction protects people against restrictions imposed by persons who are not party to the agreement.

(*e*) The removal of the restriction would seriously affect employment in an area dominated by the parties.

(*f*) The removal of the restriction would probably cause substantial reduction in the export earnings of the parties to the agreement.

(*g*) The restriction is necessary for the maintenance of another restrictive agreement which the Court has ruled to be in the public interest.

Defendants have to quantify their evidence and it has proved difficult to get agreements through the Court (*see* **61**(*c*)). If firms are not willing to submit their case to the Court they must abandon the agreement or else be fined.

60. Use of the gateways. Relatively few cases have come before the Court but the Court's decisions have not always satisfied economists. For example, the Cement Makers Federation were allowed to have common delivered prices to reduce business risk and the Black Bolt and Nut Association were allowed price fixing to save their customers shopping around, while the scrap iron industry successfully claimed their minimum price agreement kept prices down. On the other hand several price fixing agreements were thrown out. (For a list of interesting cases *see* J. F. Pickering, *Industrial Structure and Market Conduct*, Martin Robertson, pp. 287–91.)

61. Results of the Act. In the first two years of the Act over 2,000 practices were registered so it had a definite flushing out effect. In general three main points can be made.

(*a*) The Registrar's reports indicated a confidence that most markets operated without formal agreements.

(*b*) The above point hides two vital facts, viz.:

(*i*) formal agreements had been replaced by informal agreement or co-operation agreed in conversation between interested business parties;

(*ii*) price leadership had developed, i.e. firms in an industry raised their prices accidentally at the same time.

(*c*) Judges' decisions did not appear to be commercially consistent so firms were still uncertain about the acceptability of their behaviour.

On balance the Court has been useful particularly in opening up access to markets.

SUBSEQUENT LEGISLATION

62. Abolition of Resale Price Maintenance (RPM), 1964. RPM was a basic price fixing device (*see* **37**) and was declared illegal in 1964. Any company wishing to continue with the practice had to apply to the Restrictive Practices Court using a number of gateways established for RPM, e.g. the number of retail outlets would be reduced and after-sales service would be diminished. The Act was a total success and RPM is now a rarity in the British economy.

63. Restrictive Practices Act 1968. This was a tidying up piece of legislation with three points worth noting.

(*a*) Informal agreements must be registered although proof of their existence is difficult to obtain.

(*b*) A restriction is permitted if it does not prevent competition.

(*c*) A temporary exemption for agreements is allowable if they assist import substitutes or product standardisation.

64. Fair Trading Act 1973. The Act covered the wide field of consumer protection but some points were relevant to this section.

(*a*) The Act created the post of Director-General of Fair Trading, one of whose tasks was to take over from the Registrar (*see* **58**(*a*)).

(*b*) The Director-General was responsible for identifying monopolies which were acting against the public interest. He could refer them to the Monopolies Commission.

(*c*) Monopoly was defined as a supplier having a 25 per cent market share. If two suppliers acting together had this share, they would be investigated by the Restrictive Practices Court.

(*d*) The provisions of the 1956 Act were extended to the supply of services.

(*e*) The Monopolies Commission was given guidelines for its studies although the criteria were wonderfully vague, e.g. "the desirability of maintaining and promoting a balanced distribution of industry and employment in the UK."

65. Competition Act 1980. This Act kept the same anti-monopoly mechanisms but widened and deepened their powers by, for example, the following provisions.

(*a*) The Monopolies Commission will investigate efficiency aspects of the nationalised industries, e.g. the commuting and postal services of London and the South East.

(*b*) The Director-General may deal directly with companies on the question of restrictive practices, using the Monopolies Commission if the company will not voluntarily mend its ways.

(*c*) There is to be a sharper focusing on firms rather than industries thus identifying narrow or local monopolies.

(*d*) Special attention is to be paid to any restrictive practices which attempt to stifle competition from small companies.

66. EEC legislation. The ultimate ideal is for all member states to harmonise their company and trade legislation but this situation is far distant and the EEC has concerned itself with inter-state flows of trade.

Article 85 of the Treaty of Rome bans agreements between inter-state companies to fix prices, share markets or limit production, investment and technical development. Companies can justify their agreements if they improve distribution, production or technical progress. ICI was once fined for persisting with a banned price agreement.

Article 86 prohibits the exercising of market power to keep prices up or production down, or to keep new firms out of the market.

THE PROMOTION OF COMPETITION

67. The problem. Anti-trust legislation is really concerned with the discrepancies between maximum profit and social net benefit arising from a lack of genuine competition. The discrepancy shows itself through excessive prices and poor product development.

To produce competitive markets Britain has tried the pragmatic approach (Monopolies Commission, *see* **53**) and a legalistic approach (Restrictive Practices Court, *see* **58**) yet there is still unease about the dynamic qualities of British industry.

Monopoly policies have underlying them the pursuit of perfect competition but such an action itself incurs costs; e.g. too many small firms could endanger genuine scale economies, therefore a vital need is a clear-cut concept of effective competition.

68. Possible solutions. Government monopoly policy should ensure that all markets have sufficient firms to offer genuine choice to consumers and there should be realistic freedom of entry to a market. Ideas on prices are more complicated because even in perfect competition there is only one price so pursuit of price competition could be a red herring. The best course of action is to monitor price-cost-profit relationships.

To help achieve these ends three actions are suggested.

(*a*) More foreign trade should be encouraged as long as it is fair competition. There are risks to the balance of payments and employment but in the last thirty years foreign firms have been a significant stimulus to British industry.

(*b*) Company law should insist on greater disclosure of per-formance information by companies. The balance sheet is a useless guide and informed opinion has only scanty evidence to judge a firm's performance.

(*c*) Governments should adopt tougher anti-merger measures. Market domination usually comes from acuisition rather than a ompany's internal growth yet government merger policy has been very indecisive (*see* XVI). Oligopolistic markets (*see* **46**) are now so common that a harsh merger policy may be too late, but governments should quickly explore the possibilities of such action.

Fears of decreasing market competition in Britain have grown since the 1960s with the rapid increase in the number of mergers occurring in British industry. This is discussed more fully in XVI.

PROGRESS TEST 15

1. Give three reasons for the growth of large-scale industrial organisations.   (**2–9**)

2. Distinguish between vertical and horizontal integration.   (**13**)

3. What is a conglomerate?   (**16**)

4. Explain the phrase "market concentration".   (**23**)

5. Examine the costs of competition.   (**35**)

6. What is cross-subsidisation?   (**44**)

7. Distinguish between scale economies and market domination. **(49)**

8. Explain structure regulation in monopoly legislation. **(52)**

9. Outline the main principles followed by the Monopolies Commission. **(54)**

10. Suggest three methods of increasing competition. **(68)**

CHAPTER XVI

The Problems and Control of Mergers

GROWTH OF MERGERS

1. What is a merger? A merger is the coming together of two or more companies so that the overall policies of the new organisation are determined by a single board of directors. Many words besides merger are used to describe this process, e.g. take-over, acquisition, amalgamation, absorption and fusion. The various words try to distinguish between the method of merging, e.g. were the parties agreeable, were the parties of equal size? In this chapter "merger" will be used for all situations.

2. History of mergers. At specific periods of time since the nineteenth century there has been a rapid acceleration in the numbers of mergers. The variations in merger rates depend on economic disturbances, e.g. technology, economic growth, cheap capital and depression.

(*a*) The first noticeable growth was in the late nineteenth century, e.g. wallpapers and distilling, when there was a period of rapid technological change and declining profits.

(*b*) The 1920s saw the emergence of the big five in banking, four railway companies, and ICI, and the fast growth of Unilever. The prime stimulant was depressed trade with the need to reduce competition and rationalise manufacturing processes.

(*c*) Merger growth was also seen in the late 1960s, early 1970s and late 1970s, the main causes being technological change, prosperity and recession. In the same period some governments pursued an active policy of encouraging mergers (*see* **24, 25**). (*See* Table XXIII.)

REASONS FOR MERGERS

3. Marketing reasons. (*See also* Table XXIV.)

(*a*) *Domination.* A company wishes to expand its market share and feels it has not the growth potential within its own resources

TABLE XXIII. *Growth of mergers, 1965–79*

Year	Mergers	Year	Mergers
1965	1,000	1974	504
1969	846	1975	315
1970	793	1976	353
1971	884	1977	481
1972	1,210	1978	567
1973	1,205	1979	534

(*Source: Department of Trade Statistics.*)

so it seeks to merge with one or more of its competitors. This is a horizontal merger (*see* XV, **13**(*b*)).

(*b*) *Diversification.* An existing product market is reaching saturation point and the company wants to enter new markets. The easiest course of action is to buy an existing brand name in the new market (Imperial Tobacco moved into crisps through the brand name Golden Wonder).

(*c*) *Control.* A firm wishing to gain greater control of its supplies and outlets buys back or forward in the productive process. This is a vertical merger (*see* XV, **13**(*a*)).

(*d*) *Product integration.* Firms in an industry are producing the same range of products often at uneconomic levels of output with excess capacity so the companies merge and then concentrate on a narrower product range. This was the reasoning behind the famous GEC–AEI–EE merger in the late 1960s.

TABLE XXIV. *Types of mergers* (%)

	Horizontal	Vertical	Diversified
1965–69	82	6	12
1970–73	74	4	22
1974–78	65	8	27

(*Source: Trade and Industry, 14th September 1979.*)

4. Under-utilised assets. Many companies under-utilise their assets either through management incompetence or because of economic recession. Healthier, more efficient companies, spotting the asset waste and realising their low price on the stock exchange, move in to take over and exploit the assets obtaining a higher rate of return.

5. Economies of scale. Two companies join to form a bigger unit and obtain economies of scale (*see* XIII, **19**). This is an almost standard reason for merging.

6. Lack of capital. A small company's development may be handicapped through lack of capital and it asks a larger firm to take it over. Surprisingly the company which will lose its identity is often the initiator of merger proposals.

7. International competition. Many firms now treat the world as their market and they believe size is a vital factor in withstanding foreign competition. National companies, often with government blessing, therefore merge to meet the overseas challenge (*see* **24, 25**). In the coming years European mergers will develop to fend off the American multinationals (*see* XVII).

8. Fear. Small to medium-size firms fear that bigger companies may buy them out to control the market. As a counter-measure the smaller units merge to increase their own commercial power. This tendency has been very evident in the brewing industry.

9. Power. As stated elsewhere (*see* XIII, **12**(*c*)) company size generates power and status for the management and mergers are the easiest way to grow. Some critics believe that once an organisation embarks on the merger trail the process develops its own momentum. Several big companies have planning departments whose purpose is to seek out potential merger partners or victims.

10. Restrictive Practices Act. Researchers are concerned that companies, realising their trading agreements with other firms would be illegal (*see* XV, **56–61**), decided to merge and pursue their market domination as a single unit.

FEAR OF MERGERS

11. Introduction. Mergers have grown on such a scale that many critics fear the benefits that are likely to accrue, e.g. scale economies, better resource utilisation, will be outweighed by economic and social costs which are discussed below.

12. Growth of monopoly. Mergers are bound to reduce the number of suppliers in a market thus creating a potential or actual monopolistic situation with all the attendant dangers listed in XV, **27–31**.

13. Social fears. Mergers can have immense political and social implications for several reasons.

(*a*) If the merger is within the mass or local media, the problem of democracy and open access to opinion becomes an issue.

(*b*) If the merger involves foreign capital the fears of foreign control of home industry will arise.

(*c*) The merger could well create unemployment in one area while offering greater employment security elsewhere, thus possibly creating antagonisms between different workers.

14. Are the economic benefits real? Merging companies will list benefits to be derived from the merger but these benefits are seldom quantified and can only be checked long after the merger has taken place (*see* **16–17**). Disturbing evidence is accumulating which suggests that increased efficiency and better rates of return simply do not materialise.

The most thorough British research by Newbould (G. Newbould, *Management and Merger Activity*, Guthstead, 1976) showed that:

(*a*) bidding managements did not make a rational financial appraisal of their potential investment;

(*b*) in only half of the mergers studied did the acquiring company have a plan for the new organisation;

(*c*) if there was more than one bidder for a firm, size not economic logic decided the winner;

(*d*) the major motive for merging was to reduce competition or to alleviate fears of being taken over; a search for greater efficiency was not a high priority.

American evidence is equally alarming in showing the poor realised performance of mergers.

Why should hopes and fulfilment be so divergent?

15. Reasons for poor performance.

(*a*) From Newbould (*see* **14**(*a*)) it is clear that many companies simply do not research the real facts of a merger situation.

(*b*) Kitching (*Harvard Business Review*, November 1967) in an American study suggested that many mergers failed because of "size mismatch", i.e. many of the acquired companies had sales of less than 2 per cent of the bigger companies and the companies had nothing in common.

(c) The benefits of scale economies do not materialise because of diseconomies (see XIII, 19), which tend to be undervalued. There is a drain on managerial resources, worker insecurities grow, and product development is delayed (British Leyland has suffered badly from this fault). Quite simply, bigger companies are more difficult to run effectively.

(d) Economies may be achieved at head office but there are no developments at the various plants throughout the country.

(e) Mergers do involve a multitude of changes (some estimates suggest 2,000) which are bound to provide problems which can only be overcome by utilising rigorous management techniques and planning; assets which according to Newbould are not present (see 14).

EVALUATING MERGERS

16. Summary of costs and benefits.

(a) *Benefits.* Possible benefits include scale economies, product rationalisation, better asset utilisation, greater research finance, improved management, and avoidance of excess capacity.

(b) *Costs.* Possible costs are monopoly power, unemployment, scale diseconomies and Leibenstein's X-inefficiency losses (see XII, 12(e)).

17. Points for a merger cost-benefit analysis.

(a) *Identify interests.* Workers, shareholders, consumers, producers and the economy.

(b) *Effects on interests.* Redundancies, profits, prices, innovation, balance of payments.

(c) *Establish costs or benefits.* High prices (bad), innovation (good), high profits (?).

(d) *Weighting of costs and benefits.* Is £1 of unemployment to worker = £1 of added exports to the economy?

(e) *Distinguish between industry and company.*

(i) Industry: information on market characteristics, growth trends, levels of technology.

(ii) Companies: information on profits, liquidity, cost structures, management skills, production and distribution methods.

This type of exercise is costly, and much of the information may be subjective, but without such analysis any evaluation of a merger is worthless.

A special difficulty is that much of the information will be predictive, thus a true judgment of a merger can only be made several years after the merger. Should that judgment be unfavourable, how is the merger to be unscrambled? This problem was tackled by the 1979 Conservative Government (*see* **25**).

BRITISH GOVERNMENT POLICY TOWARDS MERGERS

18. Government reaction to mergers. Through the 1950s and the early 1960s the government took no action against mergers as such. Indeed in many industries, e.g. aircraft and textiles, governments actively encouraged mergers which produced bigger industrial units.

From 1964 the merger boom accelerated (*see* Table XXIII) with a new facet emerging. This was a growing proportion of mergers involving two big companies, e.g. GEC and English Electric; Boots and Timothy Whites. Fears of market domination rapidly grew and the fears deepened when the acquiring company was foreign, e.g. Chrylser and Rootes; Nestlé and Crosse & Blackwell (*see* Table XXV: increasing concentration of net assets).

TABLE XXV. *Number of firms required to account for 50 per cent of net assets in different industries*

Industry	End 1957	End 1967
Drink	12	4
Textiles	8	3
Food	7	4
Vehicles	5	2
Clothing and footwear	3	1
Paper and printing	6	3
Wholesale distribution	21	14

(*Source: A Survey of Mergers 1958–68, HMSO (1970), Appendix 10.*)

The feeling of the time was expressed by Mr Crosland, Minister at the Department of Trade and Industry.

"Mergers raise profound political and social as well as economic issues. A very large firm has a pervasive influence on people's lives. We can lay down certain principles—they are good if they lead to better management or greater economies of scale, bad if they lead to inertia, a dangerous lack of competition or any abuse of market power. The difficulty comes in applying these general concepts to particular situations." (Speech to Manchester Chamber of Commerce, 2nd February 1969.)

19. Principles behind intervention. Governments will contemplate intervening if:

(*a*) there may be a divergence of social and private interests. e.g. will the merger produce factory closures and unemployment;

(*b*) the merger is not in line with the government's view of the "correct industrial structure".

ACTION AGAINST MERGERS

20. Monopolies and Mergers Act 1965. The main features were as follows.

(*a*) The Department of Trade to investigate any merger which creates or increases a monopoly in the supply of any good or service in the UK. The value of any assets to be taken over must exceed £5 million (raised to £15 million in 1980).

(*b*) The Department of Trade to investigate the merger of any independent newspapers whose combined circulation is over 500,000. (This is designed to ensure a variety of opinion in the mass media.)

(*c*) The Department of Trade to investigate any merger involving a foreign company gaining a major shareholding in a British company.

(*d*) The Department of Trade to refer any merger to the Monopolies Commission for further investigation. The latter to report within six months. (*See* **22–23** and Table XXVI.)

(*e*) Parliament to have the power to unscramble a merger which has taken place.

(Note that the administration is not in the hands of the Office of Fair Trading.)

21. The nature of the investigation. The Department of Trade seeks information about the companies involved in the merger, the motivation behind the merger, demand factors, market structure,

TABLE XXVI.   *Recent conclusions on mergers referred to Monopolies Commission (1973–78)*

	Against public interest	Not against public interest	Abandoned
Horizontal	12	9	9
Vertical	3	3	0
Diversified	3	6	8

(*Source: Trade and Industry, 14th September 1979.*)

the efficiencies expected to accrue from the merger and any likely
effects on the balance of payments (see *Mergers, A Guide to Board
of Trade Practices*, HMSO 1969).

22. Results. Since the Act was passed nearly 1,000 proposed or
actual mergers have been investigated but only approximately 3
per cent have been referred to the Monopolies Commission (latest
figures are shown in Table XXVI). There are scarcely sufficient
findings to establish a coherent "Commission view" on mergers but
the threat of reference often kills the merger proposals.

Such evidence confirms Newbould's view that many mergers are
unplanned and the realisation that the Monopolies Commission
will require quantifiable justifications daunts the merger partners.
Sometimes companies have escaped a reference by giving the
government assurances about the new companies' behaviour, e.g.
not to use price discrimination or to restrict supply. There are
obvious misgivings about such vague promises; for how long will
civil servants monitor the behaviour, and what action follows any
breaking of the assurances?

23. Some findings of the Monopolies Commission.

(*a*) *Merger of Ross Group and Associated Fisheries.* Disallowed because it would lead to market domination in the Humber
ports without strengthening the industry.

(*b*) *Merger of Boots and Glaxo.* Disallowed because it is more
beneficial to have a variety of research interests.

(*c*) *Merger of British Match Corporation and Wilkinson Sword.*
Allowed because it would inject new management into British
Match and give Wilkinson more overseas contacts.

(*d*) *Merger of Barclays, Lloyds and Martins.* Merger between the two big banks disallowed because it would diminish competition. Martins could join either of the big banks (Barclays and Martins joined).

(e) *Merger of British Motor Corporation and Pressed Steel.* Allowed because of product integration and export potential.

GOVERNMENT IN FAVOUR OF MERGERS

24. Basis of action. This chapter has concentrated on the control of mergers but government has also encouraged mergers. Chapter XIV showed that politicians wish to produce an efficient industrial structure and big companies, because of their technological know-how and their ability to compete effectively against overseas firms, form an essential part of the structure, thus governments have been tempted to encourage the formation of big units. This attitude has been prevalent in shipbuilding (before nationalisation), machine tools, motor cars, textiles and computers.

25. Action. Labour Governments, despite their ideological fears of big business have actively encouraged mergers, via the IRC (*see* XIV, **14**) and NEB (*see* XIV, **15**). In fact IRC inspired mergers were spared formal investigation.

Conservative Governments, although philosophically committed to competition, have produced no significant merger policies although in 1980 the Minister of Trade condemned mergers for stifling market power and producing unwieldy accumulations of financial power. The 1979 administration was investigating possible amendments in company and taxation laws to ease the demerging of companies where the supposed benefits of merging had failed to materialise.

26. Summary. Establishing a realistic merger policy is complicated by a lack of knowledge of the correlations between size and desired industrial objectives. There is also a subtle interplay between big and small companies. For example, the following issues need investigating.

(a) Do big companies generate the incomes to create demand for specialist goods and services?

(b) Do big firms suffocate the growth of small companies? Small to medium companies seem to flourish best away from traditional industrial areas, e.g. in East Anglia.

Despite the unknowns of the merger equation some observers

praise the tough American policy which bans any merger which creates a unified market share of over 4 per cent.

PROGRESS TEST 16

1. Define a "merger". **(1)**
2. Give two marketing reasons for the growth of mergers. **(3)**
3. Why might fear be a reason for mergers? **(8)**
4. Outline the social worries associated with mergers. **(13)**
5. Examine Newbould's findings on mergers. **(14)**
6. Suggest possible benefits of mergers. **(16)**
7. What principles lie behind government merger intervention? **(19)**
8. Describe the main results of the 1965 merger legislation. **(22)**
9. Why might governments be in favour of mergers? **(24)**
10. Explain why a logical merger policy is difficult to formulate. **(26)**

CHAPTER XVII

Multinational Corporations

NATURE OF MULTINATIONALS

1. Introduction. So far the discussion of industrial size has been confined within national boundaries but many commentators believe that the key big company/government problem centres on the growth and activities of multinational enterprises. Simply, they are companies which have production plants in many countries but the control and decision-taking units of the company are in one country. This chapter will analyse the nature of these commercial mammoths and investigate the reasons for the large-scale worries which they seem to generate.

2. Definition. Any definition must be arbitrary but the following seems adequate: "A combination of companies of different nationality connected by means of shareholdings, managerial control or contract and constituting a single economic entity." (R. E. Tindall, *Multinational Enterprises*, Oceania Publications, New York, 1975, p. 1.) Pickering, less legally, suggests a multinational will have annual sales of at least £100 million, 25 per cent of which will be earned by overseas plants. The multinational will have production facilities in six or more countries. (J. Pickering, *Industrial Concentration*, Martin Robertson, 1974, p. 175.)

The country which contains the head office of the multinational is known as the parent country, while the other countries containing production or distribution plants are called host countries.

3. Who are the multinationals? The multinationals are in fact household names and below are a very small selection of them listed by parent countries.

   (a) *USA*. General Motors, Du Pont, Esso, IBM, Gillette, ITT, Ford.

   (b) *UK*. British Leyland, BP, Dunlop, ICI.

   (c) *Europe*. Volkswagen, Philips, Ciba-Geigy, Nestlé, Siemens, Volvo-Saab.

Sometimes a multinational might have significant decision-taking units in more than one country, e.g. Unilever.

4. Significance of multinationals. Four quotations illustrate the power of multinationals.

"To a remarkable extent the ownership and control of both production and distribution, outside of the Communist countries, has passed into the hands of gigantic corporate organisations." (C. S. Burchill, "The Multinational Corporation", *Queens Quarterly*, Spring 1970, p. 3.)

"Given an expanding world economy and the rise of the multinational corporation, national boundaries may follow the history of state boundaries in the USA which failed to confine the American corporation and prevent the growth of a national economy. It represents a move beyond international trade into internationalisation of production." (G. Paguet, *Multinational Firm and The Nation State*, Collier Macmillan, 1972, p. 1.)

"The really significant resources are now technology and management. These assets enjoy the quality of mobility as well as scarcity. Manufacturing operations formerly found in a few nations are now widely dispersing throughout the world." (R. A. Mathews in Paguet, *see above*, p. 154.)

"On the basis of output amongst the top 100 countries and enterprises with a volume exceeding £2m, 54 are enterprises and 46 are countries." (A. Sampson, *The Sovereign State*, Hodder & Stoughton, 1973, p. 270.)

In fact in terms of Gross National Product if General Motors were a state it would rank fourteenth in the world.

These are sweeping statements but seeking specificity it can be noted that in Great Britain in 1973, 13 per cent of output and 20 per cent of exports were produced by multinationals. In certain fields, e.g. breakfast cereals, razor blades and petrol, the figure rose to 40 per cent.

The problem of multinational power is treated as an essentially modern problem but articles warning of the impact of Singer, Heinz and other American corporations in Britain were written at the beginning of this century. An American businessman wrote in 1902, "When the duty exceeds the cost of separate managers and plants then it will be an economy to erect works in the country that our customers can more cheaply be supplied from." (R. E. Tindall,

p. 9.) Compare this with a modern thought: "It is just not possible for a mere exporter to become a major long-term factor in a market in the second half of the twentieth century." (President of Pfizer & Co. Ltd.)

5. Growth of American multinationals. The concept of companies seeking and developing factories in other countries grew in the second half of the nineteenth century, e.g. Bayer Chemicals, a German firm, opened, in New York in 1876, Russia in 1882 and France in 1908, while Singer of America moved into Scotland in 1867. Movement has always been two ways between America and Europe but until recently the American concerns have dominated the scene. The reasons for this are as follows.

(*a*) The general faster growth of the American economy produced a big demand for labour-saving consumer durables, which had a high income elasticity. This demand was a tremendous stimulation to innovation.

(*b*) The overall growth of mass consumer demand automatically initiated the search for new mass production techniques.

(*c*) American industry was obsessed with the idea of finding good managers, it was not content with a belief often found in Europe that management still is an inherited gift which can be passed down in families. For the Americans, management is a science rather than an art and they have devoted vast resources to obtaining efficient management techniques.

(*d*) The American anti-monopoly laws have always been severe, thus companies have been tempted to go overseas rather than form alliances at home.

Economic history has therefore given American companies the natural ingredients for growth, namely big markets, technology and good management. Nationally they grew big and by the Second World War the firms were facing tremendous oligopolistic competition. Post-1945 home competitive pressures were intensive, while in Europe living standards were expanding rapidly but labour costs were lower than in the USA. These factors made an American invasion of Europe inevitable.

Interestingly since the mid-1960s the same circumstances of tough competition, rising living standards and lower labour costs are pushing the European and American multinationals into the Third World.

6. Growth of European multinationals. The European multinationals have as long a history as their American counterparts but the scope and scale of their growth has been much more limited and significant development did not occur until the 1950s.

As with the American experience, European multinational growth has come with rising incomes, increasing management techniques and the impact of research and development, although the product mix seems different with the European multinationals producing more working-class and luxury goods. However, certain differences can be detected in the European picture.

The ownership of European companies is strongly influenced by families, banks or governments rather than private shareholders and dynamic profit-orientated management, and the Europeans have therefore lacked the aggressive stimuli to expand vigorously. In addition European businessmen, perhaps because of their trading history, have placed more weight on the value of exports. On average Europe exports 26 per cent of her GNP, the Americans only 7 per cent, so the concept of attacking foreign markets from production plants in the market is alien to the European experience.

The conservatism of the Europeans is revealed in that their first steps to becoming multinationals are often taken in countries close to their geographical boundaries, possibly because they wish to follow common linguistic and cultural patterns.

Evidence also suggests the Europeans are bigger diversifiers. Some Americans are almost single industry companies, e.g. IBM, Kelloggs. This situation may arise from the size potential of home markets.

Rather oddly the recent European multinational boom has been helped by America which was interested in attracting foreign capital for balance of payments reasons. In 1966 an office was opened in Paris to provide information about America for European businessmen. Some of the attractions offered were:

(a) access to the largest market in the world;
(b) the ease of raising capital on the Eurodollar market;
(c) a more rigorous implementation of the Buy America Act which made it difficult for the simple exporter to sell direct to America;
(d) the benefits of exposure to American competitive business methods.

However, the size of initial investment in America, at least £80 100 million, often tempted the Europeans to attack the Am market by buying into smallish local firms and utilising their capital and managerial assets.

7. Growth of Third World multinationals. Several companies in the more developed Third World nations, e.g. Singapore, Argentina, Hong Kong and Brazil, have spread their business wings across the weaker nations.

Unlike their Western counterparts these new multinationals rely, on a network of local commercial contacts rather than heavily marketed branded goods and they compete through low prices arising from a curious mix of the newest micro-technology and cheap manual skills.

Their appeal to the more backward countries has several roots:

(*a*) a greater psychological knowledge of local aspirations;

(*b*) the use of appropriate production techniques, especially a willingness to use local labour in small-scale production;

(*c*) less diffidence about involvement with the host country's public sector.

8. Summary. The multinationals have become a huge influence on the international business scene and consequently are part of the social and political landscape of nearly every country in the world (even Communist countries are encouraging their activities).

Pessimists predict that by the late 1980s, a significant share of world output will be in the hands of a few multinationals. The potential of the multinationals to create either economic good or social and economic costs is awe inspiring. The next section investigates this power for good and bad.

THE ADVANTAGES AND DISADVANTAGES OF MULTINATIONALS

9. Introduction. "It is run by foreigners. It rigs its intra company transfer prices. It imports foreign labour practices. It doesn't import foreign labour practices. It underpays. It overpays. It competes unfairly with local firms. It is in cahoots with local firms. The tec⌐   ʏy it brings to the Third World is old fashioned; no ⸂   ⸃ rn. Nobody can control it. It wrecks balances of ⸂   ⸃ ays governments off against each other. Won't it ⸂   ⸃ invest. Let it bloody well go home." (*The* ⸂   ⸃ anuary 1976, p. 68.) In this context "it" refers ⸂   ⸃ nd the passage sardonically reflects the amazing ⸂   ⸃ bout multinationals.

This section tries to investigate rationally the good and bad points relating to these international giants. The normal procedure of separating the advantages and disadvantages will not be used. Instead the investigation will centre on the main areas of controversy.

10. Balance of payments. The multinationals move large quantities of goods and capital around the world to suit their own strategies and these movements can influence countries, balance of payments and exchange rates.

(*a*) *Capital.* If a multinational invests in an overseas subsidiary, superficially there is capital outflow from the parent country and an inflow to the host country. Over the years the flows will be reversed as the debt is repaid and profits return to the head office. However, the impact of the flows will depend on the following.

(*i*) Where was the capital raised? In these days of international capital markets, there is no guarantee that the capital will be raised in the parent or indeed the host country.

(*ii*) The movements of profits will depend on the shareholding structure of the parent company and on its method of control over its subsidiaries.

Some critics of multinationals argue that the capital flows will seriously affect exchange rates but it is more likely that the capital moves in response to changes in exchange rates, i.e. it does not cause the fluctuations.

(*b*) *Goods.* Multinationals will try to rationalise production on an international level, therefore they will be moving components and semi-finished goods in and out of countries. A sudden change in production policy, e.g. if Fords switch all body-making from Great Britain to Germany, could alter a country's flow of imports and exports. In addition, a multinational may decide to bring in components from another subsidiary rather than buy locally, thus influencing import totals.

In general the balance of payments effects may be greater for a developing rather than a developed nation because the latter will be both a host and a parent country and therefore the movements of capital and goods are likely to cancel out.

11. Technology. Technology has always been a stimulus for multi-nationals (*see* **5**(*b*)) so they are going to be innovators bringing new ideas and methods into host countries. Unfortunately, many host countries will be developing nations and their technological needs are a continuous source of debate. One school of thought believes that to copy the newest Western technology will bring fast economic growth whereas the other school argues that a copying technique ignores the total differences of economic and social structures, e.g. is it sensible to use labour-saving technology when the nation's cheapest resource is labour?

Another view of technology is that it has replaced share ownership as the source of power in a company. If the parent company controls the technology its formal share relationship with the subsidiaries is a red herring. The role of the multinationals with respect to technology is neutral, the real question is society's perspective on technology.

12. Manpower.

(a) *Management level.* Many host countries believe that the multinationals prefer their management to be parent country nationals thus stifling the development of local talent. The contrary view is that modern international management methods act as an incentive to local companies. There is no firm evidence significantly to support either view.

(b) *Worker level.* This is a major controversial area revolving around multinational impact on local labour market wage levels and the structure of industrial relations. There is more myth than evidence to feed the debate but it should be noted that the multinational tradition is to seek efficiency (implying high pay levels) and the honouring of local laws. Unfortunately in Britain our system of industrial relations is built on tradition rather than the law, thus in the interests of economic efficiency a multinational might view the tradition with a jaundiced eye. (In May 1977 the workers of IBM in Britain overwhelmingly voted against being unionised by compulsion.) The relationship of unions and the multinationals is discussed in **21–23**.

13. Efficiency.
As implied in **11** the multinationals when building in a new country seek efficiency otherwise the operation is pointless. The host country is nervous about whether the invasion will kill or stimulate local companies and the host government will probably become increasingly involved in the industrial structure. As always it is dangerous to generalise about the multinational effects.

14. Markets.
Three major problems occur within local market structures.

(*a*) *Market shares.* If the multinational has a commanding share of a local market what should be the host's reactions? The response may depend on the strength of anti-trust legislation or the ability to merge local companies into a viable competitive force. An oligopolistic market structure seems inevitable with the coming of the multinationals to a country. The real local sufferers may be the medium-sized companies, for the genuinely small company can usually find a place in the market.

(*b*) *Pricing decisions.* Multinationals will operate in many markets using international production techniques, but what will determine the price-cost ratio in any given market? Cross-subsidisation may be used so that prices and profits in a strong established market are used to subsidise a price war against local companies in another market. If a multinational is operating in so many markets with a spread of production units, is there any chance of using the marginal techniques of pricing which theoretically lead to the optimum use of recources?

(*c*) *Buying locally.* A multinational will want to integrate its production techniques probably on an international scale and this will have balance of payment implications (*see* **10**(*b*)). The buying policy of the multinationals can affect the general economic well-being of local companies, e.g. in a Third World country would the multinational buy locally at high cost to stimulate the local economic structure?

15. Tax avoidance. It is claimed that multinationals can avoid paying their correct company taxes by showing false profits through the manipulation of transfer pricing. The latter is the name given to the prices charged to each other by the different parts of the multinational empire as they exchange components and semi-finished goods. Assuming that some plants of the empire will be in countries which have low rates of company taxation, the multinational accountants then ensure by rigging the transfer prices that high profits are made in the low tax countries and low profits in high tax countries. Proof of this practice would require an investigation far outside the scope of this book.

MULTINATIONALS AND GOVERNMENTS

16. Basic problem. It has been shown in **9–15** how individual aspects of an economy can be affected by multinational activity, but governments, and in particular Third World governments, have to assess the comprehensive economic and social effects of the multinational presence.

The host government/company relationship is perhaps the most controversial area of the whole multinational debate. The main worries can be grouped under three headings (*see* **17–19**).

17. Global strategy. The multinationals plan their output capacity and sales targets in terms of the world economy rather than a national one, thus a decision to transfer or expand resources is taken irrespective of local effects. Even more importantly the decision is not in the hands of the host government.

The realities of the situation may be different as resource transfer is often an economic nonsense (because of tied up capital) and governments do have the power to control capital movements across their boundaries.

18. Attitudes of parent countries. There are fears that parent country governments may persuade their multinationals to deal more favourably with politically acceptable countries or even worse use the multinationals as a front for intelligence activities. There is some evidence of ITT involvement in Chilean politics but it would be ludicrous to tar all multinationals with this brush.

19. General attitudes to host countries. The attitude of multinationals to the economic, social and cultural aspirations of host countries is often questioned. Most of the industrial giants argue that to antagonise host governments would amount to business suicide. However, it is not known how many pursue the positive policies of British American Tobacco which always uses local management and ploughs back profits into the local community.

20. Conclusions. The irony of the relationship is that as governments become more abusive and regulatory towards the multinationals the latter will find the host's economic climate less inviting and thus the host government may well lose the capital and technological infusion it so desperately requires. Some system of controls based on a mutual appreciation of each other's needs seems very necessary.

MULTINATIONALS AND TRADE UNIONS

21. Basic worry of unions. Trade unionists often treat multinational corporations as bogeymen blaming them for all of mankind's difficulties. Rational members believe the corporations could use the threat of transferring plant to less developed economies in order to restrict domestic pay awards, curtail manning levels and erode traditional industrial relations practice. However, such fears underestimate the huge cost of physical asset transference merely to curb trade union activity.

22. Difficulties of international union agreement. The achievement of effective international union co-operation faces many hurdles. Below is a list of the main obstacles.

(*a*) *Variations in philosophy.* Unions in different countries have a varying philosophical appreciation of their roles. In America, trade unions have a free market, profit orientated view of the world; a European Communist union has the opposite ideology; the British socialist unions have a confused perspective of their environment; and in Japan the unions are usually company based.

(*b*) *Variations in industrial law.* The function of the law in industrial relations varies tremendously between countries both in principle and in detail. The German framework centres on industrial law, whereas in Britain we believe in custom and practice. Thus any international agreement would have to make legal sense in all countries, e.g. sympathy strikes are legal in some countries but not in others.

(*c*) *Variations in wage determination.* Wage determination is a prime part of collective bargaining and the methodology can vary significantly in a single country let alone across nations. Imagine the problems of internationalising wage agreements between countries which have or do not have income policies. Linking with (*b*), it is essential to know if a wage contract is legally binding.

(*d*) *Union organisational abilities.* Apart from the American unions it is most doubtful if any other unions have the management skill and financial resources to organise themselves across national boundaries. Indeed most admit to the problems of meaningfully organising their home activities.

However, despite these frightening hazards unions will clearly, at the political level, join with their governments and any international body to try to control the dangers, real or otherwise, of the multinational.

CONTROL OF THE MULTINATIONALS

23. Introduction. From the previous sections, a potential conflict of interest emerges between managements that operate in a world context and governments which work on the national scene. Increasingly the multinational is regarded, without too much concrete evidence, as a sinister new form of imperialism.

The objections of states can be summarised as loss of national pride, the historical fear of absentee ownership and the growth of unknown decision takers who operate outside the democratic control mechanism. The most pessimistic multinational watchers prophesy that by the end of the twentieth century the nation will be an obsolescent concept. Perhaps it will, but there seems no reason seriously to blame the multinationals for this amazing political and constitutional change.

Nevertheless, given the unknown quality of the multinational (what really is its *raison d'être*?), the mystery will produce fear and governments will try to erase the devilry by controlling the demon. This section investigates the parameters of control policy.

24. History of controls. In the 1960s and early 1970s governments and international bodies published a host of tracts about multinational control, most of the suggestions being fairly gentle and untroublesome, e.g. local equity participation, the quicker promotion of local personnel, the use of local suppliers and the harmonisation of company investment policies with government economic requirements.

These attitudes reflected a belief that both multinationals and nation states had a part to play in world economic and social progress. Then in the mid-1970s the pace of world economic growth began to falter and the nation states searched for scapegoats and after the Arabs they chose the multinationals.

Attitudes hardened and hostility grew particularly in the Third World, the United Nations and trade union movements. There was talk of stringent controls such as states becoming compulsorily the major shareholder or the drawing up of international guidelines to regulate multinational behaviour. Some poorer countries incredibly argued that the West should give them the multinationals. The Western nations despite their own fears of the multinationals drew back from the wilder proposals but began a desperate search for their own control system.

25. Basic thoughts for control. Western countries have never rationalised their views on the costs and benefits of industrial size within their own boundaries, so their thoughts on international control are tentative.

(*a*) *Shared ownership*. This means that the host country should have an equity share in the subsidiary to influence the company's decision taking. This argument simplifies the vastly complex question of ownership and control, the cloudy relationship of shareholder and manager. Share participation could lead to apparent rather than effective control.

(*b*) *Local managers to be locals*. Some companies already follow this policy (*see* **19**) but to establish it as a principle is questionable for the manager's task is to better his company not to work for some ill-defined concept of national interest. Presumably economic efficiency and hence prosperity depends on the best managers being at the top, irrespective of colour, race or creed.

(*c*) *Anti-trust legislation*. Countries may design an active policy to prevent foreigners buying into national companies (as France did under the presidency of General de Gaulle). This policy presupposes that the government has a very clear picture of its required industrial structure, which seems an unlikely phenomenon judged by Britain's performance over the last two decades.

None of the above control points seem very useful because of the difficulties outlined below.

26. Difficulties. Any control system must overcome two extreme difficulties.

(*a*) *Power of a single country*. A single country can only act against the subsidiary of a multinational and over-reaction may drive out much-needed foreign capital. There seems a need for concerted action, which leads to the second difficulty.

(*b*) *International agreement*. If the activities of the multinationals are to be restricted, countries must act together and formalise international agreements on company, merger and industrial relations law. Such agreements appear impossible because they would involve so many countries all with highly localised traditions. Even the EEC cannot seem to evolve a satisfactory Community policy on mergers (*see* XV, **66**).

A further difficulty is that many developed countries are both parent and host to multinationals so their attitudes are bound to be ambivalent. The most likely development is that each country will bargain with a variety of multinationals to develop a *modus operandi* for the successful running of their economies.

CONCLUSIONS ON MULTINATIONALS

27. Summary. The dilemma of the nation state is that it cannot live easily with or without the multinationals. Each state must define its own relationships with each multinational for there is no single concept of a multinational or a state.

Perhaps the whole problem can be summarised by quoting Hymer: "The coming age of multinational corporations should represent a great step forward in the efficiency with which the world uses its economic resources but it will create grave social and political problems and will be very uneven in exploiting and distributing the benefits of modern science and technology." (S. Hymer in *Multinational Firm and the Nation State*, G. Paguet, Collier Macmillan, 1972, p. 63.)

PROGRESS TEST 17

1. Give a definition of multinational companies.   **(2)**
2. Name four multinationals.   **(3)**
3. Explain the growth of American multinationals.   **(5)**
4. How has America tried to attract European multinationals? **(6)**
5. What is the effect of multinationals on the balance of payments?   **(10)**
6. Describe the impact of multinationals on manpower.   **(12)**
7. Outline the problems arising from multinational pricing decisions.   **(14(*b*))**
8. What is the likely attitude of multinationals to the host countries?   **(19)**
9. Why do unions worry about multinationals?   **(21)**
10. Outline the history of attempts to control multinationals. **(24)**

CHAPTER XVIII

Nationalised Industries

BACKGROUND OF THE NATIONALISED INDUSTRIES

1. Definition. In November 1976 the National Economic Development Office published a wide-ranging investigation of the British nationalised industries (HMSO) It suggested that a nationalised industry could be defined as a public corporation:

(*a*) whose assets are in public ownership and vested in a public corporation;

(*b*) whose boards are appointed by a Secretary of State;

(*c*) whose board members are not civil servants; and

(*d*) which is primarily engaged in industrial or other trading activities.

It is a tight definition concentrating on the production and sale of goods and services. The major source of revenue is therefore the customer. It excludes such bodies as regional water authorities, port authorities, the Bank of England and the National Enterprise Board. The problem of the status of British Leyland, Rolls-Royce (Aero-Engines) and other companies dominated by government money is avoided. This chapter will concentrate on the traditional nationalised industries as designated in Table XXVII.

2. Impact of nationalised industries. The nationalised industries play a significant role in the British economy. Together they account for more than a tenth of the Gross Domestic Product and nearly one-fifth of total fixed investment. The four biggest employers (besides the government itself) are nationalised industries. They occupy a dominant position in the supply of steel, transport, energy and communications. About a third of all plant and equipment bought by British industry is consumed by the nationalised sector while they are the sole domestic customer for several areas of British industry.

The nature of the beast is summed up by W. G. Shepherd:

"The problems of the Nationalised industries are complex and

TABLE XXVII.   *Nationalised industries and the UK economy, 1975*

	Value added £m.	% GDP	Employment '000s	% UK	Fixed investment £m.	% UK
British Airways	279	0.3	53	0.2	82	0.4
British Gas	745	0.8	102	0.4	349	1.7
British Rail	1,118	1.2	254	1.0	205	1.0
British Steel	745	0.8	220	0.9	410	2.0
Electricity[1]	1,397	1.5	167	0.7	595	2.9
Coal Board	1,397	1.5	312	1.2	185	0.9
Post Office	2,608	2.8	421	1.8	923	4.5
National Bus Company	186	0.2	70	0.3	21	0.1
National Freight Corporation	186	0.2	45	0.2	—	—
Total	8,662	9.3	1,644	6.7	2,770	13.5
Other national industries	372	0.4	47	0.2	164	0.8
Other public corporations	1,304	1.4	261	1.1	943	4.6
TOTAL	10,337	11.1	1,952	8.0	3,877	19.0

[1]Electricity only England and Wales.
(*Source: The Economist, 27th November 1976, p. 15 (figures may not add because of rounding*).)

changing. With their many operations and outputs the industries are enormously diverse and they are closely involved in the adjustment problems of the entire economy with important social effects frequently linked to their actions. No single economic criterion for organising and operating the nationalised industries has been found appropriate." (*Economic Performance under Public Ownership*, Yale University Press, 1965.)

In a nutshell the British nationalised industries are very large business organisations with a vital economic influence yet they have to perform a social role and there are no clear guidelines for establishing criteria to evaluate the success of their combined economic and social achievements.

3. Myths. Serious debate on the complex industrial problem is severely handicapped by political prejudices which have created myths about the nationalised industries. Below are some examples.

(*a*) *All nationalised industries lose money.* As Table XXX shows this is not true. British Rail probably has lost most money but in all countries it has been found difficult to make profit out of running a major railway network whether it is publicly or privately owned. Simple profit levels are never a satisfactory test of efficiency.

(*b*) *Nationalised industries are a UK phenomenon.* All Western nations have nationalised industries, usually in the public utilities, and government involvement in this field can be traced back to the late nineteenth century. Furthermore, many countries have developed nationalised interests in other industries and even in individual companies, e.g. in Sweden, the alcohol industry, in France, Renault. Each country has evolved a nationalised sector best suited to its own traditions and modes of business organisation.

(*c*) *Nationalised industries are pure monopolies.* The competitive position of the industries varies significantly. The Post Office is near enough to a pure monopoly (but *see* **28**), while British Rail is in fierce competition with private road transport, and private and public air transport. (In 1975 British Rail accounted for only 8 per cent of passenger travel; the 1964 figure was 12 per cent.) The energy industries compete amongst themselves and with the private oil industry.

(*d*) *Total nationalisation leads to economic salvation.* Myths (*a*)–(*c*) are in the minds of right-wing political people; the salvation myth belongs to the left. There is no scrap of economic or business theory, or indeed pragmatic evidence, to support this piece of nineteenth-century dogma. Cruelly the industrial performance of the Socialist countries where nationalisation is total is admitted by themselves to be well below Western standards.

ARGUMENTS FOR NATIONALISATION

4. To prevent abuse of monopoly power. Competition through the presence of several firms would be very wasteful of resources in certain industries, e.g. gas, electricity, rail, postal communications and water, because the capital intensiveness of the industries would make plant duplication extremely costly. Without nationalisation single private firm domination would be inevitable and the community would be exposed to the potential abuses of monopoly power (*see* XV). Government control of monopolies never seems entirely satisfactory, therefore nationalisation puts the monopoly power into public rather than private hands.

5. Economies of scale. There is a fear that in certain industries firms might be too small to maximise scale economies. This would be serious if the industry was capital intensive and competing in world markets. Failure to achieve the economies gives low profits which further reduces investment incentives. Either the vicious circle continues until near bankruptcy, or the City encourages private mergers which might lead to the fear of monopoly argument given above. Both situations are unattractive and so the government steps in with nationalisation plans. This argument was behind the 1967 steel nationalisation and the 1977 shipbuilding take-over.

6. Control of the economy. This is really a political argument which suggests that if the government is to run the economy successfully, the traditional monetary and fiscal policies are inadequate and the government must control the major industries whose decisions on investment, prices and employment policies can have far-reaching effects on the economy.

7. Social benefits. The output of certain industries contains elements of social benefit, but the costs incurred in providing the benefit are so high that a purely profit-motivated industry could not afford to provide the relevant output. Nationalisation is therefore used to obtain the social benefits.

Good examples occur within the post and rail industries where services to non-urban areas are maintained despite the non-profitability of such services.

However, there must be limits to the social argument. Calls to nationalise big companies for social reasons are often made when large-scale redundancies are announced, but such arguments are an economic nonsense as a change of ownership does not affect a company's product demand which is the ultimate determinant of employment.

8. Government as main customer. Some industries, e.g. aircraft, shipbuilding, generating equipment, are heavily dependent on the government for orders. They are often technologically advanced industries so their demise would scarcely be in the national interest.

It is argued that if these industries were state owned it would be easier for the government to have an overall buying and production plan to avoid the uncertainties which presently plague the industries.

9. Redistribution of resources. This is another political argument based on old-fashioned doctrine. It is assumed that nationalisation means a transfer of control over the means of production to the workers who would also gain from a distribution of the profits. So far nationalisation has meant a transfer of power to the state and as will be seen in **30–51** a change of ownership has not eased some extremely complex problems of control, investment and pricing policies.

10. Summary. The case for nationalisation rests on three broad strands.

(*a*) Certain industries depend on size of operation and private control might entail serious monopolistic dangers in terms of price and output policy.

(*b*) Industries may have certain social obligations which a totally profit-orientated structure could not meet.

(*c*) A change in ownership of industry produces an economic and social Utopia.

The first point can be economically researched and debated, while the final point is an act of faith. However, the middle argument is the tricky one because it entails seeking a balance between economic and social ends, a situation which is at the heart of modern life.

ARGUMENTS AGAINST NATIONALISATION

11. Creation of monopoly. In Britain nationalisation has so far always involved a single supplier of a good or service although the possibility of substitutes exists (*see* **3**(*c*)) so the government is creating a monopoly with all its inherent dangers. This argument rejects the thesis of **4** that a government monopoly is more amenable to control. It is felt that the government has far more weapons to guard its monopoly power (e.g. the use of taxes and subsidies to protect coal against oil) and that ultimately there is no higher authority to protect the consumer against government monopoly power. Believers in this argument contend that monopoly, irrespective of ownership, is potentially dangerous to consumer satis-

faction and resource allocation. The case of the Post Office
monopoly is often cited as the number of postal collections and
deliveries are curtailed despite rising prices.

12. No profit motive. The aims of the nationalised industries are
seldom clearly defined in profit terms (*see* **23–29**), so the managements lack any incentive to improve their efficiency by the usual
control standards of private enterprise. Later sections will try to
clarify what are the aims of the industries and the aspirations of
their managements. Simply to correlate profit and efficiency is
naïve (*see* XIII) and traditional economic theory of the firm
exaggerates the role of profit in private industry decision taking.
However, a concept of working for a high rate of return seems more
reasonable than the whimsicalities of R. Pryke who wrote: "The
aim of those in charge of the nationalised industries is to meet the
needs of the consumer at the lowest possible price, to act as a model
employer and in general to help maximise the welfare of the
nation." (*Public Enterprise in Practice*, MacGibbon and Kee, 1971,
p. 460.) More recently Pryke has expressed scepticism about the
performance of the nationalised industries.

13. Diseconomies of scale. The nationalised industries are very big
and face the danger of suffering from diseconomies of scale. Over-
bureaucratisation is the chief fear and there are many signs of the
industries suffering from too much centralisation, poor communications, red tape and the other well-known evils of organisational
size. The management seems aware of the problems and all the
industries have endured many restructuring operations but the
benefits are not so obvious.

Another diseconomy can arise from market contraction with
subsequent rises in costs per unit. In private industry diversification
is the answer but the nationalised industries live in a market
strait-jacket and diversification is frowned upon (*see* **35(c)**).

14. Political interference. Constitutionally the politician is supposed to keep at arm's length from day-to-day management of the
industries (*see* **30–34**) but the whole history is marred by a
persistent overruling of sound business decisions for nebulous
political gain.

The record of intervention undermines the control of the
economy argument (*see* **6**) which is based on a quaint belief in the
economic rationality of politicians. The nationalised industries

have been used by both parties as a lifeboat to rescue the sinking economy but unfortunately this role is beyond any single group of industries whoever owns them.

15. Fears for democracy. This is a pure political argument based on the premise that democracy rests on a multi-dimension sharing of the ownership of productive resources and the greater the share enjoyed by the state, the less power there is for the people. At the extreme of a totally socialist state the argument is valid, but in Britain where the basic nationalised structure is only ever marginally changed, whichever government is in power, the fears are exaggerated.

16. Summary. The arguments against nationalisation depend on two major thrusts.

(*a*) State monopoly, given the quality of political thinking and integrity, may be even more dangerous than private monopoly which can at least be controlled by the law.

(*b*) The nationalised industries lack adequate concrete economic and social aims to guide their managers' decision taking, so the danger of resource wastage must be high.

17. Conclusion on 4–16. The supporters and opponents of nationalisation forget a vital point, viz. nationalisation cannot be inherently good or bad. This is a logical absurdity. Essentially it is a method of business organisation which ought to be evaluated by business criteria. (This does not preclude social costs and benefits.) It is not, and this absolutely devalues debate, the heralding of the Red Dawn.

The nationalisation of public utilities is easy to justify on economic grounds but the nationalisation of the whole retail trade would be a piece of economic fantasy. Real difficulties of debate occur when the nationalisation of steel, cars or drugs are proposed. In these complex arguments, economists must avoid twisting their economic facts and theories to suit their political prejudices.

Finally it must be remembered that nationalisation is only one method of government involvement with industry. The next twenty years may see more subtle and satisfying ways of realising a successful working relationship between government and industry. Total *laissez-faire* and total nationalisation are obsolete and irrelevant ways of fashioning a desirable industrial structure.

METHODS OF ORGANISATION

18. Department of state. This was an early idea in which the enterprise was organised through a specific minister and his department, e.g. the Post Office used to be run by a minister with the title Postmaster General.

19. Local authorities. Most local authorities through their committee system and officials provide a range of non-social services, e.g. buses and markets.

20. Public boards. The traditional British method of running a state industry is to create a board (equivalent to a board of directors) responsible to a government minister and hence to Parliament. The board is responsible for the day-to-day running of the industry but remains accountable to the representatives of the people (*see* **30–34**).

21. Government financial control. Since the 1960s, some private companies have received ever increasing injections of public money although governments have made no attempt to nationalise them or even effectively to control their policies.

Labour administrations via the IRC (*see* XIV, **14**) and NEB (*see* XIV, **15**) have tried to increase political control over the long-term plans of such companies, e.g. Rolls-Royce and British Leyland.

The desire for accountability was also emphasised by the 1979 Conservative Government which took the step of reinvolving the Department of Industry in the above companies' affairs.

However, whatever efforts governments make, the companies' directors retain effective decision-taking power, so the companies, although totally dependent on government investment, are not nationalised. Some new status is required.

GOVERNMENT POLICIES TOWARDS NATIONALISED INDUSTRIES

22. Intervention and its problems. The ideal way to run a nationalised industry would be to recruit top calibre management with the brief of maximising the effective utilisation of the industry's resources. Lip-service is paid to this ideal, but governments intervene in management policy, offering a variety of excuses, including the following.

(*a*) The expansion or restriction of capital investment programmes for reasons of macroeconomic policy (*see* III, **17**) rather than the long-term needs of the industries.

(*b*) The use of pricing policy for short-term political gains (winning an election) or economic goals (financing the Public Sector Borrowing Requirement) without reference to the product market or the industries' financial targets (*see* **24–26**).

(*c*) To shore up failing sectors of industry, e.g. the purchase by British Airways of unwanted British aircraft.

(*d*) The provision of loss-making services on social grounds, e.g. telegrams, commuters' railway lines.

These examples reflect the broad problems facing the nationalised industries' management, e.g. can the industries be tools of general economic and social policy? How responsive should they be to market forces? How valid are their financial objectives?

23. Period I 1948–61. This was the great maternity period, when numbers of nationalised industries were born and various statutory obligations were laid down. Broadly there was a desire to meet the demand for the products and to charge prices which allowed the industries to break even over a period of time. In fact the aims were staggeringly vague as a guide to practising management, e.g. the NCB was expected to provide coal at prices and qualities best calculated to further the public interest; the electricity industry had to provide electricity to those who wanted it and to cheapen supplies as far as was practicable.

There was no clarification of the public interest, no efficiency criteria were established. Management was therefore left in the dark and performance was disappointing.

24. Period II 1961–67. In 1961 the Government, trying to rectify the lack of purpose, published *The Financial and Economic Obligations of the Nationalised Industries* (Cmnd. 1337). Industries were required to balance their books over a five-year period after providing for interest and depreciation, at historic cost. Provision was also made for the building up of reserves. Finally financial targets were to be set for the first time, with each industry having a target rate of return on capital based on its capabilities and needs, e.g. Electricity Boards, 12.4 per cent; British European Airways, 6 per cent; Post Office, 8 per cent.

The Government also promised the Boards greater freedom to

fix prices and promised to give a written explanation of any intervention on prices. Subsequently Select Committee Reports repri-
manded governments for ignoring this policy of non-intervention.

25. Period III 1967–71. In 1967 the Labour Government published
*Nationalised Industries—A Review of Economic and Financial
Objectives* (Cmnd. 3437). The basic concern was with the tremendous increase in nationalised industry investment which was
consuming an ever growing share of scarce capital resources.

The major concept was the use of discounted cash flow techniques to evaluate proposed investment plans in order to keep
them in line with national resource utilisation. It was suggested
that no project should be undertaken if the likely rate of return
was below 8 per cent which was deemed to be a comparable rate
with the private sector. The Government also required a pricing
policy that would ensure the customer paid the true cost of
the service, although if wider social benefits were involved the
Government promised to make a subsidy towards the cost of the
benefit.

 On balance this White Paper was slightly odd for a Labour
Government, for its philosophy was definitely profit orientated
with social obligations taking a back seat.

26. Period IV 1971–74. The Conservative Government of Mr
Heath came to power in 1970 on a platform of applying almost
nineteenth-century principles of *laissez-faire* to the industrial structure. It wanted to hive off many of the periphery activities of the
nationalised industries and to make the remainder highly profit
orientated. Government intervention would be out.

By late 1972 as inflation was beginning to accelerate the
nationalised industries were ordered to peg their prices. The consequence of this policy were staggering losses in 1974 (*see* Table
XXX). Target rates of return and discounted cash flow techniques
vanished.

27. Period V 1974–79. The incoming Labour Government allowed
the industries big price increases to recoup the huge losses incurred
under the Heath administration. This commercial attitude was not
always maintained. The efficient gas industry was ordered to raise
its price levels to catch up with less efficient fuel industries while
the Electricity Board had to build unwanted power stations.

However, a 1978 White Paper still argued the need for efficiency checks if the industries lacked the discipline of market forces or the fear of bankruptcy. To this end, prices ought to reflect costs, the market environment and financial targets rather than political need.

28. Period VI 1979 onwards. The new Conservative government promised to tighten financial controls and to sell off assets to the private sector (privatisation). The latter policy became entangled in legal and financial complexities but by 1981 plans were afoot to bring private capital into British Aerospace and British Airways, while offers were invited for the assets of British Rail's non-rail subsidiaries. In addition, by the summer of 1980 proposals were launched to split telecommunications from the postal service and gently to fragment the monopolistic powers of each.

On the financial side the government became very interventionist, often denying the needs of the market. The following are some examples of its measures.

(*a*) The Government fixed tight cash limits on the industries' budgets irrespective of wage settlements and the impact of the recession.

(*b*) It continued to pour money into British Leyland and British Steel, the latter overshooting its 1980/81 cash limits by £600 million.

(*c*) The industries, particularly those supplying fuels, were forced to raise prices irrespective of market demand, ostensibly for conservation reasons, but in reality to ease the burden of the PSBR.

(*d*) Late in 1980, the Government relaxed the industries' external financing limits but made no concession to the idea of borrowing on the capital market or removing investment programmes from the PSBR accounts.

In short, the Conservative's policy on nationalised industries was interventionist but seemed totally to ignore market forces and business logic.

29. Summary. Nearly forty years on from the birth of the nationalised industries, the community and its politicians have evolved no clear and workable philosophy for them. Such is the confusion, that Labour Governments have tried to manage them on business principles while Conservatives have been blatantly interventionist for short-term economic and political reasons.

THE PROBLEM OF PUBLIC ACCOUNTABILITY

30. Introduction. Whereas the board of directors of a private company is responsible to its shareholders, the board of a nationalised industry is ultimately responsible to the electorate via Parliament. This is a nebulous concept and the Acts of Parliament establishing the industries deliberately offered no rigid solution in the belief that experience would evolve a satisfactory method of accountability. Below is a broad outline of the system that has evolved.

31. The Minister. The Minister responsible for the industry has been the main instrument of control. Certain statutory obligations are placed on him. He appoints board members, fixes their salaries and approves major policy decisions, e.g. investment programmes. He can also direct the boards to conduct the business in the public interest.

As a general rule the boards and their management take day-to-day decisions and the Minister has a big say in overall policy. Unfortunately at times of political and economic crisis, the border-line between the two decision areas disappears (*see* **22** and **26**).

Parliamentary back-benchers also complain about their inability even marginally to influence the policies of the nationalised industries. At question times, questions seem to investigate the Minister rather than the industry.

32. Select committees. Since 1951 all -party select committees have acted as parliamentary watch-dogs over the industries. They have the power to send for people, paper and records and from 1956 they have investigated the boards' reports and accounts. Their aim is to inform Parliament about the aims and activities of the industries.

The select committees have performed well for their reports are rational and free from political bias, while they have won the confidence of the boards. However, their reports tend by nature to be retrospective and it is difficult to specify progress which can be attributed to the committees.

33. Consultative councils. Each industry has a consultative council (composed of lay people) with a statutory obligation to act as general advisers to their boards particularly from the consumers' point of view, e.g. they often have the right to veto price increases. The council are organised on a regional basis but they exist in a limbo as the vast mass of the people are unaware of their existence except possibly for the Post Office Consumers' Council.

34. Problems of the system. The NEDO report (*see* **1**) identified the following four elements in the accountability problem.

(*a*) A mutual lack of trust and understanding between the industries and the government (politicians and civil servants).

(*b*) No closely identified roles for all the bodies involved in the management of the industries.

(*c*) No effective system for assessing performance particularly at management level.

(*d*) No mechanism for establishing long-term goals, backed by necessary finance, which is independent of the short-term policies of political expediency.

Ultimately public accountability can only be discussed in relation to other problems facing the industries.

COMPETITION

35. Relations with private industry. The nationalised industries and their private counterparts live in the same commercial world. At least two-thirds of nationalised output is bought by the private commercial sector and the nationalised concerns, because of their big investment programmes (*see* Table XXVIII), are huge buyers of plant and equipment. Below are some of the problems posed by the relationship.

(*a*) *Pricing policies.* Should nationalised industries sell cheaply to subsidise private industry costs or sell dear to conserve fuel or help the PSBR (*see* **28**(*c*))? Both policies distort the industries' financial structures and the nation's use of resources.

(*b*) *Buying policies.* To what extent should the industries' buying powers be used to protect and encourage the private sector? (From January 1981, such actions are technically against EEC regulations.)

(*c*) *Diversification policies.* What are the boundaries of the commercial interests of the nationalised industries, e.g. do British Rail need to own hotels, or should British Airways provide package holidays? (In 1981, the Conservative Government required British Rail to begin selling off some of its hotels; *see* **28**.) Conservatives have tended to define the boundaries very narrowly but this goes against all industrial experience because as demand patterns change companies must diversify, e.g. the major tobacco companies are into food and cosmetics. As *The Economist* said, "Without development we might still have a nationalised stage coach company with all the problems of the coachmen's union." (*The Economist*, 27th November 1976, p. 17.) The counter argument is that nationalised industry competition is theoretically unfair since they can never go bankrupt because of government finance.

36. Competition between nationalised industries. Several nationalised industries are in severe competition with each other, e.g. rail/air, gas/electricity/coal, but it is difficult to establish what is the most beneficial nature of that competition. If competition does stimulate efficiency then the public must gain, but does the consumer gain from the possible wastes of competition, e.g. different gas and electricity meter readers, or the advertising campaigns of the different industries?

The answers are not obvious and it is perhaps a problem of competition practice rather than a particular aspect of nationalisation.

PRICING POLICIES

37. Role of prices in nationalised industries. Four possible roles for prices may be determined by looking at the history of pricing policies.

(*a*) Fixed to maximise profits. In this case, theory of the firm principles would be applied.

(*b*) Fixed to provide a basic service at a price that all sections of the community can afford with the implication that a financial loss may be made.

(*c*) Fixed to satisfy the government's economic strategy, e.g. prices kept down as a bargaining ploy to seek an incomes policy.

(*d*) Fixed to strike a balance between (*a*) and (*b*). The industries are obliged to make profit but they have to meet certain definable social obligations. Thus the industry seeks a satisfactory profit given a social constraint. This fits the "satisfying" principle from the modern theories of the firm (*see* XIII, **12**).

Should policy (*b*), (*c*) or even (*d*) be used, the industry will need a subsidy which has economic consequences of its own (*see* **43**). Alternatively if policy (*a*) is rigorously applied it will prompt the question—why nationalise the industry in the first place? Clearly pricing policy cannot be realistically divided from problems of the purposes of nationalised industries.

38. History of nationalised prices. The layman believes that nationalised industry prices have always been very high relative to the private sector but reality is more complicated.

Between 1960 and 1975 the nationalised prices to the consumer rose on average 8.4 per cent per annum, while the total retail price index rose by 7.2 per cent per annum. Over the same period a price index of nationalised industry outputs, purchased by manufacturing industry, increased less rapidly than those of total basic materials and fuel purchased by the manufacturing sector.

Although the average price rise is higher than the retail index, the average masks periods when prices were kept artificially low for political reasons, big losses were incurred, then prices were allowed to rocket over a short time period, much to the consumer's horror. This process occurred early in the 1960s, 1970s and 1980s. Such abrupt price changes without reference to marketing needs totally undermine long-term planning to achieve financial objectives.

39. Price theory and the nationalised industries. For all practical purposes nationalised industries are monopoly suppliers of goods and services and using basic economic theory their price/output policies ought to give them supernormal profits (*see* Fig. 8). They sell an output of ON for a price of OP which gives then a supernormal profit of $APMB$. However, one reason for nationalising an industry is to avoid this situation (*see* **4**). What therefore should be the pricing policy of a nationalised industry?

Economic theory suggests that if we wish to maximise welfare and resource allocation then a policy of equating price and marginal cost should be pursued (*see* Fig. 9).

In this situation an output of ON is sold at a price of OP. The price is lower and output greater than in the profit maximising situation where price would be OP^1 and output ON^1.) The White Paper of 1967 seemed to endorse this policy: "The consumer should pay the true costs of the goods and services he consumes in every case where they can be suitably identified" (Cmnd. 3437, para. 18). The Government suggested the use of long-run marginal costs which would include a provision for the replacement of fixed capital. There were three suggestions for deviating from the general rule.

FIG. 8 *Price and output policy in monopoly.* The monopolist has the power to restrict the output to *ON*, in order to achieve a price *OP* substantially above the lowest point on the average cost curve. Competition would have forced a larger output, minimum average cost and a lower price.

FIG. 9 *Price and output in a competitive market.* Competition obliges the supplier to produce an output consistent with marginal cost (the extra cost of one more unit of output), equally the price it achieves. Thus *ON* sell at *OP* which equals marginal cost of *NM*.

(*a*) If there was spare capacity in an industry, the price should be lowered to short-run marginal costs to attract more custom.

(*b*) If there was excess short-run demand then price should be raised as a rationing device.

(*c*) If it is difficult to allocate costs to specific services then two-part tariffs (*see* **46**) should be used with prices proportionate to marginal cost.

However, the principle of equating price and marginal cost has been attacked on many grounds and these difficulties are discussed below.

DIFFICULTIES OF MARGINAL COST PRICING

40. Falling average cost curves. Nationalised industries are usually capital intensive, thus in the long run because of scale economies they should enjoy falling average costs. This situation also ensures a falling marginal cost curve which creates a problem for the *MC* = price relationship (*see* Fig. 10). Clearly at a price of *OP* the industry is making a loss of *PABM* which would have to be financed out of tax revenues, a situation creating two worries.

FIG. 10 *Price and output policy with falling marginal cost.* When because of scale economies marginal costs, rather than rising, continue to fall, the competitive rule of equating *MC* with *P/AR* would result in a loss of *PABM*.

(*a*) There is a redistribution of income from the taxpayer to the consumer based on no obvious criteria of equity, need or resource allocation (*see* **43**).

(*b*) Price policy might become a facet of taxation policy which is a piece of economic irrationality.

41. Measuring marginal costs. Marginal cost is an elusive concept in any industry but in capital intensive industries the problem is very complex. The time period chosen is of great significance because the cost of meeting an increase of demand of one unit in period *t* is not necessarily the same as meeting the identical demand increase in period (*t* + 1). Consider the problems facing the electricity generating boards. Assuming no change in the total number of customers, the demand varies by time of day, day of week, week of year and through the vagaries of climate. Varying output to meet these changes produces a myriad of marginal costs. Consider further the decision whether to build a new power station costing millions of pounds but which in the long run is a marginal cost!

Theoretically the industry will have a multitude of marginal costs which might be reflected in a complex tariff system. However, the information costs of calculating and metering the system make it only worth while for very large customers. In addition, if the producer is facing an inelastic demand, subtle price differences will have little effect on consumption decisions.

42. Marginal social costs. The management of nationalised industries usually accepts that it has to meet certain social obligations but nobody (despite many gallant mathematical exercises) knows how to allow for these costs within the framework of marginal costing. How are the social costs and benefits of the telegram service to be evaluated? What is the social value of putting electricity cables underground rather than on overhead pylons?

The industries often argue that their social elements should be clearly designated and then the government should pay for them by direct subsidy.

43. Subsidising prices. It is shown in **40** and **42** that governments may have to subsidise various nationalised industry activities but this policy itself has dangers.

(*a*) Large subsidies can quickly increase the volume of public expenditure, a step which, depending on the financing of the expenditure, can be inflationary.

(*b*) If subsidies are just cheap finance for the maintenance of inefficiently operated services then they represent a misallocation of the nation's resources. The continuous availability of subsidies can also undermine the rigour of management decision taking as the stimulant of financial control is removed.

(*c*) As already stated (*see* **40**(*a*)), subsidies paid for out of tax revenue ensure that the taxpayer is subsidising the consumer and yet the rationale of this subsidy is not clear on either social or economic grounds. Some Labour Party members have suggested, rather wildly, that rail commuting is a middle-class pleasure and to subsidise it creates a regressive distribution of· income. If a country branch line is subsidised then presumably the reason for subsidy is living in a pleasant area which seems a debatable excuse for handing out government money.

44. Side effects of marginal cost pricing. If the price of the output is related to the true cost of providing the output then various odd social and economic side effects could develop, such as the following.

(*a*) Coal-mine efficiencies and hence costs vary enormously for a variety of technical and geographical reasons, so if prices were related to marginal costs consumers would be charged a big range of prices depending solely on the regional source of their fuel. Consumers would bitterly resent this luck element in their coal bills and if demand was elastic the sales of the inefficient pits would collapse and the remaining pits might not be able to meet the nation's demand for coal.

(*b*) British Rail provides three basic passenger services—long distance Inter-City, commuter services and short-distance branch lines. If the true costs of the second and third categories were reflected in prices then:

(*i*) commuters might be forced on to city roads with terrifying consequences for congestion costs;

(*ii*) branch line passengers might desert the rail service which would seriously affect Inter-City because the branch lines are a feeder service.

ALTERNATIVE PRICING POLICIES

45. Average cost pricing. Average costs are easier to calculate and by ensuring prices were linked to them, deficits would be less likely to occur. Despite these attractions the problem of allocating costs remains because the fixed cost sector of total costs is very large and to allocate a percentage to any specific output cost seems arbitrary. Fixed costs are now so important that the industries can become involved in a vicious circle; as prices rise, sales drop (depending on demand elasticities) and unit costs rise thus tending to push prices up again.

In some industries average costs might be difficult to define in an economically meaningful way, e.g. **44**(*b*) showed three elements of British Rail passenger service. Would rail average costs be for all services combined or for the individual sector? If the former case was true, the branch lines would be hugely subsidised by Inter-City. What are the social and economic values of this type of cross-subsidisation?

46. Two-part tariffs. This is a popular system used by the gas, post and electricity organisations. The price is made up of:

(*a*) a fixed charge to make a significant contribution to the fixed costs, i.e. an average cost approach;

(*b*) a running charge which attempts to cover the cost of producing extra units of output, i.e. a marginal cost approach.

47. Summary. The pricing policies of the nationalised industries are infinitely complex, interwoven as they are with the vagueness of the industries' aims and the heavy handed interference of politicians, but until the purpose of the nationalised industries has been established pricing policy will not be a rational economic feature.

INVESTMENT POLICIES

48. Importance of nationalised investment. Table XXVIII gives some impression of the sheer magnitude of the nationalised industries' investment programmes. These high levels, which are inevitable given the nature of the industries, produce several problems, which will be investigated in the next paragraphs.

49. Investment levels. Because the industries are capital intensive, the level of investment will always be high but this statement disguises the fact that the actual size will tend to fluctuate wildly as big replacement and expansion programmes are undertaken, e.g. the electrification of the London–Glasgow rail link and the development of North Sea gas. The level of investment will largely depend on long-term demand forecasts and scientific estimates of

TABLE XXVIII.   *Investment levels Great Britain (£m.)*

	Total investment	Public corporation investment
1966	8,079	1,738
1968	9,182	1,844
1970	9,453	1,679
1972	9,862	1,506
1974	10,124	1,738
1976	9,562	1,889

(*Source: Economic Trends, June 1977.*)

future technological developments, both of which are areas of calculation which can be easily but disastrously wrong. For example, the electrification of the Glasgow–London rail link, from planning to completion, took about fifteen years, so its success depended on guesses of long-term rail demand. Short-term demand forecasting is hazardous but time scales of over five years rely more on faith than statistics.

The time scale can also undermine the technological size of investment plans as designers have to work out possible future production techniques; the electrical generating bodies have persistently suffered from this problem through the breaking down of new equipment and because of the raging scientific and political debate on the role of nuclear fuel.

Fear of short-term government restraints has destroyed confidence in long-term strategic planning which in turn has delayed technological progress, e.g. the 1977 Chester Committee criticised Post Office efforts in telecommunications which produced changes in 1980 (*see* **28**).

50. Raising the capital. The nationalised industries between them raise well over £1,000 million per annum not all of which can be self-financed. The scale of the borrowing raises several problems.

Each of the industries has a statutory limit to its borrowing powers and each needs ministerial approval to raise and spend the money, but they can borrow working capital without prior approval. Up to 1956 (with the exception of the NCB) they borrowed on long-dated fixed interest stock. The rates were low and unrelated to risk so there was a danger of unfinancially controlled

TABLE XXIX.   *National Loans Fund net lending (£m.)*

	1967–68	1971–72	1973–74	1977–78	1978–79
Post Office	200	296.7	313.4	−38.6	18.0
Coal	76	44.2	18.6	94.7	222.6
Electricity	379.9	194	−115.9	−58	−12.4
Gas	262.2	187.9	−38	−555.9	−666.6
Steel	175	144.5	−3	216.4	−161.6
Aviation	17.4	43.4	−36.1	−23.6	−15.1
Transport	88.2	44.5	34.7	−6.6	−0.7

(*Source: Annual Abstract of Statistics, 1980.*)

investment which would be wasteful of the nation's resources.

In 1958 the industries started to borrow from the Treasury and in 1968 they commenced borrowing from the National Loans Fund (*see* Table XXIX) at more commercial rates of interest. All the managements would like the power significantly to extend their borrowing from the national and international private capital markets. Such a course of action would give them more commercial rigour and free them from the irrationalities of government decision taking. However, although private borrowing has increased the Treasury has misgivings about the policy for three reasons.

(*a*) *Social objectives.* The social obligations of the industries make it difficult to forecast risk factors and rates of return, thus the private lender lacks the normal commercial mechanism for judging investment opportunity.

(*b*) *Market impact.* The amounts of money involved are so large it would distort the market for conventional private users.

(*c*) *Effects on economy* (*see* **51**(*a*)). The investment programmes have been used as a tool of demand management and the Treasury is reluctant to relax control over the programme. It also fears the balance of payments consequences of too much overseas fund raising.

51. Economic policies and investment levels. Throughout this chapter it has been clear that the nationalised industries have been bedevilled by government interference often based on short-term considerations. Investment policy making has been no exception to the above assertion for all British governments have used nationalised industries' investment plans as a weapon of counter-cyclical finance. Plans have been cut or invented, pushed back or brought forward without reference to the needs of the industry concerned (both Mr Heath and Mr Benn ordered power stations to be built for the expediency of creating jobs in politically sensitive areas).

This policy has so many pitfalls that governments' continuing adherence to it seems amazing. Some of the difficulties are as follows.

(*a*) *Time lags.* What is the lag after the decision to increase or reduce a programme before the economic effects materialise?

(*b*) *Relation of private and nationalised investment.* What is the effect of sudden changes in public corporation investment on private firms who are the main customers and suppliers?

(*c*) *Inflexibility of investment.* Investment is essentially a long-run phenomenon, its result determining industrial patterns in five to ten years time. Does anybody know the results of persistent short-run changes in these patterns?

Finally it must be noted that if governments indulge in arbitrary price fixing policies for the nationalised industries it can create fantasy in the investment process (*see* **38**).

NATIONALISED INDUSTRIES—SUCCESS OR FAILURE

52. Guidelines. To judge the success of any organisation it is necessary to see if its objectives have been achieved. Unfortunately, as has been seen through the whole chapter, the objectives of the nationalised industries have been both many and muddled. The ideas below indicate some areas into which government policy has pushed the nationalised boards.

(*a*) A pricing policy to promote the best use of resources and to obtain a commercial rate of return on investment.

(*b*) To promote social welfare by policies of low prices and high wages.

(*c*) To have the industries as engine rooms for research and innovation.

(*d*) To use the industries as a tool for wider economic objectives, e.g. anti-inflationary and regional policies.

Clearly they have been expected to be all things to all men and any critic or supporter can find an objective which has or has not been achieved.

53. Criteria of success. From the vagueness of aims two general principles can be identified.

(a) The industries are users of scarce resources, therefore they should ensure the efficient utilisation of their resources by effective output, pricing and investment policies which implies the seeking of profit returns commensurate with private industry.

(b) If the above was the only criterion, there would be no point in nationalising the industries as they could be organised in the conventional private way. The industries are taken over because they may have to provide non-profitable services for social reasons or to offer external economies, e.g. British Rail running non-paying rail links for the Scottish tourist industry.

Therefore any evaluation must be based on some attempt to balance (a) and (b) as extremes of either principle would destroy the other.

54. Evaluation. At the simplest level on profit terms (see Table XXX) the industries have had good and bad years but so have all private firms. The reliability of profit figures is debatable because each industry has its own accounting system. In addition, the figures ignore the loss-making social elements in the output (see **7**).

TABLE XXX.   *Nationalised industries, profits and losses, 1968–79 (£m.)*

	1968	1970	1972	1974	1975	1976	1979
Coal	35	9	−118	−112	35	46	−19
Electricity	55	65	−23	−176	−265	9	66
Gas	−13	14	15	−42	−44	25	426
Rail	−147	10	−26	−158	−61	−14	−0.4
Steel	−21	10	−45	56	89	−246	−545
Post Office							
Mail	4	−25	−13	−62	−109	148	49
Telecom.	35	61	58	−61	−195	155	236

(*Sources: Economics 1, 27th November 1976, p. 16; annual financial reports of the industries covered.*)

Supporters of the nationalised industries have made a strong case for the efficiency of the industries using measurements of innovation and labour productivity based on the fruitful pursuit of scale economies, good labour relations and realistic wage bargaining systems. Unfortunately many private firms could establish similar cases. They also ignore diseconomies of scale which could produce the poor service to consumers which has been well chronicled, e.g. disappearing gas board maintenance men.

Unfortunately, the judging of nationalisation success has become a matter of ideology rather than an evaluation of the effective use of scarce resources.

55. The future. A serious increase or decrease in the number of nationalised industries seems unlikely but a growth of companies with mixed private and public finance is a distinct possibility. In general terms the structure of nationalised industries will still pose fundamental problems, such as the following.

(*a*) What should the relationship be between the industries' financial needs and the government's own accounts?

(*b*) How can the industries generate future cash without substantial investment, yet paradoxically how much self-generated profit is needed to finance the investment?

(*c*) Should the persistent loss-makers, e.g. British Rail, be financed separately from the profit-makers?

(*d*) Should a distinction be made between financial and economic objectives? A high rate of return could be made by a pricing policy which exploits an industry's monopoly position, yet such a policy would seriously undermine the economic use of resources.

(*e*) Are the industries too dependent on each other, which means that trouble in one sector spreads across the whole fabric? For example high fuel costs endanger British Steel which hits at rail and coal; the latter raises its charges and the circle is complete.

56. The example of British Rail. The complex problems are highlighted in a thumbnail sketch of the facts facing British Rail.

(*a*) Substantial under-investment has caused a serious deterioration in the quality of rolling stock and equipment.

(*i*) Most commuter stock is over thirty years old.

(*ii*) In 1979, 2,000 new locomotives were needed but only nineteen were bought.

(*iii*) Track failure creates a rise in accidents and unpunctuality.

(*b*) Compared to Continental countries, British Rail is under-subsidised.

(*i*) Between 1975 and 1980 the real rate of subsidy to passenger traffic dropped by 4 per cent.

(*ii*) Two-thirds of costs are met by revenue, one-third by subsidy, which is the reverse of the Continental pattern.

(*c*) The industry has an industrial relations policy which produces staff shortages on passenger traffic and overmanning in freight. Despite many productivity agreements there has been little improvement in labour efficiency.

(*d*) Because of (*a*) and (*b*) and the recession, the freight business is a heavy loss-maker yet there are strong social arguments for switching freight from road to rail.

How can these deep business problems be solved by the economic actions of politicians who believe the long term is a week away?

PROGRESS TEST 18

1. Describe the significance of the nationalised industries for the British economy. (**2**)

2. Give two arguments in favour of nationalisation. (**4–9**)

3. Give two arguments against nationalisation. (**11–15**)

4. Why do governments interfere with the running of nationalised industries? (**22**)

5. Explain the effect of nationalised industries' pricing policy on private industry. (**35**(*a*))

6. Outline the role of prices for nationalised industries. (**37**)

7. Define marginal social costs. (**42**)

8. Explain a two-part tariff. (**46**)

9. Why is the Treasury suspicious of private capital raising by nationalised industries? (**50**)

10. Suggest criteria for measuring the success of nationalised industries. (**53**)

CHAPTER XIX

Government and the Regional Economic Problem

NATURE OF THE PROBLEM

1. Introduction. Throughout history differing regions within countries have had varying levels of prosperity as the free play of economic forces has produced the rise and fall of industries. In one period a region might have full employment and relatively high income levels; within a generation or two the region has begun to decay economically and its people's living standards have fallen below the national average. Alternatively a region can initially be very poor then perhaps the discovery of a valuable resource can bring prosperity to the area.

Prior to the twentieth century, governments would view these changes as natural and unalterable. They would only interfere if they thought the situation might produce political upheaval. Even then the intervention would not try to reverse economic forces but merely give help to those suffering from change. England has a long history of this assistance through the Poor Laws.

However, since the 1930s when the unemployment figures were so appalling (*see* Table XXXI) and for the reasons outlined in **3–7**, British governments have given a high priority to the economic and social problems of the regions.

This chapter sketches in the policies and discusses their successes and failures. Regional problems are not confined to Britain and the views of the European Economic Community on its regional troubles are analysed at the end of the chapter.

2. Characteristics of poorer regions. A poorer region will exhibit some or all of the following features.

(*a*) The region relies for its employment on a few traditional industries, the demand for whose products is in decline (probably permanently). These areas are suffering from structural unemployment.

(*b*) The region's industries may also have a relative cost disadvantage because of their distance from major markets.

(c) Because of the above factors, unemployment will be much higher than the national average.

(d) Levels of income will be relatively low although the effects may be modified by the transfer of money through government welfare schemes.

(e) Because of (c) the levels of demand in the region will be low thus adversely affecting the service industries whose demand is bound to be localised.

(f) Educational attainment will be lower as evidence suggests that in the poorer regions fewer children stay at school after the statutory leaving age. This circumstance will affect the skill levels of the local labour market.

(g) Many poorer areas, particularly if dominated by a big city (as, for example, Merseyside is dominated by Liverpool), may suffer from urban decay, which is often precipitated by bad planning (see 24). This produces a population migration plus the beginnings of deindustrialisation. Superficially the population exodus ought to reduce the unemployment figures but in fact whole areas become an economic and social wasteland.

(h) The "infrastructure" of the region will be poor, i.e. the quality of housing, schools, hospitals, communications and amenities will be below a desirable standard.

(i) All these factors are likely to induce in the region low productivity (*NIER Review*, November 1968) and low returns on investment (*Guardian*, 18th November 1969, p. 23) which makes it even more difficult to ease its economic difficulties.

Should a high proportion of these factors prevail in a region the quality of economic and social life of its people will be below an acceptable level prevailing in the rest of the country.

REASONS FOR GOVERNMENT CONCERN WITH THE PROBLEM

3. Waste of resources. Labour is a productive resource which is wasted if it is underutilised. This argument is open to debate for it can be argued that ever accelerating technology is undermining the conventional attitudes and structures of employment. (J. D. S. Appleton, *Labour Economics*, Macdonald & Evans.)

4. Social problems. The poorer regions are likely to have a higher proportion of the long-term unemployed. These people and their families, despite the welfare state, suffer great social, economic and psychological hardship and they become entangled in a poverty trap from which it is very difficult to escape.

5. Conflicting economic policies. A government's economic policy particularly in its demand management is trying to influence the economic conditions of the whole country. Therefore the need for separate policies for different regions can run counter to the basic macroeconomic policy objectives. For example, a country with a high rate of inflation may cut demand, tighten credit and introduce an incomes policy, all measures which will worsen conditions in the poorer regions, whereas policies to help the regions are likely to increase demand. "A more even distribution of economic prosperity would counteract the inflationary effects of regional concentrations of excess demand, thus facilitating the management of the economy." (E. Roll, *Public Administration*, Spring 1966.)

6. Congestion costs. If people move out of the declining areas to more prosperous regions they will create a growing pressure on the demand for houses, transport and social services in their new environment, thus raising the costs of living and creating intolerable social pressures. Theoretically, the congestion costs could reach a level which would tempt people and firms out of the congested areas back to the declining regions. Fears of overcrowding in major conurbations was a dominant factor in the new town policy (*see* **15**) pursued by governments over the last thirty years.

7. Summary. Regional backwardness presents so many economic and social problems that governments have felt bound to intervene with the free play of market forces. During the 1970s a new strand of thought developed which argued that the problems were created by overcentralised decision taking and consequently more political power ought to be devolved to the regions. This argument lies behind the call for self-determination or devolution which takes the regional problem into a far larger dimension. The rest of the chapter looks at the conventional problems but the new issue is briefly mentioned in **36**.

THE BASIS OF GOVERNMENT REACTION

8. Introduction. Basic economic theory offers little help to governments which are trying to ease the problems of regional imbalance. Traditional welfare theory deals with individuals, whereas regional policy is working in arbitrarily defined geographical areas with a variety of economic and social structures.

Theoretical concepts also presuppose maximising objectives, e.g. a consumer maximises satisfaction, a firm maximises profit but what is being maximised in regional policy? Is it the welfare of the people living there now or the welfare of some future population? Is the government trying to maximise the income *per capita* of the region? If so does it devise policies to raise income for a constant population or should it try to move the poorer sections of the population out of the region? Governments, being pragmatists, seem to have the simple measurable objective of trying to reduce the level of unemployment and the more subjective aim of improving living standards within the less prosperous regions.

In general terms governments have had two broad policy options, each with attendant difficulties. These options are either to move industry into the region or move the people out.

9. Moving workers out of an area. The government through various financial aid schemes tries to subsidise workers who are prepared to find work outside the poorer regions. However, the economic and social costs are very high, e.g. the cost of new housing, leaving family and friends and disruption of children's education. The size of these costs plus the difficulties outlined below have discouraged governments from making really committed efforts to promote labour mobility. Mobility costs are really the costs of human investment and finance needs to be raised to cover the cost. For capital investment an economy has capital markets but lending on human investment is risky for conventional financial institutions because there is no collateral. To bridge this gap Hartley (K. Hartley, *Problems of Economic Policy*, Allen & Unwin, 1977, p. 183) suggests the establishment of a state manpower bank to finance training and mobility.

10. Difficulties of mobility policy.

(*a*) The people with the incentive to move are probably the skilled workers and to denude an area of its skilled manpower further damages its industrial credibility.

(*b*) If the numbers that move are sufficient seriously to reduce unemployment levels, then there will be a further drop in demand levels in the region and it will suffer from a reverse multiplier effect which could keep up the level of unemployment.

(*c*) The policy if successful could create congestion costs elsewhere (*see* **6**).

(*d*) A significant migration of people would lead to a serious underutilisation of the social services already provided in the regions.

11. Bringing industry into regions. The fundamental government policy has been to persuade or bribe firms to open new plants in the less prosperous areas by the use of capital cost reducing or labour cost reducing policies, e.g. investment grants or the Regional Employment Premium (*see* **17**(*b*)). As with the labour mobility policy, questions can be raised about the wisdom of such inducements to companies.

12. Difficulty of moving industry.

(*a*) Are firms persuaded to locate in areas in which they are not maximising their efficiency according to location theory (*see* **23**)? If so, is there a misallocation of resources?

(*b*) Is there a temptation for companies to move to a poorer region to obtain all the incentive money and then pull out? Critics of Courtaulds suggested the company did this with its plant in Skelmersdale.

(*c*) In order to obtain government grants, companies establish assembly or distribution units miles from basic production head-quarters. If economic conditions deteriorate the company, like a retreating army, pulls back to its main base and sacrifices the out-posts. The regions in fact require more substantially based organisations to give stability.

(*d*) By offering companies substantial assistance to defray capital costs does the government encourage the establishment of capital intensive companies with a consequent low demand for labour?

(*e*) There is evidence to suggest that the regional inducements are most profitable to (*i*) firms in warehousing and distribution which need little labour; (*ii*) companies with simple assembly line units which use largely female labour. Neither of these types will effectively help to reduce male unemployment.

(*f*) Does anybody know the economic effects on the competitive cost structure of companies which establish plants in areas to which they would not have gone by free choice?

BRITISH REGIONAL LEGISLATION

13. Introduction. R. Turner ("Government Policy on Location", *Economics*, Summer 1966) suggested that British regional legislation has had three common characteristics.

(*a*) It defines geographical areas in which companies and local authorities qualify for government assistance.

(*b*) It defines the range of industries qualifying for aid.

(*c*) It sets out the available financial benefits.

In principle most of the legislative Acts are similar varying only in detail, e.g. altering the regional boundaries, defining new areas or changing the type of incentive aid. This section outlines the major legislation but only discusses significant conceptual changes.

14. Pre-1945.

(*a*) *1934 Special Areas Act.* Four particularly depressed areas, West Cumberland, the North-East Coast, South Wales and Central Scotland, were designated special areas and industry therein was made eligible for government assistance. However, the Act had no real effect as the financial aid was slight and most industries were so depressed they had no incentive to develop anywhere.

(*b*) *1937–40 Barlow Commission.* This body was asked to study the twin problems of backward areas and congested conurbations. They recommended the establishment of a central body to:

(*i*) redevelop the congested urban areas;

(*ii*) disperse industry from those areas;

(*iii*) promote a reasonable balance of industrial development throughout Britain.

The outbreak of war sank these recommendations and no post-war government was prepared to formulate such a strong central-ised policy although some of Barlow's thinking was found in the 1945 legislation.

15. 1945–59.

(*a*) *1945 Distribution of Industry Act.* This Act slightly enlarged the 1934 special areas, e.g. by including parts of North Wales and South Lancashire. It rechristened them "development areas" and gave the Board of Trade powers to build new factories for leasing on trading estates. There was also aid towards the capital cost of moving.

(*b*) *1946 New Towns Act. 1947 Town and Country Planning Act.* These two Acts were not technically concerned with regional economic problems but they represented a new idea which argued that the location of people and industry together with physical planning are all elements in the search for that elusive concept, the improvement of the quality of life. The 1947 Act introduced a vital new weapon, Industrial Development Certificates. (IDCs).

They are needed to support applications for planning permission for industrial development above a certain size, outside the development areas. In these non-development areas planning permission without an IDC is invalid, although the actual granting of a planning application lies in the hands of the local authority. The Department of Industry is now responsible for issuing IDCs. The IDC represents a negative control to help the regions; negative in the sense that a company refused an IDC for building in the South East may still not decide to build in a development area.

16. 1960–66.

(a) *1960 Local Employment Act.* Previous legislation was repealed and the old areas were replaced by "development districts" which were localities with unemployment rates of $4\frac{1}{2}$ per cent and above (or a district where that figure might be achieved in the near future). The new districts were smaller than the areas, thus fewer people were in localities receiving aid. Capital was provided for new buildings and local authorities were given considerable powers and finance to improve their infrastructure (*see* **2**(*h*)).

(b) *1963 Local Employment Act.* Aid was extended to places within commuting distance of the development districts and to overspill development of any city within a district, even if the overspill community was outside the district. The quantity of capital aid for buildings was increased and for the first time grants were given for the installation of machinery. The Government also promised to use its purchasing requirements to help firms in the development districts.

(c) *1964 regional planning.* The advent of a Labour Government brought a renewed interest in the concept of planning. George Brown believed the country's geographical economic inequalities had to be solved on a regional level. By magic the country acquired eight regions (Scotland, Northern, North West, Yorkshire and Humberside, East Midlands, West Midlands, Wales and South West) and each region was given the following.

(*i*) Regional Planning Board: this was a committee of top civil servants from all government departments in the region and its task was to co-ordinate government activity in the regions. The boards were also responsible for producing plans to promote growth in their region.

(*ii*) Regional Economic Planning Council: the Councils consisted of twenty-five part-time members, men and women of distinction in their locality. Their functions were to assist with the drawing up and implementation of the regional plan and to evaluate the effects of national economic policy on their region. The Chairman, in theory, had direct access to the corridors of power in Whitehall but at least one Chairman resigned because he felt powerless. However, the government's thinking soon returned to more conventional channels, although the Councils survived a number of years until abolished by the 1979 Conservative Government (*see* **20**).

(*d*) *1966 Industrial Development Act.* The development districts of 1960 were widened into development areas, namely:

    (*i*) the whole of Scotland except for an area around Edinburgh;

    (*ii*) the whole of the Northern region plus the Furness Peninsula;

    (*iii*) an area in the North West based on Merseyside;

    (*iv*) most of Wales;

    (*v*) an area in the extreme South West.

Capital aid was again increased but instead of giving money through tax allowances the aid came in direct grants.

17. 1967–70.

(*a*) *1967 special areas.* These were small parts (based on Department of Employment offices) of development areas suffering from acute unemployment, e.g. Workington and Ystalyfera, and they qualified for more extensive aid. By 1971 when new areas were so classified, 8.5 per cent of Britain's insured population were living in special development areas.

(*b*) *1967 Regional Employment Premium.* This was a system springing from the now defunct Selective Employment tax whereby employers in the development areas received a subsidy on the labour they employed. At first the measure was severely criticised for linking a subsidy not only to newly created jobs but also to existing ones and the Conservative administration of 1970 promised to abolish it in 1974. However, research showed REP was helpful to employment and it was retained for a further period until finally ended in December 1976 by the Labour Government.

(*c*) *1969 Hunt Report: intermediate (grey) areas.* The Hunt Commission investigated those areas which claimed to suffer from economic depression but did not receive aid because their unemployment rates were insufficiently high. Examples of such places were North-East Lancashire, South Yorkshire, North-East Derbyshire and Plymouth. The common economic and social characteristics of intermediate areas were:

(*i*) falling or slow growing employment opportunities;
(*ii*) slow growth of personal incomes;
(*iii*) a net emigration of population;
(*iv*) decaying environmental factors;
(*v*) poor communications.

Hunt's report acknowledged the problem and offered some solutions which were largely smaller amounts of aid than were going to the development areas. The Government accepted the report in principle, reduced the suggested levels of aid and narrowed the number of areas qualifying for intermediate status. The whole concept of intermediate areas was enshrined in the 1970 Employment Act.

18. 1970–74. The new Conservative Government with its market philosophy had no grand regional strategy, although it indicated a desire to concentrate aid on the infrastructure of a region.

Suddenly and without warning the Government, realising the regions needed a healthy national industrial structure, produced the 1972 Industry Act which granted investment assistance across the country. To maintain the regional aid differentials the Act also:

(*a*) increased cash grants for plant and machinery;
(*b*) offered assistance with employment creating projects;
(*c*) increased the aid for manpower training and mobility schemes;
(*d*) increased the number of intermediate areas (*see* **17**).

To bolster its new interventionist mood, the Government created a whole new bureaucracy of Industrial Development Minister, Board and Executive.

Although the Heath administration did not live long enough really to use the Act, the following Labour Government took full advantage of its wide powers.

19. 1974–79. This period saw the birth of fears that the whole industrial structure was crumbling, which together with accelerating inflation and unemployment rates dimmed the regional problem. The Labour Government used the 1972 Act plus short-term employment palliatives, e.g. the Temporary Employment Subsidy, and its own 1975 Industry Act which set up the NEB (*see* XIV, **15**) to shore up British industry in general because the feared economic disaster was now national not regional.

20. 1979 onwards. Regional aid was bound to suffer under the new Conservative Government's expenditure cutting policies. Its basic regional policy was announced in July 1979, the main features being as follows:

(*a*) To concentrate aid in black spots by reducing the number of areas receiving aid (in 1979 regional aid was going to areas totalling 40 per cent of the work-force).

(*b*) To keep the three areas of special, development and inter-mediate status but to reduce grants from 20 to 15 per cent in de-velopment areas and to abolish automatic grants in intermediate areas.

(*c*) To increase the difficulty of obtaining selective aid under the 1972 Act (by 1981, this policy was relaxed).

The government also scrapped the Economic Planning Councils (*see* **16**) and reduced the need for IDCs (*see* **15**).

However, the most novel policy was the creation of Enterprise Zones in selected urban areas to combat "planners' blight" (*see* **2**(*g*)). The zones were to be small sites (approximately 500 acres) on which small companies would be encouraged by the removal of bureaucratic restraints, e.g. exemptions from industrial rates, simplified planning procedures, 100 per cent capital grants and no Training Board involvement. The possible relationship between the zones and the local authorities was a matter of considerable speculation.

21. Results. To quantify accurately the results of regional policy is very difficult and even if accuracy was possible the nature of the variables behind the statistics would be open to considerable controversy. Below are some figures which serve as a rough guide to assessing British regional policy.

(*a*) *Policies a success.* The main criterion of success is the em-ployment situation. Table XXXI clearly shows that compared to pre-1939 the regional discrepancies in unemployment rates have been significantly reduced and all researchers show that the policies have created or saved jobs. G. Manners ("Reinterpreting the Regional Problem", *Three Banks Review*, September 1976), a critic of the policies, estimates that approximately 300,000 jobs were created in the period 1960–74.

Table XXXII shows a narrowing of regional income disparities across the country, which might of course indicate a decline in national economic health rather than regional recovery, although

traditionally the gap narrows in prosperity rather than recession.
In addition, a reasonable case can be made to suggest that the regions now have a broader industrial base and that their fortunes are no longer tied to the fates of one or two industries. Road and rail communications, particularly through Inter-City, and the

TABLE XXXI. *Regional unemployment rates, 1929–80 (%)*

	1929	1932	1936	1959	1969	1977	1980
London and South-East	4.5	13.0	6.2	1.3	1.6	4.4	4.6
South-West	6.8	15.8	7.7	2.1	2.7	6.8	6.5
Midlands	9.1	21.5	9.0	1.6	2.0	5.2	6.8
Northern	12.6	29.8	18.1	3.3	2.2	7.9	9.9
North-West	12.6	25.4	16.6	2.8	2.5	7.0	8.8
Scotland	11.0	26.8	17.1	4.4	3.7	7.8	9.4
Wales	18.2	37.4	30.4	3.8	4.1	7.7	9.7
Great Britain	9.6	22.4	12.8	2.2	2.4	5.8	6.9

NOTE: Between 1969 and 1977 there were slight changes in definitions of some regions.
(*Source: Regional Policy for Ever*, IEA Readings, p. 79; *Department of Employment Gazette*.)

TABLE XXXII. *Personal disposable income per head in regions, as % of UK average*

	1971	1975	1979
North	88.7	95.4	92.0
Yorks. and Humberside	94.2	93.7	95.0
East Midlands	96.1	96.5	98.7
East Anglia	96.9	93.6	95.7
London and South-East	111.7	111.3	112.6
South-West	100.8	95.7	97.3
West Midlands	101.1	101.2	95.9
North-West	96.0	97.4	96.9
Wales	90.9	93.4	93.3
Scotland	93.4	96.7	96.1
Northern Ireland	77.7	80.7	82.2

(*Source: Economic Trends*, November 1980.)

motorway network have opened up many areas while educational facilities have also increased. Infrastructures have therefore made forward progress.

(*b*) *Policies a failure*. Three arguments tend to be used.

(*i*) The geographical areas now receiving aid have increased frighteningly and about 45 per cent of the population now live in these areas. Outsiders have noticed this trend for in EEC eyes (*see* **35**) Britain, as a European regional problem, ranks with Italy and Ireland. Critics reasonably speculate why forty years of regional policies have apparently worsened the situation.

(*ii*) Nobody can deny the creation and saving of jobs, but at what cost? Estimating the cost of each created job is a nightmare; so many schemes pump money into the regions while one has to subtract from costs the savings on social security payments. Manners thought that in the 1970s about £600 million per annum had gone into the regions while an estimate in the late 1960s suggested each job created cost the Exchequer about £900–1,500. More recent evidence submitted by Moore and Rhodes to the House of Commons Committee on Expenditure (*Guardian*, 17th January 1974, p. 15) suggests the cost of each job is £6,000 (excluding extra tax revenue to the government). Is this good or bad? Is the social benefit of reducing unemployment greater than any private economic cost?

(*iii*) Have regional policies contributed to the general economic malaise? Certainly they have created a considerable charge on government spending and at worst they might have damaged industrial efficiency by tempting companies to make irrational location decisions.

POSSIBLE CRITICISMS OF THE POLICY

22. Introduction. A divergence of opinion on the success of regional policy is shown in **21** (*a*) and (*b*). Ultimately we are faced with the usual economic dilemma of not knowing what an alternative policy would have achieved. Nevertheless it is possible to discuss aspects of regional policy in which government thinking has been muddled.

23. Market forces and regionalism. Market forces are the main cause of structural unemployment and they determine the long-run pattern of industrial location. Should governments be more cognisant of location decision taking if they wish to influence these decisions? In fairness to governments it is argued that company thought in this field is by no means rational. It can be argued that many industries are footloose, i.e. the siting of their plants, within reason, is of no importance to their cost structures.

Locational theory teaches that companies must balance factors of distance (raw materials and markets) with factors of availability (labour and power) then economies and diseconomies of scale and concentration are introduced into the calculations. A location decision should resemble an investment appraisal project with the firm evaluating alternative site choices on a non-social cost basis.

However, Townroe has shown (P. M. Townroe, "How Managers Pick Plants", *Management Today*, October 1970) that companies have restricted alternatives because speed and secrecy of decision taking are important variables. The few sites are not seriously costed because companies have no simple location decision routines and managerial subjective views on their own quality of life intrude into the decisions.

Locational decisions end as satisfactory rather than best decisions with an inherent desire to build near existing plant. Companies giving evidence to the House of Commons Expenditure Committee on Regional Development in 1973–74 said regional incentives had a low priority in their location decisions. Dunlop summarised the general feeling by saying the primary consideration remained the validity of the commercial decision and Thorns argued that any financial gain was purely short term.

Governments must seek more direct co-operation with companies to understand their location motives. A quizzical mind might wonder why governments spend so much on regional aid when the main beneficiaries seemingly ignore the value of the incentives. Would a tighter IDC policy be cheaper yet more effective?

24. Role of the town planner. Within the last thirty years, governments have allowed the regional economic problems to become entangled with the town planner. Unfortunately, town planning is a pseudo-scientific discipline ravaged by the illness of Parkinson's Law and the onset of sociologists. Higher education institutions have churned out increasing numbers of planners all with the urge to plan our environment without any obvious understanding of man's social and economic needs. Local government reorganisation and new town expansion have been the powerful laxative enabling planners to run through our regions. (Warrington in

Cheshire, for example, has the benefit of five different groups of planners working on its behalf.)

Governments might have noted Marx's comments on the inherent power and importance of the economic structure of our lives. Hopefully light is dawning and even planners are talking of the role of industry and commerce in the fight to renew the nation's decaying town centres.

25. Policy changes. Industrialists have criticised governments for frequently changing the details of their policies. Two examples are given.

(*a*) *Capital grants or allowances.* Allowances are linked to company taxation and companies making high profits will receive more aid. However, the finance is paid after the time lags of the tax system and low profit companies may run into liquidity problems (as Rolls-Royce did in 1971). Grants are direct payments to companies moving to development areas, thus there is a specific link between moving and the aid, but no link between the company's efficiency and the finance. Sudden switching, as often occurs, between grants and allowances undermines the industrialist's confidence in the investment incentive programme.

(*b*) *Growth points and areas.* Conservatives have tended to concentrate aid into small geographical areas, i.e. growth points, in order to centralise the industrial growth and achieve external economies of scale, e.g. housing, education and communications. The created benefits then ripple out to larger areas. Labour Governments have doubted the validity of the ripple theory and argued that the growth point thesis would leave large areas of under-utilised resources.

26. Blanket solutions. Governments have tended to treat all development areas as homogeneous units with identical causes of under-development thus requiring identical solutions. This is an over-simplification. Scotland has suffered a vast emigration, while Wales has pit closures and declining hill farming; none of these problems are inherent in the Merseyside situation. More varied aid schemes ought to be devised and areas could utilise the most relevant help available.

27. Over-use of capital incentives. Most of the major incentive schemes are geared to reducing capital costs with the obvious consequence that they attract capital intensive firms to the regions (*NIER Review*, November 1968) where the main identified problem is unemployment. Of course the thought of creating labour intensive industries in the 1980s may well be economic nonsense given the accelerating growth of technology and high labour costs.

28. The nature of unemployment. Generalised treatment of regional problems has already been criticised (*see* **26**). Typical of this approach is the use, mainly, of a single criterion, unemployment, to judge the regional problem. Total figures of the unemployed are misleading; in terms of finding relevant industries for an area there is a need to identify the types of worker unemployed. Liverpool, for example, has an excessive supply of unskilled and semi-skilled workers, whereas many of the new companies which have come to Merseyside have had to import skilled workers to man their plant.

There is also a need to investigate the relationship between population changes and rates of unemployment. Moore and Rhodes ("Effects of British Regional Policy", *Economic Journal*, March 1973) have speculated whether regional policy has actually increased the supply of labour in the regions because the late 1960s saw a considerable reduction in the outward migration of population, yet we have no knowledge how this affected employment levels. Manpower planning is in its infancy but it could be useful in a regional analysis.

29. Basic changes in society. G. Manners ("Reinterpreting The Regional Problem", *Three Banks Review*, September 1976) argues that governments in viewing the regional problem have ignored some fundamental changes in the thinking and structure of society.

(*a*) *Economic environment.* Nobody now believes the old levels of full employment (in the 1950s, 1.3 per cent) are attainable. The use of Keynesian demand management to control unemployment is under considerable attack (*see* I, IV and V); indeed the whole question of unemployment is a controversial one. Therefore views on the nature and treatment of unemployment must be established at national level before a meaningful regional policy is possible. A growing proportion of our industry is now owned by multinational organisations (*see* XVII) and their location decisions enter totally new areas. No longer is the choice between Essex and Wales; it is Nigeria or Belgium or Ireland or the United Kingdom. Location questions have become a global problem and regional policies may have to move in the same direction.

(*b*) *Employment patterns.* There has been a basic loss of manufacturing jobs in the UK over the last decade. V. H. Woodward (*Occupational Trends in Great Britain 1961–81*, Cambridge University Press, 1975) calculated that manufacturing would lose 530,000 jobs in the period 1971–81. By mid-1981 the situation had deteriorated well beyond these forecasts. Manufacturing employment had declined by 1,028,000 jobs in the period 1979–81 and total unemployment was approaching the 3 million mark. Within these gloomy figures there were changes in employment patterns with the service industries and the public sector (basically white-collar jobs) suffering relatively fewer job losses. Unfortunately for the poorer regions, these jobs, despite a policy of relocating civil servants, tended to be concentrated in London and the South-East.

(*c*) *Socio/geographical changes.* The mid-1970s witnessed a significant fall in rates of population growth; we may be entering a period of falling population. There are also shifts in population migration, e.g. out of the West Midlands. These two facts could undermine our long-established divisions of poor and rich areas and also invalidate many of the long-term plans about resource utilisation, particularly land. For example, the inner boroughs of London are desperately poor and short of work whereas the north east of Scotland is dripping with oil money, yet it is the latter area which receives regional aid. Politicians are recognising this switch of prosperity (market forces working again) and the cry is to regenerate life in the inner cities, a life extinguished by governments and planners who failed to note the simple economic fact that small firms provide work and work helps community life (this problem was particularly highlighted by the riots in a number of cities in the summer of 1981).

30. Lack of growth. The disappointing performance of the British economy has been the fundamental reason for the lack of work in the regions. If a company cannot sell its products it will not create new work anywhere. Since 1945 the constraints of inflation and the balance of payments have caused governments to reduce the level of aggregate demand in, on average, two years out of five. Since 1979, the monetarist attack on inflation has produced almost nil growth, so the regional problem has really been translated into a national problem, with the whole economy suffering from the disappearance rather than the creation of jobs. The backward regions can only improve in a climate of expansion.

31. Lack of knowledge. Regional policy has been with us for thirty-five years, acres of words have been written, endless speeches made, yet do we really understand the underlying economic foundations of the regional problem (*see* **8**)? The following two quotes will suffice.

> "There must be few areas of government expenditure in which so much is spent but so little known about the success of the policy." (*Public Money and Private Sector*, July 1972, House of Commons Paper 347.)

> "Regional policy has been empiricism run mad, a game of hit and miss, played with more enthusiasm than success. There has been no proper evaluation of the costs and benefits of policies pursued." (*House of Commons Expenditure Committee Regional Development Incentives Report*, HMSO 1974.)

ALTERNATIVE IDEAS

32. Introduction. It has been argued that the problem of the regions is now becoming merged with national difficulties and the whole background thought of the regions is slowly changing. However, should the need for a distinctive policy re-emerge the following ideas may prove more useful than simply rehashing the ideas of the previous era.

33. Types of aid. There has been little change in the broad type of aid given; changes have come in the myriad of detail and administration, thus making the pursuit of assistance a time-wasting paperchase for industrialists. (Perhaps jobs have been created via the Civil Service.)

Would it be possible to devise a system where the company received a lump sum for each job created assuming the job lasted for a guaranteed period of time? (If it did not, money could be refunded.) Such a scheme would link aid directly with jobs and cut down the administration.

34. Mobility. There is a theoretical case for moving workers but policies have only dallied with the problem. The real root of the mobility problem is the housing situation, particularly if a person moves from a poorer to a more prosperous area. The system of allocating local authority housing subsidies to buildings and not people, plus the series of Rent Control Acts, has meant that any tenant of a private or public rented house is acting in an economically irrational way if he moves unless his new wage differential is enormous. Geographical job mobility depends on housing mobility. This fact is recognised by industry which often subsidises the job movement of its employees.

35. Adjusting labour costs. According to market force theory, wage levels in areas where there is an excess of labour ought to be relatively lower but because of national wage bargaining the regions do not develop a labour price differential. However, the government might do this in two administratively difficult ways.

(*a*) *Differential National Insurance contributions.* Companies in the development regions would pay lower NI contributions thus reducing their labour costs.

(*b*) *Payroll tax.* A payroll tax would be levied on all employees outside the development areas. Politically this would only be feasible if there were high levels of employment in the non-assisted areas.

36. Regionalism. The definition of British regions was done as an economic planning exercise (*see* **16**(*c*)) but it can be argued that if the concept was transmitted into political terms, power and decision taking could be decentralised to the regions, thus improving their economic performance. The logical extension of the argument is devolution, when a whole country, e.g. Scotland or Wales, becomes self-governing. To the economist the following two big questions remain unanswered.

(*a*) Why should the decentralising of economic decisions make the decisions better ones? Is it valid to suggest that a local allocation of resources automatically creates greater welfare? Are the decisions of town halls noticeably better than the decisions of Whitehall?

(*b*) Is the British economy big or strong enough to be split into small parts? Regional economic policies and results so far suggest the answer is "no". Cynics might argue the growth of Scottish Nationalism is simply a function of the discovery of natural resources off the coast of Scotland and the prosperity of Scotland will develop from old-fashioned economics not from political musical chairs.

EUROPEAN ECONOMIC COMMUNITY AND REGIONAL PROBLEMS

37. Introduction. The problems of uneven levels of prosperity is by no means confined to Britain and from the beginning the EEC has recognised the Community would face the problem of a mal-distribution of affluence across a wide geographical area. (In 1970 Hamburg's Gross Domestic Product *per capita* was five times higher than western Ireland and southern Italy; by 1975 the ratio was six.) The Preamble to the Treaty of Rome (1958) refers to "Reducing the differences existing between the various regions and mitigating the backwardness of the less favoured", while Article 92 states "Aids intended to promote the economic developments of regions where the standard of living is abnormally low or where there exists serious under-employment are compatible with a Common Market."

This section looks at the broad pattern of EEC thinking and policy on the regional problem.

38. Basic thinking. A prime fear of the EEC is that industry, trade and prosperity will be concentrated in the central core of the Community (in British terms the Midlands and south-east England), while the peripheral areas (e.g. Scotland and northern England, north and south-west France and southern Italy) will decline. To test this theory is difficult because these areas would be the recipients of national aid with or without the EEC.

The 1960s saw the original EEC members enjoying growth and prosperity on an unprecedented scale and regional worries faded from the scene. However, the 1970s and early 1980s have brought a distinct change of emphasis attributable to two new factors: first, the slowing down of economic growth as the Western world fought inflation; and secondly, the admittance to the EEC of weaker countries, e.g. the United Kingdom, Ireland and Greece, and the application for membership of even weaker countries, e.g. Spain and Portugal. Suddenly regional problems are back on the EEC agenda.

Several points have developed as the centres of interest.

(*a*) To what extent would competing national regional policies produce distortions in the total EEC economic objectives?

(*b*) Would the desire for a common fiscal and monetary policy worsen the regional imbalances?

(*c*) What policies and institutions could be developed to help the problem?

39. Policy. The commitment to regional policy can be seen in this statement: "The underlying gap between richer and poorer regions remains as intractable as ever. The market economy will not automatically resolve the problem even when growth revives. Without a strong regional and structural policy there can be no real progress towards greater economic integration or cohesion, the lack of which is a limitary factor in the Community's international role and influence." (1st Report European Regional Fund, 1975, p. 5.)

The basis of the policy is a fund-channelling agency and some co-ordination of national policies.

(*a*) *European Regional Fund.* The Fund developed out of the 1972 Paris Summit meeting and a report prepared by Commissioner George Thompson (UK) in 1973. The Fund was officially established in March 1975 and the first year's budget was 300 European Currency Units. (Currency units (ECUs) are the EEC standard measure and are converted into national currencies. In July 1981 1 ECU = £0.55.) To be eligible for Fund assistance investments must fall in the framework of regional development programmes prepared by member states and must be receiving national aid. Britain has greatly benefited from the Fund receiving, in 1979, 37 per cent of the allocated funds, which put her on a par with Italy and Ireland. The main criterion for receiving aid is regional unemployment rates and the Fund tries to make not only quantitative but also qualitative decisions. Table XXXIII shows the number of projects approved by the Fund and their value in the period 1975–79.

TABLE XXXIII.   *European Regional Fund, 1975–79*

	Projects	Value (ECU millions)
Belgium	232	51.08
Denmark	342	47.31
Germany	1,318	280.21
France	1,756	626.93
Ireland	558	230.75
Italy	4,506	1,418.76
Luxembourg	6	3.41
Netherlands	34	70.50
UK	2,993	986.25

(*Source: Regional Development and the European Community, EEC Publications, April 1981.*)

(*b*) *Co-ordination policies.* The Commissions are working in several areas.

(*i*) National aid should be transparent, i.e. capable of being expressed as a percentage of the cost of investment. The Commissions wish to avoid disguised subsidies which simply allow individual firms to enjoy competitive price advantages in the market. Some doubts have been expressed about Regional Employment Premiums (*see* **17**(*b*)) on this score.

(ii) Where possible there should be general policies, e.g. a common type of IDC (*see* **15**) policy to stop multinationals playing off one state against another (*see* XVII).

(iii) Evaluations are being made of the impact of other EEC policies in the regions. For example, the policy of allowing in cheap Third World textile imports decimated parts of the Northern Ireland textile industry.

(*iv*) Methods are being developed for ensuring that Regional Fund investments are cost effective in order to avoid endless sums of money going down bottomless wells.

40. Other regional aid. Member states with regional problems may draw help from three other sources.

(*a*) *European Investment Bank.* The Bank was created by the Treaty of Rome, its basic function being to contribute to the balanced development of the Common Market. It grants long-term loans and gives its guarantees to public and private institutions to finance projects which favour the less advanced regions or which serve the interests of the Community as a whole, e.g. a cross-boundary motorway or generating scheme. Its capital comes from its members and it raises funds from international capital markets, therefore its lending has to be commercially orientated although the bank itself is non-profit making. Generally the bank's loans go into infrastructure programmes (*see* **2**(*h*)). By 1980 the Bank had invested over £2,000 million in the UK. (This was nearly 30 per cent of its total lending in the EEC.) About 75 per cent of the UK loans have gone to the assisted areas. The 1980 investment was £417 million and included such projects as the following:

(*i*) mineral wool factory in Bridgend;

(*ii*) foodstuff packaging machinery factory in the North East;

(*iii*) nuclear power station at Totness Point;

(*iv*) construction of the Burnley–Nelson stretch of the M65 motorway;

(*v*) sewerage scheme for the Severn–Trent Water Authority.

(*b*) *European Social Fund.* From the start of the EEC it was realised that a common market and economic growth would require change with consequent social problems. There have been a series of studies of groups who are losing out, e.g. young workers and migrant workers. The Social Fund was set up to finance projects for helping people meet the change and most of the money goes to retraining schemes. Retraining is clearly a vital element in regional schemes, and the Fund has been a useful addition to regional aid. It must be noted, however, that in the structure of the EEC, regional and social policies are distinct entities.

(*c*) *European Coal and Steel Community.* The EEC has a fund to assist workers who are made redundant when these declining industries are nationalised.

The amounts paid out in aid from these three funds and from the Regional Development Fund in 1978 are shown in Table XXXIV.

TABLE XXXIV.   *Aid from EEC, 1978*

	£m.
ECSC Retraining and Settlement Fund	751
European Social Fund	236
European Investment Bank	827
Regional Development Fund	173

(*Source: various EEC documents.*)

41. Conclusion. The EEC is well aware of the regional problems in its midst but whether the Community can succeed where member governments have struggled is open to doubt.

PROGRESS TEST 19

1. Describe the characteristics of the poorer regions of the advanced nations. (**2**)

2. Explain congestion costs. (**6**)

3. What are the difficulties of moving workers out of a region? (**10**)

4. Outline the underlying principles of British regional legislation. (**13**)

5. What is an intermediate area? (**17**(*c*))

6. In what ways have regional policies been a success? (**21**(*a*))

7. Discuss the impact of market forces on regionalism. (**23**)

8. Why do capital incentives for the regions have draw-backs? (**27**)

9. How could worker mobility be increased? (**34**)

10. What is the European Regional Fund? (**39**(*a*))

Bibliography

PART ONE: THE MACROECONOMIC APPROACH

Beveridge, W. H. *Full Employment in a Free Society*. Allen & Unwin.

Brittain, Sir Herbert. *The British Budgetary System*. Allen & Unwin, 1959.

Brittain, S. *Steering the Economy*. Penguin Books, 1971.

Brooman, F. S. *Macroeconomics*. Allen & Unwin, 1967.

Caves, Richard E. *Britain's Economic Performance*. Brookings Institution, 1980.

Dow, J. C. R. *The Management of the British Economy 1945–1960*. Cambridge University Press, 1964.

Galbraith, J. K. *Economic Development*. Oxford University Press.

Gill, R. T. *Economics*. Prentice Hall, 1974.

Hansen, A. H. *A Guide to Keynes*. McGraw-Hill.

Hayek, F. A., *Choice in Currency*. Institute of Economic Affairs, 1976.

Lewis, W. Arthur. *Theory of Economic Growth*. Allen & Unwin.

Lipsey, R. G. "The Relation between Unemployment and the Rate of Change of Money Wage Rates in the United Kingdom 1862–1957." *Economica*, February 1960.

Morris, D. J. *The Economic System in the UK*. Oxford University Press, 1977.

Phillips, A. W. "The Relation between Unemployment and the Rate of Change of Money Wage Rates in the United Kingdom 1861–1957." *Economica*, November 1958.

Prest, A. R. *Public Finance in Theory and Practice*. Weidenfeld & Nicolson, 1967.

Seddon, E. *Economics of Public Finance*. Macdonald & Evans, 1969.

OFFICIAL PUBLICATIONS

Appropriation Accounts. Annual. HMSO.

The British System of Taxation. Central Office of Information,

Reference Pamphlet No. 10. HMSO, 1965.
Estimates. Annual. HMSO.
Economic Trends. HMSO.
Finance Accounts of the UK. Annual. HMSO.
Finance Act. Annual. HMSO.
Finance Statement. Annual. HMSO.
Loans from the National Loans Funds. Annual White Paper. HMSO.
National Income and Expenditure. Annual Blue Book. HMSO.
National Income Statistics: Sources and Methods. HMSO.
Preliminary Estimates of National Income and Expenditure. Annual White Paper. HMSO.
Prices and Incomes Act 1966. HMSO.
Public Expenditure 1968–69 to 1973–74. Cmnd. 4234. HMSO, 1970.
Value Added Tax. 1971 Green Paper. Cmnd. 4621. HMSO.

PART TWO: THE MONETARY SYSTEM
Carter, H. and Parkington, I. *Applied Economics in Banking and Finance.* Oxford University Press, 1979.
Clarke, William M. *Inside the City.* Allen & Unwin, 1979.
Crockett, A. *Money: Theory, Policy and Institutions.* Nelson, 1973.
Dacey, W. Manning. *The British Banking Mechanism.* Hutchinson, 1962.
Day, A. C. L. *An Outline of Monetary Economics.* Clarendon Press, 1957.
Friedman, M. *The Counter-Revolution in Monetary Theory.* Occasional Paper 33, Institute of Economic Affairs, 1970.
Gibson, N. J. *Financial Intermediaries and Monetary Policy.* Hobart Paper 39, Institute of Economic Affairs, 1967.
Hobson, Sir Oscar. *How the City Works.* Dickens Press, 1962.
Morgan, E. Victor. *Monetary Policy for Stable Growth.* Hobart Paper 27, Institute of Economic Affairs, 1966.
Revell, J. *The British Financial System.* Macmillan, 1973.
Sayers, R. A. *Modern Banking.* Oxford University Press, 1967.

BANKING PUBLICATIONS
Bank of England Annual Report.
Bank of England Quarterly Bulletin.
The Banker.

The Bankers' Magazine.
Journal of the Institute of Bankers.
The reviews of the London clearing banks.

OFFICIAL PUBLICATIONS
The British Banking System. Central Office of Information
    Pamphlet No. 65. HMSO.
British Financial Institutions. Central Office of Information
    Pamphlet No. 24. HMSO.
Report of the Committee on the Working of the Monetary System
    (Radcliffe Report). Cmnd. 827. HMSO, 1959.

PART THREE: INTERNATIONAL TRADE AND PAYMENTS
Friedman, M. "The Case for Flexible Exchange Rates." *Essays
    in Positive Economics*, pp. 157–187. University of Chicago Press,
    1953.
Haberler, G. von. *The Theory of International Trade.* Macmillan,
    1937.
Hodgman, D. *National Monetary Policies and International
    Monetary Co-operation.* Little, Brown & Co., 1974.
Kindleberger, C. P. *International Economics.* Irwin, 1963.
Machlup, F. *Plans for Reform of the International Monetary
    System.* Special Papers in International Economics No. 3.
    Princeton University Press, 1962.
Scammell, W. M. *International Monetary Policy, Bretton Woods
    and After.* Macmillan, 1975.
Triffin, R. *Gold and the Dollar Crisis.* Yale University Press, 1961.
Worswick, G. D. N. and Ady, P. H. *The British Economy in the
    1950s.* Oxford University Press, 1962.

OFFICIAL PUBLICATIONS
The Activities of GATT. Annual. Geneva.
*Britain and the European Communities: An Economic Assessment.
    1970 White Paper.* Cmnd. 4289. HMSO.
Britain's Financial Services for Overseas. Reference Paper
    R.4881/65. COI.
Britain's Overseas Investment. Reference Paper R.5732/66. COI.
European Free Trade Association. Annual Report. Geneva.
IMF Annual Report. Washington.

Preliminary Estimates of National Income and Balance of Payments. Annual White Paper. HMSO.
UK Balance of Payments. Annual Orange Book. HMSO.

PART FOUR: GOVERNMENT AND INDUSTRY

Allen, G. C. *Monopoly and Restrictive Practices.* Allen & Unwin, 1974.

Cameron, G. C. and Clark, B. D. *Industrial Movement and the Regional Problem.* Oliver & Boyd, 1973.

Caves, R. E. and Krause, L. B. *Britain's Economic Performance.* Brookings Institute, Washington, 1980.

Everly, R. and Little, I. M. D. *Concentration in British Industry.* Cambridge University Press, 1976.

Hartley, I. C. *Problems of Economic Policy.* Allen & Unwin, 1977.

Heald, D. *The Economics and Finance of Nationalised Industries.* Glasgow University Discussion Paper, Glasgow University Press, 1978.

Howe, W. S. *Industrial Economics.* Macmillan, 1978.

Jewkes, J. *A Return to Free Market Economics.* Macmillan, 1978.

McCrone, G. *Regional Policy in Britain.* Allen & Unwin, 1975.

Mazzoloni, R. *European Transnational Concentrations.* McGraw-Hill, 1974.

Morris, D. *The Economic System in the UK.* Oxford University Press, 1977.

Newbould, G. *Management and Mergers Activity.* Guthstead (Liverpool), 1975.

Pickering, J. F. *Industrial Structure and Market Conduct.* Martin Robertson, 1975.

Prest, A. R. and Coppock, D. J. *The UK Economy.* Weidenfeld and Nicolson, 1980.

Pryke, R. *Public Enterprise in Practice.* McKibbon & Kee, 1971.

Shepherd, W. G. *Economic Performance under Public Ownership.* Yale University Press, 1976.

Sloman, M. *Socialising Public Ownership.* Macmillan, 1978.

Sutherland, A. *Monopolies Commission in Action.* Cambridge University Press, 1976.

Tindall, R. E. *Multinational Enterprise.* Oceania Publications, New York, 1975.

Webb, M. *Economics of Nationalised Industries.* Nelson, 1973.

OFFICIAL PUBLICATIONS

Financial and Economic Obligations of Nationalised Industries.
   Cmnd. 1337, 1961. HMSO.

Mergers: A Guide to Board of Trade Practices. HMSO, 1969.

Monopolies Commission Reports. HMSO.

*Nationalised Industries: A review of Economic and Financial
   Objectives.* Cmnd. 3437, 1967. HMSO.

Registrar of Restrictive Trading Agreements Reports. HMSO.

Survey of Mergers Report 1958–1968. HMSO, 1970.

Examination Technique

Success in examination depends not only upon a knowledge of facts but also upon the ability to marshal evidence systematically in a succinct answer to a specific question. In developing an examination technique the candidate will benefit from the following advice.

1. Read the whole paper carefully and unhurriedly and make a selection of those questions you intend to answer. You should be confident that you understand quite clearly the meaning of the questions selected. Avoid those questions where it seems that you will simply duplicate what you will write elsewhere.

2. Having understood a question let it remain uppermost in your mind so that your answer is wholly relevant. Too many failures result from candidates answering questions which do not appear in the paper.

3. Apportion your time so that you are certain of answering the required number of questions. Failure to complete the paper automatically lowers your maximum possible marks.

4. Many problems in Applied Economics have a highly controversial content with no clear-cut solutions. You should therefore avoid dogmatic answers. It is preferable to present the arguments of opposing schools of thought and to arrive at a balanced conclusion. You must certainly avoid the superficial and politically emotive approach of popular journalism.

5. Plan your answers systematically so that there is a logical progression of ideas leading to a natural conclusion. Avoid arguments based upon a series of disconnected points which do nothing to support you conclusion.

6. Finally, it is important to give attention to the composition of your script. A slipshod presentation immediately creates an unfavourable impression.

Examination Questions

PART ONE: THE MACROECONOMIC APPROACH

This selection of examination questions is related to the four parts of the text. However, it should be understood that in some cases it will be necessary to refer to material covered elsewhere in the book.

1. Explain how the level of income and employment are determined in a private enterprise economy. (*GCE(A)*, *JMB*)

2. Consider the relative merits of direct and indirect taxation. What are the advantages and disadvantages of increasing the proportion of revenue derived from indirect taxation in the United Kingdom? (*GCE(A)*, *JMB*)

3. Is it possible to reconcile the views that (*a*) savings are necessary for growth and (*b*) savings create unemployment? (*GCE(A)*, *JMB*)

4. To what extent, if any, is the National Debt a burden? (*GCE(A)*, *JMB*)

5. How may redistribution of income offset the level of total demand? (*BSc(Econ)*, *Part I, London Internal*)

6. Explain the multiplier concept and discuss its implications for economic policy. (*BSc(Econ)*, *Part I, London External*)

7. Control over the money supply is increasingly advocated as a means of preventing inflation. Examine briefly the theoretical rationale of this argument. (*BSc(Econ)*, *Part I, London External*)

8. "Higher taxes will never solve our problems." (Mr Edward Heath, 22nd March 1969.) Explain how the pressure of demand on the country's productive capacity is reduced:

(*a*) by higher taxes;
(*b*) by higher saving. (*BSc(Econ)*, *Part I, London Internal*)

9. Discuss the policy implications of the Phillips Curve which relates changes in money wages and prices to the percentage of unemployment. (*BSc(Econ)*, *Part I, London Internal*)

10. How do you distinguish between macroeconomic and microeconomic theories? (*BSc(Econ), Part I, London Internal*)

11. Discuss critically recent developments in the forecasting and control of public expenditure in the UK (*BSc(Econ), Part II, Public Finance, London Internal and External*)

12. "Post-war stabilisation policy has replaced ten-yearly major depressions with much more frequent minor recessions." Discuss. (*BSc(Econ), Part II, Public Finance, London Internal and External*)

13. Discuss the influence of short-term stabilisation policies on long-term growth. (*BSc(Econ), Part II, Public Finance, London Internal and External*)

14. Discuss the influence of the progressivity of the income tax on the aggregate supply of labour. (*BSc(Econ), Part II, Public Finance, London Internal and External*)

15. What measures would you recommend to improve the built-in stability of the UK economy? (*BSc(Econ), Part II, Public Finance, London Internal and External*)

16. How would you explain the comparatively slow rate of growth in the British economy in recent years? In what ways do you consider that public finance may best be directed to achieving an improvement? (*HND Business Studies, Liverpool Polytechnic*)

17. Explain why measures to sustain the level of effective demand are not appropriate in dealing with all forms of unemployment. What alternative measures have been developed and with what results? (*HND Business Studies, Liverpool Polytechnic*)

18. Explain the belief that it is not necessarily sound public finance to insist upon balancing the national budget. (*HND Business Studies, Liverpool Polytechnic*)

19. Detail the structure of the National Debt. Examine the significance of its burden and the possibilities of reducing this burden. (*HND Business Studies, Liverpool Polytechnic*)

20. What difficulties hinder a prices and incomes policy in conditions of full employment and free collective bargaining? (*HNC Business Studies, Liverpool Polytechnic*)

21. "The acceptance by governments of responsibility for the level of employment cannot be understood without reference to the changes in economic theory associated with Keynes." What in economic thought do you associate with Keynes? (*HNC Business Studies, Liverpool Polytechnic*)

22. Present government economic policy faces a conflict of interest between short-term "stop-go" and long-term planning for

growth. Explain, with examples, why this is so. (*HNC Business Studies, Liverpool Polytechnic*)

23. Outline the main characteristics of the "National Debt". How far is such a debt a burden on a country's economy? (*IOB*)

24. Outline the general principles a government should adopt when levying taxation. (*IOB*)

25. Contrast the place of the budget in the modern economy with its position before 1939, illustrating your answer by reference to any particular country. (*IOB*)

26. Discuss the relationship between rising wages and rising costs. (*IMTA*)

27. "Since the Second World War the centre of interest in economics has shifted from the study of equilibrium to the study of growth." How do you explain the change? (*Economics, Final Part I, IMTA*)

28. To what extent can the government use the level of public expenditure as an instrument of economic stabilisation? (*Public Finance, Final Part I, IMTA*)

29. Is the short-run control over the supply of money a necessary condition for ensuring price stability? (*Public Finance, Final Part I, IMTA*)

30. "Savings and investment are always equal."
"In equilibrium savings equal investment."
Reconcile these two statements. (*Public Finance, Final Part I, IMTA*)

31. What are the causes of unemployment? Illustrate your answer with examples. (*ICWA*)

32. Why has the United Kingdom experienced inflation since 1945? (*ICWA*)

33. "Savings and investment are done by different people at different times for different reasons." Explain this statement. (*ICWA*)

34. In what ways may the budget be used as an instrument of economic policy? (*ICWA*)

35. What do you understand by the "multiplier"? Explain its usefulness to a government seeking to control an economy. (*IOT*)

36. Is it true to say that the trade cycle belongs nowadays to economic history? (*IOT*)

37. What do you understand by a full employment policy? How likely is it to cause inflation? (*IOT*)

38. What do you understand by inflation? Why do governments seek to control it? (*IOT*)

PART TWO: THE MONETARY SYSTEM

39. What factors determine the supply of money in the United Kingdom? (*GCE(A), JMB*)

40. What part do the discount houses play in the system of monetary control operated by the Bank of England? (*GCE(A), JMB*)

41. What are the main instruments of monetary policy? Assess their efficacy as economic stabilisers. (*GCE(A), JMB*)

42. Outline the chief problems involved in the value of money in time. (*GCE(A), JMB*)

43. Explain how the London discount market acts as a buffer between the monetary authorities on the one hand and the clearing banks on the other. (*BSc(Econ), Part I, London External*)

44. "Bankers cannot create anything; they merely exchange one kind of asset for another." Discuss. (*BSc(Econ), Part I, London External*)

45. Discuss fully the meaning attached to the concept of liquidity in the Radcliffe Report. (*BSc(Econ), Part I, London External*)

46. Outline the ways in which an efficient capital market can assist the finance of industry. (*BSc(Econ), Part I, London External*)

47. "Recent theoretical attempts to arrive at a definition of money suggest that the problem can be usefully pursued only as an empirical question." Discuss. (*BSc(Econ), Part II, Principles of Monetary Economics, London Internal*)

48. The experience of the 1960s seems to suggest that rising interest rates are associated with an expansion rather than a contraction of the money supply. How can this experience be explained? (*BSc(Econ), Part II, Principles of Monetary Economics, London Internal*)

49. Non-bank financial intermediaries have grown in size and number in the past two decades. What effects may this have had on the supply of money, rates of interest and the effectiveness of monetary policy? (*BSc(Econ), Part II, Principles of Monetary Economics, London Internal*)

50. "The quantity of money in the United Kingdom since 1945 has been entirely demand determined." Consider whether this statement is true and, if so, why. (*BSc(Econ), Part II, Principles of Monetary Economics, London External*)

51. "The authorities can choose interest rates or the supply of money but cannot choose both independently of each other"

(Sayers). On what basis should the authorities make their choice? (*BSc(Econ), Part II, Principles of Monetary Economics, London External*)

52. "A firm control of the money supply is both necessary and sufficient to control inflation." Discuss. (*BSc(Econ), Part II, Principles of Monetary Economics, London External*)

53. To what extent is it true to say that money is the creation of the banking system? (*HND Business Studies, Liverpool Polytechnic*)

54. Describe the structure and operation of the London discount market. Do you believe that it performs a useful function? (*HND Business Studies, Liverpool Polytechnic*)

55. The methods by which the Bank of England traditionally exercised the ultimate control over the supply of money are no longer effective. Explain and evaluate this statement. (*HND Business Studies, Liverpool Polytechnic*)

56. "The commercial banker's basic problem is to achieve a proper balance between liquidity and profitability." Explain. (*HNC Business Studies, Liverpool Polytechnic*)

57. How can the authorities control the amount of money and why should they wish to do so? (*HNC Business Studies, Liverpool Polytechnic*)

58. Describe the structure and operations of the London money market. (*IOB*)

59. Discuss the special characteristics that distinguish money from other economic goods. (*IOB*)

60. Examine the various factors which in present-day Britain set a limit to an increase in the money supply. (*IOB*)

61. Describe the demand for, and the supply of, funds in the London money market. (*IOB*)

62. To what extent is the ability of money to fulfil its functions affected by changes in its value? (*IOB*)

63. "It is impossible in practice to achieve together all the objectives of monetary policy." Discuss this statement. (*IOB*)

64. Describe the components of the supply of money in Britain and examine carefully the consequences of a reduction in the supply. (*SBI*)

65. Set out the sources of borrowing by the central government in Britain and show the importance of the savings banks in this borrowing. (*SBI*)

66. Explain the function of the Bank of England as "lender of last resort". What role does the discount market play in the fulfilment of this function? (*SBI*)

67. Consider the consequences on the supply of money of my withdrawing a deposit from a savings bank and depositing it instead with a commercial bank. (*SBI*)

68. Discuss briefly the asset structure of joint-stock banks. How is it influenced by changes in interest rates? (*Public Finance, Final, Part I, IMTA*)

69. "The discount market makes a living by borrowing short and lending long." Discuss. (*Public Finance, Final Part I, IMTA*)

70. Assess the view that the management of the National Debt is an integral part of monetary policy. (*Public Finance, Final Part I, IMTA*)

71. Outline the economic services provided by a joint-stock bank. (*ICWA*)

72. Distinguish between the characteristics of the Bank of England and those of the joint-stock banks. (*ICWA*)

73. What do you understand by the supply of, and the demand for, money? (*ICWA*)

74. Distinguish between (*a*) finance houses and (*b*) building societies, making clear the economic role of each. (*ICWA*)

75. If banks are merely intermediaries, how can they create credit? (*OT*)

76. Bankers claim that they can only lend what is lent to them. How then is it possible for them to "create credit"? (*IOT*)

77. Contrast the functions of a central bank and a commercial bank. (*IOT*)

PART THREE: INTERNATIONAL TRADE AND PAYMENTS

78. Explain what is meant by the *terms of trade* and the *balance of trade*. What relationship exists between these two concepts? (*GCE(A), JMB*)

79. Explain what is meant by "devaluation". How is a devaluation likely to affect the balance of payments of an economy? (*GCE(A), JMB*)

80. State precisely what you understand by the "fundamental disequilibrium" in the British balance of payments. (*GCE(A), JMB*)

81. Assess the relative merits of devaluation and tariff imposition as instruments for correcting an adverse current balance. (*GCE(A), JMB*)

82. Consider the relative merits of devaluation and deflation as

correctives of a balance of payments deficit. (*BSc(Econ)*, *Part I*, *London External*)

83. Why is it mutually profitable for two or more countries to engage in international trade? Can the existence of unemployment modify your conclusions? (*BSc(Econ)*, *Part I*, *London External*)

84. Argue the case for and against flexible exchange rates. (*BSc(Econ)*, *Part I*, *London External*)

85. Consider the view that restrictions on British investment can secure short-run improvement in the balance of payments only at the expense of a long-run worsening. (*BSc(Econ)*, *Part I*, *London External*)

86. Under what conditions would you expect a fixed exchange rate system to permit major trading countries to maximise their own welfare? (*BSc(Econ)*, *Part II*, *Principles of Monetary Economics*, *London Internal*)

87. "The problems surrounding the supply of international means of payment arise because the countries which are the world's bankers are also its chief traders; these problems will be solved only when these roles are separated." Discuss. (*BSc(Econ)*, *Part II*, *Principles of Monetary Economics*, *London Internal*)

88. Discuss the merits of the "crawling peg" scheme for exchange-rate adjustments. (*BSc(Econ)*, *Part II*, *Principles of Monetary Economics*, *London External*)

89. "Under a regime of fixed exchange rates a government cannot maintain both internal and external balance." Comment. (*BSc(Econ)*, *Part II*, *Principles of Monetary Economics*, *London External*)

90. "The general adoption of flexible exchange rates would increase, not lessen, both the need for the authorities to intervene in the foreign exchange market and the need for international co-operation." Discuss. (*BSc(Econ)*, *Part II*, *Principles of Monetary Economics*, *London External*)

91. Explain the concepts of over-valuation and under-valuation when applied to a currency. What are the possible remedies in each case? (*HND Business Studies*, *Liverpool Polytechnic*)

92. Explain the composition of the balance of payments and assess the relative importance of each of its components. Consider some of the measures which might be applied to the improvement of this balance. (*HND Business Studies*, *Liverpool Polytechnic*)

93. Despite the advantages of international trade based upon the principle of comparative costs, countries do in fact impose

restrictions on trade. Why is this? (*HNC Business Studies, Liverpool Polytechnic*)

94. Argue the merits of devaluation rather than deflation as an answer to balance of payments problems. (*HNC Business Studies, Liverpool Polytechnic*)

95. For what reasons do some economists advocate a rise in the price of gold? What objections are raised to such a proposal? (*HNC Business Studies, Liverpool Polytechnic*)

96. Show how the total of the debits and credits on a country's balance of payments account must always equal one another. (*IOB*)

97. "Deflation and devaluation are not alternatives. Some deflation is necessary if devaluation is to succeed." Comment on this statement. (*IOB*)

98. "For international monetary equilibrium a properly functioning adjustment process is as important as sufficient liquidity." Discuss this statement. (*IOB*)

99. Define the term "international liquidity" and comment on the main elements of such liquidity today. (*IOB*)

100. How can a country have a surplus in its balance of trade but a deficit in its balance of payments? Why must a country take steps to reduce a persistent payments deficit? (*SBI*)

101. Give an account of the objectives and principles of operation of the International Monetary Fund. (*SBI*)

102. Outline the functions of the International Monetary Fund. Will the issue of Special Drawing Rights enable the Fund to play a more effective role in the international monetary system? (*SBI*)

103. "Whatever policy is used, a balance of payments deficit can only be corrected through a reduction in the standard of living of the economy as a whole." Discuss. (*Public Finance, Final Part I, IMTA*)

104. Will export subsidies increase the competitiveness of British exports in the long run? (*Public Finance, Final Part I, IMTA*)

105. Why may it pay a country to import goods which it can produce itself? (*ICWA*)

106. How may the government finance a deficit on the balance of payments in the short run? (*ICWA*)

107. Discuss the advantages and disadvantages of imposing restrictions on international trading relations. (*IOT*)

108. Why does the economist suggest that international trade is gainful? (*IOT*)

109. "Overseas investment merely creates overseas competitors and should be discouraged." Discuss. (*IOT*)

PART FOUR: GOVERNMENT AND INDUSTRY

110. Why are monopolistic practices in general thought to be against the public interest? How has the government attempted to deal with them? (GCE(A), JMB)

111. "In the industrial structure of the UK, all competition is monopolistic, all monopoly is to some extent competitive." Discuss this statement. (GCE(A), JMB)

112. What factors encourage (a) horizontal integration and (b) vertical integration in an industry? (GCE(A), JMB)

113. Is increasing concentration in industrial markets inevitable? (GCE(A), JMB)

114. How and why has the government intervened in the location of industry since 1945? (GCE(A), JMB)

115. Examine the view that public sector industry should be run like ordinary commercial enterprises. (GCE(A), JMB)

116. What criteria of efficiency can and should be applied to nationalised industries? (GCE(A), JMB)

117. What are the advantages and disadvantages of setting price equal to marginal cost in public enterprises? (GCE(A), JMB)

118. In what ways does the functioning of a "planned" economy differ from that of a "free" economy? (GCE(A), JMB)

119. "To check and reverse the drift of population to the South-East and Midlands would be to impose an unwarrantable cost upon the national economy." Discuss. (BSc(Econ), Part II, London)

120. Should the financial targets for nationalised industries be based on the rate of return on capital earned by private industry? (BSc(Econ), Part II, London)

121. Would a policy to outlaw monopolies necessarily be in the public interest? (HND Business Studies, Liverpool Polytechnic)

122. Governments have tried to cure regional economic imbalance for over thirty years, yet the problem remains. Discuss possible reasons for this lack of success. (HND Business Studies, Liverpool Polytechnic)

123. What difficulties arise in applying commercial criteria as a measure of efficiency to nationalised industries? (HND Business Studies, Liverpool Polytechnic)

124. Discuss the assertion that a ruthless breaking up of monopolies might create more inefficiency than it would eliminate. (HNC Business Studies, Liverpool Polytechnic)

125. "No policy for dealing with the regional problem ought

to interfere with the fundamentals of economic efficiency" (Professor Wilson). In what ways might government policy have offended this precept? (*HNC Business Studies, Liverpool Polytechnic*)

126. What main factors influence an entrepreneur in his choice of locality for a new factory? (*IOB*)

127. Monopoly is usually regarded as undesirable. Outline the case that can be made against this view. (*IOB*)

128. To what extent do you agree that nationalised industries should finance their capital investment out of profits? (*IOB*)

129. How may companies with "monopoly powers" attempt to strengthen their market position? (*ICWA*)

130. Some authorities take the view that the security of monopoly provides conditions in which the most rapid technical progress will take place in industry. Others hold that the pressure of competiive conditions is more favourable in this process. Discuss. (*CIS*)

131. "The taking over of one company by another is always in the interest of the shareholders but rarely in the interest of the country as a whole." Discuss this statement. (*CIS*)

132. "The main disadvantage of monopoly is not that it causes high prices but that it is inefficient." Discuss. (*CIS*)

133. Does economic theory indicate any rules which should govern the policies pursued by nationalised industries? (*CIS*)

134. "Planning without specific targets is a useless operation for raising economic growth." Do you agree? (*CIS*)

135. "The economic activities of the state have increased and are increasing." How far economically is such increase (*a*) desirable, (*b*) undesirable? (*CIS*)

Index